Race For Obedience

By

Rev J. A. (Jim) Watson B.Th

PRESS

Race For Obedience
by Rev J. A. (Jim) Watson B.Th

Printed in the United States of America

ISBN 1-597810-59-2

www.xulonpress.com

Introduction

Rev J. A. [Jim] Watson B.Th
Box 853
Tofield AB T0B 4J0

e-mail, jim4jane@telus.net

A fifth generation Scot, born in London, Ontario, Canada, and raised in a log shack in the back woods of northern Ontario, where children were taught to be seen, and not heard. Went on to become a builder of communities.

Born again in Temple Baptist Church Sarnia Ont. 40 Years Preaching the Gospel.

The Ministry of Jesus Christ, the Son of God, remains one of the noblest and most honorable professions to which man is called. Therefore the direction is not to be entered into lightly. For the call is not contrived of some imaginary dreamed up apparition floating in the wild blue yonder. Rather it is an inner sensitivity to the indwelling spirit that identifies the need to reach out and touch others. A person receives the call to do that by giving them the complete, and ethical message of a living God, who provided Salvation through Jesus Christ, by the shedding of his blood upon the cross of Calvary, for the soul purpose for the forgiveness of the sins of all mankind.

In order to comply with this superb command of God one must attain knowledge, because it is written in the scripture;

"Study to show thyself approved unto God, a workman that needeth not to be ashamed, rightly dividing the word of truth." 2 Timothy 2: 15.

A call to serve the living God is not necessarily to a pulpit Ministry, but is deemed to be active to any vocation wherein one is given the possibility of telling the story of so great a Salvation.

For there is one God, and one mediator between God and men, the man Christ Jesus: Who gave himself a ransom for all, to be testified in due time.

Public relations:

I have strong capability to interact with people from all walks of life while building a trustworthy relationship. I prefer Senior leadership as I am a self starter with an extroversive personality. I have extensive experience in management, and promotion of community activities. I have implemented programs that have been received wholeheartedly by communities in which I served

Whereunto I am ordained a preacher, and an apostle, (I speak the truth in Christ, and lie not;) a teacher of the Gentiles in faith and verity. 1 Timothy 2: 5-7.

-Preacher, Teacher, Evangelist, Pastor, Counselor, Builder of Communities, Mayor, Federal Constituency President, Church Planter, Creative Writer.

* * * * *

Table of Contents

—⟨∞⟩—

Dedication

⸺◦∕◦∕◦⸺

I dedicate this work to my ever encouraging wife Jane, in her effort of just being there as God's most precious gift to me.

Also to a very special "The best little logger in the valley.

Preface

Country kitchens emanate a most vigorous aroma, enchanting ones healthy appetite to mouth watering level that goads us to eat more than we need. When we seat ourselves around the table to feast, often we fill ourselves to the uncomfortable zone. As believers, we too need to leave the comfort zone of secular life, to feast on the tantalizing word of the living God, to the point that we leave that comfort zone, to be overwhelmed by the aroma of salvation with eternal life. It is for that reason I believe God has directed me to the discourse of putting the word into a literary venue feast, to feed believers and non believers depicting, "The Race of Obedience," explaining the application to live God's word

The race is in the running.

A thrill of swiftly moving forward with the intent to win. The thrill of the ear, to hear those who would cheer you on, as you measure each step of intent to finish first. An elated feeling as the finish line surges into visible reach, and the completeness as we falter over the line. Yet the emptiness as we realize that someone made it ahead of us. Then comes the fever to make another attempt. And another threshold rises in the soul to run again, for the race is in the running.

The element that has brought those that would race to the place where they could run encompasses a great amount of vigorous practice with hard work to put themselves in shape enhancing all the bodily elements in order to endure the run that they may win. Although all do not receive the prize, there is a special self satisfaction of having run your race well.

Paul was of the same mind as he said he had run the race well, and knew that as it was for Christ it entailed the ultimate in reward.

There are a multitude of instructions on how to achieve the fitness level to enable one to be fit for the race. The same element can be related to the living of the Christian life. So many instructions as to the preparation to walk as we ought to walk, but each one carries a little gem within that can be related to enhancing our walk to a greater degree. With that in mind I have attempted to share some of the simple methods which I have witnessed to be working methods to the building of the Christ like body while paving the path for those who love God.

I say with the Apostle Paul, I have run a good race, seeking to have the creator of all things present me with the ultimate prize of the high calling of the Father as he hands me the trophy for a race well run.

Contemporary worshipers have condescended to the art of entertainment within the structure of the temple, which was set up for the purpose of worshiping the living God. There appears to be a slackness within the soul while fellowshipping together to acknowledge the quiet attention of the almighty and living God. Rather, we have succumbed to the noisiness of the sinner who only adheres to the sinful structure of the unbelieving world, and we find ourselves embracing the overflowing of nonsensical gestures before man made altars worshiping human talent, and achievements instead of submitting to the power of an omniscience creator, God, who was, and is, and shall be forevermore.

In my writings I have attempted to point out measures of preparation that will allow us into the presence of the awesome living God. Herein I have used the scriptures hoping to direct persons to the methodology of paving a path before us in the gold which God expects from his followers. A path that will allow those who watch us, to drop what they are doing, to take up the cross, and tell the whole world, of a loving saviour who laid down his life for our salvation.

Some exercises that I divulge for the mat are very simple. There first of all must be the exercise of accepting Christ as our saviour. I do that by ignoring the myth perpetrated by an unbelieving world to be politically correct. Instead I dress with a winning garment of being forthright with being Spiritually correct. Only then can we enter into the long list of exercises that will allow our fitness for the kingdom of heaven. In running to win, we must use the exercise of humility, and the exercise of loving our neighbour as ourselves, along with the exercise of loving our enemies. We need to regress from the exercise of the unbelieving world who judge others as being unfit.

The most valid exercise for the believer in the race is the acceptance of those whom the world deems that they do not belong or do not fit in. We need to be determined to work with them that they too might become an integral part of running the good race. Most of all we need the exercise of faith which can only be extended when coupled with the exercise of prayer. I have tried to give simple direction to the exercises that will make us fit for the race that we are required to run while existing on this old creation of a world.

There is a need to be cognizant of those with a preconceived idea of what the method for the race will unfold because of their personal input, but they wander far from the truth. There is a working plan already in effect, and set in motion by our living God.

Nothing we can say or do will add to, nor allow us to contribute, will justify our entrance into the race. When you enter into a worldly sports event you cannot change the rules to suit your own desires to enhance your chances of being a winner. So it is with God's race, we need to abide by the rules already set in place.

Set our best foot forward, build our spiritual body according to the rules of the Father, and exercise until we are fit to run for him.

Impossible, you say, remember, all things are possible with God, we do not have to borrow slick slogans from an unbelieving world. All we need is to adhere to the rule book that has already been issued, the Bible, and use it as our manual that will allow us to win in the life everlasting in the Race Of Obedience.

* * * * *

Master Of The Storm

—◦◦◦—

And, behold, there arose a great tempest in the sea, insomuch that the ship was covered with waves: but he was asleep. And his disciples came to him, saying, Lord, save us: we perish. And he saith unto them, Why are ye fearful, O ye of little faith? Then he arose, and rebuked the winds and the sea; and there was great calm. Matthew 8: 24-26.

These are times when we recall the words of Christ saying there shall be wars and rumours of war. Men rise up to justify war to establish strength in their economies. Wars are planned by Governments of the day and not by the masses of civilians. Also we see that the thoughtful men are sobered by grave confusion. Groups are fighting for world power. Independent thinking sectors rally to separate from the rest of the world while they initiate dictatorial systems of their own. Revolutionaries are resorting to terrorist activities. People, to whom poverty has simply been a way of life for years, are now demanding to be given all. Their intent is to have the world focus upon them, and feed their demands, whether political or material. There is a terrible social unrest throughout the world. We can see many areas of countries that affirm that observation. Turn your eyes to Bosnia, North Korea, Iraq, South Africa, Somalia, Rwanda, and many smaller countries where cult Religious orders strive to take control, and this is not the way of a living God.

North America has internal conflicts that simmer on the political level, and heat up when those who would de-christianise our territory for which we pay lip service to as having the freedom of religion, and the neo-socialist work day and night to take it away particularly from the Christian community. They put in their plan in which they label Christian thinking as right wing, while they label themselves as left wing. If being left means to abandon Christian principles then we as believers need to rise up armed with God's word to educate those who are headed for the fires of Hell. Again there is political conflict, a political party now in power in Quebec by electing sufficient Members to Federal Parliament, that has been responsible for the murder of elected officials of a legitimately elected Government. More, and more, we see evidence of the demand for a higher and greater standard of living while rebels are elected to implement ungodly rules.

Still we are faced with natural disasters throughout the world; earthquakes, in the United States to the south of us, and to the south of them, more in Mexico, South America, and across the sea, in Italy, India, and Japan. Even in Canada, our own country, we cannot escape the terrifying natural disasters, as Tornados threaten the once safe Provinces which we believed were havens from natural disaster because of being situated in the Northern hemisphere. Yet the Province of Ontario is often plagued with those terrifying twisted winds. Also experienced in a part of Canada deemed as is the haven from natural disaster, the Province Alberta. British Columbia's swollen rivers produce a measure of flooding in some flatlands least expected for that natural disaster; mountains send slides to destroy major highways, and entire valleys.

Most recently forests devastated by raging fires, and communities suffering loss. Similarities exist between those fires, and the more costly one was learned about that took a terrible toll in California several years in a row.

One can hear about these events through the media; whether TV. Newspaper, or radio; but we cannot begin to imagine the realistic faction of the devastation, and trauma, suffered when personally experienced. It is beyond us, to imagine how terrified people must have been at the instant of those crisis moments. Standing amidst the rubble in the aftermath of a storm gives one the sense of devastation to a greater degree than a TV. image can. Still, one cannot begin to comprehend the trauma of those who suffered the loss, or found themselves in the midst of that terror.

My wife, Jane, and I, traveled through the Tornado ravaged area of Edmonton, and district, to witness the evidence of damage with our own eyes, the aftermath of the path that was left by a destructive tornado, in an area where short hours before the professional men of science were recorded saying, it was scientifically impossible to have a tornado here.

As we gazed upon this now wind ravaged area, we realized the futility of man, and were quickly reminded that our living God was still, Master of the storm.

As devastating as any crisis may appear, you must know, and assess that God is still in control. As we look into the book of Ecclesiastes chapter 3: 1 - 8; we find that there is in fact a time for everything,

To every thing there is a season, and a time to every purpose under heaven: A time to be born, and a time to die; a time to plant and a time to pluck up that which had been planted; A time to kill, and a time to heal; a time to break down, and a time to build up; A time to weep, and a time to laugh; a time to mourn, and a time to dance; A time to cast away stones, and a time to gather stones together; a time to embrace, and a time to refrain from embracing; A time to get, and a time to lose; a time to keep, and a time to cast away; A time to rend, and a time to sew; a time to keep silence, and a time to speak; A time to love, and a time to hate; a time of war, and a time of peace;

Although this portion of scripture is one that has been commonly over saturated with negativity with new translations along with others who think they know what it means as they come up empty in the presentation of God's word.

I believe that this precious section simply portrays effort to consistently represent things that have to be done in the round of life's duties. This passage has a restrained majesty of movement, as though the river of life were two currents flowing through the same banks. There consists in this writing the permission to do, alongside of the stream of prohibition. It is part of the wisdom of life to know where to catch the flowing tide, while not wasting the hope and effort on that which cannot be done. Good timing is one of our sovereign conditions of success, from planting of the seed to charting the course for a flight.

One may find in this portion some rich experience adapted to living, but there leaps out a voice that tells us that there is a place for loss as well as for gain, for tears as well as laughter. So we who are on the cautious side rather than the side of timidity, will recognize the opportunity to accept both sides of the portion that is meted out to us. Along with the astounding brilliance that leads us into the adventure of living a full life, there comes the ominous shadows that we need to learn to accept and continue to carry on with our lives.

According to the preacher here, life is full of determined events, and we need to prepare ourselves as we go out to meet each event which comes our way. There is a pet saying that I use which I have dubbed it a Senior Saying, and that is "been there, done that."

Christian faith transcends all philosophies to give real body to true theology, which is the study of God that will direct us into the will of God.

Again the bible says in 1 Kings 19: 11b - 12; *And behold, the Lord passed by, and a great and strong winds rent the mountains, and brake in pieces the rocks before the Lord; but the Lord was not in the wind: and after the wind an earthquake; but the Lord was not in the earthquake: And after the earthquake a fire; but the Lord was not in the fire: and after the fire a still small voice.*

Here we are talking about God's way. God the Master of the Storm. God in control. God not in the storm; not in the falling rocks; not in the fire; but in a still small voice.

There are those who would have you believe that our God is a noisy chaotic God; and that he will rush in with thunder, and lightening, and some great visionary thing that will scare us awake. But don't you believe it my friends for God has been insulted by those who fail to listen to that still small voice. We fail as Christians to listen to the Master of The Storm, with his still small voice. We want to turn away when He tries to show us that He is still the Master of the Storm.

We read again in Matthew 8:25, who records a cry, *"save us we perish!"*.

My ministry takes me to many different churches throughout our country. My findings, a regrettable apathy to retain the excitement, and enthusiasm, to embrace the desire to tell the story about Jesus Christ. There is little, or no desire, to spread the gospel to the unbelieving community. There appears to be no desire to tell about the evidence of salvation through the redemptive blood of Christ. No evidence of those wanting to tell about what God has already done. There are men who desire to get closer to God, yet the miracle is that God has already come down to man, and there is absolutely nothing we can do to walk closer to God, He has already done it.

Matthew 8: 24; says this, *'behold there arose a great tempest'*.

Tempest, used here shows that there was an inability of man to manoeuvre his ship. Sailors were helpless to save their livelihood against such terrible odds. Today it could be likened to a mobile home in a hurricane or tornado.

Simply, man had no control here. The last resort was to call on Christ.

What happened here?

It is somewhat evident that this incident was to give assurance that Christ could deliver his followers from anything. We see also that the disciples under pressure panicked, then they called on Christ, save us we perish.

How swiftly the storms of life can surround us. Waves of sickness wash against us nearly capsizing our lives; death floods us with grief; and other forms of negative waves roll over us; we too need to make that same established cry, save us we perish. With treachery within our social structure, we feel helpless. Yet, our very human helplessness is here depicted, as the disciple's panic. The function of our crisis as was the function of the crisis of the disciples, is to remind us of our helplessness.

As I stood on the fair grounds of Camrose, Alberta, and watched that awesome tornado take form then touch down to rip a land apart; I was reminded of the smallness of man, and of how little power we really have. There I stood, unable by any token of the imagination, to control the element of disaster. In the sunshine we tell ourselves that we can control our destination, and imagine ourselves to be self sufficient, but in the time of storm we panic.

We need to call upon Christ to save us, or we perish. We relearn a simple truth of God, that man, is neither able, nor was he intended by creation, to live by his own resource. We then ask the ultimate question as in John 6:68, *To whom shall we go? Thou hast the words of eternal life.*

They called upon Christ, and he came to them and delivered them, portraying his role as 'Master of The Storm'.

Returning to our text Matthew 8: 27, there was an inquiry that prompted the question.

What manner of man is this that even the winds and the sea obey him?'

Here is the man that they knew as Christ. They believed on him as Lord and saviour. They called upon him in the time of trouble when they had panicked. They screamed at the man who slept on the deck, save us, we perish. He did as they expected, he calmed the waters, stilled the sea, stopped the storm. In the next instant they challenge,

What manner of man is this?

Who is this man?

This is Jesus Christ, Son of the living God. What manner of man is this? Jesus Christ the servant of man. Jesus Christ the author of Grace. This Jesus Christ with a message. This Jesus with eternal life. Jesus, saviour of the souls of men. Saviour, Lord, Christ.

What manner of man is this?

In love with mankind; and continues to still the storm. Jesus Christ, forgiver of sins; Christ, who portrayed the finished redemptive work of God.

My Christian friends, your commission is to tell others of this Jesus Christ, the son of the living God that finished the redemptive work on the cross, by the shedding of his blood, for the remission of our sins. You do not need to achieve results academically, nor achieve some professional theological status, to give this news about Christ; all you need is this small message.

John 3:16-17, that goes like this; *For God so loved the world, that he gave his only begotten son, that whosoever believeth in him should not perish, but have everlasting life. For God sent not his son into the world to condemn the world; but that the world through him might be saved.*

There is absolutely no excuse, for those claiming to be a

follower of the Christ of the living God, and allowing people to think on them as Christian, not to tell the message about Jesus Christ, the Lord, and saviour. Christ brings about Regeneration, and redemption. He will save, even when we appear to perish. Faith without works is dead. The bible very clearly states, be not conformed to this world; but be ye transformed by the renewing of your mind, that you may prove that which is good, and acceptable, and perfect, will of God. Romans 12: 2;

Oftentimes Christians get so entangled with the world they stop the transformation to the body of Christ. There is a desire to live like the world, but God sent his son to redeem us.

Is he your saviour, your Christ, your Lord?

By agony, and blood, he died on the cross that you might be free. We watch the secular world, in all its power, all its ideology, in all of its analogies, in all of its psychology, in all of its meditation, and all of its analysis, and they still remain dysfunctional in the understanding of the Christ life. The world with all their advanced technologies cannot comprehend God. They talk peace and cannot find it. As they palaver over one condition, another conflict flares.

Some time ago I was watching a TV. Programme called, Face the Newsmen, they were interviewing a lady from the Philippines who was apparently the head of some peace movement. They challenged her to explain what kind of peace she was talking about. My thought is that it is time for the Christian to challenge the secular humanist, to what kind of life they are talking about. The only message the world has is doom, and destruction, which takes the soul to an eternal hell. They have no plan to deliver God's people, into God's hand. It is time for us to fill the vacuum in their lives, and tell them the message from the word of God, the bible. It is proper that we expose the evil of the world rather than trying to find the good of the evil world. Evil is that which would separate us from the love of God. Today we attempt modify evil to an inappropriate social conduct.

Personalization of evil is alien to the modern mind. Our techno-logical science has lulled us to sleep. We are in a time warp of apathy. We cannot talk comfortably about Jesus Christ. Evil is robbed of its living terror. My bible says, that the fear of God is the beginning of wisdom. God is in danger of being depersonalized.

God must be an ideal to the secular world, but he is not just an ideal, he is the perfect person, omnipotent, omniscience, and omnipresent. He is the only one that gave his only son, Jesus Christ, so that we could have eternal life. You may achieve all the things you desire on a secular level, but know this, God is not pleased.

Evil is brought down to a sociological level of self determination, or biological urges, or psychological complex. Evil loses its frightful personality, and we lose sight of its reality. Evil verses good still exists. We need desperately to recover a boldness in biblical vocabulary There is a need to contrast God's word to the abstracts of science. The hearts of men understand it; the devil fears it; but God loves us for it. We need a vocabulary that stands against all secularism, and all humanism. All the logic of the world does not believe in a living God who sent Christ for man's deliverance. We need to exercise our vocabulary that others may know that we belong to Christ. Let us not be found in the position of having to answer God, as to why we are ashamed of his son. We can talk about swimmers, hockey players, baseball players, and many other achievers, whether in sports or the arts.

We ought then to know Christ to the extent that we can talk about him. After all that is where our faith rests. In Christ. there are those who put their faith in a piece of paper hanging on the office wall. Others put their faith in man made statues, which have been awards for their achievements. And God who gives us a beautiful eternal life as the greatest reward of all, and we as Christians have fallen into apathy. We would rather not talk about it.

God has made us to be a peculiar people. That is not to be a ridiculously strange people. But peculiar that we continue in our love for others, our love for the unlovely, and an unbelieving world, and try to give the message of the redemptive work of our redeeming Christ. Peculiar that we follow God through his son Jesus Christ regardless of, and in spite of, the names they attach to us. Simple faith in Christ always throws a curve at analogies, and psychoanalysis, and worldly terminologies. However we know that receiving Christ into ones life will change that life for the better, because they become a new creature in Christ Jesus.

You may try to shift the responsibility of talking about salvation to someone else; but you are saying to God, I don't believe you, I cannot believe that you would use me to change someone else's life.

You also may ask, To whom would or could I talk to?

There are a few you have missed already, like the grocery cashier, as you go through the till, or the bag boy, who carries your groceries to the vehicle you drive, and what about the gas station attendant, where you purchase your gas, mailman, meter reader, the person next to you in a line up, and on and on.

Are they heading for a Christless eternity, because you did not believe God?

Have you taken the message of Jesus Christ to your neighbour?

Are you able to write the names of at least ten unbelievers?

Perhaps when you complete your list you will call them now, and tell them of the saving power of Jesus Christ. It is a power that works. It is a love that sustains us. It is a life that is eternal. There is in actuality, a sequence of events that come into our lifetime, that appear to be spaciously timed into our life's journey, and we must simply deal with them as they deal us their hand in the game of life.

One can accept it in a detrimental sense of fatalism that gives us no other choice. However, it is my thinking we must face each issue at a positive action level to determine the outcome of our own desire. In the case of the believer, that which would best please God.

At whatever stage in life you are at today; whatever turmoil you encounter, or confusion, and frustration, of life you face; make that plea to Jesus 'save us, we perish'; God is there, and he will hear, and Christ will come as he came for his disciples; he will handle those difficult things for you; for truly He is The Master of the Storm.

* * * * *

No God No Gold

—◦⟨∞⟩◦—

Give me the gold that will shine brilliant in the sun for a reward.

Give me the richly strong ribbon that will bind me to my Saviour.

Give me the race of a lifetime that will commit me in depth to my living God.

Eric Liddell, an Olympic runner in 1929, who stopped the world in it's tracks when he refused to break the Sabbath day, by running for the time set by Kings, Prime Ministers, hard nosed organizers who tried by use of position of authority, and insidious insults, to persuade him that he had to fall into line with the status quo. His love for the living God was greater than his love for self accomplishment, his commitment to God was as it should be in every believers heart, the wishes of God first, and the wishes of man second. I believe that is a greater attribute than any hunk of gold that sits collecting dust on a shelf. And the world stood still as this young successful Christian stood his ground. The Sabbath is a Holy day, and he was not about to desecrate the day that God had set aside for himself. He had the courage to keep an important commandment without compromise. In his own words on his deathbed, "It's complete surrender."

In the on going attempt to de-christianise our society we find a man who held no fear of those who opposed God. Sportscasters do not consistently elevate this man as they do with other past Gold medal winners. It is because of their unbelief that they cannot understand this man 's dedication to a living God. Their mouths are still stopped, and stuffed with ignorance. They are the real commercial cowards of the day because they allow their superiors to cut out anything that pertains even in shadow to Christianity.

As believers in Jesus Christ as the son of a living God who created mankind for his benefit, we must look into the scripture to see his promise to us. One thing that he promises is eternity with him in heaven. What is heaven like? Well when we consider God's word in the book of Revelation we find it spelled out as the inspired writer paints a valuable and distinct picture as God directs.

And he that talked with me had a golden reed to measure the city, and the gates thereof, and the wall thereof. And the city lieth foursquare, and the length is as large as the breadth: and he measured the city with the reed, twelve thousand furlongs. The length and breadth and the height of it are equal. And he measured the wall thereof, a hundred and forty and four cubits, according to the measure of man, that is of the Angel. And the building of the wall of it was jasper: and the city was pure gold, like unto glass. And the twelve gates were twelve pearls; every several gate was of one pearl: and the street of the city was pure gold, as it were transparent glass. Revelation 21: 15-18, 21.

The measurement used herein is probably not relative to many of the readers of today however if it appears that these measurements consist up about a 1500 square miles. Looking about size of the city is rather a phenomenal structure. We are more and more impressed by the daring with which the book of Revelation builds up its been great description of the holy city the city of God. It is pointed out in the book of Revelation that this will be as city of gold. Some may suggest that this is simply a thought of materialism but when the material as such as this is used in this spiritual sense worsened as the spiritual instrument it becomes a part of nobility by which it is used. With all this precious metal of being used is rather unusual that each gate is made at one Pearl. This is probably because the religious of the dating would suggest that the precious stone used whether tools from the breastplates of the high priest. With that thought in mind it almost surpasses one's imagination, but I'm sure that it was intended to do that so that it was not man's idea, but only God's idea. The streets of the city were also made a pure gold which according to Scriptures seem to be as transparent glass. Remembering the prayer of Abraham in this city there will be no need for light. For the unspeakable splendor from the light of our Lord's countenance will be the supreme light. As it will be the illumination of our divine savior which will be more than enough light than we could ever used in this world.

The vision here is the far flung dream of the presence of God that is so illuminated that the darkness of evil could not enter in as the brilliance of the most precious substance would wipe away even the shadows of evil thinking. A divine place where negative can find no dwelling place. The total reward of the followers of Christ as they gather together to fellowship for an eternity of timelessness surrounded by only that which is richness to the soul.

Recognized as the final achievement of mankind where the race has been won and all the rewards are meted out in ecstatic wonderment of a new and wholesome peace for which the believer has been searching for until Christ comes. Here he reigns with illuminated light of the universe called heaven. In all it's finality, the gold city, with streets of gold, to receive only the believers of Jesus Christ, the Son of God.

* * * * *

Going For Gold

⟶⟶⟶

W e know from God's word [the bible] that after receiving our Salvation by our acceptance of the Son of God, Jesus Christ, we are responsible for working out our Salvation. When the Christian is raptured we will be brought into the presence of Christ who will be sitting upon the Judgment seat and He will present us with our reward.

Blessed and holy is he that has part in the first resurrection, on such the second death has no power, but they shall be priests of God and of Christ, and shall reign with him a thousand years. Revelation 20: 6.

He has received a special reward for his suffering and will be sitting upon his throne to reign for a thousand years upon the earth. We will have the privilege of sharing that throne and reigning with him if we spend time with him here and now to share his suffering.

This know also, that in the last days perilous times shall come. For men will be lovers of their own selves, covetous, boasters, proud, blasphemers, disobedient to parents, unthankful, unholy, Without natural affection, trucebreakers, false accusers, incontinent,{without self restraint} fierce, despisers of those that are good, Traitors, heady, highminded, lovers of pleasure more than lovers of God; Having a form of Godliness, but denying the power thereof: from such turn away. For of this sort are they which creep into houses, and lead captive silly women laden with sins, led away with divers lusts, Ever learning and never able to come to the knowledge of truth. 2 Timothy 3: 1-7.

In these latter days where TV has become somewhat of that corner modern day icon of our living room. As they find people are striving to survive for a different lifestyle without God. We are simply and urgently warned about the times in which we live. Those around about us think nothing of trespassing upon God's laid out plan in which He expects man to abide by. There arc elements displayed which project anything but Christ, and suggest a style of living that is supposed to build a template of everlasting self esteem. It is a propaganda of deception that shall lead the unbelieving soul to eternal damnation without God, and without all the substance that an unbelieving world made them seek after. We find programs produced that would strip away the all of the meter of the character and reveal about individuals or groups for what actually are. Of those of us who are the believers in the salvation of Jesus Christ are brought up short by the use supposed characters who suffer affliction from their acting. But what is brought mainly to our attention is we believe that in our day appears to be far closer the end of the time. We also believe that there will be another apart from the Godly view who will bring us to the end of an age of familiarity and usher in a new era. That era is outlined in the brief statement in second Timothy Chapter three. Most of the sin mentioned it in this portion of Scripture are simply common faults of ordinary men. So we see in this chapter that men and women were simply challenged to walking and upright manner avoiding sin in their lifestyle walk. Seen here, I am sure that the apostle Paul was inspired to encourage the people to walk in truth, and righteousness, and being careful not to fall into the trap of unrighteousness under the watchful eye of the unbeliever.

Yea and all that will live Godly in Christ Jesus shall suffer persecution. But evil men and seducers shall wax worse and worse, deceiving, and being deceived. But continue thou in the things which thou hast learned and hast been assured of knowing of whom thou hast learned them; And that from a child thou hast known the Holy scriptures, which are able to make thee wise unto salvation through faith which is in Christ Jesus. All scripture is given by inspiration of God, and is profitable for doctrine, for reproof, for correction, for instruction in righteousness; That the man of God may be perfect, thoroughly furnished unto all good works. 2 Timothy 3: 12-17.

In reading this portion of Scripture we quite often find people bemoaning the fact that this statement falls true as we view others around about us instead of realizing the importance factor of self application of fact, that even with all conflicts that we suffer, or appear to suffer, we do not come near to the suffering of Paul, and least of all the suffering of Jesus Christ. Therefore it behooves us to be careful of each action and function in which we decide to be a participant of for fear that those things we do would make the message of Christ derelict to our community.

I charge thee therefore before God, and the Lord Jesus Christ, who shall judge the quick and the dead at his appearing and his kingdom; Preach the word; be instant in season, out of season; reprove, rebuke, exhort with all long suffering and doctrine. For the time will come when they will not endure sound doctrine; but after their own lusts shall they heap to themselves teachers, having itching ears; And they shall turn away their ears from the truth, and shall be turned unto fables. But watch thou in all things, endure afflictions, do the work of an evangelist, make full proof of thy ministry. For I am now ready to be offered, and the time of my departure is at hand. I have fought the good fight, I have kept the faith: Henceforth is laid up for me a Crown of righteousness, which the Lord, the righteous judge, shall give me on that day: and not to me only, but unto all them also that love his appearing. 2 Timothy 4: 1-8.

I believe the most important statement made here in this point of Scripture is the fact that we need to always be cognizant of the fact we're in the presence of a living God when accepting Christ as our personal savior, and therefore must walk giving that impression to others by our treatment of others. The essential function of any preacher is to preach justly in that the word of God in the attempt to persuade the unbeliever to join them in that difficult march with the family of God. If you are unable to walk in this manner you are in urgent need to take it upon yourself to study the word of God. Usually, doubt will come about our stand when we accept the criticism of the unbeliever or those who do not wish to walk as God would have them walk. There is a popular prejudice against the word preach. Often my question is where have all the preachers gone?

Often, I find that there is a drive for being politically correct, I would then ask another question wouldn't you rather be spiritually correct?

You may make the statement, I live my own life, and I can live it the way I want to. The element remains that as a leader you must always be cognizant of the fact that you walk in the presence of God otherwise you deny God. It is a dangerous ground that you walk upon when you deny God with your lifestyle, with your attitude, and with your action. Remember God is always the Observer as well as the judge. We of ourselves have no right to judge others because God has not given us that office for he alone is a judge. Nevertheless in witnessing the wrongdoing a man we ought to practice forgiveness as Christ practiced

forgiving us for our wrongdoings by hanging on the cross and being raised to appear before his father on our behalf.

We believe as Christians, through death we enter into the presence of God. We believe also that prior to Christ's return we shall be caught up into the air with Him. In some circles this is better known as the Rapture. It is said that all believers shall be included in the rapture into the presence of Christ who will be sitting upon his judgment seat. This is not a tribunal seat as Pilate's judgment seat, but is similar to the judgment seat that was then used at the Greek Olympic games, to which the winner came to receive the prize.

The rewards that are to be presented at the Judgment seat of Christ by his very own hand, and are duly designated to be golden crowns. The significance of the term lies in the fact that crowns are symbolic of Royalty, and the Saints of God are to reign with Christ.

Believers in Christ are Saints, and they shall judge the world of unbelief with Christ. God's word tells us that we shall have the opportunity to receive Five Crowns, for the enthusiastic implementation of God's plan, and each one will be pure Gold.

The First Crown, the Crown of Life which is mentioned twice in scripture, first in the book of James 1:12, secondly in the book of Revelation 2: 10. In the book of James, we find these words, *Blessed is the man that endureth temptation: for when he is tried, he will receive the Crown of Life* , with the Lord has been promised to them that love him. Is quite apparent that this is a crown for those who endure. The application here is not inference to those who simply attend the Sunday morning service that actually directs itself too those who go through trials and temptations in an ongoing basis.

In Revelation 2: 10, *Fear none of those things thou shalt suffer, behold the devil will cast some of you into prison that ye may be tried. Ye shall have tribulation ten days, be thou faithful unto death, and I will give thee a crown of life.*

This particular verse reversed to the first crown as well. Here we find that they have a particular reference to fear. That is understandable for as we read verse 10 we find the number of areas that the apostle point out many areas of tribulation. There are those of whom advocate that without tribulation there is no Christianity. However I feel that if we have that desire to do the correct and obvious thing to make our Christian walk real by applying God's word we can avoid most of the tribulation Man sets before our community. In saying that, I believe that the Christian who finds themselves bowing down to fear because of self apprehension that eludes to the need of acceptance, are wrong. Intentionally being focused on adopting a selfish need, to be accepted of a man made community, will not make our plight an easy one nor enhance our ability to please our creator, the living God. Therefore lacks in the element of producing that which is right of right, and the edification of fellow believers. There are natural fears such as fear of death such as fear of being lost, such as fear of enemies, and so on. There are so many things that we adopt unto ourselves which inevitably will misdirect our following God. We must be very careful to adopt the will of God, and not the will of Man. That decision may seem to leave us in much of a lonely position. I must submit to you that you are far better off to stand alone before God than to gather a crowd around you who simply agrees with all you present to them, and still will walk away without the understanding of their need for salvation.

The crown of life by some, has been referred to as eternal life, but it is my firm belief that it is a solely separated reward, as indicated in the scriptures, for eternal life is the only gift we receive when we accept Jesus Christ as our saviour. Then the crown of life is rewarded for the consistency of living your life for Christ with the best interest of your fellowman at hand.

The second Crown, The Incorruptible Crown, *1 Corinthians 9:25, And every man that striveth for the mastery is temperate in all things. Now they do it to obtain a corruptible crown; but we an incorruptible.*

In this brief talk by Paul, he brings into focus the corruptible crown. I believe that is referenced herein is to the running of the race simply for self gain with no concern for those around us. Therefore that is what he deems to be the corruptible crown as he warns the believer not to be entangled in those kind of gains. It is thought with a number of writers that Paul here is pointing out that Christianity is no short run term, but one must be there for the complete running of the race for the benefit of everyone around about. The Christian life in our contemporary age calls for moderation in all things. I believe that often we forget this call, and having to work in the league is to lead the believing community into tribulation that is avoidable. I believe in considering this verse about the crown we must take into consideration versus 26 and 27 where Paul tells us that he did not run your fight as one that simply faking the race with unresolved action of appearance by emptily throwing his hands out to the beating of air. So many times I find the Christian people with very good intentions fail to have all the facts at their fingertips and are as those that fight by just beating the air. In verse 27 again Paul points out that he is concerned about bringing his body into subjection, for fear that he preaches to others by his lifestyle he himself to be a castaway. Sometimes our lives are overridden by elements that must be dealt with, and if we do not deal with them properly we find ourselves by our own volition castaways. Therefore all the more reason that we need to be careful about what we do, and what we say, and how we portray the word of God, and the life of Christ. Too often we avoid presenting the life of Christ to put ourselves into a better light, and all we really do is end up burying ourselves in complete darkness as our empty actions allow us to lose the privilege of ministering for a living God.

Here again, Paul points to the race that leads to a prize for the winner, but at the same time he attempts to embrace the church pointing out that each believer is the winner when they cross that goal line to which they are headed, that is eternal life with Christ.

Believers that are to run to win must be subject to long exposure to the elements that help you keep your faith alive. A good athlete practices all the rules while working extra measures that keep them in shape to win their race. So it is with the believing Christian, we must indeed be consistent in exercising for the race to win the souls of man for an eternity with Christ in heaven. Many in the wayward crowd are watching to cheer when we falter, and show weakness of our team, but God is faithful to help you win your race to eternity for we strive for the incorruptible crown of righteousness. Self-discipline, and self-control can attain this. The demands of Christ are high and exacting that challenge the reproach of the world. Salvation is the starting point, heaven's eternity the goal.

The third Crown, is the Crown of Righteousness. *Henceforth there is laid up for me a crown of righteousness, which the Lord, the righteous judge, shall give me that day: and not to me only, but unto all them also that love his appearing.* 2 Timothy 4:8,

This portion of Scripture ought to remind us that we have pledged ourselves to Christ, to whom we owe faithful allegiance. When you are reading the Gospels you will find that Christ addressed his disciples concerning this very thing. He asked them that very thing, "Will you also go away?"

This crown indicates to us that there are many rewards awaiting us if we will just walk the way Christ asked us to. We know that there will be the approval of the righteous judge, God. He tells us in Matthew 25: 21, when he says to serve its well-done the good and faithful servant. We then must ask ourselves if the task that we perform is right and proper. In our sincere consideration to walk for eternal life we can answer seriously in a positive sense when we know that Christ will greet us readily with that same statement to each one. We work for God simply because we seek his everlasting fellowship, and when we find our service to God that gives the spiritual communion with all those who have loved and longed for his appearance. Only then can we be assured of this third crown.

This is the race that is not easily won, it is crystal clear that the Christian life is a struggle, not only to survive the evil of the world around us, but to overcome the struggles we have from within. Always keep in mind that no race is won until you cross the finish line. There can be no slackening along the way if we are to keep up. We have pledged ourselves to Christ, to whom we owe our allegiance therefore we need to strive to keep a perpetual motion of that vision of fellowship with God for our crowning glory.

The fourth Crown, is the Crown of Rejoicing. *For what is our hope, our joy, or crown of rejoicing? Are not even ye in the presence of our Lord Jesus Christ at his coming?* 1 Thessalonians 2:19,

In our modern age I believe that quite often we wallow in a so-called rejoicing that is theatrical and godless. Again we must be very careful what we attribute to God and again that which we take away from him to claim as our own. When God here is speaking a rejoicing he is not talking about getting around and flinging arms, or bodies, or hands into the air. The reference is to acknowledging the fullness of the grace of God in the quietness of our achievement. The element of being very careful in your showmanship of worship that you do not simply exaggerate or imply by deliberate action on your part that you have the right to be where you are. Consider this, if you have not been called of God to minister for him you have no right rejoicing before him in any manner. I believe that modern-day enthusiasts forget about God's plan that already is in place to do it that way he wants it done, and not the way the crowds want.

Here we find there is the need to have an eager expectancy of the second coming of Jesus. We must have knowledge of God the Father in order to receive that welcome to us as believers while we stand to receive the crown of rejoicing.

How well have we come to know our Lord along the way?

I believe we know him as we learn to know and love those people around us that God has deliberately put in our pathway as we run for that high calling. If you lack internal understanding of those humans that you fellowship with then Christ will see you that you have no real love for him. If you are one of those who have no time for others on an intimate basis, it will show up when you meet Christ. There is no doubt that He will ask, "Why did you not love my people along the way?" "Why did you only find time to criticize?" "Why did you not give concern to the heart of the individuals I sent your way?" If you cannot answer Christ in the positive way you will find that you are not fit for the kingdom that God has set out for those believers That is for those with an earnest desire to love their fellowman. All the answers you need for Christ are found in the Bible, God's word. If you wish to have a humbling experience you would do well to silently sit yourself in the quietness of the pew of an empty church, and there ask yourself, "who sits here?" "what do I know of them?" "What have I done for them? or what could I do for them?" Have I ever visited with them?, have I ever prayed for them?". Every believer needs to confront themselves with the question, "what have I done for others to please Christ?"

The fifth Crown is the "Crown of Glory" 1 Peter 5:1 - 4, *The elders which are among you I exhort, who am also an elder, and a witness of the sufferings of Christ, and also a partaker of the glory that shall be revealed: Feed the flock of God which is among you, taking the oversight thereof, not by constraint, but willingly; not for filthy lucre, but of a ready mind; Neither as being lords over God's heritage, but being ensamples of the flock. And when the chief shepherd shall appear, ye shall receive a Crown of Glory that fadeth not away.* 1 Peter 5: 1-4.

This portion of the scriptures is probably the most warped writing edifice that appears in the modern churches of our day. Elders here is talking about a positive species of mankind in charge of God's work identified as Elders who were so named because they were older men with much experience. Today churches have made this scripture a lie as they divert it to an appointment or elected position where younger men are allowed to adopt the title. This becomes obvious as Paul did not make his statement glibly or thoughtlessly. This becomes evident in verse five as he then addresses the younger as he challenge them to submit to the elder wisdom. It was not the Apostle's thinking to disparage anyone in service for age and certainly not to be ashamed of being a young minister. Nevertheless there was given to the Elders a favour of accountability measure to those who followed after them.

The apostle makes his statement here that ought to lift us to the highest element of our living for Christ. First Peter five verse four says, "you shall receive a crown of glory that does not fade away." What a wonderful hope that is for each of us to look forward to. We have no right to assume some favourite place about the man we are to be part takers of all the experiences both good and bad that happens to other believers around us. We are also to be available to bring the word of God in an instant notice to those in need. We are not only supposed to be part takers of the glory of Christ, but also part takers of the glory which used to be revealed. In other words we had no idea of what God has in plans for us, but we are to rejoice in the expectation of the beautiful things he will allow in our lives. That is not to say nor even infer anyway that we will not have tribulation, because that is the instruction of God to be able to stand through the difficult times that will come if we sincerely Minister God's word to unbelievers. The instability of our society gives way to disintegration or revolution. It will be even in these times that God expects us to embrace others even in the falling apart of our society.

The Crowns spoken of in God's word are for believers to obtain. The skeptical and unbeliever have already accepted the corruptible Crown.

Saints of God, those who have accepted Jesus, and allowed Him to come into their hearts to project their lives to a lost world that they might see the package of Salvation by God's only Son, will receive a Crown from God when they are called into His presence. The faithful ones, who have endeavoured to plant God's word, and those who have made a legitimate attempt to save souls here on earth, will be awarded with a Crown. Opposition to sin of mankind without fear of presenting the gospel to the unbeliever to show that we live by Grace will receive the Golden Crown. Always the willing presenter of that Crown, is the living God.

Where does that leave you?

If you were the judge, and saw your life in Christ before your eyes, could you in all fairness, and without bribes, award a crown for that which you have accomplished for the Lord Jesus Christ. If not, now is the time to begin to produce a work, as Christ requires it. Run the race to obtain the Gold. When God hands out the final prize you will be there to receive your Golden Crown.

Whosoever therefore shall confess me before men, him will I confess also before my Father which is in heaven. But whosoever shall deny me before men, him will I also deny before my Father which is in heaven. Matthew 10: 32-33.

This statement in Matthew can be a very fearful one when we are not walking as God but have us walk. Here Christ tells it in a very simple way, if you tell other people about me I will tell my father in heaven about you, but if you insist on denying me to other people I have no choice but to deny you before my father which is in heaven. It surprises me that men attempt to go around this statement, and attempt in many ways to bypass it or simply ignore it. Yet if any portion of Scripture needed to be taken to memory and read over and over again it is this portion where Christ's tells us that if we do not tell others about him he will not tell his father about us. My question then, "How much more do you need to know before you begin to minister for Jesus Christ."

Movement upon social movement cries out calling for peace. It is a false cry for as we read further in Matthew verses 34-36; Christ warns, *Think not that I have come to send peace on the earth: I came not to send peace, but a sword. For I am come to set a man at variance against his father, and the daughter against her mother, and the daughter-in-law against her mother-in-law. And a man's foes shall be they of his own household.*

In all that we say or do it must be Christ first; as he explains quite carefully and clearly, that we need to make the absolute consideration to show ourselves worthy of Him.

At the time of our examination before Christ we shall be pronounced worthy, or unworthy. If we have denied him before men he will deny us before his Father in heaven telling him that we are not worthy of the seat on the throne. Paul clearly understood all of this for many times he spoke of the coming glory. He even forgot the things behind him that he might press forward for the prize of the high calling in God, through Jesus Christ. He was completely aware of the award awaiting him.

In our generation we experienced a king who denounced the throne in order to marry a women of his choice. She was deemed not to qualify to rule with him.

This gives a minor glimpse of what will happen at the judgment seat of Christ. There will be those who are not qualified to sit on the throne with Christ, But for those who are qualified there will be a reward, and there are designated to receive at least one of five crowns to be obtained in that reward.

Let us work to identify with Paul as he says, *But watch thou in all things, endure afflictions, do the work of an evangelist, make full proof of thy ministry. For I am now ready to be offered, and the time of my departure is at hand. I have fought a good fight, I have finished my course, I have kept the faith.* 2 Timothy 4: 5-7

Here we find there are four basic principles for workers in the church, [1]there must be stability of purpose, [2]the power to be urgent in season and out of season, [3]there must be a capacity for sacrifice, [4]there must be a readiness to share the experience of the cross as a part of price of discipleship: [a] there must be individualistic zeal, [b] and eagerness to enlist all men in in the cause of Christ, [c] there also must be a willingness to do the working goal in the enlisting souls that are willing to put their shoulder to the work. There must be curried in faith to stay the job against the opposition. There must be a willingness to go through the readiness and discouragement long after reasonable obligations have been fulfilled. Only then can they say with Paul, we are profitable servants.

How far have you come?

Those crowns that I have pointed out to you are not for the skeptical, and unbelievers, but for the Saints of God. I am talking about those who have allowed Jesus to come into their hearts, and lives. These crowns will be given for work done, even as the modern day corporations give favourable packaged for services rendered, so God's package consists of five crowns. The faithful, who have endeavoured to plant the seed of the word of God, and to those who have made that last desperate, attempt to save some soul. The crowns will be awarded to those who have no fear in expounding the gospel to a lost world. Also inclusive of those who are unalterably opposed to the sin of deception practiced by an unbelieving world, in order to emanate God's grace in the believer's life.

Where does this leave you?

If you were a judge looking at your life in Christ laid before your eyes, could you in all fairness award a crown for that which you have accomplished for your Lord and Saviour?

If not, now is the time to begin to produce the work that Christ requires for your reward. Run the race to obtain the rightful crown on that day when God stands before you to hand out the final prize for the high calling. For only you can be held responsible for your work.

* * * * *

I Run

by J. A. [Jim] Watson

Wind in my face
I love the race
The body lurches on
Sweat beads spawn
Glance behind
Losers grind
No longer fun
Aches of body run
Muscles ripple fast
If only I can make it last
It's done! It's done!
The heat is won.

Body crumples to a heap
Inner soul begins to weep
For what is now past
A victory shadow cast
What's the direction next
On to that more complex
Does it never end
My victory to defend
I'm back in the race
Wind upon my face
Worn and weary my soul
Satan takes his toll.

Victory is when
We give again, and again,
Ever present cost
Satan has lost
And I receive grace
For Christ has won the race.

• • • • •

The Shepherd's Voice

The Bible says, *the fear of the Lord is the beginning of wisdom: and the knowledge of the Holy is understanding. For by me thy days shall be multiplied, and the years of thy life shall be increased.* Proverbs 9:10 - 11.

In these words of wisdom we clearly see that one needs to learn humility with all things that they have experienced. Knowing then that which we have received is first given to us by God, and we are to use it wisely.

Scriptures also declare that knowledge puffeth up when we begin to declare ourselves to idols. I believe that there must be an underlying assumption that knowledge and wisdom, and knowledge and understanding can be two separate entities. In the modern-day it can be said that in this century of 2000 we have the bowed religiously to that false god of academics seeking an avenue of human reward. Very clearly the Bible is the word of God, and in our initial thrust we need to show others around us that indeed the fear of God is truly where wisdom begins. Often times men have relied on their own findings that they believe it apart from creation is a more consequential avenue to follow than the Scriptures. If the purveyors of truth would begin to integrate the wisdom of God in their findings they would indeed convey that there is no radical separation other than that which God has already established that man needs to know.

We must however confess that knowledge has become the golden key to the success in our contemporary lifestyles. Another way to put it would be that academics have indeed become the God of man. Man has often portrayed elements of lifestyle which lacked truthful statements because they wished to leave God out by following other philosophies that bend the truth as they continue to walk in their own way. You can have many degrees, and still be at a loss for happiness and satisfaction of living with others. God in his wisdom laid out a plan that would inevitably bring peace, Joy, and ultimate happiness to all mankind who would accept its purpose of salvation.

Knowledge not only of our books or of the educators, but experience and the expansion that takes place within the person because of the knowledge they have accumulated. The difficulty however is the ability, or lack thereof, to transpose knowledge or experience to others in a method that is usable and understood. With all the man's academic understanding it is difficult to teach others and bring them to the same understanding, and knowledge of other men. The Bible, to which we hold dear as God's word is surely that which carries the only decision of accuracy for the absolute plan of satisfaction. For of that divinely inspired compilation of knowledge must be applied to other life styles than our own selfish path of existence. We must be transparent in presenting the message that the scripture carries, and be fervent in our application. We as believers have no apparent reason to follow the lie of a secular nature patented by people who are in need of some seemingly reasonable solution apart from scripture. If we would like a showcase of how our lives have been enhanced by the knowledge we received, we need only to direct persons to the reading of the scriptures. There they will find applications for living that truly work.

It is here in the Shepherd's voice I will attempt to pass on the vapour from scripture that has caressed my soul along the path of life. Hoping that as you ferret your way in the mine of knowledge, I may be able to leave you in the direction of a worthwhile gem. Even perhaps a little nugget, and maybe only a sprinkle of the gold dust of life's worthy attribute through God's word. Perhaps you will find an open tunnel to eternal life in Jesus Christ, Saviour and giver of Salvation with forgiveness that knows no boundaries. From time to time I shall refer to elements that were a part of my life only in an attempt to relate how God led me through the abyss of tribulation.

Often the thought comes to me now, I can measure the hits, and the incredible misses in a single incident, and how God oft times embraced me in times of ultimate joy which showed up more often than tribulation.

I do not intend to set up disclosures that would solve your problems, only those happenings that may give you some direction to turn. That may be a better path than the only one you see with tunnel vision. In whatever sense it affects you or anyone else who may relate to these things remember this, in all these things I have found God's hand which shepherded me through many dark storms, but has also shepherded me through more sunshine than darkness. It is my intent to set out helpful information by supplying scriptural verses, poems, humorous antidotes, and sermons written and delivered by myself. It is my hope that even a tidbit from this writing will help some soul along the way. Also that it may be found helpful by church leaders as a document supplying direction for them as they work with unbelievers. May we always remind ourselves, that we of ourselves are nothing, without the loving, living God in our lives. All things were made by him and without him we are headed to a lost eternity.

God, our great Shepherd calls men to speak for him. My prayer is that as he uses me to write I will be careful to speak for the Shepherd with his alluring voice leading souls and servants in a better way with Christ the son of the living God.

* * * * *

The Christian's Accountability

Daniel Webster was once asked, "What is the most sobering thought that ever entered your mind?" Without hesitating this statesman of wisdom replied, "My personal accountability towards God."

If only men found an answer such as this to apply so quickly and meaningful relating to every action of their lives what a difference we would see in Christianity. Souls are often led aside from commitment because of temptation, which minimizes the individual responsibility. A positive attitude is the strength of the Christian body, and the make up of the church's active function within our society. But when we abrogate the place of trust to allow ourselves to savor the way of the unbelieving world, we find insoluble practices take over. It is the adopting the way of a sinful unbelieving world into the extremities of the operation of a religious body that often brings dismay and disappointment to the church.

The scripture gives an incredible insight as to our individual responsibilities to the church.

Be ye doers of the word, and not hearers only, deceiving your own selves. James 1:22

Apparently, the apostle here was attempting to identify that when you heard the word you must also show your testimony in action. It was not enough to piously sit and hear the word. In other words when the word is read in the temple one must extensively absorb it in such a way that they could go to put into action. And that without fear to be applied within the community immediately. That is the only acceptable way of identifying one's seriousness of serving a living God to exercise their belief in the Jesus Christ.

Again we read, *Who is a wise man and endued with knowledge among you? Let him show out of a good conversation his works with meekness of wisdom. James 3:13.*

Many times, it is apparent that the listener has not absorbed the word of God to the extent whereby they clean up their language. This is rather sad when you hear a self-proclaimed Christian using language that is adhering to philosophy having no relationship to the salvation of Jesus Christ.

When a person does that it immediately identifies their loss of the realism out the transformation that is wrought in the believer after accepting the shed blood of the salvation message. Therefore, it behooves us to be all the more careful about putting what we have heard into action by embracing those around us who find it difficult to walk a godly life.

Be patient, then brothers, until the Lord's coming. See how the farmer waits for the land to yield its valuable crop and how patient he is for the autumn and spring rains. James 5:7

For many lives this indeed is a struggle to exercise of this verse because it asks the ultimate in limitations of attitude, and application of that which we have learned. To be patient brings to mind an old Oriental saying being translated goes like this, "They run away when the road is half built." We must learn to embrace those elements within our contemporary world, with all this diversification, the harvest of righteousness does not come overnight. Therefore, it behooves us to reach out with the arm of encouragement to those roundabout us. *Confess your faults one to another, and pray for another that ye may be healed. James 5:16.*

Here's a short sentence that people find which can also prove difficult to readily apply. Our first response to this statement might very well be, after all what business is that yours if I have a fault. This is probably not necessarily the Canadian thinking, but rather would be found to any area which refuses to see Christ as Saviour as well as being total North American attitude. This thinking prevails within our communities because we have a tendency to make a god of privacy. Therefore allowing failure, as we often are unable to share our fault with one another, yet God requires that we do just that.

A most important part to claim to rectify that is the next portion which reads, *Submit yourselves therefore to God. Resist the devil and he will flee from you. Jas 4:7.*

By absorbing this portion of the word of God we tend to bring our souls to a wide awake process. This is not a process of condemnation, but an appeal for a change of mind and heart. When we realize the very little it takes on our behalf to please God knowing that even though we may have exercised defiance, when we come before Him we shall be welcomed, and lifted up because we are His creation. Submission to our creator is the necessary act we need to exercise in order to put in place our stand for Christ in our community. We are able to flow in the living water with the pattern that God gave for us. This scripture allows us to keep it simple instead of wearing ourselves out trying to paddle against the stream, and allowing ourselves to absorb the warmth of moisture in the water of God to soak into our souls to their depth of our being.

Draw nigh unto God, and he shall draw nigh unto you. Cleanse your hands you sinners; and purify your hearts ye double minded. Jas 4:8.

Drawing nigh to God does not mean to stand beside a cross, nor does it mean to kneel before an alter, rather it in more processing means an appeal of that change of mind and heart. No matter how rebellious a life we have lived, nor how defiant the application of one's life has been a drawing nigh to God he will be lifted up and forgiven for all trespasses for. In other words drawing nigh and to God would change a person in the most drastic sense. It will be visible by others and the absolute change that has taken place in your life. There will be no mistaking that you have become a person of God.

Humble yourselves in the sight of the Lord, and he shall lift you up. Speak not evil of another, brethren. He that speaketh evil of his brother, and judgeth his brother, speaketh evil of the law, and judgeth the law: but if thou judge the law, thou art not a doer of the law, but a judge. There is but one lawgiver, who is able to save and destroy: who art thou that judgest another? Jas 4:10-12.

In this portion we are simply reminded that we do not have the right to be proud of our action, because of transparent change has been an active God forgiving us to the point that we contained their lives and love one another. The genius of Christianity lies in the fact that it demonstrates renewal. There is no other concept in the world that embraces renewal. Throughout our lifetimes we constantly need to be apprised of the nature of the beast I suspect. There is no wrong-doing in being careful that we rightly deal and abide with the proper influencing aura to the point that we are not falling into a serious trap of wrong direction. However the writer here is not putting down the act of carefulness, he is simply reminding us not to grab the opportunity of setting ourselves above another simply for the prestige option. That is a direction that quickly allows us to wander away from God's initial intent of supplying forgiveness for all who will accept salvation and become followers of His son Jesus.

Beloved let us love one another: for love is of God; and everyone that loveth is born of God, and knoweth God. He that loveth not knoweth not God; for God is love. If any man say, I love God, and hateth his brother, he is a liar: for he that loveth not his brother whom he has seen, how can he love God whom he has not seen? 1 John 4:7-8,20.

Jesus says, *"let these sayings sink down into your ears."* Luke 9:44a.

Many times I have heard the so called written testimony of a believer given from the pulpit that betray God's own words. People who simply have been unable to comprehend what it is all about even while they testify. Although they shout out about the things that God has done for them, they fail in the most simple terms, and that is by loving their fellow man whom they walk with daily. Be careful not to fall into that trap with the idea that you can make a judgment call, because it is not yours to make a judgment. That order belongs to God alone.

The very word, responsible, according to Webster's Dictionary means, 1. Expected to oblige or account. [for something to someone]; answerable; accountable. 2. Involving accountability, obligation, or duties: as, he has a responsible position. 3. Answerable or accountable as being the cause, agent, or source of something [with for]: as who is responsible for this state of affairs? 4. Able to distinguish between right and wrong and to think and act rationally, and hence accountable for one's behaviour. 5. a) trust- person b) able to pay debts or meet business obligations.

Having fully comprehended the meaning of responsible, adds a whole new dimension to the Christian concept of their duty and rather puts an end to a lax structure of the belief system.

Ye have heard that it hath been said, Thou shalt love your neighbour, and hate your enemy. But I say unto you, Love your enemies, bless them that curse you, do good to them that hate you, and pray for them which despitefully use you, and persecute you; Matt: 5:43-44.

I am glad that God is the author of the scriptures. For when it comes to a statement such as this, I as many others find it quite difficult at times to love my enemies as God requires. At the time I made it a point to stop and pray about the things that I need to do, at which time I asked God for the strength to love my enemy. I hear Christian people say, "I don't have any enemies." My response is, then you are not living a real life of submission for Christ. If we would not have enemies then God would not made provision for us to love them or be delivered from them. In all that we are to be cautious that we be not buried in a world of hate, but rise with our Lord in a world that even loves the enemy through our gift of salvation.

We must promote each other, Sunday school teachers, Elders, Deacons, Stewards, Board members, members, and adherents alike. Together follow again the scripture as it says, *Go ye into all the world, and preach the gospel to every creature. Mark 16:15.*

We must be very sure and especially careful about administering God's wishes in our responsibility. Each individual is responsible for the offices and position of the church. Also there must be an assured attentiveness as we each must represent for the growth pattern of the church. Take it upon yourself to make the effort to increase the church attendance. Be aware of those that are hurting around you because of the churches unfulfilled promises. Be constant in reminding your church to be cognizant of Christian ethics of the body of believers. Your action will have a toll on every other person attending the congregation that you are in. A very special area of Christian living is the element of language. The things we say, and the application of the way we say them.

Remember to be polite, and to make others that attend to be comfortable with you around. All of these will happen automatically in our Christian walk if we adopt a positive attitude about our walk with Christ. Never deliberately set out to belittle someone else, it will only bring you down,, and send a would be believer back out into a sinful world. All this leads to our judgment on God's choice and we simply are saying God you're wrong in your decision. That my friends is a dangerous place to be.

The question then is not only, What is my responsibility?

But, What is my brother to me?

How can *I* enrich his life in God's light?

* * * * *

The Christian
A Peculiar People

—◆◆◆—

A genuine Christian provokes opposition because he or she is different from the status quo, a peculiar people.

But ye are a chosen generation, a royal priesthood, a holy nation, a peculiar people; that ye should show forth praises of him who hath called you out of darkness into his marvelous light: 1 Peter 2:9.

More simply stated, a people for God's own possession. The terms here are directed to members of the believing community, referring to laity and clergy as established under God on the same plateau with no separating differences. They are associated by reason of their calling to a new life which is destined to fulfill God's purpose. They are made up of a great company of many kinds of people bound together to use their gifts for the service of mankind. People belonging to God in a very special sense. As the scripture includes it, a peculiar people. God's relationship to these type of people that he gathers to himself is that of a bride. God relates to the church as the husband-wife relationship, because He loves the church as a bride, but that it should be Holy without spot or blemish.

For thou art a holy people unto the Lord thy God, and the Lord hath chosen thee to be a peculiar people unto himself, above all nations that are upon the earth. Deut 14:2.

We must remind ourselves that peculiar people does not elude to that of being odd. It simply is a term of scripture that denotes the fact that we are a people set apart for God's own purpose as His very own.

Who gave himself for us, that he might redeem us from all iniquity, and purify unto himself a peculiar people, zealous of good works. Titus 2:14.

Here we see a need to implement a self mastering in which we follow the things that God requires of us as a Holy people which generates a flawless attitude of man to himself and his place before God.

We must remember that the Christian is not peculiar as in oddball, or lunatic, or practice of heresy. But that God had set a special people aside unto himself in that we being owned by God set aside for him by Christ's sacrifice on the cross

Sets us apart unto God and we are his peculiar people. Saved from sin, with the love of God by the redemption of the atoning blood of Christ. In other words we have been given the privilege of being set apart for God's own people, because God says, the world hateth you for your stand on a living God who lay out the redemption plan with easy access and you accepted eternal life through it.

In the book of Mark chapter 10 we find the story of a young successful business man described in verses 17 to 19 who was not only God fearing, but was aggressive to the point that he desired to achieve even more. His disheartening answer came in verse 21,

Then Jesus beholding him loved him, and said unto him, One thing thou lackest: go thy way, sell whatever thou hast, and give to the poor, and thou shalt have treasure in heaven: and come, take up the cross, and follow me. The writer goes on to tell of how disappointed he was in this response, he was sad at that saying, and went and grieved:

Many with an achievement agenda can readily relate to this young man's dilemma. After all he was given to logical reasoning, as were we while making forward strides. Also those things that we acquired were given to frugal thinking and putting forth good deals for others as well as for our own benefit. We strive to reach academic goals, and goals of accumulation, by telling ourselves that we are following according to God's will.

Is it not factual while we were measuring God's will by saturating our lives with self satisfaction, and God has little to do with giving direction?

When he does in a way that it flows against our grain of wilful acquirement, we grieve as this young man did. With that grieving we determine that to follow God's real agenda is too costly for us, and we go with the easy flow of self-satisfaction.

It is apparent this young man knew that he could make no deals to purchase the gift of eternal life that he desired, nevertheless his reasoning power drove him to at least ask for it. He walked away with nothing because the price was far greater than he had bargained for. He was to determine that by following Christ by the carrying of the cross without any material gain was an exorbitant fee that he refused to pay.

Stay with me while we examine this young man. He had wealth. Now the Bible does not condemn the ownership of money or the accumulation of material wealth. However when your time comes to die, you cannot buy one minute more of time, neither will you be able to purchase or contract another opportunity to be saved. This young man was morally responsible. He lived a clean life, he filled his duty by keeping the commandments, and he was a good reliable neighbour. He lived with all the attributes that we might look for in a trustworthy friend. The prime attribute he had at that moment, is that which we find ourselves inundated with a premium by the media, Government, and the sports world of today, that of being a youth. The world of business demand young people with scruples, whom are vigorous, and bitten by the success bug to rise to the top. [Whatever that is]

He had social rank. He for all intents and purpose was a climber of the social ladder. Some people give up a great deal to climb the proverbial social ladder. Usually the first thing to go is service for the Lord Jesus. They turn their backs on the church, as they are unable to mention Christ to remain with social grace.

This young man had a form of religion. He fasted, he tithed, he attended the Temple. He had good sense; he came to Jesus at the right time. Again he in humbleness knelt before Jesus to ask his question. Kneeling before God, sadly, is an element that has slipped away from many of the Christian churches of our contemporary age. He had the right spirit, a spirit of humility; he came seeking the right thing, eternal life. He came to the right place because he came to Jesus the Son of God.

The meeting was not on some hidden agenda. It took place in the open. The seeker here was offered a saviour as Christ directed the young rich man to follow him. He was offered a cross but he must release himself from carrying other burdens with him. The successful young man was sorrowful because he had much substance where he came to the crossroads of life and was unable to auction off his belongings to help anyone, even to helping himself to eternal life. Although he was offered a home in heaven he ended up rejecting the saviour of mankind, and forfeited his right to eternal life although it appeared to be a forgone conclusion to walk away from this special sought eternal life, he grieved with the knowledge of his loss.

Jesus here was not saying that poverty is a requirement to enter into heaven. Rather he was dealing with a specific individual that desired eternal life on his own terms. Jesus' statement simply points to the fact that one cannot acquire eternal life for social ladder climbing. It is a given through belief in Christ and acceptance of him as a saviour that allows you into God's special circle. God never intended his action to be a social structure to work your way up to. He has already come down to man in order to meet him with the salvation package on the bottom rung to climb with him and not for him.

The Christian religion has taken on a vast numbers of "do nots" to the point that the "do's" have faded into the background along with God. This portion of scripture depicting the sorrow of the young man also shows to the modern day Christian how we organize our own condemnation with a tribute to religion. We work with a preconceived idea that we work towards God's approval. Christ showed the work was already done. Unless we acknowledge the finished work we will also walk away in sorrow. Many stand grieving about the unreachable element of eternal life. They are finding it unobtainable when trying to reach it in their own way. They simply refuse to accept the fact that God has already made a way.

Are you self made? So self satisfied with your material gain do you in sorrow recognize your incompetence to remove the sin from your life?

It has already been done for you. God requires only that you believe in the unselfish sacrifice of his only son who shed his blood on the cross for your sins. Paid in full.

There are some that would have you believe that you continue to suffer because of your sin. That philosophy bears an element of untruth. Suffering is as much a part of life as birth and death. Sin will however keep you separated from God. You will find it much more difficult to cope without God on your side. You must submit to God for the gift of eternal life. He will help you through suffering. God has not promised that he will do away with human suffering here on earth.

One of the lessons to the church through this story has to be the enormous impact of not lowering your standards. Jesus made no effort to make a deal with this man. There was no deviating, or dancing around the basic fact of the real message. Jesus did not change his message nor modify the impact of the realistic package to gain a desirable follower. Jesus did not present tricky little come-ons to gain disciples. He did not offer up coupons for the best effort. He never misplaced the cross with an overhead projector. He always presented the wholeness of his message how pitiful that the churches have failed to follow the example of Christ set down here. No pleasing of the board, or the elders, no modification for status, only a straight message be willing to let go of what you carry when it separates you from the love of God. Always the saving challenge "take up the cross, and follow me."

You suffer because you sin against God. You suffer because of your pleasures that take you away from the servitude of God. You suffer because of your material gain as it begins to point out the severance of God from your life, and separating you from the blood of our Lord Jesus Christ.

The true Christ like man stirs up opposition, because the unbelieving world says he meddles in our affairs. He reminds us that God is the Father of all mankind.

Blessed are ye, when men shall revile you, and persecute you, and shall say all manner of evil against you falsely, for my sake. Matt 5:11.

* * * * *

Hopelessness

For we are saved by hope: but hope that is seen is not hope: for what a man seeth, why does he yet hope for? Romans 8:24-25.

The world's social order often refers to hopelessness, but you need to know that there is no such word scripted by God in His holy word. Simply it is not part or parcel for the vocabulary of the believer.

Yet this apparent hopelessness administered by the unbelieving world can assume a role in many phases of our lifestyle. According to Webster's Dictionary and along with some experience the word holds deep emotional structure. Looking at the Synonym, hopeless means having no expectation of, or showing no sign of, a favourable outcome (a hopeless situation); ***despondent*** implies being in a very low spirit due to loss of hope and a sense of futility about continuing one's efforts; ***despairing*** implies utter loss of hope and may suggest the extreme dejection that results.

This allows the understanding of those who attempt suicide when there is no one able to deter them out of the channel of dejection. Our social society uses a new terminology called depression in a vain attempt to wave aside the area of hopelessness that brings on despair.

There are those that accept God with a preconceived assumption that he will cure all their ills whether physical, emotional or financial, only to be disappointed when they find out that God intended all along for them to use the faculties that they were given at creation. They find themselves in despair because of their unrealistic view of the fulfillment they expected to receive from God. Peripheral rim believers are not yet focused on the fact that God is love. In that love hope brings all things into the light of the promises of God.

Many individuals seeking a solution to personal dilemmas join a church to find the society of perfect folk, and are dismayed to find only a community of redeemed sinners who still struggle in living as they do.

I am a fortunate person being brought up in a family that literally got along well with each other as well as having built good relationship with the neighbours for miles around us. All of us enjoyed our lives together yet suffered no trauma as we separated into our own individual lives.

The church on the other hand claims to be the family of God yet creates problems walking with those who do not believe exactly as they do. Or with people who will not bend to the stipulated none Christlike rules to build ungodly rituals as laid down by men who wish to impose their own type of religious form of Temple worship. Often, those self styled worshippers wander far from the scripture message of the gospel according to God's inspired word.

Only lip service is paid to the statement to being the family of God. Most peripheral rim believers churches are more likely able to hug a tree rather than their fellow believers. There must be a major overhaul in this area of church life if there is to be an eventful show of leadership in rearing a family of believers.

Parents of the world do not fly kites all day when their children are hungry. They look to the stream to fish for food to feed them. Not so with the church. They trample their wounded to death. No recovery period given by the organized body that claims Christ only by name seldom by action. Many who claim Christ are unable to talk to him as though he is with us. They are too busy building their own secret agenda. Do we really know him? We cannot hide our lives from God the way we hide our lives from other believers. Is what you are doing sanctioned by a merciful God? Or would God be appalled at the way you treat your fellowman?

To examine these things in our life style would be a commendable start in a truthful serving of a living God. If God is real only when we can talk to him in some abstract terminology, then we have not known God.

Many believers live on John 3:16 and often quote it as a ritual to their belief, but when asked what John 3:17 says their minds are blank. It goes like this, *For God sent not his son into the world to condemn the world; but that the world through him might be saved.*

We of the Christian faith have adopted the spirit of condemnation that goes against God's redemption plan. Show me a forgiving Christian, and I will show you someone who walks as Christ requires his followers to walk. The world of unbelievers more often will exercise that idea of forgiveness and allow the person to get on with their life. In fact they are more apt to exercise forgiveness than those who call themselves Christians. Although we cannot reach out and touch God physically as we touch each other, does not mean that he is absent from our gathering. When you get in touch with God, and learn to reach out in love to others around you in the name of Christ, your language will change, your thinking will change, and you will find it a pleasure to share your faith with others.

I lived in the beautiful mountains of British Columbia for a time. One important thing I learned as I ventured to climb them is that the only mountain you cannot see is the one that you are on. I believe that would permeate a much better attitude if we considered that element when things that oppress us, or elements that persist as we make ourselves to worry building mountains to blockade the life around us. It is at that time we need to make an about face to remind ourselves that the only mountain we cannot see is the one we are standing on. While there you either continue to climb up and conquer it or you climb down to leave the element of conquering for another day.

I hear young Christians planning programs to run about saving people, They would do well to remember a couple of practical things; (1) God saves people in spite of us. (2) People are not saved because they turn to God; they are saved only because they turn from sin.

If you are truly able to adopt the ministry of witnessing to the so called unsaved people, but you must first learn to walk with them to win them first as friends who can trust you. They will hear what you say when you talk a language that they can understand, without lowering your standards by attempting to deviate to what you presume to be their pleasure. Remember that they are able to relate to intelligent conversation. If we present ourselves as concerned people, and not people of condemnation they will believe us with trust and will receive us into their lives where we will be able to lead them with our life walking in the word. Make friends by not imposing some form of matter that is highly misunderstood, but simply by being available to help with their needs and give them a listening post, you. When people find that you are genuine first in friendship as well as solid in your convictions about a good lifestyle they will pay attention to what you say. As they believe what they see in action only then will they repent of their sinful ways. The scripture says, *And with many other words did he testify and exhort, saying, Save yourselves from this untoward generation. Then they that gladly received his word were baptized: and the same day were added unto them about three thousand souls.* Acts 2:40 - 41.

The Christian contribution is not a reformed system but reborn men. The Christian task is to keep alive that which is centered in the activities of God coming into the life of man in the character of Jesus Christ. We must understand the message that Christianity does have an interest in the world that God loves, and we must in our own lives be the constant reminder that we are designated to build that world as God would have it. We must be very careful that our actions in the name of Christ do not betray the gospels. Our lives must adhere to that which was written in the New Testament.

That ye may be blameless and harmless, the sons of God, without rebuke, in the midst of a crooked and perverse nation, among whom ye shine as lights of the world; Holding forth the word of life; that I may rejoice in the day of Christ, that I have not run in vain, neither laboured in vain. Philippians 2:15-16

They kept their eyes fastened to the light that is in Christ, never once focusing on the darkness of the world. When you take that position it will not be long before that light shines through all that you do and say to penetrate even the darkest corners of the world. Christianity has always been a way of life, and today is much more prevalent as we identify being close to the end times.

It is imperative that we know that God chose us as his servants. then we must be careful to administer his word to needy souls in an honest way without compromise, yet careful not to take on God's role as judge.

If one looks closely at the life of Jesus you will find that he always initiated the conversation in an element that was understood by the person to whom he was speaking. He did not provoke them to having to rise up defensively. He first loved them, and gave of himself in humility. Only then did he identify himself to the person to whom he had befriended. Often by a simple message, I am he whom you seek. He did not use any intimidation technique to bring them into salvation. He always made them welcome to come, and they believed and came to serve God with thanksgiving in their heart.

* * * * *

How Shall We Escape

How shall we escape, if we neglect so great a salvation; which at first began to be spoken by the Lord, and was confirmed unto us by them that heard him; Hebrews 2:3.

The book of Hebrews is never far from our daily life or business of daily living. The first chapter deals with the mystery of the Godhead, and the supremacy of Christ. Then the writer, inspired by the Holy Ghost, says "Therefore," and our attention is quickly captured as we are solidly drawn to the question, "Therefore what?"

The first verse in chapter two capsules the reasoning, *Therefore we ought to give the more earnest heed to the things which we have heard, lest at any time we should let them slip.*

Our modern today Society with the "only me" attitude has generated a highly visible and severe community of political correctness which has manufactured excessive loss of a true God consciousness. There needs to be generated the art of loving our fellowman regardless of what their life may allow them to appear to be. We in the real present tense do not want to hear the reason why for fear we are the ones who may be rejected. After all, it is much easier to reject someone else than to hear their full story that may destroy all our suspicions which elate us. We glibly tell ourselves there is really no need to understand the real and true situation.

God's word always indicates that believers knowledge is always personal, and it differs from our knowledge of nature. Nature reveals her secrets equally to Saints and scoundrels while God revels to the whole person. The whole person involves the intellect, the conduct, thought, trust, knowledge, and desires of the heart.

Blessed are the pure in heart: for they shall see God. Matt 5:8

I heard a man give a eulogy at the funeral for a leader of the labour movement, he said, and I quote, "all men of labour here, and throughout the world, are better off now that this person sits up there and begins to negotiate with God." end of quote.

Let me assure you after death there are and will never be any negotiations. The ultimate settlement has been made on the cross of Calvary signed and sealed by the blood of Christ. Knowledge walks hand in hand with fate if we are to draw near to God. Fate walks hand in hand with obedience and the truth of God confronts us with making a decision. We gain and hold divine truth only when it goes to work in our own lives.

Of the many funerals that I have had the privilege to conduct, the very first one stands out in my mind. As I walked up the church steps I was accosted by a woman cursing and swearing about the deceased person. She challenged me, or rather dared me to pay a positive tribute to the deceased. For if I would pay any tribute to the goodness of this person she was threatening to stand up and scream at the top of her lungs. She declared that there was no good in this person's life. I, having no knowledge of the life or adventures of the person whose burial I was about to commence I was appalled at this attack, and somewhat taken back with the particular action of this female tirade.

In fear and trepidation I approached the pulpit, raised my hands and proposed a prayer. I then made a statement that if there be any good in this persons life we must take it and exercise it daily that it may live eternally, and if there be any evil found then it must be cast into the sea of forgetfulness. I paused for ten seconds. There being no adverse reaction I carried on with the normal service.

How we ought to praise God for those people in our fellowship that take the initiative to adhere to, and put into practice God's word in their lifestyle.

With all the counseling I have provided, with all the sick I have visited, with all the bereaved I have comforted, with all the time I have lent an ear to the troubled, not one iota of that will get me to heaven. None of those elements work to that end. Only the grace of God given as a gift by him which confers salvation by the receiving of His son Jesus Christ gives that assurance. A born again conversion from sin with a transformation to a place in heaven with him. Only by my acceptance of Jesus Christ who gave himself upon the cross of Calvary to pay the price for me. My action is to accept him as my saviour. This simple methodology confuses the world.

When your claim is to believe in God then you must also accept the Bible as His divine word from which we accept our way of divine living with moral values. Let all else be still, let human talk be hushed, let the babble of the world be silent that we may pay attention to what God has said lest we drift away.

Yet it seems that we as energetic self centered packages continue to push away that image of God from ourselves. We would rather build upon myths of fable orientation, which are encouraged by the unbelieving generations.

We attribute happiness to St Nicholas. love to St Valentine, joy to a rabbit. While in fact Christ shed his blood to give us those as our very own attributes. God gave his only begotten son that we might have eternal life, and that we might experience the peace that passeth all understanding allowing us true happiness, love, and joy in Jesus. Christian, it is sin to attribute these gifts to mythical beings, or humanistic organizations within our social structure.

Dr Maurice Rawlings a heart specialist, visited Edmonton, Alberta, to speak at the Jubilee auditorium some years ago. He was then affiliated to some degree with Creation Science Institute. Most fundamental churches support this Institute, and endorse their theory of Creation rather than evolution. They also adhere to the basic fundamental doctrines of the scripture.

Dr Rawlings pointed out that life after death is real. In his remarks along with slide pictures he presented documentation about people whom were clinically pronounced dead yet they came back to life. He explained that as he attended patients of this nature how he witnessed the soul leaving the body to go on a journey to be sent back to re-enter the body because their time had not yet come to leave this world.

Scripture tells about that very thing, *And it is appointed unto men once to die, but after this the judgment. Hebrews* 9:27.

A person needs to be aware of that appointment because before that appointed time to meet death we must come to the place where we accept God's son as our saviour in order to have our place in heaven. If we are not believers in the Son of God and his work on the cross we shall spend eternity in Hell. We like the niceties of the church we even tolerate the propriety of Religion, and we most certainly appreciate an excellent orator as he delivers the word in a message with authority. Sometimes we even like some biblical sayings, but more often than not there are many portions we simply don't want to hear. That is because when we do hear we may be within ourselves see that enforced spirit to change our ways and our attitudes about others.

God's word describes it so vividly that it leaves no room for doubt. In describing the outcome of the rich man who ignored the need of the beggar on earth we read, *And in hell he lift up his eyes, being in torments, and seeth Abraham afar off, and Lazarus in his bosom. And he cried and said, Father Abraham have mercy on me, and send Lazarus, that he may dip the tip of his finger in water, and cool my tongue; for I am tormented in this flame. But Abraham said, Son, remember that thou in thy lifetime receivedst thy good things, and likewise Lazarus evil things: but now he is comforted, and thou art tormented.* Luke 16:23-25. Also Mark 9:41-48; points out the devastating type of afterlife it will be without Christ.

Time and again I have witnessed persons asking for proof that God exists. When you produce reasonable proof those same people still have difficulty handling the truth of God because it requires a difference to their lives. Some change, but most are not willing to make that transition in their lives.

Again the ugly question raises it's head, How shall we escape if we neglect so great a salvation?

The truth of the matter is that there is no escape without accepting Christ's station as the only son of God and his shed blood on the cross. Whereby we can claim forgiveness of sin.

In Brandon, Manitoba, I had organized the Christian Service Brigade, which was an organization similar to Boy Scouts except there was a greater emphasis upon the servanthood of God through belief in Jesus Christ as saviour. I was designated as Captain which gave me the overall leadership of programming as well as overseeing the work of others involved in the program with me. In our group there was a young boy who had a thousand questions if he had one. Those of you in leadership probably can relate to that. I was very cautious and careful to relate each question to the scripture when attempting to answer each one. Finally he shouted at me, "How come you have all the answers?"

"Well, you see, the scriptures prove God," I said.

"If there be a God, let him build a stairway right here," he shouted.

"If God were to take you up on your challenge, and built the staircase you wanted, you still would not believe. You would then demand a railing, and if that were given you, then you would demand a landing. If you received that then you would demand another flight of stairs, and so on." I said.

He stormed out of the church, but returned a couple of weeks later. I have not seen him since, but others tell me that he served the Lord well in his later years.

You will not get into heaven because of your unbelief, because of your inaction, because of your being lukewarm.

I know thy works, that thou art neither cold nor hot: I would thou wert cold or hot. So then because thou art lukewarm, and neither cold or hot, I will spew thee out of my mouth. Revelation 3:15-16.

To the unbeliever, you are a sinner with no hope. To the believer, you are a sinner made Saint with hope. Dedicate you life today. Give your life over to Jesus. There is only one way to get to heaven. You must come to God as a lost sinner humbly knowing your need for salvation. You must genuinely repent of your sins. Turn around where you are at and walk against the unbelieving crowds. Your life will change for the better. God will help you walk with him. You must in sincerity trust Jesus Christ the Son of God as your saviour. God looks upon the earth at His creation, and sees each individual as different from the other as He fully intended it to be when He created man in His own image. Then it is as Isaiah points out, *All we like sheep have gone astray ; we have turned every one to his own way; and the Lord laid upon Him the iniquity of us all.* Isaiah 53:6

Then as proof to what has happened in your transformation you must confess Christ before the world.

For with the heart man believeth unto righteousness; and with the mouth confession is made unto salvation. Romans 10:10.

The book of Hebrews is never far from exposing our walk in daily life or the business of daily living. The first chapter deals with the mystery of the Godhead, and the supremacy of Christ. Then the writer inspired by the Holy Spirit says "therefore." We then are faced with the question, "Therefore what? The first verse in chapter two wraps up the direction of reason for our search. *Therefore we ought to give the more earnest heed to the things which we have heard, lest at any time we should let them slip.* Heb 2:1.

This is a statement that has immediate and eternal application for every phase of action we enter into. Whether playing football, baseball, hockey or any other game for that matter. Or if we are looking at a blueprint to build from the architects point of view. We need to take earnest heed to the things we have heard lest we lose the game or watch the building collapse because we lost the art.

Today's believers appear to have lost their God consciousness as they continue to desecrate the altar that God requires, and to fragment the word. Somewhere along the way, sight has been replaced by whim. With whim we do that which is natural, and leave God out supposing that he will latch on somewhere down stream. Somewhere along the way we have lost our love for our fellowman. We make preconceived judgments upon our neighbours pushing aside those things that God would have us do. God requires that we love our neighbours as ourselves. But it is easier to reject someone else before they reject us. We get so wrapped up in the psychological ramifications that we instantly put God away for those things that we want.

The bible indicates that Christian knowledge is always personal, and it differs from our knowledge of nature. Nature reveals her secrets equally to saint or scoundrel. God reveals to the whole man. The whole man involves the intellect, conduct, thought, trust, and the desires of the heart. Knowledge walks hand in hand with fate if we draw near to God. Fate walks hand in hand with obedience. The truth of God confronts us with making a decision. We gain and hold divine truth, only when it goes to work in our own lives. The bible is the word of God. When you claim it to believe God, then you must also accept the bible as the divine word from which we derive our way of living with moral values.

In this divine word we find Christ Jesus, God's only son. Let all else be still, let human talk be hushed, let the babble of the world be silent, that we may pay attention to what God has said lest we drift away. We like the niceties of the church and we even tolerate the propriety of religion. It goes without saying that we enjoy the leader that is a good speaker who delivers his message with authority. Sometimes we even like short bible sayings, but there are many portions we do not want to hear because I may be forced to change my ways. More significantly I may have to change my attitude towards others. If I do actually hear the portion that I would rather was left out I may have to treat people differently even if they do not respect God in the same way that I do. As I hear, I may have to alter the decision about how I choose to take action in serving God. In hearing the word we will spend more time with Jesus, with God, in his word.

God looks upon the earth at his creation, and sees each individual as different from the other as he fully intended it to be in his creation. The book of Isaiah points out, *All we like sheep have gone astray; we have turned everyone to his own way; and the Lord has laid upon him the iniquity of us all.* Isaiah 53:6.

We are the sower of the seed, and the seed is the word of God. The sower soweth the word. Mark 4;14. Here we have Christ's parable of the four soils. When you examine this text closely you cannot help but see the responsibility of the soil is for the success of the seed. Therefore if we abdicate our responsibility to the soil in which we plant the seed we promote an ungodly atmosphere that attempts to promote a solution without the word of God. Any professional organization that teaches the solution without the Saviourhood of Jesus Christ, is ungodly. Psychologists are ungodly, Psychiatrists are ungodly, social workers are ungodly, law societies are ungodly, even our courts are ungodly because they do not hold Christ up as Master, and Saviour of the world. Any institution that teaches other than what God has set forth in his word is ungodly. Some go so far as to acknowledge God, but so does the devil, and he trembles for he knows the truth of God is real. The bible says little about listening, but a great multitude about hearing. The book of Hebrews points out the discrepancies of man's law, showing the old penalties under the law, no mercy, no justice, and most important lack of Godliness, no forgiveness. Thank God the writer does not stop here, but goes on to point out the new penalties. "How shall we escape?"

This question begs two more questions, "How great is our privilege?" and "How great is our penalty?" The penalty is clearly inevitable, the punishment for neglect of the clearly supreme word of God, is Hell. It won't go away. Separation from God. Like every generation before us, our generation trys to shun it. We don't want to talk about it. Husbands will not talk to wives about it. Wives will not talk to husbands about it. Kids will not talk to their parents about it. Parents will not talk to their children about it. People have been deliberate in their refusal to bring about the subject of a living God. There has been a move to perpetrate the mythical idea that they must not offend with the gospel, therefore do not talk about it. Rather than talk to those close to us about salvation we stand by and watch their journey to hell. For that we shall be accountable to a living God. Somehow we have borrowed the idea that it is alright to watch the believers being offended by the pooh, pooh, cry of the unbeliever with ungodly elements of their lives. I say, and the bible affirms it, that we are to be bold in the presentation of the gospel. We are to preach it to every creature. It is not a matter of offence to the world, it is the matter of giving each person that comes into our lives, the opportunity to accept Christ as their Saviour. We are not to offend the believer by refusing to stand boldly upon our convictions in serving our Lord Jesus Christ. To give our message is not an offence, rather it is the right way to offer a lost world a way of life, and to please God by carrying out the work he has asked of you. If the fear of all fears in your heart is rejection of people when you tell the story of salvation, the bible says that you are better off without them.

And Jesus answered and said, Verily I say unto you, there is no man that has left house, or brethren, or sisters, or father, or mother, or wife, or children, or lands, for my sake, and the gospels, But he shall receive a hundred fold now in this time, houses, and brethren,

and sisters, and mothers, and children, and lands, with persecu-
tions; and in the world to come eternal life. Mark 10:29-30.

I am not advocating leaving behind loved ones at the drop of a
hat, but I am telling you how important it is that each person in your
life knows and are assured that you are born again into the family of
God as followers and servants of Jesus Christ. Others must see and
will see the change that Christ will make in your life by change in
your attitude, your love, with ongoing concern for the salvation of
the lost world. Others will see Jesus Christ in us by our caring for
them. They will be refreshed by our new understanding ways.
Others will rejoice when they know we hear their despairing cry for
help. Our message then takes on a realism that works as we give the
message to the right path of escape because we no longer neglect
God's creation of his own image. We can now with a love that we
never knew before present to others this plan of salvation that works
to change lives.

We must continue to emanate the fact that it does not matter
what we think man is like, but it matters a great deal what God is
like. What has God done? Well he has sent Jesus Christ, his only
son, our saviour, to this world and I must follow him. Nothing else
matters. When you put something else before you that appears of
more importance then you are joining past generations of unbelievers by shunning the saviour. Why does the gospel of grace fail to
get a proper hearing?

We need to stand together as God's army, and demand a fair and
equitable hearing. If we are given an opportunity of a fair hearing
we can then give the evidence of Jesus Christ in your life. Men have
forgotten the justice of God. Every ease loving generation sooner or
later is rebuked by some awesome judgment, and stand to cry,
"Why me God?"

Such a great salvation. How great was it? How shall we escape?
Hear this, it was so great our Lord declared it. It was so great that
God spoke through Jesus, through his life, through his words,
through his death, through his Resurrection. In Jesus we hear the
authentic accent of God. It was attested to by those who heard the
witness of the living church, through men, through history. Certainly
born of God through many miracles performed by the son of God

himself. The bible confirms the gospel today. Let us mark the flaming question in Hebrews 2:3, How shall we escape? Again read the verse. It does not say how shall "they" escape, but distinctly asks, "How shall we escape if we neglect so great a salvation?"

If you do not have salvation, you cannot neglect it. If you do not believe in Jesus Christ as the son of the living God, if you are not walking after Christ by setting everything else aside, if he is not first in your life before friends, and family, and job, or sports, then you will not have to worry about this question. If you are not walking after nor for Christ you do not have salvation. But if you have professed Christ as your saviour, then God asks, "How shall you escape if you neglect so great a salvation?"

Since the writer of Hebrews confronts the professing Christian, their neglect might include several things. Neglect might include ceasing to give earnest attention to the things of God, and his plan of salvation that we first cherished. It may include a growing distaste for the reading of his word, or a blatant willingness to be absent from the gathering of believers, and the fellowshipping of the saints. Once we have missed that one gathering to worship the second exclusion is easier to fall into neglect. Again we fail to follow God's directive. *Not forsaking the assembling of ourselves together as the manner of some is; but exhorting one another: and so much more as you see the day approaching.* Heb 10:25.

Neglect of so great a salvation may also include shallowness. The seed planted upon the rock unable to take root. A lack of enthusiasm to study in depth God's word. God does not imply that you need to understand all the theological implications of the seed. His concern for you as the soil is to take responsibility for the growth of that seed. We may neglect salvation by getting caught up in earthly things. Perhaps it is sports that take first place priority over and maybe it's party time, somebody's anniversary, birthday, or achievement celebration, and you think you shouldn't miss any of those, but none of those things ought to take precedents over Christian worship times. Let us be ever prepared to strike out "evil" at the plate. Prepare to score points for our saviour before the end of the game. Let us work out in God's word by worship with the body of believers for a victory touchdown with Jesus Christ as our coach, manager, and owner.

Sometimes we even want to pass the buck to God, trying to justify what we ourselves have chosen by suggesting that God knows that we have all these things to do. Remember this, God has already put his plan into motion, and he expects us to abide by the set down rules. Not by our own decision, but by his requirements. You must put God first in all things. He commands, come and worship for I am the living God.

We live in a contemporary society of self indulgence, and there is a desperate need to maintain a real and new God consciousness.

Can we grasp the suffering of Jesus Christ as he hung on the cross with huge spikes driven through his hands. and his feet, a spear into his side with blood, and water gushing out, as he hung there for us. Can we identify with him as he lay there in the grave for your sins and mine? Are we able to grasp the torment as he ascended into hell to conquer death, Satan's last stronghold? Do we rejoice in identifying with him as he rose the third day establishing for us eternal life?

Remember when you first met Christ how you rejoiced in all these things as they became real to your life? What an exciting time that was. for me it was as though I were flooded with a great sea of light while the world changed. I was able to run in a new light, and to leave behind a black nothingness. I was free from the bonds of sin.

Somewhere along the way we lose sight of that moment of deliverance. We lose the love for God whom by grace sacrificed so much. Yet we have an increasing deadness of heart towards Christ who sacrificed all to pay the price on the cross at Calvary. With mere religiosity we keep a ho-hum philosophy of a major sacrifice. We come to a place where we boldly say, it doesn't really matter to God, and we heap unto ourselves a number of excuses for why we do the things we do to deter us from God's requirement. He says I require you to worship me because I gave my son for you.

Therefore shall they eat of the fruit of their own way, and be filled with their own devices. For the turning away of the simple shall slay them, and the prosperity of fools shall destroy them, Proverbs1:31-32.

This does not justify the thought that to be rich is wrong.

Neither is it wrong to successfully prosper. For serving God we are bound to gain over that which we already have because God has promised that it would be so, There is however a condition found in the scriptures that says, *But seek you first the kingdom of God, and his righteousness; and all these things shall be added unto you.* Matt 6:33.

Preoccupation with the news and events of the present world rather than the world to come may also be a method of neglect. Starving people tear our hearts out in their plea for food. The sick and afflicted cry out, and we are concerned, and so we should be. Terrible things are happening in our world, and we become possessed with getting politically involved. Let me remind you that the majority of the nations with a major starving population of today's world are victims of ungodly regimes. Now they turn to those of us who serve a living God who gave his only son a ransom for many with a cry for deliverance from their plight of poverty.

There is no doubt in my mind that we need to help, but let me assure you even that must take second place to the worshipping of our living God, and in that worship we shall be strengthened to go forth with a message that will bring relief to the world. Added to that growth will be the message of reward of a beautiful city that God builds for us called heaven. We must talk about the pearly gates, and about streets paved with gold, and about the trumpet sound that we await to hear when we shall go forth like soldiers into battle. God will come for his own, and shall take us up as we meet him in the air.

What a blessed picture we can portray to a lost world. We shall be able to transpose that blessed thought of a future with Jesus to the lost that they too would desire to be there with us. Let this language be first and foremost a part of our living, and serving our Lord and saviour. Let us make that special effort to work feverishly at building a God consciousness. Let us not be blind to relative issues and relative values. The coming judgment cannot be filed away as some agreed upon passed document. We must be aware of the continuing presence of God in order to become immune to the surrounding indifference to spiritual matters. Somehow we must endeavour to display our Christ likeness to the point that it will deter evil.

We must never conform to that of the world simply because the majority approves. We must be careful to access the wisdom of God's love, and we shall find that rejection of the world is not a bad thing. It, on the other hand, may very well be the most lifting reality of your spiritual life. You must be so transformed into Christ like-ness that people will know that your conversation will be untimely about the things of eternal values.

Therefore we ought to give the most earnest heed to the things which we have heard, lest at any time we should let them slip. Hebrews 2:1.

Here in capsule form the writer talks about God's word, Jesus Christ, God incarnate in the flesh, God's forgiveness, mercy, and love. God's lifting up, and setting down, his giving out, and going forth with his caring for us as we are. Let us make sure that we have not suffered the loss of God consciousness in our daily walk with the holiness of Jesus Christ our Lord and saviour. Saying,

I will declare thy name unto my brethren. in the midst of the church will I sing praise unto thee. Hebrews 2:12.

What have you done with Jesus in your life? Where does he stand with you? Are you able to declare his name?

More important, will he be able to declare your name before the church, before the father in heaven?

For with the heart man believeth unto righteousness, and with the mouth confession is made unto salvation. Romans 10:10.

* * * * *

Living God That Hears

———◦/◦/◦———

Though life holds all it's treasures out to everyone, it is the lifted face that enjoys the shining sun.

Listen God is speaking. Do you hear? I believe as God spoke to the prophets of old he speaks to man today. In saying that one must know that you cannot walk with God and at the same time be in rebellion with him. God has no possible way of entering into the fellowship with a soul that is disobedient to him or his will. Believe me when I tell you that it is mere mockery and absolutely useless to cry Lord! Lord! while you are in a disobedient state of mind toward a living God and refusing to do his bidding. The bible has the word "listen" only once, but four pages in my Strong's Concordance listing the word hear, hearing, and heard. Those who have ears to hear let them hear, says God.

We have forgotten the original price. How much did you pay for that vehicle you purchased? How much for that room full of furniture did you pay? Or how much for that new dress, or suit of clothes? Did you get a bargain? If you did, what was the original price? Yes God is speaking to us today, and we have forgotten about the original price he paid to bring it to our attention, because we are unable to hear.

* * * * *

On The Road To Hell

by J. A. [Jim] Watson

He was a lost and lonely man
Addicted to the Devil, Alcohol
Not much more his plan to tell
Abandoned God, some years ago

Now on his road to Hell

Some say, falling to drink is disease
That theory is human's social trap
If love excelled to fellow man increased
There is only a heavenly road to map

Away from the trip to Hell

And Jesus came and saved his lost soul
The church hasn't decided to take him in
But God has made him whole
Christians who fail to measure sin

Now on the road to Hell.

God the Father sent a terrible flood
God the Son paid the price with His blood
God the Holy Spirit indwells to make it understood

* * * * *

The Seven Wonders Of Hell

I t has been noted that the preacher is a Spiritual Doctor. He knows what is ailing mankind, but as he makes his diagnosis he must tell man that he is a sinner lost in the wilderness of me-ism.

Today we are not given important information that allows us to direct our paths away from hell. As pulpits disappear as altars from our churches so has the message about Hell.

I have heard the cultured, and the educated of the so-called elite of our Noble country say that they hate the thought of Hell, and would even doubt its existence. Let me share with you that I hate the thought of prisons, electric chairs, hangman's noose, I hate the thought of adultery, Homosexuality, theft, murder, rape; I hate the thought of people starving to death because of political warfare, and Terrorism in foreign countries which has now been experienced in North America. I hate the thought of poverty stricken homeless people in our own country caught as pawns in the Political forums. These are loathsome things; nevertheless they exist as a hideous reality. So it is that God has laid the responsibility of it upon my heart to tell you about the seven wonders of hell by reminding you of one of the bibles most fragmented stories over the years. As a rule it is only partially revealed to this generation.

The total of the original story is found in Luke 16:19-31. *There was a certain rich man, which was clothed in purple and fine linen, and fared sumptuously every day; And there was a certain beggar named Lazarus, which was laid at the gate, full of sores, and desiring to be fed with the crumbs which fell from the rich man's table: moreover the dogs came and licked his sores. And it came to pass, that the beggar died, and was carried by Angels into Abraham's bosom; the rich man also died, and was buried; and in Hell he lift up his eyes, being in torments, and seeth Abraham afar off, and Lazarus in his bosom. And he cried and said, have mercy on me, and send Lazarus, that he might dip the tip of his finger in water, and cool my tongue; for I am tormented in this flame. But Abraham said, Son, remember in thy lifetime thou receivedst thy good things, and likewise Lazarus evil things: but now he is comforted, and thou art tormented. And beside all this, between us and you there is a great gulf fixed: so that they which would pass from hence to you cannot; neither can they pass to us, that would come from thence. Then he said, I pray thee therefore, father, that thou wouldest send him to my father's house: For I have five brethren; that he may testify unto them, lest they also come into this place of torment. Abraham saith unto him, They have Moses and the prophets; let them hear them. And he said, Nay, father Abraham: but if one went unto them from the dead, they will repent. And he said unto him, If they hear not Moses and the prophets, neither will they be persuaded, though one rose from the dead. [kjv]*

1. The wonder of its existence:

In God's original plan there was no provision for Hell. The bible says that it was prepared for the Devil and his angels. The reason that men go to hell is that they allow Satan to lead them. Let us examine the scriptures to see what is said about these things.

And to you who are troubled rest with us, when the Lord Jesus shall be revealed from heaven with his mighty angels, in flaming fire taking vengeance on them that know not God, and that obey not the gospel of our Lord Jesus Christ: Who shall be punished with everlasting destruction from the presence of the Lord, and from the glory of his power; 2 Thessalonians 1:7-9.

Judgment of God will be manifested at the time Christ returns when at that time there will come into place the visible revelation of God's purpose in the sacrifice of His son.

For if God spared not his angels that sinned, but cast them down to hell, and delivered them into chains of darkness, to be reserved unto judgment; 2 Peter 2:4.

It appears here that the denying of Christ's sacrifice carries punishment even into the heavenly bodies. Here we are literally shown that there will be no acceptable excuse for the lack of accountability in living for God.

And whosoever was not found written in the book of life was cast into the lake of fire. Revelation 20:15.

The ultimate and severe destruction of evil. That action which has challenged God has no right to be, and shall be thrown into the midst of the burning flames because it perpetrates destructive evil abhorred by God to the point that it is known as the second death.

2. The wonder of its severe character:

The person whose mind was so warped that they ended up committing murder will remember the face of their victim, and recognize them from hell. In today's church, a committee would not allow hell to be a functional part of Christianity, but God created it, and it stands in the way of those who would change Christian philosophy to their own benefit.

V24, The thoughtless rich man cries out. "I am tormented in this flame."

I was personally involved in a raging forest fire such as is often portrayed by the electronic media. The flames leapt to the top of those towering evergreen trees creating an explosion to say the least is a startling experience. The terminology is, "the fire crowned" and we found ourselves trapped. I was the foreman, and suddenly I found myself responsible for the lives of seven men who depended upon my decision to deliver them safely from this fearful situation. Crowning fires are treacherous, and have taken their toll on human life. Although those brilliant multicoloured flames may be fascinating on TV, let me assure you they are not that beautiful when you find yourself at their mercy, trapped, with no visible way of escape. I directed the men to douse all their clothes in water even their heavy Mackinaw jackets. After having followed that procedure I instructed them to wrap their heads in the heavy wool jackets and to run through the blaze for all they were worth on the backfire trail. I am evidence of the survival of myself as well as all seven men of whom I was responsible for. At that time each of us were elated about our escape. It seemed to me at the time simply the use of common sense because survival was at stake. How often are we at the crossroads of life when we need the common sense factor to deliver our fellowman to the salvation of Jesus Christ.

That brings me to the third wonder.

3. The wonder of no escape:

v26, *and beside all this, between us and you there is a great gulf fixed: so that they which would pass from hence to you cannot; neither can they pass to us, that would pass from thence.*

In the incident I just used as a factual illustration I was able to manufacture an escape that proved successful. There is an exit from earth through death. There is an exit from heaven as Christ came down to sacrifice his life for our sins. Moses and Elijah came down to the mount of transfiguration. However we are told that there is no exit from Hell.

4. The wonder that it never ends:

Moses led the people out of bondage from Egypt. Abe Lincoln, is credited for putting an end to slavery in United States. Those who are overcome with sickness get well. Others who sorrow in the loss of their loved ones, eventually stop weeping outwards, and after tragedy fades, there is boisterous laughter. Everything appears to have an end to its existence, but there is no end to Hell. The rejection of Christ is the only unpardonable sin. All other sin is forgiven but when we turn our backs on the creator of man, God, we shall find ourselves entered into an eternal pit of damnation which God named Hell. There is no exit and it never ends.

5. The wonder of its inhabitants:

*But the fearful, and unbelieving, and the abominable, and murderers, and whoremongers, (*homosexuals and lesbians*) and sorcerers (*psychics*), and idolaters, and all liars, shall have their part in the lake that burneth with fire and brimstone: which is the second death. Rev 21:8.*

There are no questions applicable here to ask about the what ifs or could have beens. The dark blanket of disapproval has been spread, and will only be uncovered by God as He casts away into that eternal flame of damnation those who have not accepted His son as their personal Saviour.

You do not have to be a great sinner in the eyes of the world to be lost. Many good people according to the world's standards will be in Hell.

There will be husbands who had Christian wives. There will be children who had praying parents. There will be those who were almost persuaded. there will be those who put off salvation with the excuse that they didn't have the time to deal with it right now. There will be those who said "I hope so." While they depended on their works building a resume of their own goodness. There will be those that simply ignore Christ, and the message of how he gave his life upon the cross making a certain path of forgiveness through his shed blood. There will be those who were care givers, and shelter keepers, and social workers, daycare people, policemen, lawyers for sure will be there. Some politicians will be there, and because of your lack of witness you may find your good neighbour there, as well as some of your family.

6. The wonder that so many are going there:
Enter ye in at the straight gate: for wide is the gate, and broad is the way that leadeth unto destruction, and many there be which go in thereat. Matt 7:13.

You may know a number of Mountains that some will have to climb to arrive at their destination of a burning hell. I, for my own benefit have listed here a number of mountains that people will climb over to get to hell. 1. Church, 2.the gospel, 3. the bible, 4. conscience, 5. better judgment, 6. love, 7. prayer,
8. holy spirit, 9. the cross, 10. Christ.

Foothills sometimes a sea of tribulation to overcome before starting that mountain climb. Those foothills might encompass, hesitation, doubt, envy, criticism, lack of concern, bad attitude, and other elements that separate us from the love of Christ. The sad part is that people will wrack there bodies, and risk their souls, struggling over wild terrain, and climb over the mountains that I previously mentioned as well as others to end up in Hell.

<u>7.</u> The wonder of prayers in hell:

v27 of Luke 16 reads, *Then he said, I pray thee therefore, father, that thou would send him to my father's house*:

You see, he had a problem, he waited too late to cry for mercy. My Christian friend, you must see in this portion of God's word the need to testify to the unsaved, or the unbelieving sinner, because he will be recognized in hell. God loves you; that is why he saved you. *For God so loved the world, that he gave his only begotten Son, that whosoever believeth in him should not perish, but have everlasting life. For God sent not his son to condemn the world: but that the world through him might be saved.* John 3:16-17.

My God is not willing that any should perish. What about you? Are you able to love the unsaved enough to bring them to Christ? Or are you willing to allow them to wallow in the pits of hell? Oh! my friends I plead with you today to hear the cry of the perishing; "help thou my unbelief."

Christian, renew your covenant with God today. Have a burden for unsaved souls. Allow the Holy Spirit to direct you to someone today. Pray for the burden of a soul to be laid upon your heart today. Claim souls for salvation that their blood will not be upon your hands for the sake of refusing to talk with them about God. Pray for the ability, and the wisdom, to lead them to a saving knowledge of the Lord Jesus Christ. Show them how they too can have assurance of eternal life and be in heaven with their living God the father along with our saviour Jesus Christ. Renew your commitment to your Lord Jesus Christ now. Give him complete control of your life, and watch your world expand while you reap the rewards rejoicing.

Are you afraid that you may not know what to say? Hear God's word. He gives you one of the simplest messages a person can deliver in John6:37. *"Him that cometh unto me I will in no wise cast out."* No limit is set about duration of this promise. It does not merely give a message with time limitations that will be applied at some later date nor does it imply qualities of academic proportions. It is a very simple and precise statement issued by God himself that allows each person to come, as they are, right now.

But suppose someone comes, and accepts but slips and sins afterward. God says if any man sin we have an advocate with the father, Jesus Christ the righteous. Suppose those who become believers backslide? God says, "I will heal their backsliding, I will love them freely: for mine anger is turned away from him." What then happens if the believer falls into temptation? God is faithful, who will not suffer you to be tempted above that which you are able; but with temptation also make a way of escape that ye might be able to bear it. But the believer may fall as did David. Yes but he will purge them with hyssop and they shall be clean; he will wash them and they shall be whiter than snow. From all their iniquities I will cleanse them. I give unto my sheep, saith he, eternal life; and they shall never perish, neither shall any man pluck them out of my hand.

What say you to this oh trembling feeble mind? Is not this a precious mercy that coming to Christ you do not come to someone who treats you well for a season then discards you. He has given us the power to become the sons of God. He will receive you without condition, and you shall be his forever. Receive no longer the spirit of bondage and fear, but the spirit of adoption.

Oh! the grace of these words, I will in no wise cast you out.

* * * * *

Loving Friends - Farewell

—⟨●/●/●⟩—

I want to just talk with you as friend to friend, because I love you. We have not come to praise mothers, and not to praise fathers, but as a tree is filled with gifts, and as Peter walked on water in obedience to heed the Master's call. God is love. My inroads to your lives are because of God. We could ask the question, why does God bring people into our lives, and take them away again?

I believe, he does that in order to show you how to use your very own gifts that he has given to you. To enable you to appreciate what they are, that you may be enabled to exercise each gift to a greater degree than you realized was possible. Perhaps the saying from scripture, where two or three are gathered together in my name there I am also, will take on a more meaningful fulfillment for your lifestyle.

You have changed. We do not change each other, we set examples to lift each other up in the walk of following Christ. God's holy spirit is the one who makes the change in our lives, and changes our attitude toward our fellowman. There is a ministry in receiving. You have received me, and I you. You say that I am versatile and flexible, perhaps it is because that I understand the path that you now walk, for I have been there to walk the same walk for God to give me a greater understanding of my fellowman. There are times when you will think that you walk alone. Not so! says our Lord. Lo I am with you always.

I have walked with Prime Ministers, Premiers, Senators, Members of Parliament, Cabinet Ministers, and writers of Philosophy, and Religion. Writers of songs, and poetry. I have walked with both Radio and TV personalities, and stage entertainers. Also I have walked with the poor, the drunkard, the murderer, the unbeliever, drug pushers, harlots, users, the damned, lustful, atheist, agnostic, arsonists, thief, the large and the small. I have addressed small gatherings as well as crowds of thousands.

Does all this make me more of a Christian person than you?

Not at all. Not in the eyes of God, I am a sinner saved by his unmerited grace. The difference that you discern is, experience, different than what you have experienced, accompanied with aggression, and knowledge in that which I have attempted to deliver to you that you may absorb the real and true message of a forgiving Saviour. There here are two sets of experience, it does not elevate one higher than the other when we use the experience to nurture others. The intent is simply to bring each one into the family of a living God. I like to think of it as having a touch with Jesus.

Have you felt the touch of Jesus?

How wonderful it has been to share with you even a minor portion of my life in Christ for a very short time. May God's grace continue to flourish amongst you until I am called to return and minister to you for even a short moment.

* * * * *

Praise From Incarceration

━━◦୭◦୭◦━━

Testimony giving account of the modern day justice system leaves much to be desired. Consistent occurrence of false imprisonment of many people of the North American society which is touted as a Democracy, we witness too many times the abuse of incarceration. We have a right at least to ask the question, have the times changed? Here when we read in Paul's account we find reason to pause.

Each age emphasizes a facet of truth. Paul, in Acts, was a prisoner in a place where they had experienced a phenomena that some writers explain away as an earthquake. I like to believe that it was an exact movement of God's hand to deliver Paul, and his fellow believers from a very precarious situation to establish fear in the heart of many for moving against the servants of God who claimed Jesus Christ as His son and their saviour. It has been a major observation that life and death are one even as the river and the sea are one.

And at midnight, Paul and Silas prayed, and sang praises unto God: and the prisoners heard them. Acts 16:25

There is no evidence as to the hymn that was being sung here however the words of praise given in harmony with songs of praise proved to have a transforming influence upon the jailer. Paul, being incarcerated for his belief in advocating the salvation through Jesus Christ, found himself in a position to bring a soul to Jesus even under these devastating happenings that surrounded him and other prisoners. Instead of scrambling for safety as many of us would today, he stood his ground to take time to lead a soul to Christ. Sometimes we are so caught up in our woes that we fail to see the apparent need for the gospel within the turmoil that we find ourselves in. Here we see that through honest heartfelt praise affected those around Paul and Silas. Their actions, in disaster, spoke volumes to those who witnessed their stand. Without a shadow of doubt brought forward the glory of God to the point that their adversary the jailer sought to be saved. I am always impressed with the simple message here from Paul, *Believe on the Lord Jesus Christ, and thou shalt be saved, and all thy house.* Acts 16:31.

If one reads this very carefully noting all the events that surrounded this statement. The keeper of the jail was about to kill himself because he thought that he had lost all the prisoners; But Paul saw him and called out to identify that all the prisoners were still with him. I am sure that today the norm would be to allow this guy to go ahead with what most prisoners would feel he justly deserved. Then a believer took charge, and commanded him to stop his own execution without any fear of what the repercussions may be, and it turned around many lives. For the jailer and his whole house was promised salvation.

We see here two movements at work. The unsaved jailors in fear, both of the prisoners now loosed, but even a greater fear of their employer who would surely put them to death for losing control of their keep, even through an earthquake was to blame for the situation. Paul, the leader of the Christian community, and the jailer , leader of the unbelieving community. Also present was the affirmation that you cannot be of both camps. The Socialist cannot stand as a Socialist by himself, as the Christian cannot be a Christian by himself alone. We can only adhere to that in which we believe when we engage other people. Paul quickly seized the opportunity, and invited acknowledgement by the jailer. So often we fail to render the need to apply the acknowledgement level to the unbelieving Socialist of our modern day unbelief in Jesus Christ.

A point established here, is to walk with our living God, a person must become a part of the Christian movement It is not a hiding place that will nurture all of our wounds and heal all of our hurt feelings. There must be a positive action on the part of the believer. The seeker , who is not yet complete in acceptance of Jesus as Saviour, must be encouraged to become involved in the church fellowship in order that they may move from play school status into a real learning structure.

Singing has always been a part of the worship in our religious heritage, an element that existed even before Christ's appearance here on earth. There is nothing quite as reasonable and soul settling as praise to God in a good hymn singing fellowship. In saying that I must insist that we must be cognizant of the error of allowing music to take the place over and above the word. For God requires the acceptance of the word that He has set down for our direction in worship of Him and to love our fellowman. Also we must be very careful that the music we allow in our worship time actually brings the message of the cross to the forefront. Otherwise we allow the world to destroy our quietness before God.

If it is your intention to walk with Christ as a believer there are important exercises to follow. As you walk in two worlds one secular, where you earn your keep at whatever vocation, and the other Christian, where you must develop your new world with love, loyalty, and sacrifice. It is an invisible world where you must acquire spiritual eyes to recognize those things unseen. You will also be required to develop spiritual ears that will help you understand the theology of prayer asking God to forgive you while you take into account all the blunders you will make in the baby walk in your beginning with him. Know that he is already willing to forgive all things, but he desires you to ask for that forgiveness even in small things.

It is imperative that you know that you cannot be a Christian privately unto yourself. Christ repeats himself by his challenge for us to tell others about the gospel that purchased us. Neither can you be illiterate and understand the fullness of God's word. Your knowledge of Christ cannot remain dormant to remain in spiritual inactivity. You need to exercise with the information you collect in your walk. When you accept the Christ walk you will as others before you have to explain the cross. It takes words, and wisdom in gentle terms abounding in a special love for your fellowman.

When Paul, and Silas, exercised their faith through the gift bestowed upon them by God, which was at this point a song of worshipful meaning, that embraced all other prisoners. The jailer and all of his house are identified as accepting the saviour. This new Christian went to the authorities and was able to convince them to release Paul and the others. When he brought the news to them Paul insisted that those in authority of ungodly acts must come on their own to release him and the others. He refused to leave until the leaders did in fact come to talk to them. The word given and being allocated in a responsible manner goes on endlessly even as we read the story again today.

Sincere unexploitive worship will render earthquakes to the saving of the soul. There was a right attitude in that short time of worship, and souls were saved. No music just singing with the word. There were no fluorescent lights, no overhead power point projectors, no enticing fixtures of any kind. These believers were in Jail. Mistakenly they would never be invited to today's activities in the church. After all, committees made up of people who know the right way would have them designated to be watched for a year or so before including them into the fellowship, and then forget about them altogether as they faded from a seared conscious altogether. Even though their faith was right with an attitude that excelled before a living God, and it excelled in love and adoration before a loving God.

The jail keeper asked the question, "What must I do to be saved?" He was given the answer, "believe," and he believed. Not only did he believe , but he was changed. Prisoners that he had inflicted with punishment, he now washed their wounds. Those he treated with disdain now he fed with a new love in his heart. How great a lesson here needs to be absorbed by today's Christian community.

In relationship to that miraculous change do we then simply trifle with Christian love, with Christian life, with life living ethics.? Or do we become more sincere, more meaningful, exercised with staying power.?

Courage can be an elusive emotion, however when we capture even a remnant of it we can sing in one accord the praises unto a living God that will make miracles happen in our lives. Let us capture, and put forth in a major way an enthusiasm for Christ.

The persons that follow the worldly ways are unrelenting followers of Satan, and are watching, and waiting to hear your words of praise that will change their lives.

* * * * *

Let God Love

Beloved, believe not every spirit, but try the spirits whether they are
of God: because many false prophets are gone out into the world.
Hereby know ye the spirit of God: Every spirit that confesses that
Jesus Christ is come in the flesh is of God: And every spirit that
confesses not that Jesus Christ is come in the flesh is not of God:
and this is the spirit of the anti-Christ, whereof ye have heard that it
should come; even now already it is in the world. 1 John 4:1-3.

Here the writer, moved by God, points out one of the most
emphatic areas of our Christ like walk to test the spirits. All
too often we accept situations and apply our own evaluation as to
the acceptance rather than God's.

When the spirit is right it will generate love, caring, and self-
lessness in our thinking and in our action. *Beloved, let us love one
another: for love is of God; and every one that loveth is born of
God, and knoweth* God. 1 John 4:7.

We do not have to ask the question, does God love us? because
he has acted in human history to make known his great love for us
through his son Jesus Christ shedding his blood on the cross of
Calvary that we might know a greater love hath no man than this.

We add to that super structure that took place upon the cross
through the gathering of the church to feed the hungry, cloth the
naked, welcome the stranger, to care for the poor and afflicted, and
heal the sick, while we plead for peace. The knowledge that God's
attitude toward us is one of love has been confirmed again and
again into the twenty-first century. Jesus bled and died for us so we
can know the love of God. If only we could come to the place

where God is given access to our lives and we allow him to love us so much more would be accomplished.

Many of us are aware of the parable of the prodigal son. It is a story about a father who had two sons in which he encompassed both with a great love. These sons , however, had a difficult time letting their father love them. The youngest one demanded that his father give him the portion of inheritance that was due to him. When the father conceded to respond in a positive way the younger son left home to live in an unfamiliar land against his father's wishes. The parable goes on to show how his money was spent without any plan in sight. The young man found himself without money and without friends. As soon as he was broke his so-called friends left him high and dry. Without wisdom that only comes with age and experience, he soon found himself in pretty tacky situations. It was then that he realizes that even his dad's servant's received a much better living than what he had at the moment. Finally coming to his senses he decided to return home to ask his dad for a servants job with that he set out and returned home.

The father spotted him traipsing down the road and realized that he was finally coming home. He did not take the "I told you so" attitude, instead he ran out to meet him and embraced him to welcome him back. Then he took the extra step and celebrated the homecoming. He gave the repentant son a set of new clothes, a fine ring of the family symbol, and a great feast. More important the son had come to allow his father to love him.

Well, the oldest son who had stayed home to help with all the work was not too happy with all this fuss. He refused to attend the celebration. But the father in his love sought out the older brother. When the two met the older brother challenged him about killing the fatted calf for a rascal that had spent the farmer's hard earned income. He said, "I have been with you all the time and you never gave me a party so that I could invite my friends. You never gave me a ring or bought me expensive clothes. You give this scoundrel a celebration.

The father tries to explain, "Your brother was lost but now is found, was dead and now is alive again. You are always with me. Everything I have is yours.

The younger son had found his father's care oppressive, and ran off and wasted his inheritance. The older son rebelled too. He felt that he had earned a larger share of his father's estate. In this parable Jesus shows us two ways in which we often refuse to let God, our heavenly father, love us. We rebel against the way of life that our father has called us into. We refuse to come to his house on a regular basis to pray with him; we do not want to be our brother's keeper; we do not want to look upon anyone in need as our neighbour; we do not want to love our enemies; we do not want to turn the other cheek when we are mistreated. The demands are too much we want to go our own way. We flee the church, we stop praying, we stop loving, we stop living the Jesus way, we stop giving of tithes and offerings of substance, but worse we stop giving of ourselves to further the love of God.

When we decide to be honest with ourselves, after a long abstention from worship, we come to realize through our own experience that no other community other than that of the church can supply such an energy of lasting love as they. The church is designated by the living God to produce the consistency of compassion and continued challenge to fellowship in God's love. In that fellowship one with another we shall produce the very best of ourselves and our fellow human beings for the absolute tribute in service to worship God through Jesus Christ his son.

The scriptures say, *Beloved, let us love one another: for love is of God; and every one that loveth is born of God, and knows God."* 1John 4:7

A prime similarity of Jesus with the Christian of today, they did not like him because of those he associated with, the sinner, people of low degree. They were particularly offended when he chose the company of the not-so-religious of the day, or when he chose to be with a sinner rather than a Pharisee or scribe. In other words, he failed because he chose to be with the not so academic. He chose to be with those whom society viewed as not climbing their ladder of success. He was willing to be of help to the underdog.

So it becomes adequately clear that letting God love us depends on our readiness to let God love others as he pleases.

You see in the parable of the lost son, the older brother practiced legalism. It was better noted as a perverted religion he kept the letter of the law but denied the spirit. Sad to say, but there a majority within the church of the same mind of the elder brother. We call them stewards, deacons, elders, and segment leaders of our church. In this contemporary age they walk in the fog of contempt towards God's commandments that instruct us to love others as we love ourselves. Instead of a positive attitude towards those who would follow Christ and serve him, they permeate an awesome negativity toward newcomers to congregations. They have a tendency to substantiate their behaviour on bad attitude toward the wayfaring strangers that are found in their midst and make a human assessment rather than implement the love of God.

When Paul was ready to allow God to love him, he became one of God's most useful vehicles and a worthy vessel.

Now comes the day for you to choose to allow God to love you. Are you willing? Are you able? Are you ready? If your answer is yes then prepare for a great change to take place in your life as it did of old when the apostles and disciples allowed God to take them and love them.

God is trying to love you. Let him love.

* * * * *

Random Thoughts

—⟨𝄢𝄢𝄢⟩—

Family are the most important people you will ever know. They are your people therefore they rate the best from you. They deserve politeness, kindness, and your good manners. the same things you are happy to share with company are first due your family. When a guest comes along you are bright and interested in all their goings and comings, as well as their well being. In their need you will be helpful to them. When your friends issue you an invitation to celebrate with them you manage to be clean, set your hair in place and dress for the occasion. At home with the family your idea of behaviour is any old way is good enough. That thinking is pure nonsense. There is no one in all the world who will appreciate you as your own family does. Return their compliment by looking your best when you are alone with them. They may never challenge you for your lack of courtesy to them. When your with them act as though you care and you will be surprised at the way they will appreciate your respect for them.

Help, Lord, for the Godly man ceaseth, for the faithful fail from among the children of men. They speak vanity everyone with his neighbour: With flattering lips and with a double heart do they speak. Psalm 12: 1-2.

The sunset, like some magical frayed paint brush, presses itself against the western sky in an awesome array of beauty which makes you realize only God could perform such an awe inspiring miracle. Remembering the Psalmist who said *"Only a fool saith in his heart there is no God."*

Even so it burns my soul to ponder the inadequacies of the organized church and brings me to wonder if the setup machinery run by committees and such, could possibly be used as an instrument of God. After all Christ did turn his back on the religious order of the day. The then known church with all its fervour for the soul, and the coming messiah had not pleased God, but still functioned as an organization. With all its rich wisdom and deeply entrenched moral standards they fell short of God's requirement to love their neighbour, and love their enemy. In those times if you even swore in the remotest sense of the word you would be put to death by the stoning committee.

The question then must be; do our churches lack the vision of a saved world, and if they do not, then whom shall they save?

If the answer is yes, what is it they lack? Further what must be done to enhance their position to find God's favour? Should God return to take the world to task for all the errors?

Should we perhaps try to find our own favour with God by refusing to identify with any of the existing organizations as they are?

Of course we in our infinite wisdom and regenerated soul, realize that our relationship to God is a very personal one. Truly a need to experience with Jesus Christ. Why then does the church as such create so many anxieties amongst its own?

The answer in reality is simple when we examine the light in which we view the church. There are those of us who would view it as functional political machine that cannot relate to the individual. Others would say it is a body made up of various committees to portray a religious form to society as a whole. Some would even tell you that it is a society within a society that adopts the terminology, "Religious" to fulfill the need of the innermost being, and some deny that the innermost being exists.

These ideas that overlook the simplistic truth that God always puts forth in scripture. One of these ideas is that the church is only a group of believers gathered together to worship a living God, whom saw his son give his life for the remission of sin, and witnessed his resurrection as he rose victorious over the grave.

Somehow when the church is mentioned we have a tendency to think in terms of building or organization. Let me assure you, it is not wrong to have either a building, or an organization, in order that we may work and worship together. As we worship we are to further the gospel with increasing love and trust of our fellowman. there is a sentiment that we could do without buildings as Christ says where two or three are gathered together there I am also in the midst.

Many errors of the Christian ministries come because of a warped conception of what the church is. If there is blame to be placed we try to put in on the shoulders of pastors or preachers of the congregations. However each one must take some of the responsibility because we need to know God's word. Then if there is some leader who fails to inform the gathering the truth about what the church really is we are to hold them accountable. We cannot hold any one person responsible until we take it upon ourselves to establish the real meaning of the church. The church is you, and me, together or walking alone worshiping a living God.

Having made that statement let me make it very clear that many pulpit committees, and boards of management at the organized church level must shoulder a measure of blame. It is often the personnel of these bodies that abrogate their responsibility of informing the hired preacher as to their stand on what a church is. Many have the attitude that this is the responsibility of the Preacher, but the Preacher is one who is called to Preach the word, not to establish it, because God through Christ has already established it. Many of the church problems come from the leaders that lack understanding of the function of God's elect. They still believe that they somehow maintain the inalienable right to tell the preacher what to preach. The question then is, When do we allow the spirit to move the speaker, and when does the church body allow their pastors to submit to the grace of God?

They have made the decision to issue the call to a person who under God's guidance will help them worship as they ought. Many boards are boards of forgetfulness as they attempt to manipulate pastors to do their bidding.

It is as though the "called" leader is some interpretive genius that somehow is going to bring the new concept to the local body. He would then sanction the board members position of leadership by bowing to their demands. of some heroic stance not yet experienced by other believers. When the called person fails to exalt the lifestyle of the board rule, he is deemed to be somewhat less than what they expected God to send.

What then is the roll of a called person?

Scripturely speaking, he is called to preach. However the contemporary interpretation of "the call" comes with a variety of titles; pastor, preacher, counselor, organizer, youth director, and he must be wise. He must come with a multitude of experience, as well as lead the singing, chair all meetings, and he must relate well to the community. He must comb his hair right, and dress properly. Oh, yes, he must drive the appropriate car for the ministry, "a clunker." We will not tolerate too many changes, he must be shy, he must be aggressive, and he must not expect too much help with his work from anyone here. After all why would we help when we know that God called him to do all things by himself. He must not be over thirty-four and under fifty with twenty five years experience.

I walked today where Jesus walked, with jagged pebble cutting my tired feet. I looked up to see an illumined figure before me. The brilliant sun made the heavy armour shine magnificently to project the strength within. A Roman soldier. The well tempered armour projecting all its protective and glamorous being, and emanating a strength not to be matched in that day could only bring disaster to the Lord and his followers.

How very sad that today we see the brilliance of the world, and fail to recognize it as a disaster to the Christian way of life. Our shining soldier to fear we hear called humanism. or humanitarianism. Often used to disguise a Godless mission.

We intently listen to the cry from these religious poachers, "You are your brothers keeper." While there is an element of truth in that statement there is another defining truth that must be discerned, that is if those persons are not believers in a living God, they are not your brothers. Do not lose sight of that truth.

Our responsibility to the unbeliever is simply to preach the salvation message whereby they must repent and believe in the Lord Jesus Christ as their saviour. We must tell them about God's plan of salvation. If they refuse to accept that message, they cannot claim to belong to the family of God. For it is by His own word says they are not of God when they believe not.

How do we judge a preacher? The truth of the matter is, you don't. What then is the role of the deacon or the elder of the church body at the local level?

One of the very good things any committee, or board members, should remember is that they should first list their priorities of operation. One of those priorities should be to head off any criticism of the Pastor. In other words you are to be a defender of the faith of which your Pastor is the primary leader. Defend also the man to whom God has answered your prayers with a call. You do not have the right to change your mind about the pastor after you have prayed for God's direction to send you a Pastor. When that pastor is before you honour God by respecting him to lead in the work. As a church leader you should take it upon yourself to see that the spiritual things in the congregation are attended to, then the financial elements that arise in and through the mechanics of the operation of maintaining properties in order to keep the grounds to gather worshipers together.

Another very important element in keeping your operation successful is to seek out all the talent within your congregation. See that each talent, of each person, is put to use in a functional way. You will be surprised at the talent that exists just waiting for someone to ask for it to be used. You will also be surprised at the rate in which your congregation will grow when you allow the new found talent to function in the family of God, because they were allowed to participate in the ongoing growth of God's work.

Another key to success is to absolutely eliminate all sarcasm, and criticism of talents used within the church structure. After all God called even you.

Whilst I am rambling on about what some of the church leaders ought to do, allow me to list a number of things that should be adhered to if you are one of those that are going to be making speeches or some form of presentation to groups or congregations.

First of all, do not believe that everyone will hear you. Smarten up, use a mike, and stop being stupid about the need for it.

Secondly, do not underestimate the intelligence of your audience. If you think you are there because you are more intelligent than anyone else, forget the presentation.

Thirdly, do not talk down to your group or congregation from a "supposed" higher level.

Fourthly, Always assume that what you are about to say is going to carry a very specific impact on someone else's life. That life may change, hopefully with your presentation the change will be for the better. That must be a conscious analysis when making any presentation to any group whether large or small.

Fifthly, When you make a presentation, whether it be in the form of a sermon or graphic arts, you must remember to say something tangible. Allow your hearers to get a message that will help them with whatever project the desire to go ahead with. Many speakers ramble on, and on, and say nothing. You must deal with specifics to leave a message that is usable for your hearers.

There are those that would caution you against a predictable one, two, three, point message. Let me then assure you that it is much better to present a one, two, three, point message, and draw a specific conclusion, than to ramble on saying absolutely nothing. Those to whom you speak deserve more than empty platters of academic trash. Your points, and specific conclusions must in fact give direction to someone.

Sixth, Be prepared to defend any statement you make. In other words, know the background of your presentation. Do not make suppositions that make no sense. Be solid in your statements. Although I would be careful not to do away with suppositions entirely, because if you have a situation of which you are reasonably sure of the outcome then suppositions would be in order. Be ready to defend your statements.

Seven, Always set your crowd at ease before delivering your message. Even if it means in your eyes becoming a lesser person. Often in doing this you will find that the crowd will elevate you automatically. In other words do not show that you overrate yourself, by the same token do not berate yourself before your audience. No one cares at that moment what you think about yourself they have come to hear not to sympathize.

Eight, maintain a good volume while speaking, learn to manipulate the mike to your advantage. Let the audience hear what is being said. There is nothing worse than trying to listen to someone who feels bad about being there to speak then trys to cover it up by whispering the message or refusing to use the mike that your host provides because they are aware of the acoustics. Speak up; and when you think you are loud enough give another push up to speak a little louder. After all there is a beautiful deaf person out there that has come just to hear you.

There are those who will try to convince you to speak normal. They will tell you in public speaking to use your normal voice. Nothing could be further from the truth. When you speak to any audience you must speak in a projected voice or you will not be heard. This does not mean that you need to shout and scream and holler to be heard; but it does mean that you should use your stomach muscles rather than your throat muscles, and project your voice as a singer does that you may be heard clearly throughout the auditorium whether it be small or large space.

Nine, When using gestures use the full sweep gesture. In other words allow the gesture to emphasize the point that you are making at the time. Too many movements of no consequence will distract and take away from your message.

Tenth, You must be very careful about facial expression. Upon delivering your message, your facial expression must not be contradictory to what you have said. Your face must always express that what you have said is the truth.

Eleven, Remember people are not looking at you. They are listening to you with their eyes. They are there because they are interested in what the speaker has to say. If that speaker is you, do not insult their intelligence by assuming their judgment of your ability.

Twelve, Always generate enthusiasm to an audience by letting them know that they are special to you, and that you went to great lengths just to prepare for them.

Lift up your eyes on high, and behold who has created these things, that bringeth out their host by number: he calleth them all by names by the greatness of his might, for that he is strong in power; not one faileth. Isaiah 40:26.

* * * * *

The Mystery Mixture

—⟨∘⁄∘⁄∘⟩—

Let both grow together until the harvest: and in the time of harvest I will say to the reapers, Gather ye together first the tares, and bind them in bundles to burn them; but gather the wheat into my barn. Matt 13:30.

Although the previous parable to this verse has been literally mutilated by academics, and theologians alike, there really is a simple explanation here to the churches who are quite transparent in a different treatment of those that they deem not to fit in. God says, "Leave them be guys, I have a plan. They can stay until my harvest time is at hand; because if you toss them out now, you will hurt the sincere believer, and I cannot tolerate that system."

The tares that were sown in this particular field was a seed that produced mock wheat, just as the church produces mock Christians. There is no useful base for their existence, but God implies that it is more dangerous to pull them out of the congregation than to.allow them space to grow. When someone is slighted by the church there is more damage done than if that person had been allowed their say or given space to exist to allow God to carry out his plan at harvest time.

The church has created more damaged goods from their ranks than any other organization in the world. Christians have a tendency to trample their wounded to death. We are plagued by preconceived ideas of how things should be, and more often than not, that preconceived idea is pregnant with untruth, and lack of evidence towards that thinking, because we forget to consider first, God's way.

When we look more closely at this parable in Matt 13:24-30; we will identify the good and evil of the world that exists side by side. Servants in this story had gone out to the field where they expected to find a rich yield from growth of a prime seed. Instead, to their astonishment, they found fake wheat amongst the prime grain. Tares among the wheat is how Christ describes it. Here is the mystery, "how did it get there?" They determined that it had been planted by an enemy.

The great thing about being a follower of Christ we are never put into the position where we have to guess what Christ was talking about here. We simply do a fast forward to Matt 13:38. *The field is the world; the good seed are the children of the kingdom; but the tares are the children of the wicked one; The enemy that sowed them is the devil; the harvest is the end of the world; and the reapers are the angels. As therefore the tares are gathered and burned in the fire; so shall it be in the end of the world. The son of man shall send forth his angels, and they shall gather out of his kingdom all things that offend, and them which do iniquity; And shall cast them into a furnace of fire: there shall be wailing and gnashing of teeth. Then shall the righteous shine forth as the sun in the kingdom of their Father. Who hath ears to hear let him hear.* Matt 13:38-43.

There has always been wrong dwelling in the proximity of right. We recognize that fact when we look at the contemporary events of a world that appears smaller while the events of evil appear to be so much larger. Nevertheless, sin is still sin, but this is God's creation. Man consistently disobeys his creator, and God has within his own perimeters allowed for that with his own method of dealing with the unbelieving people who think they have control of this evil world, but God smiles knowing his plan works. Even so he has made a way of escape from any punishment simply by asking our acceptance of that which his son lay down his life for us. If we accept the forgiveness that came with that we shall be deemed the good grain to be harvest in the proper manner stored by God's grace.

Look were we may, tares are amongst the wheat, and good is still being elbowed by evil. There is always wrong that will be dwelling in the proximity of right. We are sure that God did not fling the world from his fingers to let it shift for itself. Jesus emphatically taught that this is God's world, and he is forever concerned about it and active within it's boundaries. With all the actions of churches, with all the stabilities of the missionaries, with all the dedication of the saints, and with all the blood of the martyrs; In spite of all the heroism of the centuries in the cause of righteousness; Sin has not been driven out of one single nation, city, town or family. Go where you will, inside Christendom, or outside of it, and you will find tares growing among the wheat. We are able to apply our lives to the church for which Jesus died, and we will always find that unsolicited mixture of tares with the wheat.

I have heard men say, "Find the perfect church and I will join it." My response to that type of person is, " I found the perfect church, but I joined it and it is no longer perfect." Besides that if there were such a place it would be an embarrassment to us. The church who maintains the adherence to the scriptures as originally translated from the original Hebrew or Greek with a clear message of salvation through the blood of Christ, is the church that is in fact the hope of the world.

I once witnessed a man lying broken and bleeding upon the London & Port Stanley railroad track street crossing in St. Thomas, Ontario. There was evidence there that the man was blind, and had inadvertantly walked directly into the path of the train. Near his torn body in a savagely ripped black suit, was lying a white cane only carried by the blind, and it was apparent that although he may have heard the train coming there had been a miscalculation of the distance or location on his part, because it appeared that he walked onto the track and the engineer was unable to stop in time to avoid this tragedy. Had I been there a moment earlier I would have been able to stop him from meeting with such a loathsome end. Nevertheless I was not there in time, and I only saw him after he had been hit by the train, and I could only stand there watching him die writhing in pain.

There was no doubt about his dying. The fact that I was aware of his injury did not serve the slightest hope to find a remedy. He must die. In a sense I was reminded about this parable. The tares must die. Only the master decides the time.

The servants were after getting rid of the tares, and that is certainly what Jesus seeks in the heart of the individual. He is on a crusade against evil. It is Christ's purpose that evil should be utterly damned and destroyed. There is no conflict here between the Master and the servant as to the goal, but the method. Servants say pull them out by the roots. Now that sounds very practical. Tare pulling is one of the most appealing methods of that which is both-ersome to the crop, in spite of the fact that Jesus does not sanction the method

First off, the proper method of setting aside the tares requires wisdom, with a power of judgment that we do not possess. Tare pulling destroys the flourishing grain beside it. We used to abolish members who were deemed by those whom we judged to be worthy, unfit for the healthy growth of our church. Some even whine that this is no longer done. I for one, am glad that a quick dismissal of personalities has been for the most part abolished. I will live more comfortably as a servant of Christ when this type of action is totally done away with. For if love will not win them, ostracism certainly will not accomplish any good thing. The method suggested by the servants was positively negative. We must maintain the solution of the Saviourhood of Jesus Christ, the son of God. Let both grow together until harvest, but for now focus your attention on the wheat. As a believer you must always speak a posi-tive gospel as you live a positive life for the community around you. It is ever new, and ever true, be not overcome with evil, but over-come evil with good. This is sometimes a hard pill to swallow when we think that we need to discard someone from the church for the betterment of the church. God says an emphatic No! He does not fail to tell us when we follow the wrong direction that permeate a positional move other than Christ would have it.

How did Jesus overcome the evil of the world? He showed everyone he met kindness with his godly attributes affecting the complete community. Nowhere in scripture do we find Jesus turn-ing anyone away. He showed mankind the solution through the power of salvation, that the mixture must be left to face the binding up and casting into the fire.

* * * * *

Attending To
The Believer's Work

Therefore let no man glory in men: for all things are yours; Whether Paul, or Apollos, or Caiphas, or the world or life, or death, or things present, or things to come; all are yours; And ye are Christ's; and Christ is God's. 1 Corinthians 3:21-23.

There is a need to be careful of putting men in the place that belongs to only Jesus Christ, Lord, and saviour. Every preacher, pastor, or minister is exactly what the term applies, a servant of the living God. This does not mean however that the congregation becomes your master. But when planted into the leadership role of a church setting you do become a curious servant, one who carries out God's bidding. You will know that servants are but channels through which God speaks to his people. God, could do his work without us, but he has chosen to work through his creation, man. He has given each minister, the privilege of making known to all with whom we come into contact with, the availability of God's riches with the blessing of God's grace. Our holy privilege, and a very responsible place.

We must continually be empathetic with John when he says, *"He must increase, and we must decrease."* John 3:30.

My expertise with employing management, and staff has allowed me to train the new and the old with on the job training. I was often privileged to observe newcomers that excelled in that which they were taught. Often those people became a threat to established workers when promotions came, and short term people were elevated to positions of authority over the long time plodder. Some would be happy to see others rise to management, but there were those that felt slighted because their lack of knowledge in certain areas did not allow progress. Rather than being elated for someone that was capable of filling the position, they would suffer a setback when they recognized their own inadequacies. I would then bring the art of the area they were interested in and encourage them to try again for promotion. Most of the time it would be accepted. Other times the discouragement would be too great and they would move on to another place of employment to apply their skills.

John had been a leader in spreading the gospel about the coming Christ. He had built for himself a credible following. People trusted him and were enamoured with his leadership. He had produced an incredible setting for Christ to take over. When Christ was ready John was not caught up in senseless emotion because of allowing Christ to take the role over him. He made the simple, but necessary announcement about the greatness of Christ over his own unworthiness. A marvelous testimony of John's witness and work. In his sincerity of worship he was able to watch his saviour excel in the gospel while he gave account of a lesser position. As John watched Christ excel it was in no way demeaning to him. He was gracious enough to allow the transition of leadership. John could allow the transition because he had worked hard for God's word to be put forth, and in doing that he knew his place to be filled by the greatness of Jesus Christ. This is an art many Christians of our day still must learn. God did not just call one person to fit one job. He called many to bring the gospel to the unbelieving world. It is not whether you are better than the next person, and it has nothing to do with you being a lesser person. It has everything to do about serving God in the way he desires you to do with the talent that you have. After you settle your soul to that idea you will be able to spread the gospel.

For the preaching of the cross is to them that perish, foolishness; but unto us which are saved, it is the power of God. 1 Corinthians 1:18.

One of the very essential ingredients of the gospel is the preaching of the cross. Many churches have pushed the cross aside in their churches, to replace it with an overhead projector. We set aside the altar to replace it with a worldly stage like setting, the visible cross has lost its prime importance. I believe churches will suffer for that particular action. They will make claim that they must do these things to attract people to the sanctuary. Before I became a born again believer I worked at the local famous, and renowned dance hall where many of the large bands of the day came to play there music for entertaining the world while they danced. There was not one church that decided to bring in the rhumba, or the jitterbug, or the bunny hop, to attract me to the sanctuary. there were however believers who knew that men like me needed to hear the gospel, and when they couldn't talk to me on the street they sent notes to me about my need through friends. The long and short of it, because of believers that never slacked off from giving the word, and never doubted that God's word would work, and I was saved. Those same people later shared with me how they spent time in prayer in the early morning, and again late at night. For this God showed them the result of their work.

Paul pleads for the people to pray for his ministry. We are all members one of another. One is not to tower above others; but by the same token recognize the talent that God has bestowed upon you, and put it to use by letting others know that you are God's choice with that particular venue. Together we are to bring forth fruit, to the glory of our Lord Jesus Christ.

You are god's building. *What! know ye not that your bodies are the temple of the holy ghost which is in you, which you have of God, and you are not your own? For you are bought with a price; therefore glorify God in your body, and in your spirit, which are God's.* 1 Corinthians 6:19-20.

Paul here primarily challenges those that would be involved in undesirable acts of fornication. He challenges believers to be constantly cognizant of the fact that they belong to God in whole, and not just in part. Being aware of that will allow our hearts the direction to which we treat those around us whether believers or unbelievers, in an effort to be a solid witness for our living God.

There are very few that can do foundation work similar to that which was implemented in the days of Christ. Perhaps church planters may touch on the base when they enter a city to make what we call "cold calls" to start a work. Seldom though are we able to grasp the founding empathy of the early Christians witness. Too often we find that enterprising givers of testimony begin building on another's ruined foundation when they should be sensitive to the issue of building on a principle foundation which has already been laid by Jesus Christ, and embedded himself as the chief cornerstone as well as the foundation of all that we live for.

Now if any man build upon this foundation gold, silver, precious stones, wood, hay, stubble; Every mans work shall be made manifest: for the day shall declare it, because it shall be revealed by fire; and the fire shall try every mans work of what sort it is. If any mans work abides which he hath built thereupon, he shall receive a reward. 1 Corinthians 3:12-14.

Here in verse ten, Paul makes an astute observation of the degree in which the work for the believers base as a directive required in the structure of the building, a master builder. The believer needs the wisdom to read the blueprints set out by God himself. In reading that blueprint, the believer 's building will take form to have a visual confirmation as to the outcome, having authentic appearance of value that will make others desire it.

If careless unconverted people are brought in they hurt, and hinder the way of Christ. Therefore it becomes imperative that you build in a very meticulous manner, and know that projected errors will thwart the value of what you have built. Ask yourself these questions; How am I building? What am I building? Will it pass inspection to be acceptable for others to relax in, and enjoy?

You may build on gold which speaks of divine righteousness, silver which speaks of redemption, or precious stone which indicates reward.

The authentic contractor for development will shake his head at the suggested building material. Today's structure include brick, mortar, stone, and vinyl, plus other synthetic substances, and to build otherwise would not be wise nor accepted.

That being a true assessment we must approach Paul's warning here as direction of two desperate worlds, the spiritual and the non-spiritual. The consequence of building upon a foundation that is lasting and is undergerded by Jesus Christ. The second element that

Paul includes in a spiritual sense, that which is on a faulty foundation shall reap destruction. Wood, hay, stubble foundations will be destroyed by fire.

Everything that has been done for the glory of God will be looked upon as gold, and has God's approval. Everything that has been a result of a renewed life through our acceptance of being redeemed through the precious blood of Christ and we have accepted redemption will reflect as silver. Our work to fulfill our commitment in our walk will show as precious stone. This is the reflection of the spiritual building put forward by Paul.

The world is filled with the "me first" attitude which emanates so much selfishness, and so much ungodly behaviour that has spilled over into Christian communities to permeate an unchrist-likeness, merging us into a position whereby we must begin to judge ourselves. In other words we must examine our lives to see if we project any offence that will turn others away from God. If so we need to ask God for forgiveness.

A great deal of action that is called Christian may only be the energy of the flesh, and although , you put on a Christian tag to it, there may not be a link to Godliness, particularly if the work is offensive to some. If the work is legitimate it will bring glory to God, if it is only a comfort zone for the flesh, there will be no glory to God at all, and that can only reap disaster to those who try to implement their selfish work ethics.

How do we feel if others are preferred before us? This is a good question to ask ourselves for a test to see if our work is building for God, or self pleasure, or simple church imagery. The bible says, only what's done for Christ will last. It will be Christ himself that apprises us of the difference.

Every man's work will be made manifest. The believer will stand before God for his work to be tried, and revealed by fire as to what "sort" it is. Notice the word sort. Not how much work or how little work. The secrets of the heart will be made manifest as God tests your stand by the light of his word. This will be in addition to salvation. For we are saved by grace, but this will be for faithful service to Jesus Christ. If the work is done in the wrong attitude with only self in mind or some status point trying to be reached, God says, "I will destroy them." The foundation is Jesus Christ the son of the living God, and to build on any other thing does not please God. Many times we find people trying to justify a different direction taken because they believe in themselves and man made wisdom. But God says, "Let no man deceive himself. If any man among you seemeth to be wise in this world, let him become a fool, that he may be wise. For the wisdom of this world is as foolishness with God: for it is written, He taketh the wise in their own craftiness. 1 Corinthians 3:18-19.

You are working toward your reward. What will your reward be? Perhaps at this point there is no reward, but it is never too late to do something about that. So turn around, change the attitude, work to bring the lost into the fold. Remember your works will be tried by fire.

* * * * *

Confessions Of A Failure

⟶⟿

The pressure of things to be done drive us to distraction. We dart from hither to yon without giving a moment to stop and smell the roses. At times the pressure is so great that we believe the only solution to be is to quit what we are doing and go on to other things. While following other things that entice us to new venues also keep us hopping from stem to stern. Always busy with never time to do the things that we ought to do. At the end of the day there is no significant sign of what should be accomplished, and difficult to explain what it was that we were really so busy at. Life passes by like a large ship to the horizon, and we forget what colour or how big it was after it floats out of sight. Somehow we seem to be left behind all that is important. The intoxication of activity keeps us going without consideration as to where and why.

And as thy servant was busy here and there, he was gone. And the king of Israel said unto him, So shall thy judgment be; thyself hast decided it. 1 Kings 20:40.

When we find ourselves too busy to worship God, through Jesus Christ, there shall be a judgment upon us for our decision to follow the secular rather than the spiritual. There is a need to grasp the patterns that God has laid out for your life. When we begin to lose that which we believe we have accomplished by our own will and skill soon deteriates into nothingness until we do a priority check of our lives. It is when you examine accomplishments at that checkpoint of your life, God's priorities take on a much clearer concept to form the picture of where you are at with him.. God delivered from the tribulation of the world's ways in order for you to identify the means from the ends

In this portion of scripture in 1 Kings 20:39-40; we see a person who has failed to perform the duty set upon him, that is to keep an important prisoner safe from harming the king. As guard of this prisoner he walks with a purposeful manner as one who knows his task. His credentials were acceptable to the party that gave him the responsibility to keep the prisoner.. He is the type who is pleased to receive the honour of the confidence in him to handle the situation. We see this same man the next day has lost that which has been entrusted to him. He lost his job and is no longer given the capacity of trust because of his slackness. The prisoner that was incarcerated and was considered dangerous had escaped from him, therefore he had to be removed from that trusted position. One might question this soldier and ask him if he had been overpowered and had the prisoner taken away by his colleagues, which may excuse his loss. He responds to the query, he escaped because I was too busy to watch him.

What could be more important task than saving your country from terrorism, or your home, or your honour?

"Oh," he says, "nothing in particular. I was just doing this and that, busy here and there, I just didn't have time to watch him all the time he was in my custody."

This soldier was then sentenced to face the death penalty because of his lack of integrity to do the job as it was required.

This man had not cut any ones throat, he had not stabbed anyone in the back, he had not stolen anything. He was not being punished for what he had done, rather he was being punished for what he had not done. He had failed to carry out the responsibility assigned to him. How foolish are they who believe because they display a religious behaviour believing they are safe because they have done no wrong. A man is much more frivolous and foolish when he thinks in his own mind that he is a Christian simply because of the fact of the things that he refuses to do, instead of the redeeming qualities he carries out knowing that the task he performs is required by God.

When you fall into the pattern of so many to fail in your duty to the living God the rug will be pulled out from under you. The Lord teaches us this over and over again as he gives the words of instruction in the scripture.

What was wrong with the fig tree that he cursed it?

It was loaded with poison. It had nothing but leaves, bearing no fruit. Therefore Jesus cursed it.

What of the rich man and Lazarus?

There was no indictable offence added to his life because of breaking the law. He simply refused help to a hungry man that hung around his gate. He never verbally abused the man. He simply ignored him as he walked by him daily. It was because of his deliberate neglect of man's need he awoke to find himself in a Christless eternity, the flames of Hell.

Five foolish virgins had brought their equipment, but had neglected to service it with the required substance, oil, they failed in their duty. "Inasmuch as ye did not—-"

Taking all these characters into consideration, they had not failed because of ignorance. Nor did they fail because of lack of knowledge as to their duty. All knew the requirements set out before them.

What then was the reason for such major catastrophe in each of their settings?

Their greatest need for success is even as our greatest need to please God in service, that being the will to live up to that which we already know.

The reason that you are Godless, is not because you do not know better, it is because you are unwilling to do better. There is no person in God's Kingdom that does not know enough to do their duty. It may be that you are unaware as to the precise task that he has called you to, but you do know this, there is an absolute difference between right and wrong, and that you need to be conscripted on the side of right. To help, not to hinder. To bless, and not to curse. To lift up, and not to cast down.

God has a task for every person that surrenders their will to carry it out. If you are not sure as to what that task is, know this, that God let you know what it is, and will also make it possible for you to carry it out. "To them that ask it shall be given."

"In all thy ways acknowledge him, and he shall direct thy paths."

In all these situations we must assume by their actions that there was no visible attempt to fulfill the requirements of the task that was set before them. Each one in their selfish action produced the element of failure. If your goal is only to look good with performance, without an attempt to fathom the risk, you too will end up in failure.

I would not in any sense imply the pressure of that worldly myth that you can be anything you want to be. That is a lie of the devil. You may want to be great in areas that are highly unsuitable to your ability. You cannot be tone deaf and become a great singer. You cannot be colour blind and become a great painter. All dreams do not become a reality, and are certainly not the way to eternal life. As individuals capable of dealing with life there will be pitfalls that will take you to the depth of despair. Dreams and talent can drive you along very different roads if you disenfranchise your ability that locks into the puzzle of success. In Christ, every person has ability to be developed through grace to perform the task to which they are called.

Why is it then that people fail in their tasks that are meant to establish their worth?

It is not ignorance, or laziness, or inability to do the things that God has directed they do. The answer is found in the scripture when the servant says," As thy servant was busy here and there."

He was one of those persons that has so many things to do, so many engagements to keep, so many functions to attend, and so many burdens to carry that he cannot do his on duty.

Too often I hear this cry, "I'm so busy." Is this your folly?

You are busy six days a week. You are earnest about amusing yourself. You do a thousand and one things that you have committed yourself to. All good things that must be done, and if you don't do them, surely they will never get done. While you are busy here, and there, the peace of God slips out of your life. While you are busy here, and there, you neglect the Sunday school, and the church. While you are busy here, and there, you lose interest in the word of God. That allows you to lose the sense of god out of your life, and you slip into a life of Christless indifference.

The solution that brings the only remedy is to listen to Jesus. This is his message, "Seek ye first the kingdom of God and his righteousness, and all these things will be added unto you.

* * * * *

The Way

Jesus saith unto him, I am the way, the truth, and the life: no man cometh unto the father, but by me. John 14:6.

The simplicity of the plan of salvation is its problem. Surely it is too easily understood and undertaken to lead to such a worthwhile destination. If there was a four year course in college or university to acquire eternal life where the tuition was high and you had to pay an extra ten-thousand dollars to receive a diploma in it, the so called elite of our day would make a bold attempt to corner the market to keep others away unless they would produce a greater, more exorbitant price dollar wise.

Thank God, his word says, "without money, without price," because Jesus paid it all.

That very fact is the stumbling block of the business world of today. The colourful perpetrators of logic in marketing are not able to comprehend someone that would in actuality lay down their life to save their friends as Jesus purported to do. More likely the marketers of our day would better buy the cutthroat message of the thief and murderer whose caring for others is not at all visible.

They stagger and stumble over the terms of salvation, free grace, undying love, truth in commitment, and selfless devotion. These elements do not fit into normal process of co-habitation with our fellowman. We undertake to measure God by our very own non-value destinations.

The academic elite of our society would have you believe that the youth of today has so numbed their brain as to past terminology they are unable to absorb the meaning of simple words like sin, repent, turn to Jesus, as he says come unto me all ye that labour and I will give you rest. That is hard to understand that we can rest in God. The brain drain is not to another country, but is sucked away by the teaching of multisyllabled words that portrays the gobbledy gook of the so called academic scholars. They speak of integration of personalities. They mean that a man must be renewed into a new creature, reborn, twice born, but it is taught that it is unacceptable to use simple words.

Scholars have renamed sin. they call it maladjustment. It may even be called glandular abnormality, anomalous, malevolent hyperbolism, by which personality is disarranged. Academics will tell you that our youth understands that, yet they cannot comprehend the little word that separate them from eternal life, sin. Nor are the younger new generation able to grasp the meaning of salvation that is a simple turning away from that which is destructive to their fellowman. We live in a day of evil words that drown out the righteousness of a living God.

Man's wisdom is often shallow as well as artificial pitting itself against the wisdom of God. Hath God not made foolish the wisdom of this world.

Young people do not need a new high sounding vocabulary, rather the new generation needs to discover and embrace the old ways of a living God. A simple trusting faith God's only way. You may reach phenomenal academic heights where no other individual can touch your achievement. You will experience a great darkness at the end of that tunnel for education, nor cultural greatness even with a disciplinary process can produce the peace within the soul. That is something that only God issues as a gift to be accepted without struggle. No person has ever yet been able to save themselves by virtue, truthfulness, honour, sobriety. Being a decent individual cannot merit salvation of your soul. There are no social, economic, moral, or political behaviour that will lead you to salvation. Each person can only receive salvation by the unmerited favour of a living God, it is called grace. There is no path by which you are able to obtain it by endeavours of your own. It is a gift of God lest anyone should boast. It only becomes ours through faith, and belief in one who lay down his life to pay for all our transgressions. Jesus

Christ, the only son of God who was crucified at Calvary on a cross in our stead. He made the purchase, it is only for you to accept the paid package in faith believing. Only then will you receive eternal life, and peace of God will flood your soul.

Faith is as much a part of life as breathing. we use it every day going to and from places that are familiar to us. We have faith that we will reach our destination unharmed, We have faith in returning home to be with those we love and it happens. We have faith that our children will grow up to be successful, and in most cases that is true. The same element must be exercised to meet with God to spend your eternity with him. There he will see that you will shed no tears. There will be no more pain or heartache, but you must first accept his only son Jesus Christ.

We are not saved by any good that we may accomplish not even when you claim it for Christ. You will not be saved by being a trail blazer in your lifestyle. You will not even be saved by the Jesus way of life. Nor are we saved by our daily walk or conversation. Not even by walking in the steps of Jesus. We are saved by faith in Jesus Christ. Salvation is in Christ. If we could acquire salvation by doing what Christ taught us to do, or live the way he lived, then Calvary would not have been necessary.

The way, the simple way, the easy way. the way in which we need not err, is simple faith in Jesus Christ the son of the living God.

Salvation does not belong to schools, or to the educational programs of our universities, nor to the wisdom of men. It is a plan of God to redeem men from their low estate of sinful nature, to elevate them to a heaven bound plateau with eternal life. In God is my salvation, He only is my salvation.

Doubting Thomas, like many of today's generation, seeing he did not see, hearing he did not understand. Jesus did not rebuke him. He simply said, "I am the way." At once Thomas understood as his hardness vanished, his eyes opened to see the realism of the saviour who opened the way for him to enter into the favour of God. Thomas now saw with a new vision the person of Jesus, his nature, his humanity, his deity all embraced in this presentation he was making, I am the way. The total of all of Jesus was a great road that led to a greater land where the heart of man would know no heartaches, no sorrow, no more weeping in tears. Here was Jesus before him leading him to that city with many mansions which are built for believers. Jesus is there the light of that new city. A city of eternal joy. When the place he is preparing for his own is complete, he will come again for those who love, and trust, and follow him.

Do not become confused, this is not an interpretation. I am not quoting from some student of the man Jesus, nor am I giving you the opinion of some theologian, I am simply giving you easily understood words of Jesus Christ himself, "I am the way."

Are you following that way?

It is a necessary way. Not an easy way, but the way you must go to obtain eternal life. Persons who have made that decision to follow the way of Christ do not need to waste time picking out the flaws of the false cults or pagan gods, but they must go about with the word of God in their hearts. We may destroy every false work in the world and do no positive good.

The victory is open to us, because Christ said, "I am the way, walk ye in it."

* * * * *

The I Will's Of Jesus

Nevertheless I tell you the truth; It is expedient for you that I go away: For if I go not away, the comforter will not come unto you; but if I depart, I will send him unto you. John 16: 7.

I believe it to be a valid discovery, that people oftimes promise with absolute and sincere intentions of fulfilling a promise, only to find that time with it's unpredictable interruptions does not allow those promises to be kept. Those people, in most cases give their word, are trustworthy to carry out that which they have promised. In other instances they fall short of being able to fulfill what they have promised. There is one whose word is always dependable, and good. The word of Jesus. When Jesus says, "I will," we may with certainty know that it will be done.

Let us look into the word to consider the "I wills" of Jesus.

[1] The "I will" of absolute reception in salvation. Him that cometh unto me, I will in no way cast out. John 3: 7

This is the promise of the reception of sinners. Jesus is simply saying here that no matter who you are, or what your sins are like, or how far you have wandered away from God, if you simply turn to come to Jesus he will not cast you out.

We are all aware of the many secular service clubs, lodges, or civil organizations, that exist to entertain those of the same mind in society. Gatherings from ex-servicemen to the fellowshipping of ex-drunks. All the organizations whether good, bad, or indifferent, make some claim of providing a helpful element to society. To belong to these social structures who claim to be of some great benefit to the social order, a person must pay a fee to become members of each organization. In most cases you must be recommended for membership or fill out an application to be exalted from the normal drone of life to a new lowly place in the club. After making up your mind that this is the place where you decide that you should be, and you apply to join there is a possibility that your application could be rejected if you do not measure up to the fall under the shadow of their political maneuverings or comply with the imposed restrictions of the organizations criteria.

Although many churches have followed the same worldly order of select membership, and reject would be members who will not adhere to their political game within church boundaries, Jesus makes no restrictions. He will always have room for those who will come to him. He offers a come as you are salvation. Jesus says, "I will in no wise cast you out." I must warn you though that he will change your life for the better. However if you would be only a tag-along-believer attempting to do things your own way, you will get left behind.

This simply means that you are to leave your sinful life behind in true repentance to place all your faith in Jesus Christ son of the living God.

If you are not a child of God today, this is his I will for you. He simply says, "Come to me leave all your sin in the past, and I will be your saviour, I will not cast you out."

[2] The "I will" of Jesus Christ as the church foundation. And I say also unto thee, That thou art Peter' and upon this rock I will build my church; and the gates of hell shall not prevail against it. Matt16: 15-18.

Amidst the bustling community there was gossip of the social concept. There was some question as to who this Jesus was , and as Jesus walked with his disciples in the exchange of conversation he asked a pointed question. "Whom do ye say that I am?"

Peter, the ever bold one, again spoke without fear or expectation of favour and said, "Thou art the Christ, the son of the living God." Matt16:16.

Jesus said, "Upon this rock I will build my church. The rock of his divine sonship. I will build my church, and the gates of hell shall not prevail against it."

Even today, Christ continually builds his church and every believer is a portion of that building. You will find us in complete agreement when you suggest that is poor material with which to build, but I remember working in a sawmill when the fist board came off the log. It didn't look like good material to build a house with. However after due process throughout the rest of the mill that board looked to be top of the line material. The same is true of those who first accept Christ, he will mould you and make you to be top of the line material if you allow yourself to follow his process that is already in place.

The positive God fearing church stands today because it offers what no other institution offers even though it oftimes lacks in presentation or practice, the offer, forgiveness of sin to the sinful soul. It offers through Jesus Christ, peace that cleanses the soul. It offers strength for the walk with Christ every mile of the way. In their presentation of Christ through lifestyle of their own offer a blessed hope for eternal life free from heartache and tears of sorrow, in heaven with God. It can offer these things only because it is Christ's way to touch God's creation. It is the one and only agency in the world in which Christ has chosen to work through that of which he himself is the foundation.

There is too much wasted time spent on man made institutions that last for a short time and add little or no element to living of life. Many man made institutions make it a practice to annihilate the Christian concept altogether. To use their own terminology they are in denial. They deny that conversion works, they deny that God exists, they deny that preaching is a viable structure of life given by God, they continue in their denial of the created being when there is absolutely no evidence that would uphold any other structure. It is a thrill to take note that the Christian church has stood for two-thousand years. It started from the persecution of others within closed doors. We are still withstanding the persecution because Christ is the beginning and the end.

Early Christians had courage, and conviction applied only by their unrelenting conviction to the truth of God. Could the practicing Christian of today grab even a fraction of their depth of ambition or even a fragment of their commitment today we would see an impenetrable surge in the overturn of the shallowness we see practiced in the world today. As believers we should not look at other church organizations to deem that it is they who are shallow, because you, as a believer, are the church. Check your own oil before you change it for someone else.

The Holy Spirit that was sent to us by Jesus Christ after his ascension has given to us the nurturing spirit to embrace those around us that need encouragement in the word. People do not need a dictatorial impact shining through from the church, they need to see the love of God which they cannot find elsewhere. As we exercise a caring reach-out-to- touch nature, there will be a growth in embracing the living God. We have inherited that desire as it came down through the ages from the early Christian movement.

Jesus said "I will build my church." Are you helping him? Are you building or tearing down? Are you seeking others?

[3] The "I will" of the indwelling Holy Spirit. Nevertheless I tell you the truth; It is expedient for you that I go away: for if I go not away, the Comforter will not come unto you; but if I depart, I will send him unto you. John 16: 7.

The work of the Holy Spirit on earth has proven to be quite a controversial interpretation during these latter years of mixed but somewhat surface Christianity. The religious practice of some newer Christian followers is like the snowflake. It can fill the air with a clean newness, but evaporates the moment it settles upon the warm ground.

There are those who would have you believe that the Holy Spirit drives your body into reckless contortions to bring glory to God. Nothing could be farther from the truth. Once you have come to the place where you have accepted Jesus as your saviour, you will be directed by the Holy Spirit to leave your sinful life behind as he convicts people of sin. You will not have to wonder about what it is, for the Spirit will make it very clear to you without unacceptable contortions. There will be a light in your lifestyle that allows you to focus upon the right and wrong of life. You will no longer turn to dark abysmal thoughts of hopelessness. The Holy Spirit will lead you to observe the cross in a while new concept, and the event that took place for you. The Holy Spirit will lead you in depth to whole thinking about others while giving you a message that you may pass on so they too may accept your saviour. The Holy Spirit comforts the Christian, and leads you to comfort others, that is why he is called the comforter. The Holy Spirit will then lead you to God's word, the bible, and give you a new understanding as you read and consider the ways of Jesus Christ.

Christ says you are the light of the world, and the Holy Spirit shows you where to find the switch to turn that light on. We in our own dim intelligence try to read with understanding God's word only to find little or no meaning, But when we allow the Holy Spirit to work that switch to turn on the light we will find deep truths illuminated as understanding flows through our soul as never before.

Serving in our own strength we are nothing, the Holy spirit inspires us because Jesus said, "I will send my spirit."

To be without God is to be without hope. To come to God we must first accept his only son Jesus, and the son who sits on the right hand of his father interceding for us sent the Holy Spirit to dwell within us or we would still be groping in the dark.

The "I will" of closeness of the walk in companionship. Teaching them to observe all things whatsoever I have commanded you: and, lo, I will be with you always, even unto the end of the world. Matt 28: 20.

When you determine your work for God as a ministry you know that you are not alone. You have the presence, and power of the living Christ, the son of God. every person is not called to the pulpit ministry, but I believe that every believer in Jesus Christ is a minister. Whether you are called to preach, teach, sing, or care for others, and uplift and encourage those round about you, you know you are not alone for Christ says, "I am with you." Jesus is interested in every element of our lives. He promises to be with us everywhere, from our place of business, to the horrible sinful dregs of society. He goes with you to worship in fellowship with other believers. He will be with you at home having your quiet time or fun family time. He will be with you when you are caring for the elderly or with children in the learning institutions or at play. This very thought needs to sustain you when you hear Jesus say, "I will be with you." He keeps this promise to us from the time we give our hearts to him until the time we rest in glory we have a wonderful companion, and his name is Jesus.

The "I will" of his attractive power. And I, if I be lifted up from the earth, will draw all men unto me. John 12: 32.

Jesus, was specifically referring here to the method of his death upon the cross which today is history which is needed to lift the followers up in spirit and in truth. Many contemporary churches disregard the cross by replacing it with the overhead projector. Jesus upon his resurrection had challenged workers to take up their cross to follow him, and he is still today drawing all manner of people to him. Hearing those expounding the gospel from the pulpit may grip your heart to draw you into a type of ministry. After two-thousand years Christ is still drawing.

In illness, or disaster, you may promise God your life if he would just deliver you from your situation. He answers your prayer and your wishes to be delivered then you begin on your own way forgetting that God has listened and delivered to you your wishes. You know that you where drawn to him in your time of need, but you should know that he does not leave you nor forsake you, and will continue to draw. It is when you fail to respond to his urging that he lets you go to suffer the consequences of your rejection of him.

I knew a specific man who made a promise to God, and failed to keep his promise. This man was a logger who was hired to fall trees in the forest industry. Fallers where hired to cut trees down with a saw called a crosscut saw. Today fallers use a totally different invention that is far more satisfactory for the work involved. The new machines are known in the industry as chain saws. Trees which were cut down in the bush by fallers had all the limbs removed before shipping to the sawmills to make lumber to build houses with. This particular venue was one of the most dangerous jobs in the bush. Often when a tree was fell, on the way to the ground it sometimes would have a high limb snap off and dangerously plummeting to the ground apart from the tree. Several of these instances would end with striking the man below, and killing him. Sawmills usually put two men in a falling crew in that they would look out for each other.

The man I knew worked at this job by choice to be alone at his work. He spent much of his time cursing God in the most profane methods that he could put to his lips. One day as he was falling trees he came upon one that was rather twisted, but with a few choice curses he decided to cut the tree down. As it fell it twisted and kicked the stump which knocked it into a different path than the intended fall. It rolled and twisted itself towards this faller, and he was unable to move quick enough to escape the powerful timbers twisted fall, and he found himself with legs pinned to the ground. As he was unable to escape from that by himself he began to tremble and to pray. God heard him for at camp someone realized that this fellow had not made it back to camp at his regular time. Aware of the dangers that befall men one of the crew picked up a buddy to set out to look for the missing faller. they found the place where he was pinned under the tree and worked to free him, but one of his legs was badly damaged so they loaded him into a truck and took him to the nearest hospital. that's when I came into the picture. He called me on the telephone asking that I visit him in the hospital as he wanted to talk. I obliged him and made a special trip to speak with him. When I arrived he filled me in as to what had happened. Out of that he shared with me that he wanted to pray about it. Knowing this man for some time I was rather surprised at the request. He then told me that the Doctors had made a decision to amputate the leg. The thought of losing a leg was an extremely traumatic event for him. He could not visualize himself being of any worth to society, or to himself without a leg.

Recognizing his real dilemma he turned to God and pleaded with him to allow him to keep his leg. With that pleading he promised God that he would live a committed life and dedicate his whole future to him if only God would spare his leg.

To the utter amazement of the Doctor, the leg stopped deteriation, and began to mend. It was truly a miracle that Doctors deemed to be that of unexplainable scientific phenomena. I knew it as God's answer to an undeserving sinner. God deployed his handiwork, and it was real

It was several weeks later the man was able to leave the hospital walking on his own two legs. He felt no more pain, and as life went back to normal for him, he forgot about his promise to God. By his own admission, he even tried to run away from God by moving from one end of the country to the other. But there was no way of escape. Years later for no known medical reason the leg began to deteriate, and this man finally had to have it amputated. I received a very sad letter from him to remind me of our prayer together yet he admitted his disobedience to God. His statement was that God had collected on his broken promise.

The one thing this man did not see was all the damage along the way that was caused from a broken promise. It was responsible for bad friendships, and broken homes, destroyed children. It generated envy and strife, it created hatred, and mistrust. Amongst those things it left a string of lost souls behind. But the most amazing thing to me is that God called in his debt. So when you make a promise to God make sure that you fulfill that promise even as God has fulfilled his promise to you.

There is another true story of an Indian woman who gave her heart to the Lord through a missionary that had taught her in her youth. Upon reaching adulthood she too forgot her promises to God. Eventually she lost one leg. Her cry again was to God. For a while she began to serve him again, and again as time moved on she forgot her promise to him. She fell by the wayside, and went to shack up with a man to live in sin. She got caught up in the lie of contemporary living, that everything is alright as it is. She took to imbibing in alcohol, drinking moonshine, wrapped in the tobacco habit giving herself to many men while shacked up with her male mate.

As time slipped away on her, she put God far, far into her background. She went blind, and was plagued with many sores, suffering greatly throughout her remaining years. She died on a broken promise given to God, with no love, no hope, no peace that passeth all understanding. Be careful what you promise God. Jesus says "I will draw all men unto me."

The "I will" of our hope in Christ's empathy. And if I go and prepare a place for you, I will come again, and receive you unto myself; that where I am, there ye may be also. John 14: 3.

This is our blessed hope that he is coming again to receive us unto himself where we shall be for in an element that is so great that it is difficult to comprehend, for an eternity. Endless time in the presence of our Gracious benevolent living God.

This thought has always been a mainstay in my life. Knowing that whatever transpires in my life there is a place of no return filled with all the comforts that one can not even begin to imagine. What a glory that will be for me. When Jesus comes for his own all the jagged edges of life will disappear, and everything will be made complete. He will take us to a better home, and give us a more satisfying work administered with a perfect love. Yes he promises that if we suffer with him we will rule with him in heaven.

Every year we work ourselves up to a frenzy in this country about the football team who wins the Gray cup, or the hockey team that wins the Stanley cup. People are enamoured with the pennant won by the so-called world series players, when there in fact is no world organization for baseball. We watch hoards of people become hysterical over the Miss America pageant, and further punish our emotional instabilities over academy awards for those who perform in ungodly displays all for a replaceable tin cup. Or a dust gathering ornament offered by the apostles of debt in an attempt to display the ungodly as an acceptable route. The person holding an icon of reward that has no great value as far as monetary supplement of life.

Yet one of the greatest rewards that will ever be presented to mankind goes unheralded because we are caught up in the self satisfying syndrome with the creeping paralysis of the unbeliever thinking it was all meant to be this way.

This type of thinking is a diversion from what God meant it to be for he has planned the ultimate great event. That is the day of his coming as he said, *"And, behold, I come quickly; and my reward is with me, to give to every person according as their work shall be." Rev 22: 12.*

Friends, Christ is the lamb slain from the foundation of the world. He was crucified for your sins and mine. He died to save us, and rose from the grave to give us victory over death that we may know we have eternal life through him. As you think of his sacrifice does not gratitude swell up in your heart? Do you love Jesus too?

I have covered a few "I wills" of Jesus, won't you say I will to

Jesus, and take him as your saviour too? Renew your life for service for a living God who cares for you and loves you with incomparable passion.

* * * * *

Mistaken Offering

And it came to pass, when he saw her, that he rent his clothes, and said, Alas, my daughter! thou hast brought me very low, and thou art one of them that trouble me: for I have opened my mouth unto the Lord, and I cannot go back. Judges 11: 35.

In a special but highly familiar colloquial expression, here is a man who let his mouth run before putting his brain into gear.

Jephthah, a leader who needed to conquer his enemy promised God an offering in loose ended conversation without counting the cost. He was so taken up by his selfish need to conquer his enemy that he had not fully considered God's original plan. As he arrived home wrapped in his own self evaluation from his conquest he hadn't noticed the lack of attention until he arrived at his own doorstep seeing his daughter running, and dancing in delight to see him with her friends by her side. Here we see the true transposition of guilt played out as he speaks, "Alas, my daughter! thou hast made me very low."

When he saw her he was reminded that he had made a very thoughtless bargain with God. So empowered by his own selfishness he set out to do the thing that he decided was necessary without considering the consequences or the cost. He had not learned that you do not barter with God in good faith without counting the cost. Jephthah was not out of the ordinary he was the nations leader, and saw the need to conquer the enemy, which he was sent to do. He discovered an element of weakness in his ranks, and sought a way to remedy it by approaching God. He did not gather his subordinates to sit down and talk it out. He refused to allow God to work out the outcome in his own way. No, he called upon God, and offered his own selfish plan believing there would be a crowd ar home to meet him with victory gifts, which was quite a normal practice, for victorious conquerors. However there was no one on the street to meet him. No gifts for him to accept for God had withdrew the encouragement of the crowds to leave that which He desired for a sacrifice after Jephthah's bargain, that turned out to be his daughter.

How familiar this action is in the light of the contemporary church moving away from God's projected plan as well as the one that has been laid down before us through Christ. We make promises to go all the way with God if he would only do this, or do that, which is our own selfish desire. When he gives us our way, and we claimed to be blessed by what has come to pass until we see God come to collect what we promised him then we find it too costly. This is where Jephthah is to given credit if he deserves any credit he deserves it when he saw the most difficult task before him was to fulfill his promise before God he carried it out. Today we shy away from carrying out God's will even after we have promised that we would carry it out. Our enemies become those who are in the church who will neither relent in carrying out God's will, nor take time to restructure their lives into the pattern which God requires.

The modern day church has adopted an aura of condemnation to nurture the emotion of hate towards others. There is a major change to our fundamental practice of worshipping the living God. We rally around the self satisfying elect groups to find a comfort zone in our lives. In doing that we endanger our stand before God because we essentially say we are unwilling to do God's will at any cost. Our vows to God have become only as mystical dreams that we never expect to come true, but when our promise to God becomes a reality before our eyes we do all we can to back out of it without any apology to God. That is because, as Jephthah, we have the wrong concept of what God requires. When people get into situations that are difficult they quite often try to get out of it the best way they know how even by seeking the unusual way of God in their lives. It is not unusual to discover them making a bargain with God if he will deliver them from a distasteful situation, or a scary situation. An often heard phrase is that every person has their price, and with that we attempt to buy God off. Okay God, if you will fix this part of my life here is what I will do for you. Sorry, God is not buying it, for he declares when they ask they do not understand the devastation that they bring upon themselves. We somehow work on a preconceived idea of the response that God will make. First off he has done it all for you in his plan of salvation. Now he expects you to act on your own by not making moves that prove to be disastrous, but moves that will allow your life to project the salvation of Jesus Christ.

When you are into a situation whereby you need to deal with God you must remember that he created all things, and without him was nothing created, and the only thing that is acceptable to him is absolute submission of self because it is you he wants, and nothing else will do.

You may find yourself in Jephthah's place where he had to sacrifice that which he loved greater than himself, but even though the price is great he would not go back on his word he kept the promise of his morbid sacrifice. Where today can we find one who is so dedicated to the living God that they would put their own welfare at the bottom of the list.

"I have opened my mouth I cannot go back." was his wounded cry.

With so many of us smug church members, we are so prudent, so wise as we set ourselves above our fellowman. we have so much admiration for ownership, and possession of all our faculties we are in danger of dying of self control. This man in the heat of enthusiasm made a solemn pledge to the Lord. A pledge that was inevitably to make him give up the most infinitely precious thing in his life. While some of us in our prudence will not make a pledge of even a meagre few dollars, here we see a man torn inside by his decision but undaunted in accomplishing for God what he had promised to do. When we find ourselves in the position where it is hard to commit even though we have laid down rules to do so, we would rather change the wording of our constitutional right than to submit in order to keep a vow. We refuse God what is rightfully His by suggesting that we are unaware how things will be next month, next year.

Jephthah went to battle from the altar of prayer. He reaped the victory that he had asked God for. In many Christian lives prayer has little importance other than to show people who meet in the group how well we are able to form our words, and call it prayer. We see God as a handyman to tell our troubles to, and not someone to whom we make a vow to keeping that vow after we find that things haven't gone so well in our favour.

All the, greats, in the bible are absolutely blessed because of their enthusiastic giving. The widow and her might so measured her love for God that she gave all that she had, and found herself overly blessed for her thoughtfulness. Mary, who knelt at Jesus feet used the most expensive material that money could buy in her giving honour to Jesus. It was their ultimate giving of their own love by putting their own needs last without being intimidated about what others would think of them. God made them immortal through his word.

Jephthah made his vow and went into battle, and God gave him the victory as he had asked. He headed home without a welcoming band or a crowd of well wishers welcoming him back from the fields of battle. He is stopped in his tracks, his heart is torn with ache as his daughter becomes visible to him he realizes for the first time the penalty for making a vow from self admiration.

Had this been any person of the modern day church venue they would have rendered themselves in need of a psychological analyses to show them the way out of their promise to God. They would have lost their place in God's plan by excusing themselves by some logical ethical explanation. Jephthah was not driven by public speculation or he might have excused himself by saying the vow was made under pressure therefore he could not be held responsible, but he did not abdicate his responsibility to God although it was a painful lesson he carried it through.

Is there a time when you have been delegated to a less than welcome situation? Perhaps it was downright frightening. does a storm of heavy thunder and lightening strike terror in your heart? When you are in that storm do you make some promise to God if he will just deliver you safely through? Then in the aftermath you never carried out your promise? A promise is a vow. Think of the vows you have made as members of your church, and have forgotten them, or just found them to tiresome to fulfill your obligation to carry them out. Some of you have made pledges to your church or some needy Christian organization, and you simply went on to ignore them.

It is check up time. What have you done with your vows? You have promised to renounce the devil. You have vowed to keep God's Holy Word, and to do his will by keeping his commandments. Have you been honest with God?

You have made a vow to uphold the members of your church and follow those instructions in God's word that tells us to;

And, be ye kind one to another, tenderhearted, forgiving one another, even as God for Christ's sake hath forgiven you. Be ye therefore followers of God, as dear children; And walk in love, as Christ also hath loved us, and hath given himself for us an offering and a sacrifice to God for a sweetsmelling savour. Eph 4: 32; 5: 1-2.

Actually , gentleness goes far beyond what is supposed to be a manly reaction. It is the stepping outside of who we are, and adopting the Christlike position of not seeking out whether the person was good or bad, only that they would clearly see the way of Salvation through the acceptance of Christ as Saviour.

Here one must envision the very act of the cross that impaled the ethics of man to allow God's ethics to soar above that which we could imagine.

If a man say, I love God, and hateth his brother, he is a liar: for he that loveth not his brother whom he has seen, how can he love God whom he hath not seen? 1 John 4: 20.

Sunday Christians have flagrantly trampled those rules that were set forth by God. Lord help us to say, *"I have opened my mouth unto the Lord and cannot go back."*

* * * * *

The Kingdom
Of Heaven is Like

Another parable put he forth unto them saying, The kingdom of heaven is like a grain of mustard seed, which a man took, and sowed in his field. Matt 13: 31.

Truly this parable depicts the invitation of hope. We may experience a small beginning, but when consistent in our attempt to achieve we will see mighty growth arise from our struggles to a place of recognizable reward for our efforts.

Jesus was taking time to explain very diligently, and carefully to get his disciples to attempt to understand what heaven was like. The empathy of the disciples was rather shallow as Jesus had to use illustration upon illustration for them to absorb what he attempted to have them learn in depth. Jesus delicately pointed out that there were those who would appear that they should be with the crowd because of their visible identification was near to the right type, but they in fact were interlopers into the field of God's work. Jesus portrayed how the responsibility would be taken on by God to ferret out the phonies. In his major parable of the tares and the wheat, Jesus was quite deliberate in setting out the outcome of those that didn't belong, the tares [look alike wheat] would be bundled up, and cast into the fire to be destroyed.

Another parable spake he unto them; *The kingdom of heaven is like unto leaven, which a woman took, and hid in three measures of meal, till the whole was leavened.* Matt 13: 33.

Believers should not get caught up by the number three here. I believe the word Networking applies to this quite admirably, for we see the woman with three small sections of leavened dough by which she in her work added it to other larger mixtures until all the manufactured product was affected by the content to grow to a much larger size. Perhaps a good indicator of how we should treat God's word in order to effect our surrounding communities.

Again, the Kingdom of heaven is like unto treasure hidden in a field; the which when a man has found, he hideth, and for joy thereof he goeth and selleth all that he hath, and buyeth the field. Matt 13: 44

I am impressed by the imperative commission of evangelism this verse directs us to. Pointing out the field in order that our vision may be to recognize the truth of the sought after treasure. For the contemporary believer it may be the lost Soul just waiting to be plucked from the baron place by the hand of the harvester of God's commission.

The kingdom of heaven is like unto a merchant man seeking goodly pearls: Who when he found one pearl of great price, went and sold all he had and bought it. Matt 13: 45-46.

The finder here was not a person of untold wealth, nor was the person endowed with Academic wisdom, this person was deemed to be your run of the mill dock worker even without a Union. In the poverty of the Nation would be accepted as one with the lowest type of income. In his challenge of a heavy work load he attempted to give of his all, and lo, and behold he uncovered a great treasure. He then set out to secure the ownership of the substance. The intent of this Parable description was to wake us up to the fact that God expects us to take ownership of that which He has given to us freely.

Again the kingdom of heaven is like unto a net, that was cast into the sea, and gathered of every kind: Matt 13: 47.

Here again all shall be gathered into the net and pulled ashore the bad with the good, but he will designate heavenly agents to separate those which prove useless to the kingdom and they will be cast into the fire to be burned and there shall be weeping and wailing and gnashing of teeth.

In these parables that Jesus gives it is evident that there are many who gather in the peripheral rim of Gods overall plan. We love the comfort zone more than we love God, or our fellowman. Although we find the parable with very likable context of the good guy, and a lovely place to be, I believe we miss the whole point when we fail to see the outcome of those hangers on group that are there only because its a nice place to be. They have gathered to supplement their "me" syndrome of self satisfaction, instead of adopting God's way to love their fellowman while spreading the gospel of Jesus Christ.

As these parable have an interrelated meaning to them let us take a closer look at the pearl of great price.

An interesting fact that is often overlooked, because of the great find, is the setting that claims the merchant was seeking. He was intent about where he was going, and the reason for his action. This merchant possessed the knowledge of the product that he sought. Also he knew where to seek the good product that he wished to have. This merchant first of all had a definite purpose of his search. He knew at what mark to aim, and what goal to set. Often in the Christian walk there is an abiding indifference with a lack of direction, and a lack of cognizance of destination.

I learned of the death by suicide of a young merchant who was found in his garage on a Saturday morning just before Christmas day. He had arranged the car to run emitting gas fumes to take his own life. There was a letter found telling of his specific plan. He was a young married man with small children. All outward appearances showed him to be very astute as a successful business man within the community. It was believed that he had everything to live for. He also appeared to be quite in control of his life as well as his business, but he took his own life.

The evident question on everyone's lips was, why? I submit that even though he had many elements at his fingertips he had lost the sight of real purpose in his life, and he had to escape the boredom of purposeless living.

Purpose makes for power, we cannot be indifferent to purpose with destination or direction. We must have a purpose that will give us character which makes us stronger in the passing years.

Another factor about the merchant of the parable is that he was a connoisseur of the merchandise he sought. In other words he knew what he was after and he sought the best for his market. The pearl was the most precious jewel of that day in his area.

The very best is in reach of all our hands if we are willing to take the risk and pay the price. Often we do not attempt to try for the very best or we would reach out and take what Christ has to offer, because we are too willing to settle for the second best. We are prone to invest our lives in secondary issues. The question of right or wrong has almost been eliminated from our vocabulary. There has been a breaking down of old sanctions, and a flinging away of practiced standards, and restraints. All of these new directions impose numerous questions. Are the ends worthwhile? Are they important or are they trivial? Are they of supreme value or are they again secondary? How about you, what are you after?

If you win the prize or find the most select jewel of your life, what would you have?

You have only one life to invest what field are you buying with it.

This merchant was so familiar with the product that he immediately recognized the best when he found it. He knew also how important it was to be a good judge of values. A person who would succeed in any business must be somewhat of a judge in order to judge the value of the merchandise they wish to handle.

Again and again we see people moving from real values to make insecure purchases of immovable stock. Too often we can find the modern day believers at the garage sales of lesser value, than seeking the authentic purchase for a costly price. What are you adding to your spiritual warehouse? That which is of good value or that which will initiate loss. No wonder Isaiah shouts at his people with a frantic earnestness, *Wherefore do you spend money for that which is not bread?* Is 55: 2.

We are confused by the crowds who are madly scrambling after things that they are told they should have or that they somehow deserve, by the media ,who has little or nothing with care about life in whatever form. Yet we decide because so many are seeking to obtain whatever they have been enticed into, that it must be of necessity of great value. We must only seek values that meet our greatest needs. Real values abide, life's, faith, hope, love, concern and caring of others. When we attribute our growth to these things we will see a great expansion in our warehouse of blessings. One cannot establish a dollar value on any of these elements, for they in and of themselves are priceless. May God truly grant us an eye for those values that are real.

When the merchant, that Jesus talks about, found the priceless pearl, he knew what it was. He was not fooled by the outward appearance. It dimmed all other pearls. His long search had ended. He held the very ultimate in value in his own hand, and recognized it.

Now, we exercise the witness of wisdom becoming effective as he identified the value he stopped at nothing to purchase it. The word says, he sold all he had to make the purchase.

Some instead of buying begin to talk about the beauty of the pearl, or get caught up in the world of, if only, and get lost in a fraudulent world of wishes. The possession wish, but they refuse to buy because they deem the price to be too great. The priceless pearl is not for those who simply wish for it. It is for the person who regardless of the cost wills to possess it. Then there are those who finding it find the price far greater than they wish to pay. for that reason they try to persuade themselves that it is not so wonderful after all.

I remember in school a story about the fox and the grapes. the same principle can be applied here. The fox could not grasp the object through his own initiative so he abandoned the effort and satisfied his ego by suggesting to himself that the grapes were sour anyway and he wouldn't like them so he passed on by.

Remember the reaching of the promised land as ten spies ventured out to see what was the greatest feat to overcome in conquering this land. All they could see was giants, and that dimmed their hopes of being conquering victors. They returned to camp with a defeatist attitude therefore gave a report with their short-sightedness, and full intention of giving their evil report saying that penetration of the land was nigh impossible.

Their fear of overcoming obstacles in their way is a very common fear that possesses people in church leadership today. They reject new ideas by scoffing at the dreamers of change for better serving our living God. Church leaders are prone to enter the era of rejection, and condoning condemnation of those who dare to upset the status quo, because they lack the courage to make true servanthood a reality in today's lax worship style.

How many are negating the program of Jesus Christ the son of the living God? Who are these wanna-be's, that scorn the worship of God without an altar, which in fact is required by God?

Not because they have found a better way to worship, but because they lack the courage to follow in the steps of the saviour to fulfill His requirements. Lacking courage, we lend ourselves to criticizing the criticism. Many stoop to using it as a smoke screen to hide behind cowardly projections, and non-sensical empty visions, that are totally related to an obscure non-Christ likeness.

Their are others who do not buy because they are waiting for the price to be marked down. They want to claim it, but they believe they can wait until it's cheaper. Let me assuredly guarantee you that day will not come.

This was a merchant of experience, he ask how much, and when advised as to the cost he replied, "I will take it." His answer was firm, without hesitation, he prepared to make the buy in selling all that he possessed. Establishing an initiative to raise the funds required to make the purchase. His mindset was to obtain the world's greatest prize to add to his stature as a bonafide merchant.

Is this story your story? Have you purchased the pearl of great price? Or are you still wandering in the wilderness making excuses as to why you do not want any part of success in your Christian life?

I realize that there are those out there who, according to the politically correct, are decent folk, and for all intents and purposes are respectable. You go to church, perhaps take some minor leadership, teach Sunday school, sit on the board, or work on one of the many groups that help the church to grow numbers wise; But the question that needs to weigh upon your hearts is thus, "Can you sing out of your own experience, Jesus is mine?"

The evaluation needs to be in place "Am I Spiritually correct" in adopting the action that I must take.

Have you ever fallen upon your knees, as did doubting Thomas, before your risen saviour, Jesus Christ, and cried, my Lord! and my

God! Can you join with Paul in saying, *"I know whom I have believed, and am persuaded that he is able to keep that which I have committed unto him against that day."* 2 Timothy 1: 12.

If you are unable to embrace these words by applying them to your life, then you have not been willing to pay the price.

Christ is asking from you, and me, not for your money, not for your work, not for your prayers, not for your tears, he is asking for an unconditional surrender of your soul to receive his gift of salvation through his shed blood on the cross at Calvary.

When we give all, he gives all, the pearl of great price. there is no other way to have a blessedness with God. You must have a definite purpose, seek after the very best, be a judge of excellent values, and pay the price that God asks.

* * * * *

Is One Sin Greater Than Another?

—◦◦◦—

W hat is the greatest sin in the world?

Some will say it is murder. Some will elude to Sexual abuse, and you may name me others that seem to be the worse sin of all. Yet Paul who was responsible for the murder of many believers, was saved by the grace of God, and in turn became one of God's most powerful sources for the Christian ministry. Others will say that theft is the greatest sin, yet the thief on the cross was told by our Lord, "Today thou shalt be with me in paradise." Again there are those who will determine that the greatest sin is adultery. Then we must examine the women at the well who had five husbands, and she was right in believing that Jesus was the promised Christ, and her soul and body was saved.

What then is the greatest sin?

Simply the rejection of Jesus Christ as the son of the living God come to be our saviour. Are you a sinner who has not yet received Jesus as Lord.? God loves you, he gave the life of his only son upon the cross of Calvary for you. He offers to save your soul from the fiery pits of Hell to give you eternal life in heaven by his wonderful plan of salvation.

You may have nothing to do with him as you trample him under your feet. You may attempt to give him no thought, but in so doing you have committed the greatest sin above all, and you will pay the highest price.

If you have the conviction of sin in your life you will feel the need to seek forgiveness of the living God. Sin is not some theological abstraction, it is evil at it's worst, out of which the burdensome weight of the worlds injustice will be heavy upon your shoulders as sin sits upon your doorstep. It is the threatening lowered moral standings of our youth. It is greed for filthy money that is tainted with blood, that fills our broken underworld economics with the racketeers. It is the impatience with discipline that breaks up our home. This sin crouches at the door of self esteem to corrupt our thinking. Sin is as real as the flu, or cancer, with its corrupting influence raising a stench making the air difficult to breath. We face the downward sickness of the soul which sin has developed. We face numerous acts which we could identify as those which put God out of your life. Today's trend to same sex marriages is simply lust of the flesh. God identifies with it this way;

These six things does the Lord hate; yea, seven are an abomination unto Him: A proud look, a lying tongue, and hands that shed innocent blood, A heart that deviseth wicked imaginations, feet that be swift running to mischief, A false witness that speaketh lies, and he that soweth discord amongst the brethren. Proverbs 6:16-19.

In rejecting Christ, a person shuts the door on their highest potential. We need to say yes to Jesus, for rejecting Christ we put ourselves in the way of all sinners whose destination is fire and brimstone in the lake of fire. In rejecting Christ, we designate our life to the devil's side. There is no in between, no pretty goodbye speeches, just the devil and his torment outside of Christ. John the Baptist said, *"Behold the lamb of God which taketh away the sin of the world."* Paul says. *"In him dwells the fullness of God."* Peter said, *"Thou art the Christ the son of the living God."* Nicodemus said, *"Rabbi, we know that thou art a teacher come from God?"*

Polycarp said, "Eighty six years have I served him, and he has done nothing but good."

Tolstoy admitted having lived most of his life without belief in anything, but finally when he found Christ he was deemed to admit to the absolute transformation which his life underwent. He admitted that when his faith came to him and he fully surrendered to Jesus to accept Him as Saviour he found that when he fully believed in Jesus, his whole life underwent a sudden transformation. Life and death ceased to be evil and innstead of utter despair he now tasted the fullness of joy, and happiness.

Successful, and famous preachers often employ the same finding and can only respond with "All that I think, all that I hope, all that I write, all that I live for is based on the divinity of Jesus Christ, the central joy of my poor wayward life."

If a man were even somehow able to touch the hem of His garmet there would be instilled into the soul that relentless pursuit of souls for the heavenly Kingdom which he offers that is all inclusive in the plan of salvation. Even a rag from the body of Jesus, worn in contempt, despite ones self, he would look greater, and be better."

Each individual believer must learn to commit their soul into the hands of our Saviour in full confidence. Each believer must forge ahead with the message of this great Savior careful not to harbor any thought of turning back.

Books could not begin to contain all the wonderful thoughts and experiences of the great men who identified their success in ministry as they made that life changing decision to follow Jesus. In rejecting Christ, a person seals their doom forever.

The wicked shall be turned into Hell, and all the nations that forget God. Psalm 9: 17.

Here, in the scripture, is the sharp knockout punch given to those who believe that there is another way on the highroad. Given the choice to thrive in the lower echelon of living losing all respect for God and his way.

Hell from beneath is moved for thee to meet thee at thy coming: it stirreth up the dead for thee, even all the chief ones of the earth; it hath raised up from their thrones all the kings of the nations. Isaiah 14: 9.

In the stranger world of translators that somehow try to penetrate the ideology with their own relieving thought, but the writer here makes no mistake about where the unbeliever, whether king or pauper, will end up. They will end up in torture of a flaming Hell where those who have gone on before await to taunt the new tenant about their easy fall into the pit, and show amazement at that person being one of those who fell.

He that believeth on him is not condemned; but he that believeth not is condemned already, because he believeth not on the only son of God. John 3: 18.

It is to be noted here that nowhere in the scripture does God give the believer the right to condemn anyone. We are to cherish, and nurture each soul unto salvation, only God has the right to condemnation of the unbeliever.

He that believeth on the son hath everlasting life, and he that believeth not on the son shall not see life, but the wrath of God abideth in him. John 3: 36.

This appears to be an invasive wrath into the unbelievers lifestyle. Nevertheless we should be elated to see the challenge put forth here. It gives the believer the absolute confirmation of our salvation, while it confirms to the unbeliever what has been offered, and what is at the very gate of eternal life. Either with God for eternal happiness, or without God into eternal damnation into the flames of hell.

The same shall drink of the wine of the wrath of God, that is poured out without mixture into the cup of indignation; and they shall be tormented with fire and brimstone in the presence of the Holy angels, and in the presence of the lamb. Rev 14: 10.

But the fearful, and the unbelieving, and the abominable, and murderers, and whoremongers, and sorcerers, and idolaters, and all liars, shall have their part in the lake which burneth with fire and brimstone: which is the second death. Rev 21: 8.

Are you sealing your doom with your rejection of the loving son of God, Christ?

Man in the image of God with his idealism of being self sufficient leads to his own doom.

Where is hell?

At the end of a Christless life.

* * * * *

Appointed For That Great Day

—*◦/◦/◦*—

There will be a day when Christ returns to receive his followers who are appointed unto himself, that will be a great day, and there are some who are not prepared.

And the times of this ignorance God winked at; but now commandeth all men everywhere to repent: Because he has appointed a day, in which he will judge the world in righteousness by that man whom he hath ordained; whereof he hath given assurance unto all men, in that he has raised him from the dead. Acts 17: 30-31.

One needs to remind themselves of the very important question to ask, "Is the empathy of the teacher or preacher lost in an intellectual gathering?"

Although they may appear to be more difficult to bring over to the redemption team, I believe always that God deals with the heart. As teachers or preachers we lack the perception of God at work. It is always a great day when we witness people who accept Christ as their saviour in what could be described as a silent conversion. A decision made on their own by recognizing their need. With a persons non intellectual maneuver while taking a breather from the chaos of life, was reached out and touched by Jesus, and were transformed by the message of the gospel, does not take away the necessity of telling the word as God requires. there is no measuring stick to a message. Sometimes it seems to roll over the crowd like water in a ducks back, but that is only a guess on our part. No one can truly measure the impact upon the soul.

Many born again believers look forward to that great day of Christ's return. However as one searches the scriptures it is possible to find various numbers of great days in the bible. It was one of those great days when God created the heavens, and the earth. Another great time was when God conferred with his heavenly colleagues to say, "Let us create man in our own image."

Man in his own adoption of self satisfaction wandered away from God to do his own thing only to find himself in such deep turmoil that God disowned him. Then God approached Noah with a contract to build an Ark so that he could wipe out all these selfish sinful people. And Noah built as he was directed to do and God wiped out all his creation with a flood with the exception of Noah and his family along with the animals that God had directed to the Ark.

Another great day to remember was when God asked a young virgin to have his child as the last covenant with man. He pointed out through a messenger, that she had found favour with God. She conceded that God could do with her what he would, and God produced a child with her, commanding her to call him Jesus. And she did and the whole world today celebrates his birth as our Saviour , and Lord, of our lives. For we acknowledge him as the only son of God. Jesus grew all the time knowing that he had to be about his Father God's business, because he was quite aware of his journey towards the cross. When Jesus was crucified for our sins he bore terrible pain, and shame on our behalf, but it was turned into victory over death when He arose.

Jesus ascended into heaven to sit on the right hand of his father to make intercession on our behalf. There he would discuss with his Father the day of his return to receive us unto himself. The bible tells us of other great days like when we shall see him again. He also tells us of the reward that will be ours for service in the name of Jesus Christ. One day that ought to concern all of us is the day of judgment when both saved and lost will stand before God to be judged. The righteous unto righteousness, and the unbelievers and evildoers will be judged unto damnation. what a day that will be when God separates the saved unto himself and allow us to enter into an eternal life of joy and peace. I look forward to that day.

There will also be a judgment day for the Christian believer, and if they were serving him with commitment in a productive lifestyle they shall receive a reward. On the cross the Lord took all the punishment for our sins, and wiped them clean away. Believers will not suffer in eternity for sin, but unbelievers will enter an eternity of suffering for rejecting the Saviour while they had a chance to serve him here on earth. God says that those who reject Jesus by failing to trust in him is condemned already right here and now.

Some of you are giving God small corners of your life with only scraps of your time, and only the smallest fraction of your money when you ought to be giving your very best.

Those who have decided not to trust in Jesus make up thousands of excuses, but those excuses will not be valid when you come face to face with Jesus at the judgment seat. Now is the time to give of yourself to Jesus. Tomorrow may be too late.

But as it is written, *Eye hath not seen, nor ear heard, neither have entered into the heart of man, things that God has prepared for those that love him. But God has revealed them unto us by his spirit: for the spirit searches all things, yea, the deep things of God.*
1 Corinthians 3: 9-10.

We are aware that our eyes have seen some pretty wonderful things here on earth. The great handiwork of God etched in our Canadian Rocky Mountains of Alberta. Particularly the portions from Jasper, through to the Banff corridor. Through the mighty David Thompson route, and on to the breathtaking view in the Kananaskis country. One is unable to comprehend that it would be possible for our eyes to see even greater beauty than this. Eyes have seen magnificent sunsets and sunrises that portray God's hand as he whisks his own paintbrush across the horizons. the most articulate artist must relinquish his thought of making a picture as beautiful as God has. The eyes have seen the beauty of our great water falls such as Niagara, and the beauty of the lines marking the tremendous entourage of great lakes, and waterways such as the St Lawrence river, or many others as the Sinclair, Columbia, Yukon, Thompson, and Fraser rivers. In all of these natural beauties that can be seen with the eye, none can compare to the marvelous things that we will behold when standing in the presence of God.

Also the ear has heard some marvelous sounds, songs of the birds, sweet melodies by human voice, laughter of children, but we have heard nothing that will match that which will ingratiate our ears in the presence of God at the entrance into eternal life with our Christ.

A great crowd will be there. the young and the old, the rich and the poor, the good and the bad, they all will be there. You will look into the faces on many whom you failed to witness to. You will watch them be condemned to an eternal hell. The graves will give up their dead, and we shall all stand before the omnipotent God for the judgment.

The comfort zone is picturing yourself on the outside looking in at that great throng before the throne while you watch the proceedings, but your dreams are dashed when you realize that it will not be that way. Your comfort zone will be shattered when you eventually realize that you now must stand to receive the sentence passed upon you.

The kings of the earth, and the great men, and the rich men, and the chief captains, and the mighty men, and every bondsman, and every free man, hid themselves in the dens and in the rocks of the mountains; And said to the mountains and rocks, Fall on us and hide us from the face of him that sitteth upon the throne, and from the wrath of the Lamb: For the great day of his wrath is come; who shall be able to stand.

Revelation 6: 15-17.

Some will attempt to escape as it points out in the preceding scripture. Where will you be? Are you ready to stand before the throne of God? Or will you be with those that scream the words predicted for rocks to fall upon you, and mountains to hide you as it says in in the bible?

Be assured of this one thing, rocks will not fall upon them, mountains will not hide them. Only god fearing people will escape this judgment, no sinner can escape the judgment seat of the great white throne.

Some good men are depending on their goodness to get them to heaven, or in the contemporary vernacular, to appease their Gods, like the man upstairs, or the greater power, whatever that might be. Well my friends, it is sad to say that when you reach that final stage you will discover that nobody will be allowed access to the kingdom of God by the works of achievement by the flesh. Only those who have mastered the simple faith in God through the saviour Jesus Christ will be let in. Otherwise your membership is not valid.

The believer will be seated at the great welcome banquet before the Lord. They will receive their reward for their service to Jesus Christ. It will be a life of endless joy, and that will be truly a great day.

The lost will find themselves placed into a pit with eternal torment.

My friends this does not have to be your fate. God has no pleasure in the death of the wicked. He loves you in spite of your sin. The arms of Jesus are wide open to receive you and to save you. Now is the accepted time, take this time in your life to accept him as your personal saviour, and be prepared for that great day when he will allow you to be received into his presence for you to feast at his table with joy, and love when we enter that final step into eternity. Be sure that you will walk through the gates of heaven into eternal bliss. Do not put it off for you have no guarantee. If you refuse to allow God to transform your life you will be walking through the gates of Hell into eternal torment.

Take his gift of salvation today, and be sure or your rewards without condemnation in an eternal Hell without God.

The choice is yours. Believe in the Lord Jesus Christ, and thou shalt be saved today.

* * * * *

I Walked A Smile

J. A. [Jim Watson

Today I washed a tear away
For I walked a mile
And gave away a smile

Today I washed a tear away
Said "Hello dear"
There vanished fear

Today I washed a tear away
With smile I hope to stroll
And heal a soul

Today I washed a tear away
Walked an extra mile
Gave away a smile

The soul was full of woe
But the Spirit said to go
And today I washed a tear away.

I placed a smile upon a child
Eyes lit up calm and mild
Again today I washed a tear away.

* * * * *

Friend Of The Sinner

Then drew near unto him all the publicans and the sinners for to hear him. And the Pharisees and scribes murmured, saying, This man receives sinners, and eateth with them. Luke 15: 1-2.

Amazingly, the opening verse here reveals a distinctiveness in the love employed by Jesus, for he sought the lost. In other words he kept company with those whom had not yet had the privilege of hearing of that which he had to offer, salvation of the living God.

This is an interesting scripture in that these actions are visible in the contemporary churches of today. Have then the modern Christian churches become the pools of vile concoction that turns them into the Pharisee. Without compassion for souls; only a about structural impact of the rules set up by the organization fetish. Jesus was speaking here to a group just like that. They were more concerned about activities to make them feel good, and about their authority, than was their concern for God. They were aware, and practicing all the moral attributes, but were not following the long expected Christ. He was not recognized by this group who for years claimed his coming. In this gathering that had come to give Jesus a hearing because somehow within their own lives they believed they had really messed up. Some of them were the social rejects of the day, but many were the secular society of the day trying to prove this Jesus wrong. Others were there with no religious affiliation whatsoever. The Pharisees condemned Jesus for that.

Is the modern church different from the make up of the Pharisee?

What the Pharisee didn't point out is what makes the similarity with today's churches to exist. They ignored the fact that Jesus was fulfilling the need of those who came, He offered them the Love of God even though they were not of the religious order. It shows here that their needs were being met. Their hopes had been long dead, but now were experiencing a resurrection of that hope. It is a gathering that would bring much joy to sincere Christian workers of our day to see a gathering of large numbers of unbelievers just to hear the words of Jesus. But the scribes and Pharisees were not happy campers in this lot. They were filled with indignation, and caught up with condemning criticism against Jesus. Their criticism, "This man receives sinners." Jesus seizes the opportunity and makes a text out of their criticism and preaches in parables.

We find in Luke 15, the parables of the "lost." The lost sheep, The lost coin, The lost son, The lost brother. These writings are truly united into a single relative story by the word, lost. This chapter is one most singly precious and important chapters given to the believer today. Let us look further into the saying projected by this writing of Luke.

This man receives sinners.

Who are the sinners?

They are those who are lost, also they are out of the right relationship with the

Son of God, Jesus Christ. There are four indications here of loss. First the sense of the stray sheep, which had for all intents and purposes had just wandered away. It had not fallen to its death, nor had it been devoured by a wild beast. It had simply lost its sense of direction. It had been distracted by some other form that took it away from the flock out of range and unable to hear shepherds voice.

There are multitudes today who are lost in the same manner. They are flung away from old authorities, but have found no new ones. They miss the commands that give them peaceful and reassuring direction. They have become spiritually, and morally adrift. they are between two worlds, one dead, and the other powerless to be born.

Secondly, there are those similar to the lost coin. The coin was not lost because it ceased to be silver. It was not lost because somehow it managed to become a lesser metal. Neither was it lost because there was no identification on the face of it. The image, and superscription was still clear on the coin to show it was a valid monetary exchange for goods, and accepted by all of the nation. It simply was lost because it was out of circulation. It was redundant in rendering a service to anyone. Although it was still the property of the owner, it was utterly useless as if it didn't exist. The sin here, according to Jesus, is uselessness.

Every parable of judgment was given, not against those guilty of some positive wrong, only in those that had failed to carry out their duty in obedience to the requirement of God the Father. The man who buried his talent. The bridesmaids with no oil. The rich mans attitude towards Lazarus, he was one who moved among the needy, and failed to meet those needs, and worse still he failed to see the poverty, and hunger that existed. All these utterly condemned, and still there are the same lackadaisical believers amongst us today.

Sympathy from this type are often with the church in a must be on the membership role to count. Yet they do not pass for legal tender in any enterprise to reach out and touch the lost for Jesus. No matter how elegant, or pristine they appear to be in their personal presentation, Jesus says they are lost.

Thirdly there are those who are lost as the prodigal son. Simply, demanding what we believe to be ours, ahead of time, they leave the safety net of established believers. They in disdain leave the fellowship of comfort, and straight direction with wise instruction. Those prodigals turn to foreign teaching of social structure in a society. Giving tribute to organizations that fall short in the teaching that God exists, and requires those who will follow the letter of His law. Soon they find in the casual order of other beliefs they can find no peace or satisfaction let alone the comfort, and embracement of God's grace. Thank God when we see the prodigals recognize their error of the way to return to the Father's house in humility, and refresh themselves in the sumptuous feast that is prepared for them.

Fourthly, there are those who find themselves lost as the older brother who remained at home. Here we see that the older brother who appeared to remain faithful to the organization could not accept his father's love, nor did he recognize it when he had it all the time. He harboured resentment without forgiveness, and refused to tolerate the return of the wayward believer. He resented the celebration in return of a lost soul returning. The older brother identifies with many modern day Christians as he shoulders responsibility of the ongoing day to day chores to be done to keep every thing in tact. He also harbours that which is evident in many working Christians today. That is the emotion of resentment that conjures up jealousy of others success when they eventually buckle down and do the right thing for the Father's house.

The older brother's God, was a material god. He loved himself better than he loved others. His resentment runs deep as many modern day Christians. One can hear the loud whisper, look at what I have done, rather than being thankful that God has seen fit to send other workers to help. There is nothing that will destroy a church quicker than the jealousy of the saints. Some outsider is welcomed by a few, but it only takes one long time member to begin with jealousy that will eventually destroy what the church has to set out to do. More and more of this is seen when we recognize the church as adopting the ways of the secular world.

The plan of the world cannot encompass the work of a living God for it is made of a garment that does not fit God's requirements. We need to look closely at the requirements that God lays before us to indwell our soul. Only then we will be able to welcome the return of the wayward soul. If we choose to remain outside of our Father's will, we will be destroyed. The older brother was consoled by the father here, and showed him that he already owned all that he had. God does the same for us even when we stumble, and grumble he will embrace us to encourage us in the work.

How did the lost sheep go astray?

It did not become angry, it did not do so intentionally, as he was in no way upset with the shepherd or the rest of the flock. The sheep got lost because of carelessness. It became interested in another area of the field. It did not notice itself far away from the rest of the flock. This sheep was absent from evil, but it caused sheep to wander without conscious act. The stray was not aware of its lost condition.

The same case applies to each of us. Few of us break with God to throw away our convictions deliberately. It is always little, by little, we leave church attendance on a regular basis, then sluff off bible reading, after which we become slack with prayer in the home. Then we adopt a shroud of cloud around sharing, and caring in Christian fellowship. Some time goes by before we find ourselves on the peripheral rim of Christian fellowship with the sense of God slipping from our lives.

Therefore we ought to give the more earnest heed to the things which we have heard, lest at any time we should let them slip. Hebrews2: 1.

There are those who are lost as the coin is lost. Through the carelessness of others. There are those who are lost as the prodigal. Through the stubborn determination to have at the time they are non-deserving, and also to take their own direction in hand not knowing were to go, and inevitably choosing the wrong things for growth under God.

How does Jesus feel about those who are lost?

He receives sinners.

When does he receive them?

When they repent.

They see Jesus afar off, and decide to turn around to go to the meeting place to hear his word. They were ready to listen, and they gathered in a crowd together to hear how their God had sent his only son to redeem them with his blood. The religiosity of the community witnessed this with only harsh criticism of this newly discovered channel to a living god. But they came to hear Jesus, and he received them, and taught them a new life.

* * * * *

No Confidence In The Flesh

Brethren, I count not myself to have apprehended: but this one thing I do, forgetting those things which are behind, and reaching forth unto those things which are before, I press toward the mark for the prize of the high calling of God in Christ Jesus. Philippians 3:13-14.

Many people of latter life have a tendency to adopt a saying of "Been there, done that." In that, there is a lack of comprehension of what we have acquired, and that of which we have left behind. That which we have learned in the past must in fact stir us to waken us up to put self aside, and allow a new creation within to occur. In that light we would totally commit ourselves to walking for the living God.

We live the Christian life in a daily walk with Christ seldom looking behind at our steps, which is not at all a fault, because we need to look ahead to the eternal reward that will be administered by God himself. When we are called to move into a new community we seek to attach ourselves to the body of believers where we know the gospel is preached. We then are ready to identify with the new group and exercise our everyday walk with Jesus. In our new adventure we often are asked that dreaded old question;

"How long have you been a Christian?

Oftentimes it is an innocent question with someone attempting to put us at ease in a group. On the other hand that group may have been praying for a spiritual leader, and they are only hoping that you are the answer to their prayers. The same question can also be a subtle attempt to put you on the spot. Other times people will ask the new person to lead in prayer to see how well they form their talk to God. This type of inquiry is an affront to God, and should never be allowed to be applied in a group. Many questions to newcomers are a subtle way of finding out their past, which in essence, is none of your business. The portion of scripture given here in Philippians 3: v13, and v14, challenges Christians on this very subject. We are not to be concerned about peoples past, but rather as to how we can add to their lives for an excellent future.

The apostle Paul was a man with a past. It was not the kind of past that we ordinarily think of when we refer to Paul, but he did have a past, and here in Philippians he lists his background. He says first of all he was born a Hebrew. His family background was set in the right place. He had all the right things done for him, at the right time at home. v5. He had undergone religious ceremonies according to the Jewish tradition He had also trained in Jewish law, and had risen to the office of Pharisee.

Paul claims that his life as a Jew was blameless, meaning, that before he served Christ he had kept the letter of the law. Again Paul's past was an all out massacre of the believers in Christ, but Christ had dealt with him on the road to Damascus, and he was miraculously saved as he has brought down by God's light. Paul never forgets his past, but he never allowed it to deter him from spreading the word about his saviour Jesus Christ.

When we are saved, born again, we are expected to walk away from our past, and get on with the ministry of God's word. That is the glory of marching on with Jesus. We put our old life in the burial ground of forgetfulness. That may be a difficult statement to grasp hold of when elements keep popping up from time to time. Tale bearers attempting to shattering the new area that you try desperately to build upon. You must then present it before the Lord in prayer, because man will attempt to destroy your work' Only God will answer your asking, and help you build a solid foundation that shall not be broken. It may not be that which you dreamed it to be. Nevertheless, it will be what God wanted. If you are persistent and do not refuse to challenge others who are determined to keep God out of your life. It is always the perfect idea to keep your eyes focused on Jesus, to forge ahead with God's plan, to spread the good news of Jesus Christ, his only son and our saviour.

You as a born again Christian must live a spiritual life. Cast a shadow over the argument given to deal with the selfish humanism that exists as some foreign God. This is man's selfish philosophy that is supposed to deliver you, but cannot because it lacks the power of the shed blood. We must subdue the human instinct to find another way for there is no other way but Christ.

Although you have been transformed by the spirit of God it does not mean you know all things for the eyes of the world are blinded by Satan. Neither are we able to see all things, but we shall see things in a much different light when we live by our new spiritual insight. You may make mistakes along the way as you are in a learning process, but God will guide you with His Holy Spirit who moulds, and directs, those who walk after God. Remember we are still fallible, and do not see ourselves as we really are.

There is an oriental legend about a man who found a mirror, and did not know what it was. Looking into it with great amazement he came to the conclusion that it was a picture of his father. He took it home to revere it in a private shrine as an object of his respect, and affection.

As chance would have it, his wife discovered the object of his devotion, she gazed into it and said, "Just as I thought, another women, and pretty ugly at that."

How often we fail to see ourselves as we really are, and when we do get a glimpse of ourselves we do not recognize the picture.

We know what it is to commit an ungodly act, and we know how to have a distaste for that which we have wrongly committed, but a far greater moment is that knowledge of absolute forgiveness in Christ.

The place to begin forgiving ourselves for our trespasses is to learn to forgive our neighbours, and friends as we accept God's forgiveness we must apply it to others. Hear what the gospel is saying about the love of God who is for us not against us. Do not waste your time hiding in shame or guilt of something you have done. Confess your sin before God, and he will forgive you because he loves you without condition. It is saying that "God is love," that we believe he forgives, and restores. We must learn to accept that we trespass and will continue in our human element to trespass, and in so doing we ask daily for God's forgiveness of our trespasses against him, and he will freely forgive you.

Once a man slips and falls on the street, he does not stay there, he picks himself up, dusts himself off, and gets on his way again perhaps more careful about his walk or where he places his feet. God loves us, and accepts us, while he renders to us a new power for a new life with a new purpose, in a new direction. Behold all things have passed away, and the new has come with the grace of Jesus Christ, Lord and saviour. Continue to walk forward into a new path and keep looking to Jesus.

The only truly supernatural, is that of the living God, who sent to us his only begotten son to die on the cross at Calvary where with his shed blood he rendered forgiveness for all trespasses.

We live in an era when supernatural is attributed to some far out theatrical presentation. We have had so many ridiculous pro- grammes with the almost identical story line on supernatural beings showing us how ugly the so called other forms of life are that it is almost laughable as hoards of people rally to this utter garbage. The problem is that these theatrical imageries have brought the viewer to an immunity to the supernatural phenomena of a living God. We must somehow bring the message of our God to the point where once again the hearers will recognize the forever presence in all of our living.

We serve a God who oftimes seems silent, but he is always emerging in the events of our lives that are not foretold. Each of us accumulate wisdom in stages because our growth and learning is in stages of growth. There is no stronger evidence of the supernatural than the transformation of a soul saved by grace. The believer finds the transformation in accepting Christ as saviour when they realize that the new find will work in their lives when they are ready to let go of the old, and that is accomplished by giving ourselves wholly to the new life before us.

Our view of creation must be persistent in our word and in our walk because it alleviates the practicality of Christ in a sinful world. In the finality of life on earth we shall meet him to be the link whereby we will receive the cure from always falling short. At the entrance gate to eternity, Jesus will direct us onto that highway to

God where we will be received in all our inadequacies, and be given our place in that eternal home. Heaven.

You will not be able to put right all the errors of the social structure, but with Christ you can bring a few into the fold, and God will transform them. So don't waste your life trying to straighten out all the evils of the world. Simply walk in faith, and Christ will draw all men unto him because of your effort however insignificant you may deem it to be.

* * * * *

Foundation Of Dust

And the Lord God formed man of the dust of the ground, and breathed into his nostrils the breath of life; and man became a living soul. Genesis 2; 7.

This statement gathers more substantial weight as we read about the "Potter's clay" the Jeremiah 18:3-6.

In the sweat of thy face shall thou eat bread, till thou return unto the ground; for out of it was thou taken: for dust thou art, and unto dust shalt thou return. Genesis 3: 19.

Reality kicks in when we accept that after man's disobedience of God's initial plan, it brings God to the alignment of a solution for the survival of His creation. To those who like to understand that work was a curse, I would like to point out how God, our creator, again became active in creation with a solution in order that man may get on with his own living, not as God had originally planned, but for the lack of a better terminology, a bail out package. This package also gave him an opening for help from his creator.

Always God's hand was at work to implant upon the minds of wayward men a part of the divine revelation. Which first brought man into being as his own creation in the image of heavenly beings. But that through man's own disobedience he received a work ethic to be followed as an accounting for his sin against God. Often we are shown the frailty of God's creation, but never does God impose that upon us for our own actions. Rather, God is always there to deliver us through our faith in him with a refusal to deny him. Always bringing to remembrance how we were created as well as for what purpose. In the book of Job we find several scripture that remind us by Jobs response to his friends, of how we need to stand firm to expound that which we were created to be, lover's of God working out our own salvation. God is not a master who cracks the whip at every failure to remind us who he is. However he does make a stand for us against those who would intentionally harm our character. So it was with Job as his friends tried to assassinate his character to imply to Job that he had done something wrong or God would not allow his situation. Although these were the types of men who literally would have done anything for Job, they totally misunderstood God, because God does not punish for mistakes however displeasing they may be.

God's faith in man is a very thrilling and uplifting fact in the very first account given in Genesis were the evidence of this fact is when God says, "Let us make man in our own image." God so trusts man that he commits an unfinished world to him, when he says, "have dominion over —-." His faith in his own creation has not been all that disappointing to him. As man has conquered a major element of the spirituality, which God intended, he should know that he is trusted by his creator. God is well pleased with the progress made by man in materialistic progress.

We see God's faith in man throughout the scriptures with the climax being in Jesus Christ as he sanctions that faith by the offering of his life. It is noted that the word was made flesh and dwelt among us, and to see him was to see the Father.

We know that Christ's attitude towards men was the attitude of his Father. Christ's unquestionable, undeserving love, was also the love of God. Christ in his actions here on earth was to make an absolute contribution showing the fullness of God's love. The son of man came to seek and to save that which is lost.

Here Jesus sets out two fundamental issues. First he asserts man's lost condition. He knows that there is no trust that man has not considered, and no action of trespass that he has not followed through the temptation path. Jesus understands that man is the fallen product of sin, and therefore is in need of the plan of salvation that he has come to implement. As long as man is steeped in self esteem, and self worth he remains apart from Christ. Therefore, Jesus knowing that his mission, as he sets it for himself, is to seek out the lost to offer them the plan of redemption. If the application that Christ brings to the unbeliever is accepted then the second part is activated, the soul is saved. As we hear the announcement of Jesus' mission, so we see the fulfillment of the mission. He gathered about him a circle of men that he fully trusted in spite of the fact not one of them was outstanding in their field. Their commitment was to help Jesus to seek and to save that which was lost, and to be obedient in the word. We must understand here that Christ had chosen each person individually, and not collectively. Let me assure you that these men were less than impressive in the hour of Christ's greatest need.

They left his side after receiving great instructions from the master. The outpouring of spiritual insight hardly phased their thinking. These outwardly strong warriors showed to be inner weaklings in the hour of crisis for their leader. Yet it was to these men that Jesus said, "You did not choose me, but I chose you."

Not only did Jesus believe in his friends, he believed in their influence on those outside the circle. They embraced together the outsider, who are still today, cast aside by the modern nominal Christian bodies. In faith of the outcasts, Jesus stood alone, and believers still make Christ stand alone to embrace the sinner, because the corporate church has failed to learn that acclaim, and will be required to give account of itself before God the Father.

The religious leaders of that day could not comprehend the positive need to embrace the unbelieving world of outcasts. They simply dismisses them as a dead loss without any room for them in the fellowship of God worshippers. But Jesus could not share their shameful attitude, and that is why the leaders of the religious order hated him.

We all are guilty at one time or another of demanding of our fellowship of friends, and neighbours that they hold the same prejudices that we do, and hate the same people we hate with the thought of strengthening our own comfort zone.

Jesus refused to share contempt for the outsider, as a matter of fact he went out of his way to bring them on side. His secret, he loved them before he met them, and his caring for the outsider changed the world of the day.

Jesus believed in his friends, and he also believed in the outcasts, but even more phenomenal than all that he loved his enemy. When they hung him on the cross he prayed for them, *"Father forgive them for they know not what they do."* Luke 23: 34.

Even now, Jesus believes in you. His just faith in you is your eternal hope. He made us, he knows what we are, and what we could become. He believes in us, we ought then to believe in ourselves, and in so doing believe in the only begotten son of the living God that you might have everlasting life.

* * * * *

But This Man Has
Done Nothing Wrong

—◦/◦/◦—

And one of the malefactors which were hanged railed on him, saying, if thou be Christ, save thyself and us. But the other answering rebuked him, saying, Dost not thou fear God, seeing thou art in the same condemnation? And we indeed justly; for we receive the due rewards of our deeds: but this man has done nothing amiss. Luke 23: 39-41.

We see here the picture which portrays Christ in His ultimate outreach of love. He fully embraces the community of unbelievers, even to the lowest estate. He portrays a willingness to deliver those who truly accept Him as their saviour and as the Son of the living God. Here is imposition seen often when we can see life illuminated by the brilliance of the light of death. Sometimes it magnifies all our expectations to meet Jesus face to face, but more interesting is when the unbeliever wonders if they should have listened to the Preacher of eternal life.

The picture here, three crosses, three young men had been sentenced to die, the centre cross was Jesus who had determined to lay down his life for the lost souls. On one side an individual who was still plotting to overthrow the system, and with a purely selfish interest asked Jesus to use his power of the kingdom to get them all of the cross. The young man on the third cross spoke up to challenge the first with an unusual question, "Do you not fear God." Here is a dying man, this thief who did not want to die, but he arose to the defence of Christ even in his hopeless situation. And Christ responded to him, and promised that he would be with him in paradise.

The need is of the heart and soul, the thief was aware of his wicked life that he was leaving behind, and his inability to do anything about changing it. Here was a thief who became a penitent man. Hear his justification, "We are here justly, we are guilty of the crimes we were charged with, and we receive what is coming to us. On the cross his heart had recognized the forgiving Christ, and he exercised his hope in Jesus simply asking for forgiveness, and he received more. He received the right to eternal life because of his honest remorse for his wayward life.

Christ's plea even from the cross was, "come, come unto me." The dying thief came to Jesus in soul and spirit. Although his enemies shouted victory as they spiked him to the cross, but even here a miracle is performed as he saves the soul of a dying thief.

The King of Kings, and Lord of Lords, renewed life as he gave his on the cross. The spikes, nor the sword, could delay the action that was set forth in that hour. He voiced that he had power over death yet he was the first of the three to die. He said that his father had given him all the power over heaven and earth, yet the spikes held his body firm. You see he knew for his plan to work he must go to the grave to complete the whole picture so he gave up the ghost, and died.

During their time together the young thief turned to Jesus in probable confession of his guilt ridden life, and he asked simply for Christ to remember him to his Father, and his approach was wholly acceptable as Christ responded in a positive way, "today you will be in paradise with me." Jesus, who had cleansed the leper, fed the multitudes, raised his friend Lazarus from the dead, performs another miracle in doing more than could be expected. A wonderful response from the centre cross. Three long hours of silence towards his jeering enemies, gave this simple answer to fulfill the need of a crying soul. How very little he had asked for, yet in return as always, Christ gave so much, love, pity, mercy, forgiveness, salvation, all packaged in eternal life.

In this modern day, and age we do not face crucifixion, but we do face death whether it be violent or peaceful, it still is as much a part of life as being born. Although the death we face will not be as radical as a cross it is in fact a gift from God. Nothing to be afraid of, only something to be ready for, this God given gateway into eternity. We live presently in the world of the flesh with multiple endings and disappointments, At death we enter into God's world as God's love transfers us through death to His world of ultimate peace with no more heartaches, no more tears, only the unimaginable measure of love. This old body returns to the dust from which it came, and we shall put on new bodies to live eternal.

When born as a baby into life on earth we call it birth. When we pass on to God's heaven we call it death, because it is a new transition into our new world, heaven.

How to face this?

Assurance that you belong to your Christ and saviour for he has gone to make a place for you, in that you may walk hand in hand with him who is the master of all life, both in this world and the world to come. Nevertheless we are required here to walk with an unfaltering trust that he sustains us. We are as assured now as when he uttered those words to the thief on the cross, "Today, thou shalt be with me in paradise."

We know very little about heaven. Jesus spoke in the parables to give several stories as to what heaven was like. But in our infinite capacity we are unable to absorb the full picture. We need to draw to our bosom the scriptures that touch on life after death. For they tell us that we shall be with him, we shall see his face, we shall hear his voice of unfettered welcome, and we shall work, and worship in the light of heaven that allows us to see in the brilliance of his love.

And I heard a great voice out of heaven saying, Behold, the tabernacle of God is with men, and he will dwell with them, and they shall be his people, and God himself shall be with them, and be their God. And God shall wipe away all tears from their eyes; and there shall be no more death, neither sorrow, nor crying, neither shall there be any more pain: for former things are passed away. Revelation 21: 3-4.

The last heartbreak has been experienced the last tear has fallen. But in the Holy City of God, broken sadness turns to the joy of accompanying Jesus to the Throne of Heaven.

The dying thief came late, but not too late, he made a decision in the eleventh hour. You may not be given that opportunity. Accept him now as your saviour, Christ, Lord.

* * * * *

Dead To Sin And Alive To God

—⟨⟨⟨⟩⟩⟩—

Let not sin reign in your mortal body, that you should obey it in the lusts thereof. Neither yield ye your members as instruments of unrighteousness unto sin: but yield yourselves unto God, as those that are alive from the dead, and your members as instruments of righteousness unto God. Romans 6: 12-13.

An explosive new idea comes to light to those who wander on as in a day-fog suggesting that anything that happens is alright when in fact they need to realize that immoral wrong doing is totally against God's will. Instead of nodding approval to all events and actions of the unbelieving world there needs to be an action to adopt a new attitude to life. Let us not attempt to divorce the theology , the truth about God, in working out the truth about Jesus Christ, the Son of a living God we need to be cognizant of moral results in our daily lifestyle. High doctrine cannot be separated from everyday common action in ones moral attributes. They must be Holy, and Christlike as to not lend to the unbelieving world's credence that anything goes. As a believer who has accepted Jesus as Saviour you must know that sin has no right to remain in the mortal body. The redeemed of Christ cannot permit the members of its body to be seized by sin and used as instruments of wickedness for weapons to advance Satan's cause against God.

We see here an urgent need to yield ourselves to God making every member of our body to be obedient instruments of righteousness. Show the unbelieving world that you mean business in your new walk with your saviour, and that you intend to do it the right way, God's way. When you translate the daily substance translated by the renewing of the mind your whole being will establish that you meant business when you allowed God to embrace you in your new walk. You may derive enormous strength knowing that sin now has no dominion over your life since you now are no longer under law, but under grace. Remember, that does not allow you to break the law only respect it from a higher level.

Herein lies the difficult area for those who believe they are following Christ the best way they know how. However this portion of scripture must be consider to the point of total absorption into the soul and lifestyle of the Christian walk, to die unto sin and to live unto God is essential. Although it may appear to be somewhat of a struggle when you first begin let me assure you that the greater your cognizance of God the easier your daily walk with him.

When we make that excellent choice to live our lives to please God there are things we decide to leave behind. Oftimes we wonder if it was the right thing to do, and we look around to see if we could still use any thing we left behind. Then it is about time we run our gaze across the horizon to remind us what is finally gone, and stopped hindering us in our walk. We need to regularly take stock of that which remains to remind us how the clarity of our new life has measured out to us much gain.

Sometimes we run into our promised land to find huge giants in theological structure who heap unto themselves all the fetters of the world yet claim Christ. That can shake the ground beneath us, but we must stay true to the course that God has set us upon. Even though each believer is to minister to others, we are not all called to a pulpit ministry, we are not all called to be evangelists, and some of those who claim to be evangelists do not even know the meaning of the word let alone the ministry. Remember to be yourself for that is why God received you unto himself because he needed someone of your personality on his team. So carry on with your love, and your caring for others. Do not measure your ministry as big or little, you must measure it as what God gave you to do for his development of your life. People who portray blatantly their own success may not even be in God's richness of life. They may be climbing aboard the bandwagon with their own agenda, and trust me when I tell you that God is not pleased. Upon investigation of those lives who claim God by their own success you will find them confused about God's work. They will put forth familiar words mixed up with reality from their mouths, and they will fail to show that Jesus Christ is the way, the truth, and the life, and no man goes unto the Father but by him.

God is not some passing phase in some generation, he is the beginning and the end. He created all that we know and see, and that which we have not seen. Christ in his own words confirms that as he says, "There are many things I need to tell you, but you are not yet ready."

God is not flitting back, and forth like some star wars hero, and orbiting meaninglessly around in the stars. He is ever present to those who believe on the name of Christ his son. People cannot pile upon God the blame for a half-hearted faith. If you are set aside by a waning faith it is because you have become spiritually lazy. Nothing to do with God. For that you must take the blame and carry the burden until you recognize God as your deliverer. Then he will stretch forth his hand, and lift you from the miry clay wherein you have mired down, he will lift you up back into the solid battle field. Also he will forgive you for stumbling along the way. If you were perfect there would be no need for your salvation. God knows that.

Why must Christians sink back into the doldrums when they are challenged for living their changed lives?

Must we sit back in fear and trembling when someone challenges our Christian stand by asking non-relevant questions about our salvation?

The fact is that we are allowed not to respond to silly questions that try to throw us off track. But when these questions come, remember God's word, "A soft answer turneth away wrath."

How very important it is to fully absorb and comprehend, in baptism, the dying to self, and living unto God. Let us not betray those who have helped us thus far to walk with God, and we need to continue in a positive lifestyle to show forth Jesus Christ as Lord and saviour. There is no need to bow before the world in fear and trembling because of the worlds empty questions in an attempt to destroy the faith of believers. Christians need to respond with their own questions like,

"Where on earth did you come by such a silly question?" or ask, "Did you find that in the bible?"

They will see then that you are solid in your belief and may indeed seek you out to find the way to that which you hold so strongly.

It is irrelevant how life begins or ends, or what anyone tries to prove about the working of the mysteries of the universe, for if they refuse to accept the gospel of Jesus Christ they thrive on ignorance in this world, and are headed for a fiery hell in eternity. We cannot think for a moment that somehow the political world or their economics or art, or leisure time of the modern person will in any sense contaminate the love of Jesus Christ

The complexities of life that are always there as a product of the sin of the unbeliever that continuously generates to them an indwelling fear of all that is. The fear filled with anger, implying action to hurt others, the dark face of evil, none of these will ever snuff out the gospel. If you believe it will then you had better stop to check the reality of your faith.

Jesus did not promise popularity to those who took up their cross to follow him. In the new testament we learn words that describe the very people that live around about us.

If you strike the heart of others with the Godly life you live, there will be many attempts to cast into your mind the doubts of the unbelieving world. You must never buckle under to that kind of pressure. Usually the end product of that type of person is the fear of death. The Christian is able to confront that type of thinking for we believe in the resurrection of the soul to put on new bodies. When people begin to denigrate the existence of A living God, you may ask a simple question,

"Does love stop transforming the lives of people?" "

"Is there no more laughter or tears?" or

"Has all the depth, and meaning that Jesus lived, and died for , left the earth and vanished to be no more?

Even unbelievers who are honest have to say no to all these questions.

Whenever I have stood my ground for the gospel of Jesus Christ, my soul has been flooded with a sea of peace, because the truth establishes a real place with your life in the world. When I in some limited way let the, dying on the cross, kind of love have its own way with me, my life reaches heights, and depths, it has never reached before. I believe in the resurrection of Christ, and therefore of each believer who follows Christ, because life is the free gift from God, "The gift of God is eternal life." This is where each believer should be as well. Begin now, and let the love of God measured through his son Jesus Christ, make all things new for you. Resurrection is not something that you look forward to, it is here , and now as you live and breath, you are a part of it because God has made it so. To the unbeliever, arise from your death of sin, accept Jesus Christ as your saviour, and make him Lord of your life. By so doing you will renew your life into a more positive direction. You will be able to say, no, to the temptations that drag you down as a part of the worldly ways, for Jesus will take you by the hand and lift you up.

* * * * *

Old Forms, New Faith

—∞∞∞—

No man putteth a new cloth unto an old garment; for that which is put in to fill it up taketh from the garment, and the rent is made worse. Matthew 9:16.

In my youth it was not unfamiliar to have clothes that were patched up to wear. This was a norm in the settling years of Canadian territories. Too far to travel to buy new clothing, and with only minimal income, and only a catalogue to order from we often waited extra time for new items. Mothers across the country had come to the rescue to patch up old clothes. Jesus too, was familiar with the need to patch clothes for the convenience of alleviating the poverty of the day if nothing else. I do not believe that his analogy was to show women how to do patchwork. His picture here was adopting old styles from the old religious order and practicing them under the new found robe of a Christian lifestyle. Jesus warned against such practices lest Christianity be tainted with the same brush as the Phariseeism. The believer was encouraged here to leave the old behind, and keep the new in a measure of pureness. Theologians have a tendency to miss out or perhaps in a lack of understanding the attempt of the poor to survive, tend in their wisdom to skirt around this issue of the patch for there is little written about it. Either it has been deemed unimportant, or there has been a major lack of understanding about patchwork. I believe that because it was mentioned by Christ we must apply some important values to the act. It seems perhaps that the religious orders of the day witnessed their well laid plans as falling apart under a presentation of the Saviour of the world, and attempted in some way to make

Jesus' teaching relative to what they had already taught. However, Jesus readily comes to the rescue of His followers to show them that when they now had a new robe for attire they need not patch it. For this was the Royal robe of a Holy God.

The youth of the modern day have a tendency to change things without regarding the cost of the action. That is why the scriptures are very clear about not putting novices into office of responsibility. Young people know little or nothing about the transactions that were needed in the generation before them therefore pay little heed to adopting patches that are unnecessary. Although there is an unmeasured amount of comfort in old clothes, there is the undying fact that they do wear out and must be at some point discarded.

Why then does Jesus even elude to such a parable as this?

It was because John the Baptist came to him with a question of *Matt 9: 14b. "Why do we and the Pharisees fast oft, and thy disciples do not?"*

The real question here was why Christ's disciples were passing up tradition. Jesus was aware of their misconception as to what really had transpired when souls believed and were transformed into the newness of life. For Jesus had not come to remake, or replace the Jewish religion, but to transform those who renewed their faith in God. It had absolutely no significance to the Pharisee other than when the transition took place Jesus warned them to treat the new life as a new way, and leave the old cast away. Jesus wanted to make it very clear here that he hadn't come to correct all the evils of the world, but to make all things new. It is wise to take note here that Jesus in no way included the political lie of expediency to include the need of compromise. Jesus in essence saying that to compromise would destroy both the old, and the new together, but the change to the new were fasting adds nothing. The gift of God in Christ is given once for all Although they are experiencing the new way there must be a change in form. As the seed is planted it changes its form to become fruitful grain. As the grain is harvested , although a product of the seed, the changing form must be dealt with. *The gospel of Christ is the same yesterday, today, and forever.* Heb 13: 8. We are able from time to time change the form, but the content cannot, and must not be changed for it is instituted by our living God.

Christ here shows his intent of making changes to the forms of the new direction he had brought to mankind. He wanted to make it very clear that there are some things that are not tolerated by God, and he was redirecting the form of worship to the new believers in hopes that they would carry a better and more viable attitude to those around about.

God, through Jesus, gave a new heaven, and new earth, where righteousness dwells.

We are still prone to hold up Christianity as fixed, and static, rather than living with it as something beautiful, and abidingly new. Too often we fail to realize that Christ has been here not only to mend, but to give a new way of salvation to make a new person of those who receive him as God's son.

Jesus came here to lay down his life in order that we shall be able to confess. "old things have passed away, and behold all things have become new."

Where Jesus differs in his implementation of our new life, is the way, apart from the religious order of the day, is the method to which the needs of people are to be met. Our human living is a faction that needs to be mended for man has not arrived, and the world is not yet what it aught to be. We need more people of this modern day to put on the new garment to be presentable to the living God. Our old garments are soiled with wrongful works that will not achieve the happiness we seek. Old garments have been stained by the corruption of the world who has forgotten about God. Old robes are tattered in the vain worship of self with an empty altar. Now our garments are threadbare for it is time to find that new garment and be clothed in righteousness of Christ.

God has never closed his eyes to the needs of man that were created by a self chosen path of separation from God. That was his purpose in sending Jesus to bring people back on track as to the plan that has been set in motion, to seek and to save that which is lost.

People of the world turn their backs on such magnificent love to wallow in the muck of immorality as they experience spiritual bankruptcy. Man creates bad economics as we wither away under the debt system by which all the world adheres to, with the attitude of failure of yesterday, with contemplation that it will be here tomorrow also. There are those who pay lip service to Christianity who are so caught up in the world of don'ts that they forge the do's. They have lost the sight of the more rewarding way of Jesus.

Are you a Christian of this day so caught up in the negative attitude that you fail to see the need of the event that Jesus be required.

Are you discouraging other Christians in following a victorious life in Jesus?

Or are you simply living a so-so Christian nominal existence to the point you are sucking away the richness of God out of your own life as well as everyone else's. Perhaps that we are so caught up in the negativism of humanism that we forget that we are here to tell the world about the supreme sacrifice that gave us eternal life.

If Christ has become less and less in your life perhaps you had better reconsider your relationship with a living God by asking yourself these questions;

Does your Christian message, to others, make them want to be a part of the family of God.? Does your life make the hearers of the message you send them want to change from their old ways, to meet the human need in the light of Christ's salvation to mankind?

If you are not emitting a Christlike style in your visible life, you need to make those changes now. Tomorrow maybe too late. Let your style say, here is a positive life a worthwhile walk. I want to be a part of that society that teaches and believes while they show the way of eternal life through Christ.

There are those of today's modern communities who think Christianity is a negative way of life, because they only think in terms of what it forbids. If they were to join a Christ believing church, where the thinking is about what they are separated from a lost world. Those things which are destructive, and downtrodden the church deems to be sin and forbidden simply by the word of God. A favourite leaning pole of the Christian community is that there must be a sharp distinction between the things of the world, and the spiritual life.

Some think in terms of separating the secular from the sacred, religion from business, most of all we must certainly separate religion from politics. I believe that this type of thinking is not only archaic, but should have been buried with the unrepentant thief. The

Christian life can, and should be, lived to the fullest with any chosen vocation. For the believer it goes without saying that God should be the central focus in whatever walk of life we choose. One who decides to make the walk with Christ, needs to know the what, and why, of that which they are joined to. There is a parcel of religiosity that would keep you separate from the existing life you walk with real people who are not necessarily believers. It goes without saying that sometimes the actions towards their fellowman by unbelievers can often put the Christian to shame. That is not to say there is no consideration of separating ourselves from any immoral action in the community, but we ought not to shun the people from our community. Hate the sin, but love the person. We need to live so close to God that we don't have to tell them the difference they will see it in our lives. It will allow those who observe our lifestyle to ask questions of it, but then we need to be ready with the answer that it is Christ in our life that makes the difference. When you compromise your righteousness living you disappoint the unbeliever therefore you actually lose their trust.

I have heard people say, "I am not religious, but I am a Christian."

If they mean the first part of that statement the whole verbiage is an outright lie. Religion is not a separate thing from being a Christian. Although you must identify with the Christian religion. To call yourself Christian, and deny being religious is a devil's lie of foolishness, and Godlessness. God says, "Be ye holy as I am holy," and this allows us to be religious with the complete wholeness of our lives. To pray for God's kingdom to come, and knowingly attempt to retard that kingdom by refusing a portion of it is sheer hypocrisy.

Then there are those who claim that religion is a place to hide their defects. Religion does far more for us than to cover up our ugly defects. If we are honest before God, our acceptance of Christ as our saviour, and Lord will find him removing the defects of our lives. Again Jesus does not mend the garment but he remakes it to a royal status. He gives to us a gospel of regeneration. It is an old gospel, but it is the only truth that still meets the needs of our day.

To some this experience comes suddenly with a seeming flushing of the soul while we shed tears at his acceptance of such a sinner, for others, it comes as the dawning of a new clear day with it's brilliant sunrise. Others as the seed germinates in their heart it simply may appear as the slow coming of spring. The manner of the coming is not of importance, it is that you have allowed Jesus into your life that carries the greatest importance. You will be given a new reason for living the right way from the transformation of the new birth.

The disciples had come to share the same divine nature that will now be within you. Their hearts were filled with Holy passion, and it is for this reason that Christ decided to lay down his life for us on the cross of Calvary.

Jesus selected a small handful of special men who in their learning with Him as He watched them grow. It is said that they were sometimes contentious, giving argument to one another as they framed the work to be put into place under Christ's own directives. The amazing part of their story is to know that they walked with the King of Kings who would be their Lord, and saviour. Many times as they talked, there was misunderstanding. Christ in ultimate patience spent time explaining over, and over, to each of them his purpose for being where he was at this time.

I often hear the statement from so-called Christians that Jesus is walking with me, or ahead of me, or before me. This too is one of Satan's comfort lies, for Christ has risen, and he sits on the right hand of our Father, and intercedes for each and every believer.

Just what has Jesus done for you? What does he mean to you this very moment? Is he just an extraordinary example of life or is he your Christ, your Saviour, your Lord.

Allow him into your life to loose you from your sin, and hang-ups. Also allow him to initiate your soul with real peace as you stop trusting in superficial remedies, while crying, peace, peace, when without him, there will be no peace. Stop being self centered, and start being Christ centered so that you may find power in your personal service. You may have a power that can be accounted for in the terms of Christ.

Only what's done for Christ will last.

* * * * *

Lord, Lift Up Thy Light

—⟨⟨⟩⟩—

There are many that say, Who will show us any good? Lord lift up the light of thy countenance upon us. thou hast put gladness in my heart, more than in the time that their corn and their wine increased. I will both lay me down in peace, and sleep: for thou, Lord, only makes me dwell in safety. Psalm 4: 6-8.

The world knows too well the meaning of tribulation. Were we to dwell upon the Media tycoons who bombard us with mountains of negativity, whether true of false, we would all join the weeping prophet. Often we feel the plight of the Psalmist who questions God about allowing the broken self of man into His presence, and yet goes on to promise God his service even though he feels unworthy. He then takes upon himself the rest that God, somewhere down the line has promised him, and sleep in safety. He is able to commit his life to God as he knows the way will be because of his obedience to the Holy.

What did Jesus do for the eighteen years of his life of which we have little or no record?

He was a carpenter, taught by Joseph of Nazareth who married Mary, upon instructions from God, after he was apprised of her being with child. We are suspicious of anyone who does nothing, while we honour people who work. We picture Jesus as an ideal worker. None know for sure what Jesus accomplished with the work of his hands, but many have been the product of his keeping in the transformation he initiated into our lives.

When I was a small boy not yet in my teens, I looked into the faces of the adults around me and saw many sad faces. I made up my mind at that young age, that when I grew up I would attempt to make people smile, helping them to lift up their countenance. God cannot settle into an unsettled hustling, bustling soul, who is paying no attention to his word. He instills peace to rest in a weary soul that will allow him time in our lives. He will not enter into our fray uninvited. We must stop, and consider God. Invite him in so that he may instill his peace in your soul in quietness.

There was a time when man's life fitted absolute into his work method, and the quality thereof with a fervour that has since been lost. To simply waste away the day doing nothing betrayed his existence. For the question is still asked,

"Why are we here if not to produce something of valuable time?

To be unemployed in most peoples eyes was in fact considered as a sin. The inner self speaks, we must do something with our time, and one was moved to find that which would keep them busy. In our modern times leisure has become more available, and we are not locked in to the slave like society. More, and more, we find society breaking away from the absolute work ethic, and the believer must learn to minister to this type of community. Leisure time is not a sin for even God says, "Be still and know that I am God." One problem that is quite evident in many believers is their inability to identify with others in close proximity. There is a tendency to withdraw unto self, leaving others out in the cold even though they may be seekers. Believers, must learn to spend some of their leisure time with the unbeliever. When one refuses that role they will be correct when they claim the Church shuts them out because of a prejudice to their behaviour.

Today's modern church has difficulty dealing in public relations to the point of stating Christ's position. Persons of leadership appear to be selling their own agenda with a very narrow point of view. Usually, that type of leadership has little to do with the way God has laid it down in his word. The myth persists that man's worth is determined by his productive values, because we are respecters of persons, and that persons office determines the amount of respect we show. They must belong to the who's who column of wall street, and the apostles of debt on Bloor street, who determine a man's worth through the investment measure, or dollar worth. Because it is they who play the market to their tune.

The believer in Christ must indeed learn to play to the glory of God by sincere obedience to the written word. Our youth do not attempt to emulate the worker in the religious structure. As a matter of fact, we who now are the leaders in the religious field, have driven our youth to hold up the myth of heroism into the sports world. Someone who flaunts the law is made the hero by the media, and it appears to draw our youth into living a devil's lie, to perform in an unlawful manner. Few people can tell you the name of the church treasurer, or the name of the board chairman, or even the name of the deacons or elders of the Church. Yet on the football team or the baseball team they can almost name every player along with their statistics of achievement. Not so within the boundaries of the Christian communities. We appear to the outside world as cowards who hide away in our little cubby hole of worship for one hour on Sundays, and are afraid to tell anyone about it. Even our youth.

Churches seldom publish the virtues of playing to the glory of God. The Christian is too busy playing the separation game. We separate the men from the women, the boys from the girls, the babies from their mothers. We separate the Sunday school attendees from family worship. We choose worship teams, that neither worship, nor work as a team with the congregation. Believers should understand that every person who enters the Sanctuary is a worshipper. We are overcome with the idea to be busy in churches. Christians on the peripheral rim of obedience only wish to display their busyness so that all can see their works. People seek others to praise them in quiet ways, and if they do not praise them for what they attempt to do we ostracize them from our fellowship. We are unable to give empathy with the psalmist as he joyfully makes the comment, "Thou hast put gladness in my heart."

I believe in my heart that there are times when we need to be simply silent before God, doing nothing except allowing Him to speak in his still small voice to our heart. Many involved Christians assume the aura of guilt when they listen only, for they have some preconceived idea that proper devotional exercise is in depth reading of scripture with concentrated profoundly worded prayer. Others have suggested, [which I doubt] that the only way for correct talk with God, occurs in the doing of certain deeds. Although there may be a measure of truth to the inclusive elements of these thoughts, and performances, these are only fragments in truth attached more likely to inaction of the religious person.

Psalmists were truly busy men putting together the elements of God's attributes in song.

Come, behold the works of the Lord, what desolation he hath made in the earth. He makes wars to cease unto the ends of the earth; he breaketh the bow, and cutteth the spear in sunder; he burneth the chariot in the fire. Be still, and know that I am God: I will be exalted among the heathen, I will be exalted in the earth. Psalm 46: 8-10.

In all our exuberant attempt to do things to show people how we serve God to our liking, God sees and hears for the psalmist tells it best, *O Lord, thou hast searched me, and known me. Thou knoweth my downsitting and my uprising, thou understandeth my thought afar off. Thou compasseth my path and my lying down, and art acquainted with all my ways. Psalm 139: 1-3.*

Quite often I have heard a portion of this psalm used at funerals, but I believe it carries a very strong message for every day living according to God's wishes, and desires. There always needs to be a daily careful consideration of the application to ones own walk by applying non-fragmented portions of scripture to our lives. In doing that you will find the needed strength to carry you through each day. You will then be able to honestly adopt the Psalmists peaceful notation, *I will both lay me down in peace, and sleep: for thou, Lord, only makest me dwell in safety. Ps 4: 8.*

* * * * *

Fleeing From God's Calling

The word of the Lord came unto Jonah the son of Amittai, saying, Arise, go to Nineveh, the great city, and cry against it; for their wickedness has come up before me. But Jonah rose up to flee unto Tarshish from the presence of the Lord, and went down to Joppa; and he found a ship going to Tarshish: and he paid the fare thereof, and went down into it, to go with them unto Tarshish from the presence of the Lord. Jonah 1: 1-3

I believe that God called me to preach the gospel of Jesus Christ, and the message of Salvation which He brought through His sacrifice upon the cross of Calvary. Often as I observe all the terrible happenings in the world, whether terrorism or schoolyard bullying, I often turn to someone with tongue -in-cheek, and say, "If they had just come and ask me, I could have told them it was wrong."

Here is a book that should be read, and absorbed by every modern day Christian. Whether you adopt it as an actual happening, or do as the skeptics love, that is to hammer their personal opinions, in that it is only a parable or a story of illustration, you must still accept it as God's word which must be applied to that event that can throw you into a whirlwind of tizzy about God's will in your life.

It tells the story so vividly of the walking screaming idiots who want the world to think they are following God, even when they do not have to do as he says. Truly a vivid picture of many of our contemporary Churches. Jonah gets orders from God, to go and preach to the people of a special sin filled city. Jonah says, "Yeah, I hope you don't think that I'm going in there where all that sinful nature is showing up? No way." He even went to the trouble of buying a ticket to hastily evacuate the place where God had directed him to be. His though was that if he would put some distance between himself and the city of Nineveh, he wouldn't have to do as God instructed him to do. He thought he could get out of his calling if he moved to a different part of the country God would give the job to someone else. But that didn't happen. God created a storm to rock the boat that Jonah used for his escape. Many Christians are feeling God's anger in the storm today, but they do not have the courage to let men throw them overboard to fix the problem. That is because the modern day Christian would be satisfied to let the sinner go to Hell than having to tell them the story of Jesus who came to seek and to save those who are lost. But most of all I want you to tell them of the judgment that has fallen upon them for disobedience of my word. To Jonah, God made known his will, and the purpose behind that will, but Jonah tried desperately to do anything but carry the word of God to the people whom God desired to have his word spoken to.

The word of God is coming to men and women today, and there is not one single soul committed to Christ who will read this, and not be reminded that there was a time when they too went astray from the true word of God that had come to them in a definite way to direct them. The element of attack that attempted the de-christianisation of the world is taking its toll among the younger generations. We cannot find those steeped in faith but only the loss of faith prevails the present modern day society. This generation has lost it's spiritual significance, and is deprived of any significant meaning, and without conviction have lost the profound thrust of the gospel with the related meaning to eternal life.

Jonah fled, not because of fear or cowardess, but because the instruction from God had given rise to conflict with what he desired to do. What he wanted, and what God intended where two entirely different things. He tried to remove himself to the other end of the country as though distance would somehow lose sight of God, and the chore he was to perform would be forgotten. Not so with God. When he requires a person to take up the cross he will go to great measure to see those that he called will be certain of the call.

God had required that Jonah leave his comfort zone, but when

Jonah found God's direction uncomfortable he made an unwise move to give rebuttal to the giving of the message to people that he didn't care for, the dwellers of Nineveh

He did what many borderline Christians do, he went into the hold of the ship, and fell asleep, thinking it would all go away by the time he awoke. God would not allow him to take refuge to lay the blame at someone else's doorstep. A storm was created to toss the ship to and fro with immediate danger of being broken into pieces. It is interesting that the commander of the ship woke Jonah up and scolded him for not being on deck to pray to his God for deliverance. In the final analysis Jonah did not deny his God, and he wouldn't allow others to suffer for his indiscretion of misdirection of God's orders, he said, "It is my fault for I have been disobedient to my God. The only solution now to save yourselves is to cast me into the sea.

It is sad that Christians today have difficulty confessing that their own fault is causing the present turmoil, and allow themselves to be cast into even greater turbulence by their confessing the truth of their error of handling the situation at hand. Somehow we need to see the common bond with those whom we dislike, and be truthful about our ill treatment towards them. Then we will see a turn about with friends, and enemies alike, in our furtherance of a God fearing lifestyle.

The essential thing of Jonah is that the word did come for his service to be put into action. There were no committees, no soldiers in demand, no payout for the action, only the knowledge that the message was an essential part of God's plan, and God was not going to let it be washed aside. The message was simple, "Arise and go —- and cry against it for it's great wickedness against me."

God does speak to us, and moves upon us, he calls us, commands us, and stirs us up to do his will. Jonah did not wish to undertake this mission. His commission was not born in reluctance, but he saw nothing in these people of Nineveh. In other words he determined from his own knowledge that it was of no use to preach to this bunch of sinners in the odd city. We are often hampered by that decision. We feel that it is absolutely useless to preach to some people, but thank God, he intervenes into our selfish thinking. In stubbornness we still maintain there is no use trying to make Christians out of our neighbours.

We often forget that God made no mistake in his creation, for within man he built a frequency of an insatiable desire with a hunger, and insatiable desire with unquenchable thirst that none can satisfy but God.

To Jonah, the call was unwelcome because he had a fear that the people may repent, and he did not want that because he dislikes them. After all, wasn't God the God of Israel only. It is often quite apparent that the trait within us is to believe that another's progressive advancement may be a detriment to our own lives. It is equally human to feel that another's downfall, and disgrace in some way adds to our own uplifting of placing our own crowns of achievement upon our heads for others to see. However such actions are utterly false in spite of clinging to this type of thinking throughout the centuries. It is quite disheartening when we witness many doing the same as Jonah. Finding the application of God's way so distasteful that they decide whatever the cost to cast it aside will be worth not falling into line with the right thing to do. So it is we read, "He rose up to flee —." There are only two places one can go. One, the place where you can have your fellowship with the almighty, and living God completing the circle of the will of God. Secondly, the city at the end of the road with rebels, whose streets if we ever walked them, would walk without the fellowship of God.

Which city are you choosing to dwell in?

The city of disobedience, or the city of obedience. Wherever you make your home you can always rise in the fellowship of God. If you decide that this is not the time for you to walk with him, then be prepared for the unrelenting storm as he attempts to bring you back to the road he has chosen for you. the choice is in your hands.

Jonah was given a second chance to respond to his task. The same Lord will allow you to have the second chance also when you realize that you have been following the wrong path all along, and you wish to renew your promise to God, he will deliver you to continue, and to finish the task that he had set before you.

You may be as Jonah, a bit angry for being where your at, nevertheless God was able to allow him to evangelize Nineveh, and he will also be the same for you even when you hate the people as did Jonah. He believed that they did not deserve to have the chance to repent, but God's hand was over and above the hateful human heart, and he required that the message and evangelization be done under his authority. It is the ever present Kingdom of Heaven embedded within the believing Christian forever fighting against the brute powers of the sinful and unbelieving world.

What has all this to do with you in your days of hatred of your fellowman?

Are you able to box yourself into a corner against the magnificent grace of the living God?

I do not believe that any person is able to hold out long in that position, for God will attempt to put things right. All you need to do is accept your second chance to follow in God's will to carry out that errand he set you out to do. You are in a losing battle when you believe that you will win in any argument against God.

Do not attempt to be under God's grace if you intend to continue being a detractor of human brotherhood. We must work together, one with another putting aside our personal likes and dislikes to put in place the glory of God. We are all slow to learn on the battleground as we face destruction unless we change our ways. In selfishness we attempt to save ourselves, but God chose us to save those around about us, and put self last. If then, we cannot save others we shall certainly perish being unable to save ourselves.

* * * * *

Can Religion Stop War

——⟨⟨⟨⟩⟩⟩——

From whence cometh wars and fighting's amongst you? come they not hence, even of your lusts that war in your members? James 4: 1.

The human race seeks righteousness which receives the instinct of right relationships. Those relationships can never be absolutely secured without a great deal of effort. It is when the enemy decides to override our security and peacefulness we rise up to war against someone else's takeover .

Wars are started by Governments of Nations, and not by individuals. Political manoeuvring, in order to release more money into the gross national product which creates jobs, is the hidden agenda, and truth becomes the scapegoat of the public coffers. Wars are instituted as an economic measure regardless of the propaganda that is released to the media. Governments of Nations come together and plan to go to war with little or no concern for human life. It is only dollars and cents that have any value in the decision. If the leaders of the country were really concerned about the outcry of the people, why doesn't the Prime Minister of Canada, or the President of the U.S. put prayer back into the public schools. They claim Christianity as part of Democracy and is as Canadian or as American as you can get. But either office pays little heed to the word of God that says "Thou shalt not kill." They pay absolutely no mind to the aching hearts who love God, and desire their children to have the ability to pray in public places. People also want their children to learn to love their fellowman as the bible teaches. Again neither the Prime Minister or the President with all their power, couldn't care less about your children having the right to pray at the school level. This is a proven fact, because they shut the Christian practice down when they wanted children to pray to a living God.

The American Government took three long years to decide to get into World War Two, but in the final analysis they came in after they were challenged about selling arms to the German, and Italian armies. They needed the look good, and feel good image to make economic adjustments towards our allies, as well as their general public.

Nations are crying out for relief from the ever crushing burden of debt while at the same time spending ridiculously astounding amounts preparing for war. In all fairness, the blame cannot be shifted to just one man for it is the system under which we depend to survive which has become ungodly. To the Christian the war must go, but the solemn fact is that religion alone cannot stop war.

Nations will fight as long as their minds and hearts continue in the selfish act of wrongdoing. Man, shall rise against man, as long as he refuses to share the love of the almighty living God. God is love. As long as man's attitude of one towards another is of suspicion, and mistrust there will be individual badgering, and fighting as well as war of Nation against Nation. Some have made the issue that if another war broke out churches would have to shoulder the blame. I am not sure I buy that statement as an absolute, nevertheless those churches who have stopped loving their fellowman including their enemies are blatantly flaunting Gods own commands in the face of our Saviour Jesus Christ, and will have to pay the price.

War is a planned economic injustice from the top down, and not from the grass roots up. Churches of this modern day have become players of middle of the road politics when it comes to the war factor. there are only one or two church bodies that absolutely defy the war act, and they are usually punished by being sent to what is called interim camps. These are formed for conscientious objectors, and are a black eye that leaves an ugly scar on real democracy that was the supposed element that was to be protected with war tactics, and it tore the element apart.

The active believing church cannot shoulder the blame for the actions of thoughtless, and power hungry governments who in fact go against God's wishes. They practice Satan's inhumanity to man.

Remember it is the peacemakers that shall be known as the sons of God, not the warmongers.

If the spirit in the souls of believers across our continent can shape our community with the effectiveness of Christ. Only then we can effect the Nations of the world while bound to the eternal love of God. For it was He who sent his own son to die on the cross for our sins binding us in a bond of love. I say together with that love the Christian religion can stop war. Each believer must do their part to make Christianity what it should be. Do your utmost to gather, and fellowship with the church to which you belong. Build a strong efficient body of believers who will be willing to commit themselves to the work of Jesus Christ. After which we may believe in the lasting goodwill of all Nations refusing to compromise our faith in a living God.

If we believe we can stop war then we must be ready to apprise ourselves about world conditions remembering that God warns us to put our own house in order first. Otherwise we will be unable to direct anyone else if we display chaos from our own stand for Christ.

We must make a vocal stand opposing neo-socialism that intends to de-christianise the world pushing the believer in Christ aside to set up their own destructive regime. We cannot allow them to gain ground for they are ruthless, and Godless while they will attempt to destroy all that you believe to impose upon you a dictatorial system under the ruse of democracy.

Neo-socialism is a theory that is propagated to control all people by taking away their freedoms, and their beliefs. Their main purpose is to destroy the worship factor which is now practiced by the Christian church. May God help the Nations Governments who become opposed to free enterprise. If we are to succeed in this war against Christian worship, we need to be careful to remove all prejudice towards other nationalities. We can do that by claiming the name of Jesus Christ as our saviour above all else. Do not get caught up in the false fight for peace, because peace only comes to the human soul through the acceptance of Jesus as the son of God. For it only Jesus that gives the peace that passes all understanding. The real evidence of being able to do away with war shall come through the presentation of the evidence that will bring true revival of faith in Jesus Christ throughout the world.

The bible reminds us that "Now" is the day of salvation, and in that we must move away from the sleeping religious fathers of our day, and become alive with a shout of glory, to awaken believers across our country to make them understand that the time is at hand to give God's word loud and clear. We must take upon ourselves the responsibility of making a great noise with the word of God. Only then shall we overcome those who intend without doubt to destroy the Christian worship. Claim the strength, and power, and the glory, in Christ Jesus to overcome the enemy who would take away our right to cling to our saviour. Salvation is not an escape from a lost world full of tribulation, it is a new life given for us to live with the Majesty of God in an eternity without heartache, or sorrow.

You are on the road to solve all the problems of the world like unto peace and war, rest assured my friends the only way that will be found is when you learn to tell the unbelieving world about Jesus, only then shall we find that golden age ahead.

When you ask, how?

The answer is simply, Jesus Christ the Son of a living God.

If you ask, When?

Softly the answer comes, now is the accepted time. When you accept the obvious plan of a living God, you will usher in the golden age for all of his creation.

Will you take time right now to consider Christ for your life, for he can stop wars, and move those mountains in your life. Only Jesus can make all your desires come true to benefit you as you wish. One God, one Christ, one Spirit. Let each of us play our part for God in the silent, and hidden places of our heart. God awaits your acceptance of the gift that he has prepared for you, his son Jesus Christ.

Ye lust, and have not: ye kill, and desire to have, and cannot obtain: ye fight and war, yet ye have not, because ye ask not. James 4: 2.

Accept him now, and experience a peace that you never dreamed possible even though you have sought long and hard for it, simply say yes to Jesus.

The pursuit of selfish ambition causes turmoil as we war against the moral issues of the day The cause of war arises from persons who are in pursuit of the same achievements, but are unable to agree on the arrangement of procurement therefore creates conflict because they are unable to share the goal. To eliminate war, there must be radical redirection in the goals sought by each person, as well as each Nation. There must be a possessive desire to seek the "Kingdom of God and his righteousness."

It is difficult to accept, after two-thousand years Nations are unable to accept the absolute secret of ending turmoil, and presenting absolute peace is found in one short phrase of scripture,

"For what shall it profit a man if he gain the whole world and lose his own soul?" Mark 8: 36.

In the majority of cases the conflict comes from within the person. when we find our stability to subdue that within ourselves then we will apparently own a measure of control. The one, and only way to overcome this conflict within is to submit the whole spiritual realm of self to Christ, and allow him the power to change our manipulative conflict into victory over evil projections by giving control to God.

Righteousness implies right relationships with other people. Therefore we need to examine our lives as Christian when we are at fault for locking people out of our lives we perpetrate enmity against God. For God is love. Let us not be at war with those that are in Christ, but let us be ready to be defenders of the faith by making our stand together in faith through Jesus Christ our Lord, and saviour.

* * * * *

Attitude Of The Mind

J. A. [Jim] Watson

Preacher walked the platform deck
Stretched out his hand to those elect
Rolling beautiful platitudes benign
He stoned the hearer without a sign
Placing words together, careful to be kind
People you see, it's the attitude of the mind

Moses stood, at the burning bush with pride
Talked with God standing by his side
Commander of courage, shouted, 'here am I Lord'
Having conquered many, with hand upon his sword
Found heavy responsibilities now to him assigned
Cried, 'who am I Lord ?' in his attitude of the mind

Chief ruler of the temple, found himself in flight
To obliviate the Christian had been his plight
When upon the road to Damascus came
An ominous Holy voice that called his name
And a flash of sovereign light ruled him blind
Paul began to change, his attitude of the mind

Daniel ruled by hand of a king whose law
Had brought before him his worship flaw
The word was read, stood as an iron rod.
Friends stand by the word of a living God.
Stand now before a blazing furnace thrice refined
Witnessed stronger, in their attitude of the mind

David, when he was only a small boy
Dreaming to soldier would give him joy
The Philistines came to slay an army of men
With a slingshot David stopped the giant then
In victory we will always be able to find
We overcome simply, by the attitude of the mind

Golgotha's hill, there a crowd on bloody trail
A cross was carried, and women began to wail
Soldier called to Simon, worker so forlorn
To carry cross of Saviour, bleeding, and torn
Here, the bearer of that heavy cross may remind,
To carry our Christ's load, is the attitude of the mind.

Paul took Timothy to evangelize the land
Timothy was young, and couldn't take a stand;
A challenge to the church, to nurture the man
To disciple all believers, was part of God's plan
Creation set out to change what God designed
His voice was firm, it's the attitude of the mind.

Men of God were sent to all lands and nation,
To tell the people of Christ's great salvation;
Whether we be with mind that is weak, or strong
Arise, within our heart, to sing a joyful song
When hearts give out, and we from earth declined
We'll be received by God, for attitude of the mind.

* * * * *

That I Might Gain

⟨⟨⟨⟩⟩⟩

For though I be free from all men, yet have I made myself servant unto all, that I might gain the more. And unto the Jews I became a Jew, that I might gain the Jews; to them that are under the law, as under the law, that I might gain them that are under the law; To them that are without law, as without law, [being not without law to God, but under the law to Christ,] that I might gain them that are without law. To the weak became I as weak, that I might gain the weak: I am made all things to all men, that I might by all means save some. And this I do for the gospel's sake, that I might be partaker thereof with you. 1 Corinthians 9: 19-23.

Accepting to follow Jesus Christ we admit that as Christ freed us from sin we acquire a new bondage of service to a Holy God. In living our lives as the light of the world there is a need for sustained discipline as we absorb Paul's writing under God's direction.

In this particular section of the scripture, Paul sets out a particularly tight agenda of how he has lived his life to please God by attempting to draw men from all walks of life to faith in Jesus Christ. The commission he bestows upon his discipleship is not an enviable task, but it is the direction wherein when you take it you are not liable to fall into the traps the world sets up for you to fall.

Everywhere the Apostle Paul went he was dogged by leaders of the day who hated this new message of God's doctrine of grace. They, in vigorous fashion, plied their trade in attempt to break down the commitment of those that had accepted Christ as their saviour under Paul's ministry. This is a very familiar scene that is continued in today's modern corporate structure. People who believe in Christ are flatly denied access by the corporate structure for they fear the moral attributes of God. Consistently their leaders will tell their workers to leave God out of the scene. If that employee refuses to comply they will find themselves without a position in that particular corporate frame.

In order to be a spokesperson for the Lord Jesus Christ, we are often required to present academic credentials to show those in worldly authority exactly where we received our authority to speak as we do. Although academic standings sometime help us up the ladder in theological circles, it is absolutely unnecessary for the transformed believing person to achieve an academic standard in order to speak for Christ of the living God. One only needs to accept Jesus into their lives, and he says, "Open your mouth and it shall be filled." The believer will be wisdom to speak with their sincere acceptance of Jesus Christ as their saviour. Some will expect you should be able to work wonders, and do miracles, but that will not happen for it is not a part of God's plan. Do not end up trying to manufacture some event just to impress the skeptics. You need to show that you are chosen to serve the same as Paul, not by the world's sadistic standards, but by doing the things that Paul did to "by all means save some." That applies two things, first humility, and second it will allow you to bring God's word with love to the unsaved. That will lead to the salvation of many other unbelievers. You will be asked about signs, and you again must use Christ's admonition here,

"O ye hypocrites, ye can discern the face of the sky; but can ye not discern the signs of the times? A wicked and adulterous generation seeketh after a sign; and there shall be no sign given unto it, but the sign of the prophet Jonah. Matthew 16: 3b-4.

Paul had seen Jesus Christ after his encounter on the road to Damascus where he was struck blind. He then beheld a risen saviour sitting on the right hand of God. It was then that he received his worthy commission to preach the gospel to all nations. For the Lord said to Paul,

"But rise, and stand upon thy feet: for I have appeared unto thee for this purpose, to make thee a minister and a witness both

of these things which thou hast seen, and of those things in which I will appear unto thee; Delivering thee from the people, and from the gentiles, unto whom now I send thee, to open their eyes, and to turn them from darkness to light, to light and from power of Satan unto God, that they might receive forgiveness of sins, and inheritance among them which are sanctified by faith that is in me. Acts 26: 16-18

Paul here does not pretend to speak of miracles. He had performed miracles as the other twelve, but there was a far greater sign that accompanied his ministry, and that is those that had come to the saving knowledge of Jesus through his ministry. He claimed the seal of his Apostleship was the very fact that these believers, and workers now existed, now exemplified by their work in the Lord.

The evidence that Paul was truly an Apostle of the Lord, and a servant sent by God, was found in that wherever he went the spirit confirmed the message he gave forth unto the communities of unbelievers who became also servants of Christ.

The same message convicted men of their sin to lead them into a definite faith in Christ. Paul's message from God, gave them assurance of their forgiveness, and justification for the abundance of their salvation. They were at peace with the transformation that had taken place in their new lives for God.

He was asked the same questions that you may be asked when you talk about the power of our saviour.

By what authority do you give this message?"

You will be able to quickly respond, "By the power of the blood of Jesus Christ the only son of God and my saviour. The transformation in your life will allow you to perform with only the pleasing of Christ in mind. Even that thought will make you a different person. There were those who challenged Paul's vocation because they deemed him to be only a tent maker. God does not segregate vocations in order to elevate Christianity. The birth if Christ reached to the lowest of the low, and the highest of the high. None found an extra special favouritism to receive Christ. To god all men are on the same level, they are in sin, and need the forgiveness of his son Jesus Christ. Until they accept Jesus as their saviour they are simply sinners in a lost world without Christ, and their need for their salvation remains.

Paul came to these people when they were vile, and unbelieving pagans living ungodly lives so he refused support from them as he continued his work at a secular job. His choice was to be a labourer among them to support himself and his companions to deliver the gospel at no expense whatsoever to those he was preaching to. It is a reproach upon the church as they turn to a Christless world to beg, and wheedle money from ungodly people to support the work of the Lord Jesus Christ, with no fundamental belief in him nor his work. At the same time Paul shows here that it is quite right, and proper that servants of the Lord be supported by the church of the living God.

If a man is a soldier, the country that employs him in that vocation pays him with all expenses. In our dispensation there is no distinct order for priesthood, because all who are believers are ministers and belong to the priesthood of believers. Yet they that give themselves to the ministering of the word are to be sustained by the people who are also believers in that work. Even so the Lord has ordained that they which preach the gospel should live the gospel.

Paul says, " I preach the gospel, but I have nothing to glory in I am a servant, my master sent me to preach., woe unto me if I preach not the gospel."

In this contemporary society of preachers, that word may have been rolled aside somewhere left to be forgotten about. For we seldom hear the mention of great truths that people are saved by.

Is it not a sad fact that many today who are looked upon as evangelistic preachers never tell sinners that Christ died for the ungodly, they seldom proclaim the saving power of our Lord Jesus Christ. Seldom can one find the cross being held up exalted as the only means of redemption for the poor sinner.

Though I be free from all men, yet have I made myself servant to all. Here Paul says that he is above all a simple servant to Jesus. It doesn't matter what man may think of me, it doesn't even matter what category man may submit me to, I still am a servant of Jesus Christ whatever else my lot in life may be, I live for him from whatever vocation he would settle me into, I shall speak for Jesus.

Are you a servant of Christ?

Are you ministering his way or are you being swayed by some hierarchy in the religious organization?

Do you freely minister to the needs of the unsaved soul?

The world today would have you believe that you cannot be all things to all men, yet Paul in all his academic expertise, and his warrior like training, and his term of religiosity, when he came to know Christ he determined to be all things to all men that by all means he might save some.

Are you there, ready to accept the same challenge?

There still are a multitude of Godless souls wandering around in that lost condition, and God wants us to go and preach this gospel to them that some might be saved.

Will you, just now, become an obedient servant to all, for a living God of love?

If you said yes to that question, let us go now to save souls for the Master by preaching the good news of the gospel of Jesus Christ. God is prompting you. He has given you a proven manual to make his plan work. Do not question yourself about the position you are in. If God is directing you to speak to someone then he has already decided that the position your are now in is the perfect place to work from. So open your mouth that it may be filled. When you decide to take the risk to testify of Christ, you will be surprised at the outcome, and how much more at peace you soul will be.

Walk with the knowledge that God embraces you in every step, and as you give the message of his son he will open the heavens to pour out your reward.

* * * * *

The Highest Good

———◦◦◦———

Happy is the man that findeth wisdom, and the man that getteth understanding. Proverbs 3: 13.

He who has found wisdom has found that which is above all things. This scripture comes with the highest commendation for those who find wisdom. One of the deepest longings, and desires of people is to find that ultimate path that leads them to happiness. People would soon forget or at least put aside their woes and degradation if they could find that familiar escapist, happiness that fulfills the deepest longing of the heart. This happiness is not sought after by an elite few, but it is sought after by children, boys, and girls alike. The same is true of men, and women, farmer, and industrialist, the teacher, the housekeeper and most certainly needed by the Doctor, and the lawyer. You will also find it sought out by the deacon, as well as the minister. Also the writer, and the editor seek it to the same degree. The list goes on of those who would seek absolute happiness, the poet makes it warmly flow to the thinking heart while the philosopher tries to bring it within reach, and the painter unfolds it in his art and the sculptor captures it in his mould. You should not feel out of place trying to locate happiness for it is sought by peasant ,and prince with the great fervour of the search, with the poor, and the rich alike. Indeed men do seek happiness. The search for it can raise us to great heights of euphoria that fly us to the highest good.

I do not believe that people are moved entirely by it, nor do I believe that society is founded upon the sordid principle of selfish happiness. I also believe that the right kind of happiness is the proper item that all should seek. It is right to desire happiness but not at the cost of making others unhappy.

Then to what points of the compass must men look for this happiness?

Some look for it above, some look for it below, some look for it in the grandeur of the soul, others look for it in the abhorrent act of licentiousness. Multitudes who seek will never attain the level they need to lift them up to a peaceful plateau because they seek amiss. Many people are deceived by false ideas of what, and where happiness is to be accumulated.

How then shall I depend on being happy for it is a goal I have attempted to reach for most of my life?

This is a universal question that is rather practical. The text in Proverbs 3 throws a light on a worthy consideration while at the same time points a finger at the futility of many false sources. Happiness does not consist of things. Many people believe that to be rich is to be happy. Nothing could be further from the truth. Many business tycoons who appear to all the world as successful often end up taking their own lives. Henry Ford a highly successful Automobile tycoon spent a better part of his life on a diet. A Dr Hett who claimed he had a cure for cancer was calling on a home when someone shoved a gun in his face telling him to not come there again if he wished to live to help other people. Later he was rejected by his colleagues who did not accept his cure. He lived on to be highly successful with both financial, and scientific success in the field he desired without reaching that ultimate goal of happiness. Many successful people of the world end up being lonely, and sit with an empty feeling after they have achieved what they set out to do, but all they had accumulated was wealth. One man has said. success is always just a little bit more.

Unfortunately it is that little bit more that often causes a larger part of the misery, and discontent making people unhappy, and unsteady. That bit more robs us of our usefulness, our culture, our character, and our individualism. Neither does happiness consist of worldly fame or honour. There is the story we learned as children in the public school of Scimitar's Sword that hung over his head tied only by a thread that produced the saying, "uneasy hangs the head that wears the crown."

I remember another story of an old Persian King who was always very sad. He spent much gold on remedies for happiness to soothsayers to no avail. In an effort to solve his total depravity of his goal he searched far and wide for the remedy that would make him happy. Finally he talked with one wise man that simply advised him that he could cure his sadness if he could wear the coat of a happy man. The king sent out word throughout the kingdom asking to find a happy man, but none came forward. In desperation he summoned all his soldiers to his castle, and sent them on a hunt throughout his kingdom to find a happy man and bring back his coat to the king.

Well the king's men hunted high and low without success. They were about to call off the hunt, and return to the castle when lo, and behold, they heard streams of laughter, and much singing generated by one man. Aha, they thought, finally we have found a happy man. So with only the skill of a soldier they crept up to were they heard the man laughing, and singing while frolicking along. Here they decided was truly a happy man, but alas, he was too poor to own a coat.

Neither is happiness found in the pursuit of pleasure. Happiness, it has been well said, is a thing to be practiced. Happiness dwells in performed duty. If you seek happiness you will not find it. Always be careful to submit yourself to activities that will enhance others, and happiness will come of itself. It never comes through as a substitute, nor will it reach you by proxy. Happiness, according to God's word, comes by wisdom that takes you to the highest good, and add to that understanding, and happiness comes by itself.

One of the areas that people pursue in this modern day is the pursuit of security. There is a preconceived idea that if we can attain a measure of security somehow that will generate happiness. More often than not, it only generates isolationism with severe loneliness. Human life on earth has always been insecure for no one can foretell what may happen to you for the next minute, "neither death nor life shall separate me from the love of God." That is an eternal security that is given to us through our faith in Jesus Christ. The problem is that most people work towards unhappiness. Each step they take to achieve happiness only loads another burden to their unsaved soul. As a baby cries when first born, one would think they were born unhappy. Many simply have unhappiness thrust upon them, but the vast majority achieve unhappiness. they alone are to blame for their own wretchedness. It is the result of trying to achieve the spiritual by works instead of faith. People will try to find happiness in wrongdoing, better known to the believer as sin, and sin not dealt with by receiving Christ will generate a burdensome soul into an unhappy situation. In modern day terminology, many lesser evils can cause unhappiness like trivial irritations, noted in the habits of others. When a man believes himself to be better than he actually is, and finds no one to agree with that his ego will be damaged. We worry, and fret over things that never will come to pass. We worry about imaginary evils. Much of which may be brought on by negative suppositions of the electronic media that pushes a word form of unrealistic pictures before our eyes as they explain what might have happened rather than to tell us the truth about what really took place with the real cause and effect. Listeners appear to thrive on the supposed negative given by the media with their assumptions which in the majority of cases never occur at any stage of the game. It all appeals to our ungodly nature to borrow trouble to which there is no solution. Even more important than knowing the false source of happiness to which people resort, is for us to know the positive ways through which happiness can be won. The bible says, do not be overcome with evil, but overcome evil with good. There is an old fashioned way of overcoming evil, it is by being good. Again the scripture points out, *The fear of the Lord is the beginning of wisdom: and the knowledge of the Holy is understanding.* Proverbs 9: 10.

Happiness comes, not by what we possess, but by what we are, a people who have conquest over sin with God's peace firmly implanted in our heart. All those who contain a measure of joy must share it for happiness, and selfishness cannot flourish on the same branch of the vine.

How to be happy, simply have faith in God, and trust in your fellowman. forget about self, think with your mind, and heart on Jesus Christ, and how he has transformed your life into a greater element than you ever thought possible. Leave your cares and worries at the foot of the cross. Do not continue to drag them with you along the way. Make every duty a privilege and share your pleasure making two people happy. Contemplate cultivation of simplicity while practicing self denial. Do not dwell on the mistakes or failures of the past, look forward to a new walk with your saviour Jesus Christ. Keep the faith so that it becomes relevant in every day activities that are positive in building your relationship with your God. Begin, and close every day with Christ as you cultivate the sense of his presence in all things.

The Lord by wisdom hath founded the earth; by understanding hath he established the heavens. By his knowledge the depths are broken up, and the clouds drop down the dew. Proverbs 3: 19-20.

* * * * *

The False Accusation Against Jesus

———◦⌀◦———

And they led Jesus away to the high priest: and with him were assembled all the chief priests and elders and scribes. Mark 14: 53.

A false accusation causes division in the existing community. People divide themselves into one of those two sides. There are those who recognizing the damage and wickedness of the spreading untruth, and those who justify going to the other side by telling themselves the devils lie that if a person is accused there must be some substance to it. Nehemiah had a false accuser who tried to destroy him. His name was Sanballat. Fortunately, Nehemiah was able to stand his ground, and win his right to finish his work for God. The Apostle Paul was falsely accused by the Jews as they planned to kill him for telling his story about Jesus. John the Baptist was falsely accused and was beheaded on the whim of a jealous woman. Moses was falsely accused by Pharaoh and still remained consistent in following God to deliver His people out of Egypt. Being falsely accused is still rampant to this day as a devil's tool. Churches have destroyed many an innocent person by upholding the worldly axe of false accusation. Seldom have I seen it dealt with in a truly Christ like way. It appears that many Church organisations fail in the fortitude to even hear the whole story. They would much rather adopt the cast them out attitude, rather than to stand firm as the Apostles did. I have learned that one does not keep their eye on man, but always looking to Christ will steer one around many pitfalls, because man ill always disappoint you.

As Jesus marched before his accusers we should see that he was not on trial, but he was there because the Church of the day was on trial. This picture makes one concerned about the church of today to wonder why they have come such a short way as they seem intent in adopting the ways of the existing world rather than to stand for Jesus Christ, the son of the Living God.

To this point in the scripture we have seen Jesus at the last supper with his trusted twelve where he broke the bread to share with them, and then poured the cup that all may drink of it as symbol of his shed blood. He prophesied Peter's denial by saying "All of you will fall away." Peter in anger denied that he would ever fall away, but he did not understand the human heart as well as Jesus knew it. In Mark 14: 27 Jesus says, *"All ye shall be offended because of me this night: for it is written, I will smite the shepherd, and the sheep will be scattered."*

Jesus was aware of the conflict of the dark forces of evil that will attempt to dominate our lives when we follow him. The only escape from that evil is to allow ourselves to be absolutely dependant upon God looking to His deliverance, because when we begin to think that we have the answer on our own we are then subject to attack from evil around about us. Always Satan seeks the vulnerability of the soul. As soon as we drop our guard by failing to submit to Christ's solution we fall, although we shall not be utterly cast down. One observation I make with this portion of scripture is that it is quite obvious to me that it was not Jesus who was on trial here before the then known religious community, but it was in actuality the religious community themselves on trial before Jesus. In this common day with the modernization of the church worship structure we find that in a very real sense Christ is again brought before the tribunal of modernism who attempt to de-christianise society, and again religion has to be tried by Christ as many are examining him to determine whether or not he has any place in our world of common infrastructure without the spirit. Yet in the deepest, and finest sense we find it is not Jesus on trial. Rather our whole civilization is on trial before his judgments. If we fail to measure up to the standards of Christ, if in our blindness we condemn Him to be only merely a peripheral figure on rim of our godless world, we shall likewise perish. Another aspect of Jesus' life calls for continual remembrance, that is, God challenges the religious order of our time to wake up and smell the roses.

Why did the institution of the Church fail in the hour of visitation from a living God?

The religious order of the day had substituted itself to be in the place of God. Sanhedrin became an obstruction to God's will. Much the same identity today even of our Christian order, the institution of the day fear the loss of their privilege financial, and political, with no attribute to God whatsoever. The hierarchy of the church will not give way to the plan of God's salvation, with humility and reverence of putting others before themselves as God would have it.

We empathise with Christ as we picture his walk to Mount of Olives with his disciples beside him after giving them a lecture that they did not relate to in a deep sense. They chose to hear the surface message as many hearers are guilty of doing, but don't let it move me in any way for I may have to make a real commitment to show my love for God. We hear him enter into discussion with Peter who argues that he will not turn against Jesus by denying him. Nevertheless, Jesus exchanged conversation with him, but did not withdraw his prediction. As they walked to a quiet place for a time of prayer they came to Gethsemane where he asked Peter, James, and John to stand watch while he prayed. As he prayed his heart wrenching request to his Father to let this cup pass from him, he arose, and walked back to find his disciples asleep on the watch, and he was disturbed about their action so he returned to pray the second time, and when he came back to his disciples they had again fallen asleep. Again he prayed, and for the third time the disciples had fallen asleep, and the compassion of Christ showed forth in this his most terrible hour as he simply said, "sleep on, take your rest."

We watch as we see Judas come to betray Christ with a kiss, and Jesus was arrested. We are impressed with the grace and glory of the shepherd as he calmly accepts the forgone conclusion of why Judas was here with the soldiers for it was inevitable that Christ lay down his life to salvage the creation, man. When someone rises to his defence by cutting off the ear of a slave, Jesus said ,no. and put the ear back on to go in his peace with his captors.

An illegal gathering takes place of those who in name are supposed to represent God. So they gathered unto themselves a crowd of false witnesses to make sure that they would not allow this man his freedom. Even then the witnesses could not get their stories straight, but they ruled on prejudicial testimony, and false accusations to find Christ guilty. Yet they feared this Christ because what he advocated was God's own principle that would unseat all of them. The high priests, the chief priests, and the elders with the rulers, a subsequent verse says, "the whole council." In other words the Sanhedrin had met, and came together for a special meeting of the minds to sort this whole matter out to deal with this Christ. this indeed was an illegal assembly of that day. At a normal meeting of this kind their rules of constitution did not allow them to pass a sentence on the same day as the meeting of the assembly. In spite of their own laid down rules of order, they at once quickly came to the decision that this Jesus, was worthy of the death penalty. They then send him before Pilate who pleads with Jesus as he says, *"I adjure thee by the living God thou tell us whether thou art the Christ, the Son of the living God. Jesus responded, Thou hast said: nevertheless I say unto you, Hereafter thou shalt see the son of man sitting on the right hand of power, and coming in the clouds of heaven.* Matt 26:63-64.

This was a legal structure of administering the oath. Immediately after this the priests commit another illegal act, by rending [to rip with violence] his garments. They spit on him, flung a cloth over his face, which was a symbol of death, while the cloth still covered his eyes, and called for him to identify who it was that had struck him.

Here we witness the ultimate in ignorance, or more politely, there was a lack of wisdom, for as Paul points out that none of the rulers of the world had known, for had they known they would not have crucified the Lord of glory. Also we witness the overpowering light of God's love that embraced the cursing disciple. From that standpoint of intellect while gazing upon these scenes, of ourselves embrace a revelation. First we see the whole truth, and intelligence of the Lord Jesus Christ thrown to the proverbial garbage can, as the religious people put Jesus away from their minds. A fundamental wrong was enacted here that is often found prevalent within Christian circles today. Everyone prejudged the case, and were determined to put Christ out of their life by putting him to death. People of the religious order of the day had been mastered by an unholy passion to put to death without further consideration or consultation to put the prisoner at the bar to death. They went so far as to collect people unto themselves whom they could manipulate into their belief that Jesus must die. The truth did not matter to them in this instance, nor were they concerned about false statements, they were only concerned about making a judgment that would be accepted by self appointed authority. The modern day lawmakers stand by the same rules that put the falsely accused Christ to death. Guilt or innocence does not play a part in the working justice systems of our countries. The same irreconcilable justice was meted out to Christ as the social structure of that day acted against the law of the living God.

They could not simply lay hands on Christ to dispense of him without a mock trial. They dare not do such a blatant, and open act whereby they could have suffered a setback of all their evil works. Instead they set out to gather false information and it is done even today by our lawmakers. Their information gathering had to point at some lack of discrepancies of the leaders movements which would have an element of truth that they could twist to their advantage in the conviction of Christ. Then they set out to corroborate witnesses that would lie because the oaths of the day were meaningless. Even though they knew what was wrong they went ahead from a political prospective to crucify Christ.

In the book of Mark it is twice recorded that the witnesses did not agree. That should not surprise us at all for we know there is no harmony in falsehood.

Let us look at Peter for a moment in this hour. there is no doubt that he loved the Lord, but he followed afar off. He held the right impulse, but made the wrong move as he denied the Lord that he loved, insulting his own intelligence. as he was further challenged as to his connection with the convicted Christ, he turned to profanity, and made an oath that he did not know Jesus at all. An insignificant maid pursued the question infuriating Peter to the point that he even lied about his faith when challenged.

He did know Jesus, and he was violating his own love by contradicting that which dwelt within. Peter here was wounding his own soul. Peter's love for Jesus never waned, and his faith in Jesus never failed, because Christ had covered him in prayer about his faith, that it would not fail. His hope failed, and his courage failed as he stepped for a moment into the dark to ponder the loss in his life that was apparent. They were taking his Jesus away, and it left him numb with bewilderment. The final thrust for this daring disciple was not his denial, but the shedding of tears as Jesus looked upon him he crumbled in despair.

The last note of this small revelation of a broken disciple that loved his Lord is the action of grace meted out to him in restoration from the broken tears. From those tears God's face rises to become radiant suggesting to wayward hearts everywhere that belief, and love, even through unutterable folly, God makes a way to which his banished may return to the active role as servant.

A cross to the left of Christ with the unrepentant thief indicating the selfishness of the unbelieving world who only think on there own predicament. The cross to the right of the saviour where the thief asked only to be remembered in the kingdom, and received Christ' full hand of grace to be with him.

There is a need to draw our attention to the centre cross, where our saviour lay down his life, for our sake, and give us an entrance into God's presence, a new way of life, with the significant factor of undeserved love and humility. The centre cross with all it's ruggedness presents the glory, and splendour of God with his outreaching arms to encircle the world, and placing us on solid ground with eternal life in our grip. He, Jesus, who was falsely accused by the modern day religious order that bowed down to the hierarchy of the days social structure rather than recognizing the son of the living God who brought to us a plan of salvation to enter into heavens gates.

Are you today the Pilate of Christ's day who washes his hands of the whole incident even when he was absolute in surety of the innocence of this man, but didn't have the backbone to declare him to be free?

He sought a scapegoat for his actions.

Are you the joiner of this type of Christian community?

The type that condemns a person simply because you want them to take the fall for others unbelief. Or will you stand up, and cry for the innocence of Jesus, and declare him as your saviour, Lord, and Christ of your life.

* * * * *

Reaping The Harvest

Say not ye, There are yet four months, and then cometh harvest, behold, I say unto you, Lift up your eyes, and look on the fields; for they are white already unto harvest. And he that reapeth receiveth wages, and gathereth fruit unto life eternal: that both he that soweth and he that reapeth may rejoice together. And herein is that saying true, One soweth, and another reapeth. I sent you to reap whereon that ye bestowed no labour: other men laboured, and ye are entered into their labours. John 4: 35-38

There has been a long drought in the church in regards to revivals. Seldom do we see a mass application of souls who generate their ambitions toward the following of the Lord Jesus Christ. When we observe the technology in our living rooms of the evangelistic programs in place, we witness those that make their way up front, and deem them to be seekers. Seldom do we witness in our modern spectrum, the soul that is transformed by the receiving of a saviour to transform a life. Even more discouraging is the fact that we seldom find those invited to the local church in hopes that they through our witness will find Christ to invite him into their lives. We may wonder why that can happen. The answer is simple. We are afraid to welcome the unbeliever into our midst for fear it may upset our comfort zone. We would be better off to consider how God is going to react when he discovers how badly we treat his creation. God has planted the seed, he simply asks us to help with the harvest.

I have never met a farmer that did not work hard toward or for the harvest.

In the fall of the year harvest is one of the continuing events that must take place to sustain the country's food supply. The beauty of the golden grain with the wind billowing through the firm heads of grain making it appear as a floating sea of gold has absolutely no meaning unless the grain is harvested to feed uncounted millions in this, and other nations.

The often untold story is the mass intensive labour that goes into the making of such fields. There is the disking, ploughing, seeding, fertilizing, spraying for destructive insects. A constant vigil as to the maturity of grains growth within the plant. A vigilant eye as to the formation of the grain. The sustenance with water. The persevering guard against vermin that could destroy the product. A generated consistency to assure the proper production of the plant.

Often it is a lonely walk in the field, with a wary eye which conveys an ever present awareness of the growth. Also, a weary nurturing hand readied for intense labour of harvest.

I have never met a farmer that sits in the farmhouse or his barn, waiting for the harvest to come to him, the farmer willingly goes out to the field.

And he said, Lord, I believe. And he worshipped him. John 9: 38.

Herein is the essence of worship. No doubtful disputation, no human diversion to what has been offered, just an all absorbing act that moved the man to say, Lord, I believe.

So much time wasted on saving wolves, seals, gophers, and whales, while there are over four billion people in the world today frightened, concerned, lonely, and hungry: Who is going to save this endangered species, the lonely, the aged, the youth?

We establish a self image within our hearts, and it takes a storm of destruction to remove it in order for us to see others, as God would have us see them. We must turn our eyes to the harvest. Christ implored us to see the harvest as he pointed out the fields are ripe for harvest.

Let us then see the harvest; Confused youth, drugs, booze, sex.

We must see them. We have looked at ourselves long enough. The world is virtually dying of the same old thing the sin of unbelief. We need to go and harvest the fields. We need to minister to those who have not yet come to Jesus Christ, nor accepted him as saviour. It is not a vocation, it is a calling. Never forget, God's plan is a plan for the harvest.

Can we see the harvest?

The homeless, the hungry, migrant workers, mentally disabled, innocent bystanders, the falsely accused. Haunting, hurting, humanity! Help us, O God, to see them as you see them. Our own occupation with us is not justified. The Lord of the harvest has a plan. We find in Acts 10:1-13; a man named Cornelius' was given a vision of God's plan, then the following part of that chapter shows Peter also was given a vision. Because Peter was attempting to progress for God by his own standards, and here he had learned that he was not to refer to any man as common nor unclean. How often does this present day generation of worshipers fall into the same trap that Peter found himself in. Attempting to satisfy God by judging others when God informs them that it is a move which is unacceptable.

Join the threshing crew of God. It is not God's plan that things should get worse. It is the result of sin.

The bible says, 2 Timothy 3: 13, that evil men shall wax worse and worse, deceiving and being deceived. Jesus says, John 14: 2 - 3; In my Father's house are many mansions: if it were not so, I would have told you, I go to prepare a place for you. And if I go and prepare a place for you, I will come again, and receive you unto myself; that where I am, ye may be also.

Salvation, not Alienation. Only God can grow the harvest. Jesus Christ is the Lord of the harvest. We must prepare ourselves as harvesters. The tyranny of the present, crowds out the important issues of harvesting. Financial wizard, counselor, man of prayer, good board member, visitor. Evangelism must take priority. We go to the scripture for what we believe, and to the world for methodology. We tell the world to repent, and preach the gospel. The world tells us to repent, and practice the gospel.

Stop planting seed. One does not do seeding while the field is yielding or even while the grain is ripening. Nor does one seed as the new sprouts push their tiny heads through the ground. It is time to harvest. Pray for labourers of the harvest. Live, and breathe, and move, in every phase of evangelism, in order that evangelism is or becomes the very fabric of the church.

God's plan is for salvation of the soul. You are called to be a minister for Christ. The Minister must learn that the 'fundamental sin' is 'not to preach' the gospel. You may be tempted by sins just as many other people are, but the fundamental sin of your life ministry is false preaching, false teaching, false theology.

If a builder of a bridge were to build his bridge of cardboard, he would be prosecuted, he would be made responsible for the consequences, and criminal action would be taken against him. How about our ministry for Christ?

Do you like our preaching of the gospel to others?

What if our teaching, and theology are like building bridges with cardboard?

What if the bridge we build leads men to destruction rather than salvation?

What if what we teach, and proclaim is contrary to our calling?

What if the sole reason for our existence as servants of Jesus the Christ of the gospel, is obliterated by ourselves?

We are capable of sinning in many ways, like other people, and it is good and right to remember this; But the work by which we must be tested as servants of the living God, and in which we must constantly examine ourselves, is in our witness to the unbeliever.

There the question is; what is the substance, and responsibility of our proclamation?

John 3: 16-17; *For God so loved the world, that he gave his only begotten son, that whosoever believeth in him should not perish, but have everlasting life. For God sent not his son into the world to condemn the world; but that the world through him might be saved.*

These two verses should never be voiced in separation from the other, because the complete quotation gives us the reason for salvation, and furthermore the complete reason for acceptance of Christ as saviour.

Here is the perfect scripture to begin working with. For some so called Christians, it is the only scripture they are able to remember is John 3:16. However the problem is that we appear to get stuck there. Be careful to move on to the next verse to see the complete picture. V17: For God sent not his son into the world to condemn the world; but that through him the world might be saved.

One of our problems is that we have already condemned the

person, or persons, that we believe God has given to us to witness to. How can we, in the light of verse 17 of the third chapter of John's gospel, give an honest testimony about the Christ who does not condemn the world while we condemn those around about us?

It often appears that we dress with the pullover of condemnation because of spiritual laziness. We do not want to take time to hear the situation of the

person. We are prone to the condemnation factor. God's word continues in John 6: 37; *All that the Father giveth me shall come to me; and him that cometh to me I will in no wise cast out.*

Christians and their churches would rather cast out than to deal with this portion of God's infallible word.

Psalm 5: 8; *Lead me, O Lord, in thy righteousness because of mine enemies; make thy way straight before my face.*

Many times I have travelled through or stopped at Lake Louise Alberta it being one of my very favourite places to visit, and is one of the world's spots of First class beauty. Around the lake there exists a magnificent backdrop of some of the most beautiful Mountains in the world. Around the lake itself is built a strategic walking area that takes you close to the sheer rock wall. Imbedded into those rock faces are hand holds, for those who would dare to attempt to scale the cliff from the pathway up. There have been those who have gone some distance, but there are those who have drawn up to one or two holds, and froze, needing someone to help them back to the path. The beginning was so enticing that those who froze made the same attempt as those who started, but went on. How very like the attempt to testify with your life for the gospel of Christ. Sometimes we freeze being unable to move on without help. Perhaps because we hadn't stopped to count the cost of the intense labour there was to be to finish the task.

The fields are ripe even now, unto harvest. Are you prepared for the unseen consistent labour to produce the harvest for your Lord.

You started with Jesus. End with Jesus.

* * * * *

Eternal Fellowship

That which was from the beginning, which we have heard, which we have seen with our own eyes, which we have looked upon, and our hands have handled, of the word of life; for life was manifested, and we have seen it, and bear witness, and show unto you that eternal life, which was with the Father, and was manifested unto us; That which you have seen and heard declare we unto you, that you also may have fellowship with us: and truly our fellowship is with the Father, and with his son Jesus Christ. And these things write we unto you that your joy might be full. 1 John 1: 1-3.

The Christian life is certainly no innovation nor invention, it is simply God's implementation of a successful plan for his creation to obtain eternal life. God's plan is never subject to the changing of the times to be thwarted by that which is momentarily popular. Jesus was not here because of some popularity of the time, but because God chose to reveal himself in history to attract back his creation to the path of righteousness. The invitation is to live eternal life in the age that we now experience. It is apparent that we need to realize that eternal life is the now situation. Not has been, not will be, but today in the present, believers live in eternal life with present possession. Those who interpret immortality as a future element rob the Christian of their most important and richest gift. A man may know whether or not he possesses eternal life, and if he does not possess it before he dies it is not likely that he can possess it after the body is extinguished.

1 John 5:13, *These things have I written unto you that believe on the name of the son of God; that ye may know that ye have eternal*

life, and that ye may believe on the name of the son of God.

Through this writing we will scan the whole chapter one, plus other biblical references that may cultivate this portion of God's word. Beginning with verse two that reads; *for the life was manifested, and we have seen it, and bear witness, and show unto you that eternal life, which was with the father, and was manifested unto us;*

Here we witness that the invitation of the gospel, is to live in eternal life. To live in a newness of life as we exist from day to day. Old things having passed away upon our reception of Christ, we are to live in this new dimension of eternal life. Simply a new way, not a new age. The contrived philosophy of the New Age movement is one of the most damaging elements to Christianity today. Beware of the slick slogans, and comfort zone settings they offer. According to the scriptures, all is not well with the world. God requires an active commitment of service to him. Isaiah puts it best *'All we like sheep have gone astray and we have turned to our own way'*, Know that God is not pleased with that outcome. You are not okay, and I am not okay, unless we are born again, and living within the fellowship of God. Too often we find those who look at eternal life as that which is somewhere in the future, and yet unattainable. However we must allow ourselves to be cognizant of the fact that we are in that eternal life now, of which our fleshly garment only plays a very short term within God's structure. We choose to spend our eternity with God, or Satan, when we lose our present form in death. If we accept Christ as the son of the living God, then our choice leads us to time in heaven with the almighty father. It is when we reject Christ as our saviour that we choose to stay in the sinful state of man, and are headed into eternity with Satan and his followers who will be cast into the lake of fire and everlasting torment.

This invitation to the eternal does not mean future in terms of time; but what is the character of life that Christ lived. Many of our contemporary orators express the exposition of eternal life as though it was some future episode, which we may experience. By the remotest suggestion of that impact, robs man of the now gift of God, which is eternal life. This life is intended to be lived with God now to express a qualitative life rather than the quantitative. To suggest in some way more life or less life, is to take away from that which God intended. Man's need is not to add years to his life; But to add life to his years by living now in his eternal life.

Millions long for eternal life, via the mystical fountain of youth. Billions of dollars are spent daily trying to produce a method of longer life to no avail. Multitudes long to live forever for personal gain; But give those same people a space of empty time on a rainy afternoon and they are beside themselves for something to do. Teens cry, life is boring, nothing to do in our town or district, it is a hollow cry. I am reminded of my friends who went on a trip in beautiful British Columbia, and as they traveled toward Prince Rupert they stopped in the city of Terrace at which point they sought out the Tourist information booth to ask about a side trip to Kitimat where the Aluminum production plant was. To their chagrin the clerk informed them quickly, oh there is nothing there, your drive would be a waste of time. Needless to say their enthusiasm was dashed, so they made their way to a nearby cafe and mulled over the situation while at least enjoying the coffee. Then came decision time, and they chose to go to see Kitimat, and find out what a nothing settlement was. To their surprise the clerk had been wrong, and tasteless in her judgment. They found there a vibrant city settled on the coastal Pacific waters. They enjoyed the scenery, the sea, the mountainous terrain, and the cordial tour through the smelter plant to learn of one of Canada's major industries. They enjoyed the campsites, and the playgrounds, as well as the friendly attitude of the inhabitants; it was the highlight of their journey. This virtually hidden city had fulfilled their desires with activities they enjoyed.

Many unbeliever is like the tourist clerk that gave the nothing message, and when we finally disregard the wet blankets of our social structure, and decide to venture into the presence of God through His son Jesus Christ, we will find our joy and expectations filled to a greater capacity than we could ever imagine. So let us begin by correcting those who claim, "there is nothing there."

If God would only give me mortality! The good news is that he has done just that; and you must begin that life today, and live in the presence of God now. Along with His gift of eternal life he has also given us wisdom, knowledge, strength, education, and the ability to walk with these things as He directs our paths. Also he gave us a mouth to speak with, ears to hear, feet to walk, hands to help, and eyes to see; But we consistently refuse to use them. With all this we turn away, and ask God to give us something else, whatever we might envisage that to be. Still God says he will give you the desires of your heart, but he then goes on to tell us what those desires should be, and we have a tendency to push that part of his word away. Make sure those same personal desires do not destroy you. When you desire from God be very sure you will be able to live in the presence of a living God now.

Eternal life is a present transformation from our acceptance of Jesus Christ as saviour. Christian faith not only declares the resurrection after death; but also indeed declares the resurrection with Christ now. Salvation is already set in place for you to accept, so in the same instant is eternal life already set, and we are to live it in the presence of the almighty, and living God. In doing that we come to a place where we realize that the fear of God is the beginning of wisdom.

When I speak of a biblical fear of God I do not refer to a cowering type of fear; I speak of a fear that ought to be established in one heart about trespassing against that which God has already set in place, and the things that we do becoming a denial of God. One must fear to the extent that you will at any cost witness of your life in Christ and the changes it has wrought, and the love it has generated, for God is love. If you fail in your testimony for God you may lose what you already have. As I peruse the biblical standards I find those mentioned that would not adhere to God's word, and God stopped struggling with them, and turned them over to a reprobate mind.

When the Christian lives eternal life through faith and love, they become a source of light to others. That is what its all about; your impact upon others. The words you use, the actions you take, the elements you allow or disallow into your life, will identify you as Christian. Better still it should identify you as one who loves God and serves his son Jesus Christ. Give of yourself without giving materially, love without having to hug, be joyous, and caring even in the light of your own crisis. Be always ready to reach out to others with the word of God. Practice being humble, and you will be surprised how popular you will become. Cease from complaining, that does not project the love of God. When you begin to practice these positive actions your life will be infectious to others, and people will automatically look to you because you live eternal life now.

You do not have to become physically involved to reach out to touch someone. You simply touch them by word, and deed, by action on you part to set others at ease by the very life you live. The eternal life of God's promise we find in 1st John 1:3 the writer points out the eternal life he speaks about in verse two is in fact the path to fellowship with other believers as well as having fellowship with the Father, and his son Jesus Christ.

Here we may arrive at the conclusion that fellowship is both the goal and the source of the proclaiming Christian. This coincides with the message found in Hebrews 10: 25; that states, *Not forsaking the assembling of ourselves together, as the manner of some is; but exhorting one another: and so much more as you see the day approaching.*

Christ's death upon the cross has already closed that gap between man, and God, and brought him close to us. I as a servant of God cannot shed my blood to save you from your sin, Christ has already done that. I cannot send someone to you that will save your soul, or make things right with you before God, because he has already done that through his son, Jesus Christ, and it up to you to accept him as your saviour.

Eternal life means divine, and human fellowship to abide together in love, and to be lived in the community of believers. The fellowship with the Father as well as other believers, are both the goal and the source of proclaiming the message of the gospel of Jesus Christ.

The very nature of the human demands fellowship. Human nature was created for fellowship. People seek fellowship at various levels. We watch them latch on to the ever changing cultural tastes in hopes of finding life's ultimate solution to happiness. The ever present thrust towards achievement in academics in order to stand in intellectual circles. Those with political aspirations, seeking the approval of their fellowman. There is the ever-noisy group shouting for the elevation of social causes. Some simply seek their fellowship in the beer parlour or nightclub, or some sleazy portrayal that has been deemed the ultimate outcast of our normal society. But the fellowship with the Father in heaven, as well as those who believe in the Son, is the richest type of fellowship that alone fulfills the purpose of life.

Christ was crucified as he found it not robbery to be equal with God. The bible says, he made us heirs and joint heirs with him; which allows us to become the children of God. Somehow we have difficulty conceiving that God would give us access to his estate as sons and daughters. The fellowship of men with one another and with God through Christ, is what must take place in order for you to claim to be a child of God. Individual religion is a contradiction in terms of human fellowship of believers in our Lord and Saviour Jesus Christ.

Fellowship with man, and with God, is the Christian community gathering together with one another to worship in awe and fear of our living God. The problem arises when we have our church bodies caught up in some form of cheap socializing, and allowing our temples to become places of entertainment rather than having them be a meeting place to be still and know our God in the fellowship of believers. Let us stop trying to project God by a cheap subsidy of friendliness, and a diffused congeniality. The true nature of the fellowship within the church body is simply stated by Jesus as he compares himself to the vine and tells us that we are the branches.

In the book of the gospel of *John, chapter 15: 16a* we read; *You have not chosen me, but I have chosen you, and ordained you, that you should go and bring forth fruit, and that your fruit should remain:*

Christ is very straight forward here, he says that we must produce fruit. Those that would choose first to seek after gifts must realize that without the production of fruits, there are no gifts. The true mark of a churches fellowship is self sacrificing love, that ties in with a self sacrificing life. These are manifested in mutual care, mutual service, mutual labour, mutual helpfulness, and mutual love in mutual prayer.

1John 1: 4; *And these things write we unto you, that your Joy may be full.*

God motivates the joy of the Lord. It is a holy door. It is an expression of wonderful happiness from the soul of the believer towards all. Fullness of joy brings about the memory of our conversion, and the change it made in our lives. It reminds us that following Christ is a way of life. A newness within that gives us pure contentment with whatever may be.

1 John 1: 5 This then is the message we have heard of him, and declare unto you, that God is light, and in him is no darkness at all.

Here a clear concise non threatening statement that tells simply who God is. A being without darkness. Easy to approach in the light. A God who is purely visible to those who would see. We need a test for our faith, even as we need a test in our academics of intelligence, or aptitudes, and physical health. The test for our life of faith is in the statement that God is light. God needs a person of faith to respond to that light. As the light needs the eye to see, so God needs his creation to respond to the word he has given. God is made visible by his very creation of nature. We as believers need to respond to all that he has given. To his work, to the light in him, and all that he has given for us, and to us. We must recognize the visible character of God in Jesus Christ. To walk in that light requires vigorous honesty with God, and the acknowledgement, and confession of sin. To identify with darkness will illuminate the sin in ones life. A person walking in darkness will begin to separate themselves from the Christian community. The saving revelation must be the light of God's truth so bright that others are drawn to it from the darkness of the world. Christ reaches out to the weary as he says 'Come unto me all ye that labour and are heavy laden, and I will give you rest'.

Do you know why he wants to give you rest?

It is because of the work that you have done for him. Perhaps you have struggled with the world so long, and are unable to find rest, you grow weary from your burden of sin. Hear his call now and he will take you in, and you will find that elusive rest is depleted, and you can now rest in the arms of Jesus, because God made it possible.

We need to fellowship with a living God who has already laid out the plan for our walk when we accept Christ Simply, one must accept and walk that path, and tell others the good news of having fellowship in your eternal life now with God, and your community of believers.

* * * * *

Facing Real Life

—⊂∅∅∅⊃—

He was in the world, and the world was made by him, and the world knew him not. He came unto his own, and his own received him not. But as many as received him, to them gave he power to become the sons of God, even to them that believe on his name. John 1: 10-12.

I have heard it said, get real, know real life, we must be realistic. When one makes such a statement as that I wonder, do they mean that to be real one must walk the way of the drunkard, the idolater, murderer, or the realistic way of the wife beater, or the husband abuser, the homosexual, the one who curses God and man.

Where I to pursue that question of what is real life, I am sure that you could give me some very different analogies or explanations as to what real life is to you. Let me assure you my friends that negative, godless, hurtful living is not real life. Whether you are hurting someone else or simply destroying your own life, that is sinful living. That is a very shallow life, a boring life, perhaps even a life of depression. It is a life where man is always trying to prove to himself, and to others his greatness. It is an empty life, and a fruitless life. When you are living the right kind of life, you do not have to waste your time proving it to others, because in itself will produce good fruit. Real life, and realistic life, is a life that is lived for Jesus, the Christ, the Lord.

When Christ came in the flesh there was no spectacular grandeur, as expected by others in position of power. There was no ceremonial garb of acceptance by the chosen elite few to usher him in by the officiating capacity of those who ruled. Christ's plight was to arrive with the initial seeming failure, everything looked down, and evil appeared as a way of life. Nothing was to be expected from mankind as they triumphed in their evil deeds to embrace wrongful victory. Nevertheless the sky was lit up with brilliance never before witnessed as a choir of Angels announced his arrival to the lowly shepherds, into a world which was lost in perpetual sin. Even under these circumstances, Christ's intervention survived. Today while in some places it appears to be losing ground, in other places it is leaping out across the world faster than it ever has before. The world is still engulfed in the one, and same darkness that prevailed when Christ arrived. Primarily because in this world of plenty the need to commit ourselves to God becomes more vague as man continues to enjoy the pleasures of sin for a season rather than work to spread the gospel to those who have not heard. Even that bleak darkness thrust upon Christ at Calvary did not overcome it, nor will the difficulties by which we are faced make evil turn to that which is right. We are not to flaunt our humanity upon some unsuspecting weaker element of society. When Christ was born there was an element of immediate rejection, which gives rise to the question, why is it that men even today wish to have none of Christ?

John 1: 10; *He was in the world, and the world was made by him, and the world knew him not.*

The world at that time was looking for a political leader of social reform. Society was in same turmoil as we see today they cradled in their hearts and minds a preconceived idea of what the coming Messiah would be. A selfish attitude prevailed of a me-first attitude. As it is in our contemporary society we are swallowed up in a false pride that avails us nothing. Our accomplishments carry little staying power, and we are subjected to utter confusion when confronted by the element of A God who would present us with an escape route called salvation. At the time of Christ's coming men were also rattled by the same innovation that offered to deliver them from the bonds of sin. This sudden presence of divine originality confused them. This Christ that came, was less than the ostentatious personality that they had conjured up in their expectations. They were upset because he had not met their standards of acceptance. This is a normal practice amongst so-called believers. If someone fails to meet their preconceived standards they are shut out of the circle. Therefore the world continues to be confused by the expounded philosophy of the free love of God who considers all men. The believer has been unable to project to the unbelief of the world that they are not received by God for what they are. Neither are they received for what they could be, but God accepts them where they are at. In that acceptance by God, he transforms, and delivers them into the typical transformation from worldly pleasure to that which Christ offers, forgiveness of sin with an attachment of everlasting life. Always we are surprised when there is not some special protocol to follow when meeting our King, nor is there some special way in which we ought to appear. It is a fearful thing when one moving in daily routine brushes up against our Christ, and fails to recognize him. However we push on resenting progress, and not realizing with progress we can oftimes oppose the incoming of a better way.

The Lord Jesus Christ, instead of coming as some physically damaging and destructive conqueror by slaying of others before him, presented himself quietly in gentleness. Instead of establishing himself as man leader of men, he applied love to the weary of hostile environment, he invited them to rest.

Come unto me" Christ says, *"All ye that labour and are heavy laden, and I will give you rest."* Matt 11: 28.

That is real life; Eternal life. It is not the way to which we are accustomed, or the way we expected, because we cannot comprehend that this is the road that God would travel.

It is surely not the way we assumed He would take. We have built ourselves an elite social structure to elevate God to a place unreachable by man. We being insensitive attempt to build our own image of who God is, and what he should be, and how his plan should work. We leave love aside, we do not care about people we believe are not worth liking. Yet here Jesus establishes a new way of life. A way that caring must take precedence. Others must always come first before our own selfish interests. To remember that God's ways are never stereotyped is an essential factor of our established walk with Him.

Men said to Christ, be realistic, get to know real life, curse like men, hate like men be prejudice like men, be angry, be blatantly foolish, that is real life. Had Christ given in to that concept, had Christ allowed himself to be persuaded into such a course, many would have followed eagerly. But for the spiritual things they had small taste, and in spiritual mission they could see no hope. All that which is characteristic of this our generation, and we see in John 1:11, some did not receive him. We are not told why; but it probably for the same reasons that we hear today. Life is full, and interesting, and he was crowded out, or he did not appeal to them.

The gospels make it plain that many held aloof from Christ for more sinister reasons. They resented him, and they made it a point to actively dislike him. What he offered in no way attracted them, and his claims on them upset and irritated them. There were those who did receive him; and what resulted in their case was something so amazing that only God's hands could have done it.

Romans 3:23; *For all have sinned, and come short of the glory of God;*

They resented Jesus for His intrusion into their lives. They liked the lie they were living.

Like the atheist who calls himself a theologian lives a lie. Theology is the study of the word of God, and relationship between God, and the universe. A specific form or system of this study as expounded by particular religion or denomination. No atheist could begin to understand God's word. In the first place, being a non-believer, and having no part of the indwelling of the Holy Spirit, the word would not be revealed to him or her. They actively disliked Christ, and as you tell this gospel, you will attract the same dislike. Truly there is good news, of power and status for those who accept Jesus through the salvation plan he created by the shedding of his blood.

John 1:12; *But as many as received Him, to them gave he power to become the sons of God, even to them that believe on his name.*

For the way Christ effects in a soul of those who trusts him is something far more radical, and fundamental transformation reveals nothing less than the creation of a totally new being in place of the worldly attitude of destruction and unbelief. We shall find within ourselves that which one could never attain in the old state of mind. The believer becomes so different of that of our past living desserts the soul as we obtain a more understanding form of thinking. God passes on to this creature some of his own nature whereby we may grow up into His characteristic ways. We might call it regeneration. The natural man receives not the things of God. But here, in Christ, we break through the limitations of nature, as we become new creatures in Christ; with new aims, and standards, all of a sudden our neighbour matters. Our efforts to this point have proven futile; of a sudden we are given the power to become the sons of God. Let us be realistic, to be without Christ is to be without hope. In him, man becomes a new creature, behold all things pass away. You will possess new life, new attitude, new reason for living, and then you will know it is real. You were born in sin but by the shed blood of Christ that has been taken away, and you stand forgiven and are transformed into the newness of life..

Oh! - I know the hue and cry. Its all right for you preacher, but you don't know what I have been through. Let me assure you I can take you down a few roads of my life that you would not survive without Christ. So don't give me that easy road theory that the world likes to hang on the Christian, instead of dealing with the issue of where you are.

You may counter, I have no education in that area, that will not be good enough my friend; God has already dealt a blow to that thinking; Let us read his word in *Amos 7:14; I was no prophet, neither was I the son of a prophet; but I was a herdsman, and a gatherer of sycamore fruit.*

You want to be impressive; be for God where you are, and with what you are, not for what you might be, or could be, or wish to be. The kingdom of God is at hand, Hell's gates are wide open, souls need to know about the Saviour of the world, and you are elected, by God, to tell the story of his son Jesus.

Amos 7:15; And the Lord took me as I followed the flock, and the Lord said unto me, Go, prophesy unto my people - - -

The word prophesy here means, tell the people God's word, tell them the consequences of not following God, eternity in hell; Mark 9:44, 46, 48; *where the worm dieth not, and the fire is not quenched.*

It is the first duty of any believer in the sonship of Christ, is to cry out the message to the world of unbelief while standing tall for

253

a living God who has redeemed his creation from the pits of hell. Stand in the face of criticism, and barrages of wilful attempts to demoralize your testimony of the truth of man's need to be redeemed. Of course it will fly in the face of those who are unbelievers who will make attempts to discredit your stand, but if the Christian refuses to stand against the immorality of thoughtless social order we stand to allow those to win who would de-christianise our Nations. The person who is truly Christ believing, is one who has become lesser in the eyes of the unbelieving world. Also they will feel less at home in the world of unbelief who are without sensitivity for a lost soul. The active believer of Jesus Christ will sense that they are moved less by the things that do appear. As a believer you will lose confidence in the weight, and power of sheer non-spiritual political farce. You will find an absolute assurance of those eternal verities that are hid from the wise and prudent, but are revealed unto babes. In your stand of testimony to the salvation of Christ you will begin to understand God's word as he tells you to be all the more aware of those things that *"eye hath not seen, nor ear heard!"* Cor 2:9 You will find yourself more, and more, at home in that greater, and better part of life which has until your transformation been out of sight.

Where will you spend eternity?

There is no compromise with God: Get real! Let's be realistic, walk the life of Christ in real compassion with sincerity in applying the word by consistently repeating the message of salvation put forth by Christ.

* * * * *

In The Service Of God

———◦◦◦———

If any man among you seem to be religious, and bridleth not his tongue, but deceiveth his own heart, this man's religion is vain. Pure religion and undefiled before God and the Father is this, To visit the fatherless and widows in their affliction, and to keep himself unspotted from the world. James 1: 26-27.

Two essential ingredients here are stated as a requirement of being religious. First one must have compassion to those around you, and secondly you must abhor worldliness which fails to recognize God.

Contemporary society has been inundated with the idea of emphasis upon ritual, when they think in terms of religious attachment while practicing some unorthodox performance to enhance an acceptable stand with the approach of God. We find in this verse almost the elimination of such an idea to approach God, because we see here the caring approach to our fellow human being with a sensitive approach to the need of our neighbour without displaying tribute to some out of reach device. Simply the scripture tells us to be there for someone else while being careful that our own approach is undefiled. James includes the two most essential ingredients to be held in the Christian walk, they are an attitude of complete compassion toward our fellow human, and our lack of ungodly worldliness. We must be cognizant of enhancing our truth about walking close with our living God.

When a person serves people as a servant of God, there ought to be a depth of obligation that includes a quality of empathy, and care not otherwise found in man's service to man. For we find in the secular world that personal service or favour is predicated upon mutual good pleasure. In other words, many have the colloquial concept, you scratch my back and I'll scratch yours, or I will do you a favour, if you will do a favour for me. In our contemporary Christian communities this attitude has gained credence with many as they attempt to integrate worldliness into the church community. However, the thrust of the servant of God should include, that being those who claim Christ as their saviour, must be benevolent, seeking the good for others, even if they prove to be unresponsive, or resentful towards us.

But love ye your enemies, and do good, and lend, hoping for nothing again; and your reward shall be great, and ye shall be the children of the highest: for he is kind unto the unthankful and to the evil. Be ye therefore merciful, as your Father is also merciful. Luke 6: 35 - 36.

Jesus is not asking for feelings and emotions that we cannot control. He simply points out that we must love our fellowman with a love that is exceptional because it expects nothing in return.

James, a servant of God was under obligation to measure his conversation very carefully, being careful to speak only the truth, even though the hearer might find it unpleasant to the ears. For as he taught God's word he knew that there were those who would seek their own benefits from this new gospel of Jesus Christ, the Messiah who had indeed come and returned to sit on the right hand of His Father. He remembered the prophet Isaiah was able to endure much criticism for the way he preached, and wrote of his God from the people he knew he could save.

It is because these men recognized that they were indeed God's servants, and because they knew, where they were at with God, it was impossible to discourage them. Missionaries have often found suspicion, instead of a cordial welcome, amongst those whom they have wished to help. Without the love of God in their hearts, and without belief that their prime obligation was to their Lord Jesus Christ, they would hardly persist in their service. Jesus transformed or made over the thought of service, from something that was embraced as perhaps menial, to that which became the heart of His life style, and His plan to further the gospel.

Too often we take the word service, and reduce it to, "that right of mine" to receive from the community level in the Super Market, or at the hairdresser, or the service station, or from other persons that give to me convenience for what I desire to have. A high conception of service can only be maintained when it is rooted in God. His Son Jesus Christ, as our Lord and Saviour, is the secret to happiness. Yet the ideal of happiness, which many cherish, may look to a state of ease.

James; has a different ideal of happiness, because he holds a different theory of the meaning and purpose of life. The purpose of life cannot be obtained by luxurious comfort, but only in the achievement of a Christ like character. Therefore, the Christian can count it sheer joy, when he or she meets with various trials and tribulations. When crisis is met with courage, it produces steadfastness of character. Christians are not distinguished by their immunity from trials, which are common to the secular unbelieving world, but in the way they accept, and absorb the handling of those difficulties with patience and understanding, by the transposing of adversity, into a spiritual victory.

James 1: 4; But let patience have her perfect work, That ye may be perfect and entire, wanting nothing.

Here, that which is set apart from the material universe, becomes the goal that does not allow us to settle for less. With our Christ likeness, we shall not settle for a complacent self righteousness, derived from false satisfaction, that somehow builds a hope that we have already arrived at Holiness. This verse may be disturbing to those who believe you can be closer to God when you are accepted into membership of a church body, because James points out the real situation of the Christian maturing in that he or she will be secure in the knowledge of Christ's salvation when we allow patience to work in our following of Jesus.

To remind God as the man in Mark 10: 20; Master, *all these have I observed from my youth,* is simply not enough. The perfection, to which we are called, is not the negative absence of transgression, but the positive presence of inclusive love.

James 1: 5 - 8; if any of you lack wisdom, let him ask of God, that giveth to all men liberally, and upbraideth not; and it shall be given him. But let him ask in faith, nothing wavering. For he that wavereth is like a wave of the sea driven with the wind and tossed. For let not that man think he shall receive anything of the Lord. A double minded man is unstable in all his ways.

Again this idea is often thwarted by the modern day Christian communities in the sense of demanding the requiring of academic status, rather than to have simple God inspired wisdom that comes from the greatest weapon that the Christian has, and that being prayer.

Prayer is the recourse of those who desire wisdom.

Why is prayer necessary for gaining this wisdom?

Because, in the Christian understanding, prayer involves confession of moral insufficiency, and inadequacy, and aspiration, towards the perfection of God.

James 1: 12 Blessed is the man that endureth temptation: For when he is tried, he shall receive the crown of life, which the Lord has promised to them that love him.

The Christian life must always be one of extreme moral endeavour. Faith in God does not exempt any one believer from struggle. It simply enables one to endure unto victory.

James 1: 13 - 15; let no man say when he is tempted, I am tempted of God: for God cannot be tempted with evil, neither tempteth he any man:

Who is to blame?

From Adam to Eve, to contemporary man, the alibi for succumbing to temptation is invariably, 'It wasn't my fault'.

If God made me this way, why should I be held responsible for acting according to my nature?

In today's social structure we are taught to adopt the ideology that someone else is to blame for my bad behaviour. My moral decadence must be plied to the feet of those who trained me, for I am not to take the blame for my derelict attitude. Besides all that, these moral attributes deny me my freedom of choice. And if I take it upon myself to live a better more loving life style, how then will I revoke all my responsibilities. James here is uttering a warning to his fellow Christians. That warning is against using worn out old excuses for wicked conduct, that God has never accepted, and will not now accept. In other words, 'Don't blame God'. Furthermore do not blame the nature that he has given you for the sin that you may commit.

In becoming a Christian, does one have less of life or more?

It is all too common an impression; that we must lose more than we can gain. These verses in James suggest that obedience to the word of God, is truly the only path to freedom.

James 1: 26; If any man among you seem to be religious, and bridleth not his tongue, but deceiveth his own heart, this man's religion is vain. Pure religion and undefiled before God and the Father is this, To visit the fatherless in their affliction, and to keep himself unspotted from the world.

Jesus in directing man's relationship, is based upon a simple and sincere devotion to a living, loving, God.

How else could I impress upon you the sincerity of God's requirements, than to close with this verse from Micah 6: 8; *He hath showed thee, O man, what is good; and what does the Lord require of thee, But to do justly, and to love mercy, and to walk humbly with thy God.*

* * * * *

Light Against Darkness

Be ye therefore followers of God, as dear children; And walk in love, as Christ has also loved us, and hath given himself for us an offering and a sacrifice to God for a sweet smelling savour. But fornication and uncleanness, or covetousness, let it not be named among you, as becometh saints. Ephesians 5: 1-3.

Ephesians 4: ends in an appropriative manner as we read verse 32; *Be ye kind one to another, tender hearted, forgiving one another, even as God for Christ's sake has forgiven you.*

The last clause here has become the point of departure for a wider thought, that is somehow God here, becomes the model for us to imitate. The American standard version translates the first verse of chapter five, to read, Therefore be imitators of God, as beloved children. Imitating God can be applied to our following of Jesus as the ethical example and applying to our lifestyle.

What Would Jesus do? Is a very good direction for each of us to ask.

Imitation is a legitimate, and powerful motive in human behaviour. Children imitate parents, or someone with whom they are impressed with, such as their favourite TV character, or their neighbour, or teacher. Leaders of our nations are often successful because they imitate some impressive leader in history. To imitate God would be a good practice, however I believe it could lead into some very difficult and even austere situations whereby we would need to cry unto the Father to bail us out. Let this mind be in you.

Eph 5: 2; Walk in love as Christ has also loved us, - here is an impacting phrase that can direct each believer into a special walk with others. In an attempt to imitate Christ may be the wrong direction. For we are to walk as he walked, not with some cheap imitation of love, but with strength of a new simplicity of the indwelt love of God as our wholesome self to be like him in our daily relationships. No one can follow Christ's example except they who by faith have found Christ as Mediator, and Redeemer, and by His saving Grace is armed with power to set forth on a pilgrimage after His example. The author points out a very definite danger in the early Christian church. Christian love is not a product of ethical self culture, but a response to an act of God - Christ loved us and gave Himself up for us. A wrong impression of Christian freedom, Revolt against strict moral demands of religion, this has been a frequent fact of history.

In the ancient world it took common form in spirituality which thought matters pertaining to the body as indifferent. Hence laxness in sexual morality could be condoned as bodily indulgence which need not touch the spiritual attainments. This can indicate how dangerous the word Spirit, and Spiritual, can be if loosely employed. The contrast between Spirit, and body, when the former is ranked higher than the latter is derivative of Greek philosophy, and not of the thought world of the Bible. The Bible knows nothing of the Spiritual religion in the Greek sense. That is why the body realism of the bible is so often shocking to us. The bible does not accept the worship of beauty, or of truth, or of goodness, for a substitute for a worship of a personal living God of righteousness and Holiness. No one in the Bible is excused from the humbling appearance before God as a sinner. There is no evasion of moral matters.

Eph 5: 6; *Let no man deceive you with vain words: for because of these things cometh the wrath of God upon the children of disobedience.*

The wrath of God is not a very popular theme in modern preaching. The New Testament is often misinterpreted as picturing a kind of new God, who can be controlled with the God of the Old Testament. By abolishing the wrath of God, one robs God of His righteousness. The writers of the New Testament never dreamed of repudiating the Old Testament. The New in the New Testament is simply God's sacrificial Love as revealed on the cross. We would do well whenever we speak of God's love to always prefix the adjective Holy, "Holy Love."

Forgiveness before God is costly precisely because it dare not be immoral. We are simply sinners saved by Grace suggesting that we remove ourselves as far from sin as possible. Wrong has not been turned into right because of God's forgiveness. Nor have God's standards of righteousness been lowered to the level where divine wrath no longer applies. Forgiveness is the gift across the chasm of violated Holiness. Repentance on man's side makes the giving of the gift of salvation possible. But where there is no repentance, the wrath of God comes upon the disobedient.

Eph 5: 8 - 14; *For ye were sometimes darkness, but now are ye light in the Lord: Walk as children of light: [For the fruit of the spirit is in all goodness and righteousness and truth;] Proving that which is acceptable unto the Lord. And have no fellowship with the unfruitful works of darkness, but rather reprove them. For it is a shame even to speak of those things done of them in secret. But all things that are reproved are made manifest by the light: for whatsoever doth make manifest is light. Wherefore he saith awake thou that sleepest, and arise from the dead, and Christ shall give thee light.*

It is important to read these passages with the ability to discern between the believer and the unbeliever. There are those who walk in the shade from the light along with those who prefer the absolute darkness in order not to see the intelligent moral fibre of a living God. The scriptures say that men love darkness rather than light for their deeds are evil.

Here the contrast between the unethical involvement in the immorality rather than righteousness, and the true activity of identifiable Christianity. The important verb in this passage is, walk. There is no person that I know of that wishes to be exposed to their wrong doing. They make rational judgments of others because of fear for their own exposure. Many walk in the attempt to project an image of whom they are not. A picture of thin veneer is built to protect the true actions of the real person, yet being in Christ in a sincere way the veneer is no longer needed, and falls away to show the real person that walks upright. For whatever reason people put on that false image there will be no escape from God's perception of the humility that is practiced by those who generate a special love to God's creation. The Christian can walk without fear because they have exposed themselves to God's light, and their deeds are made manifest.

Another contrast is found in the second chapter of Ephesians;

Eph 2:12 -14; *That at that time ye where without Christ, being aliens from the commonwealth of Israel, and strangers from the covenant of promise, having no hope, and without God in the world: But now in Christ Jesus ye who sometimes were far off are made nigh by the blood of Christ. For He is our peace, who hath made both one, and hath broken down the middle wall of partition between us.*

In the former passage from chapter five, we see the contrast between the past, and present conditions was stated in terms of relationship to God, and to the community of God's people; here it is stated in terms of character, and social influence. You were in darkness. Darkness was not merely their environment, they themselves shared the nature of the Evil world, which surrounded them.

Conversely; You are the Light, not merely enlightened, but partaking of that nature of light which now surrounds them. And so giving light to others.

Matthew 5: 14 - 16; *Ye are the light of the world. A city set upon a hill cannot be hid. Neither do men light a candle, and put it under a bushel, but on a candlestick; and it giveth light to all that are in the house. Let your light so shine before men, that they may see your good works, and glorify your Father which is in heaven.*

These are the words of our Lord Jesus.

Philippians 2: 15; *That ye may be blameless and harmless, the sons of God, without rebuke, in the midst of a crooked and perverse nation, among whom ye shine as lights of the world.*

Live as befits your nature, let your light shine. The writer is insisting on the moral significance of light as opposed to false mystic interpretation.

Why ?

Eph 5:10; *Proving what is acceptable unto the Lord.*

It is my perception that our contemporary churches are not willing to prove that the word which they present comes only from God. Rather it portrays only man's self identity which is supposedly worship, but puts aside God's written application of Holiness. Here we see that God is unequivocal in his direction for needing the proof of the authenticity of representation. It is our responsibility to make sure that we are not absorbed into the worldly status quo. There needs to be proven moral, and Godly substance to that which is used for worship of the living God.

No observer of human life can fail to note how desperate, for most men, and women, is the fear of exposure. We wear masks projecting a different person than what we really are. For the Saint it may be the mask of humility, the criminal fears betrayal. The adulterer fears retaliation of jealousy, and the sense of shame is of great importance to man, and that creates self delusion in the hearts of men.

The Christian is a person who has exposed themselves to the light.

John 3: 20 - 21; we read the words of Jesus, *For every one that doeth evil hateth the light, neither cometh to the light, lest his deeds be reproved. 21.But he that doeth truth cometh to the light, that his deeds may be made manifest, that they are wrought of God.*

Judgment is the very thing Christians have learned to accept as the gateway into a new life with Christ. Repentance can be joyous acceptance of the searching light of God's Holiness. The Grace given to Christians can bring with it a shaking off of burdens. Christians walking in the light can taste the glorious liberty of the Children of God.

Romans 8: 21; *Because the creature itself also shall be delivered from the bondage of corruption into the glorious liberty of the children of God.*

A forgiven sinful past is in the hands of God, and need not be paraded before men. Christians who wish to indulge in a testimony of unseemly autobiography might well heed the message in verse twelve of Ephesians five; *For it is a shame even to speak of those things which are done of them in secret.*

This is complimented by the verse that follows, all things that are reproved are made manifest by light. By that instructive sins, thus shining as lights in the world.

For whosoever doth make manifest is light, and accordingly it becomes those who are the children of light, who are light in the Lord, to discover to others light which is diffused by the Holiness of your lives, and by your exemplary walk in their lives

* * * * *

Reality Of Change

Behold I now show you a mystery; we shall not all sleep, but we shall all be changed, In a moment, in the twinkling of an eye, at the last trump: for the trumpet shall sound, and the dead shall be raised incorruptible, and we shall be changed. 1 Corinthians 15: 51 - 52*:*

Here we can determine that which comes into our lives is a portion of God's assignment, if not for our betterment, then truly for our learning to walk upright in the family of God. We as Christian followers of the living God have been given the authority to speak to warn others of the impending doom that is there when God is mocked, or left in the background. You see we are given the freedom to choose or reject. When we choose to serve God we are given access to eternal life. If on the other hand we reject his word we shall suffer the consequences in the long term. Our decision to follow God through Jesus Christ will generate changes to the way we live as well as the way we think. Make no mistake with Christ's transformation you will definitely see a change.

We live in a modern age of a very visible uncertainty. We look about us, and it appears that the world is falling apart, because of, seemingly, one disaster after another is upon us. The war mongers are planning another war or two, the apostles of debt are falling like rocks in a mountain slide of bankruptcies, yet those seeing it from another prospective only see it as inevitable change taking place as history is in the making. When we stop to consider today's events that appear catastrophic, there is much to be compared to bygone cultures that have also been uprooted by change. One certainty that we can attach ourselves to, is the fact that change is a certainty, even a way of life; and for sure, the world around us is changing.

Places change; That field path where we took a shortcut to our activities in the community, now a sea of enormous houses, complete with asphalt driveways and cement sidewalks, seldom found alleys as they build back to back. Peppered with new kinds of street called cul-de-sacs. Unheard of in our days of youth. Large towns now grown to be big cities; small cities, now a metropolis. Former bush land, now a cement jungle of skyscrapers, and shopping malls. Wagon trails, once winding, and difficult, through our swamplands, now broad twinned highways, by, which a major portion of our goods are transported over.

Yes places change.

People change. There was a young fellow in our school that hardly spoke two words, and often others would come to his defence for his own protection. One time visiting my hometown I decided to look him up, and reacquaint myself with him as an adult, if for no other reason but to assure him of my continued support for him, and to offer help if he was having difficulty. To my surprise, I located him, and he held a management position for a multi complex corporate firm, no longer a timid soul. People change.

My curiosity was fired up to search out other timid souls, to find that some had gone on to be politicians, preachers, teachers, and took no back seat from anyone. I stood in the old schoolhouse, and saw how little the children of today are. You see, we just thought we were big when we were children in that bustling rural schoolhouse. That once prune faced girl others teased you about, now a raving beauty. That sports hero, now a broken addict, dependant on drugs, and alcohol, and blaming the rest of the world for his woes.

Yes people change.

That radical, impatient fellow, with a bad temper in school, now a preacher of the gospel, calm, and content, with his lot in life. Poverty stricken children, attending school with no more than lard on two slices of home made bread to sustain them for a day, now have come into money, and it has changed them.

Yes money changes people.

Oh yes, there are those who are bitter, because they have none, but those who may have by hard work or inheritance gained prestige through the dollar, often leave others behind, and cut them out of their lives. Families, and friends, can be divided by money, particularly when an estate is involved, or someone has failed to write a will. Then we see the biblical prospective fulfilled, Son shall rise against father, and daughter against mother. Hearts are broken, feelings run high, and irreconcilable damage is done, because people change. With access to money, often finds access to power.

Power changes people also. Nothing is more evident than the elected official who finds themselves in a bind with the promises that they have made, and are unable to fulfill their promises or commitments. They begin to enjoy the luxuries of office, and they change. However the people around them will also change, in attitude, in their perceptions of the office, and in their expectations from that office. Yes power changes people. My personal involvement in the political structure allowed me to watch people change as they where elevated from one position to another whereby the level gave them more power.

Certainly **there is a change to people by illness**.

Strong vigorous people become weak, and are unable to function. Strokes take away the beauty of the flesh, and sometimes of the soul, as it takes away the voice, and the use of the limbs or other functional parts of the body. Cancer will take a healthy body, and eat away until it is skin, and bone, and acquires a great deal of pain. People change from skinny to fat, from great joy to great depression, from trust to deceit, from laughter to bitterness.

Culture change. I can remember my father ploughing the field with an old one-furrow plough, pulled by an ox. There are not many people living in North America today who can remember farming with the ox. Time passed, and dad saved enough to buy a horse, and eventually a small tractor. Not at all like the powerful machines used on today's modern farms where tractors have cabs with air conditioning, stereo players, cb's, and wireless phones. Yes cultures change as the **customs change**. We have gone from the oxcart to the speeding automobile; from the propeller aeroplane to the dynamic jet that breaks the speed of sound. My dad spent five years in the Royal Canadian Air Force, a greater part of that time he was a Master Mechanic who serviced these mighty war planes. He always gave the message, that which you are allowed to see, is always twenty years behind that which is on the drawing board ready to be released. One can barely imagine the things yet to come.

Technology ever consistent to change. When one considers the technology used in the strategy opposing Iraq, we can only hope that which we cannot yet see will be used for the good of mankind and not to our detriment.

Also I remember the first telephones with what was called a party line, that had fifteen families connected to one system, and you could listen to fourteen different families as each made their calls or someone called them. Each call would ring on all fifteen phones; and many did listen to the other calls. Homes that subscribed would receive a large wooden box to hang upon the wall. Within this box was the apparatus to receive, and send your voice. The exterior of this ungraceful wall hanging ornament, had a long protruding, cone shaped, fixture that stuck squarely into your face as you spoke into it. At the side of this box was a fork like piece that held another cone like ornament attached to a long wire, and was to be held to ones ear in order to receive the other parties voice. On the opposite side of this box there was placed a small toy like crank, this was to be spun rapidly to notify the operator to whom you wished to speak. It also made a ringing sound that could be heard by your fourteen neighbours; and that often became the invitation to pick up and listen.

Today we can call anywhere in the world with a simple push of a button.

You may screen the calls you wish to receive, and reject callers that you do not wish to talk to, and never touch the phone. We can make calls from units that have no wires whatsoever. Now we have conversations anywhere we wish with an instrument that looks like a third ear, it is simply called a cell phone. What a miracle of change there has been in that one instrument alone.

The radio, from the crystal set honed into one station, as you received the airwaves with a set of headphones, was attached to three huge batteries to assist you in hearing a fading crackling voice. Now, to the ghetto blaster tuned to hundreds of stations, and the only reason you wear the headphones now, is to lock the rest of the real world out, or because the neighbour complains about the loud noise.

Medicine has changed along with the application of health treatments.

Years ago they tried to bleed the disease from your system; later they boiled them; now they freeze for the same issues. There is no repercussion today when organs are taken from the dead to the living, while years ago it would have been attributed to witchcraft, and those practicing it, would be burned at the stake. Society condones people receiving new hearts, new lungs, and new livers. The changes in health procedures are phenomenal. Yes **procedures change**.

Even our **instruments of writing have changed**. The straight pen, with a single nib, dipped into an inkwell skillfully used by the masters, was left behind for the greater invention of the fountain pen. Then came the ball point writing instrument. It was given great opposition by the so-called elite of the day.

Bankers would not allow cheques or documents of any kind to be signed by this new ball point writer. Lawyers rejected it, educators were down on its use, and refused to encourage it. Even the governments were guilty of refusing to receive documents signed with this new instrument. Today the ballpoint pen is an integral part of our society. It is the victor of change. Not to mention the tremendous change from typewriter, to the computer age, in which we now live.

There will also be some spiritual changes I would like to talk to you about, as recorded in 1 Corinthians 15: 51 - 52; *Behold, I show you a mystery; We shall not all sleep, but we shall all be changed, In a moment, in the twinkling of an eye, at the last trump: for the trumpet shall sound, and the dead shall be raised incorruptible, and we shall be changed.*

This thought here has definitely taken wings as it soars into the heavenlies to give us the intuitive sight of God's purpose for his people.

We must also look at *2 Corinthians 5: 17; 'Therefore if any man be in Christ, he is a new creature: old things are passed away; behold, all things are become new.*

When a person makes the ultimate decision to come to God's

altar, and accept his son Jesus Christ as their personal saviour, there is a change. That change will show in your lifestyle, and give you an inner peace that you never before experienced. I cannot explain what your feelings will be, however I will share with you what the change was to me. It was as though darkness fled, and left a brilliant white light in my life. I saw the difference in life, and my world had changed into something worthwhile. I did not witness some heavenly apparition surrounding me. There was no great heavenly music to trumpet me to the family of God. God had confronted me about my life so it was only me, as I said yes to Christ, and received all this new insight to life, as God laid a message upon the preacher's lips to touch my soul.

I still am amazed at the change, receiving Christ, made in my life. When you say yes to Jesus Christ, he will change your life. Your attitude will change, and the way you view all things around you. People, and places, love, and joy, will take on a new meaning.

When Jesus was here; he touched people, and changed them. The blind could see, the lame could walk, the leper was made whole, and the demon possessed became happy. Still today, Jesus touches people, through the new birth. When you accept Christ, you are saved from sin, and eternal damnation, to the lake of fire and brimstone. Christ needs to change you to be an active witness to the gospel of salvation.

In the gospel of John 1: 12; We read; But as many as received him, to them gave he power to become the sons of God, even to them that believe on his name.'

Isn't that a marvelous promise?

Too often we only think of Christ as the one crucified, but he was also resurrected, that we might have eternal life. As Christians we believe that. However we must venture further along, and realize that God says we shall be his sons. What a marvelous changes that will be.

There is also a change in growth in grace.

2 Peter 3: 18; But grow in grace, and in the knowledge of our Lord and Saviour Jesus Christ. To Him be glory both now and forever. Amen.

Growth in this area can only come from worship as we gather

together in our churches in faithfulness, in tithes and offerings, by bible reading, and daily prayer. All these things will give you assurance of growth in grace, and knowledge.

Satan is a real person, and is the father of lies. He will have you read anything except God's word the bible. When you make up your mind to spend time reading God's word, Satan will bring other things into your life to discourage you from that time, and try desperately to interfere with your time with God. Simply apply the words of Christ, Get thee behind me Satan, saying this in the name of Jesus, Satan can do nothing else but flee. You must set a time aside to read God's word. With that we are promised growth daily, by prayer, by communication with our Father in heaven.

Daniel stood praying to his living God at the window, in a loud voice. He was commanded to stop. He refused, and was cast into a den of lions. God shut their mouths. Daniel had victory in prayer. A change will take place when we are dedicated to prayer.

Today people try to stop the Christian from praying suggesting it is an infringement upon their rights. They fail to recognize the right of the Christian to pray as he or she will, and they totally ignore God's command to pray to him for a blessing. We need to continue disturbing the unbeliever with our fervent, and unceasing prayer. Daniel was willing to give up his life and go to prison, before giving up prayer. Prayer is the greatest witness of God's action.

Luke 9: 29; tells of prayers changing even Jesus.

And as he prayed, the fashion of His countenance was altered, and his raiment was white and glistening.

A prayer in touch with God changed his countenance; changed the very aura around him. If prayer can change even Jesus, think on how it can change your life. One must, at any cost, seclude themselves daily, and commit their life to prayer.

Another **change will take place when Christ returns** for us.

In our text 1 Corinthians 15: 51-52; we read; Behold I show you a mystery, we shall not all sleep; but we shall be changed, in a moment in the twinkling of an eye - - - .

I have met clergymen who have admitted to their ignorance of the second coming of our Lord Jesus Christ. Man may portray all his wisdom, and all his knowledge, but it will not put him in the good grace of our saviour. Men who claim theological status, and cannot tell you about Christ's intention to return, simply know nothing of the bible.

The next semi - intelligent question may be; When is he coming?

Many have predicted, and dared to set dates, because of their ignorance of scripture, and disbelief of God's word. The bible is explicit when telling about the return of our saviour Jesus himself made it very clear.

in Matthew *24: 36; but of that day and hour knoweth no man, no, not the angels of heaven, but my Father only.*

Again in the same chapter verse 42, Christ re-emphasizes.

'Watch therefore: for you know not what hour your Lord doth come.'

How sad it is that Christians fall into the trap of giving the time of Christ's return, when he has made it abundantly clear, man does not, and cannot, know these things. May God forgive their sacrilegious trespass. It is an absolute that you can rest assured, when someone stands on a time, and date, of Christ's return, and calls it prophecy, they are cult, and non Christian. They spout that which is not of Christ. They are of the lot that will cry, Lord! Lord! and shall not enter into the Kingdom of Heaven. They claim to receive a message from God. But their message, when God finally speaks to them will be that of Matthew *7: 23; And then will I profess unto them, I never knew you: depart from me you workers of iniquity.*

The devil believes in God, and trembles. We do not know when Christ's return will be, but upon that great calendar of eternity, the Father has circled a date. The angels do not know, but on that day, Jesus will come for his own.

Are you able to say, even so come Lord Jesus, without fear of being left behind?

What will happen when he comes for us in the air?

Hear the great words from 1 Thessalonians 4: 16 - 17;

For the Lord himself shall descend from heaven with a shout, with the voice of the archangel, and with the trump of God: and the dead in Christ shall rise first. Then we which are alive, and remain shall be caught up together with them in the clouds, to meet the Lord in the air: and so shall we be ever with the Lord.

Our text tells us that **we shall all be changed**.

What kind of a change?

Why it will be the change every Christian has looked forward to, and wants. No more sorrows, no more heart aches, no more tears, no more loneliness, no more worry, no more arguments with those that reject your saviour, no more physical pain, no more sickness, all negatives will disappear, and no longer be a part of our lives. What a beautiful change that will be.

Hear the word of the Lord, 1 John 3: 2; *Beloved, now we are the sons of God, and it doth not yet appear what we shall be: but we know that, when he shall appear, we shall be like him; for we shall see him as he is.*

I have had people tell me that they have seen Jesus. My simple follow up question to that is, What did he look like?

Generally I have been met with a surprised expression, and little or no explanation, because they really have not seen Jesus at all. Others believe the artist's concept, such as De Vinci, or the more widely used concept of Solman's. The fact remains that these are simply conjured up ideas of what the artist perceives Christ to be. We may assume that Jesus will be a person of beauty and love, and of tenderness and compassion, But know this, he is altogether lovely, and we shall be changed to be like him. There are many great Christian leaders today, but none like Jesus. There are some that we are not sure we would like to be in heaven with, but thanks be to God, we shall all be changed.

How long will this change take?

Why it will happen in the twinkling of an eye. Believe God, it will happen as he has set out his plan and put it in place. All of our bad points will vanish. Although we were in an unworthy state, Christ saved us, and made us worthy, through the shedding of his blood. He washed the slate clean. He took away the guilt, and the right to dump negatives into our lives.

We are living in a world of change. But there is one who never changes; he is the same yesterday, today, and forever. A changeless Christ, in a changing world. He is the same loving caring Jesus. Is he saviour of your heart and life?

The change comes when we allow Jesus to work in us. He ever knocks at the door of the unbelieving heart. He can change your life, he can change your future. Trust him just now. He is able to direct your destiny with his forgiving love. Any changes that you work in your life, holds no credit with God, he loves you as you are, and only your acceptance of his son as your saviour, will allow a real change to take place in your life. A wonderful thing about Christ, he loves me where I am at, in the present, not for what I will be, but for what I am now. Again we read in God's word.

Matthew 11: 28; *Come unto me, all ye that labour and are heavy laden, and I will give you rest.*

Christ offers you a rest that will change you. No other man made programme could come close to what he offers for you. Come and serve him, while you can.

Accept the challenge to serve the Lord Jesus Christ today. He says, for this cause I lay down my life. He is not willing that any should perish; but that all might come to repentance. Be ready for that change to take place in your life, and walk assured of eternity with Christ.

* * * * *

Dearly Beloved

How that they told you there should be mockers in the last time, who should walk after their own ungodly lusts. These be they who separate themselves, sensual, having not the spirit. But ye, beloved, building up yourselves on the most holy faith, praying in the Holy Ghost, Keep yourselves in the love of God, looking for the mercy of our Lord Jesus Christ, unto eternal life. Jude 18-21.

Verse 3; *Beloved, when I gave all diligence to write unto you of common salvation, It was needful for me to write unto you, and exhort you that ye should earnestly contend for the faith, which was once delivered unto the saints.*

Three times Jude addresses the readers as beloved, vss 3, 17, 20. Paul used the same terminology frequently in connection with a synonym for brothers. This word is used in three senses in the New Testament; 1. It describes Jesus as peculiarly the object of God's love in his role as Messiah. 2. It expresses God's attitude towards those who have been reconciled to him. 3. It is used of the relationship Christians sustain toward one another.

But, beloved, remember ye the words which were spoken before of the Apostles of our Lord Jesus Christ; But ye, beloved, building up yourselves on your most Holy faith, praying in the Holy Ghost.

Although there tends to be much controversy about the Holy spirit, I believe that it is supposed to direct us in our approach to God the Father as he brings us to the praying position to surrender our helplessness before the mightiness of our Father. So Jude instructs the believers about those entering in to deceive the established believer with an attempt to abrogate the action of the Church. He sees here some of the action that is evident today. The world practices compassion without giving the credit to God for his gift of this emotion. While the unbelievers put to work the identification of the church, they change the rules to deny the acknowledgement of the heavenly Father. One must admit that the actions of some unbelievers toward their fellowman's need, often put the Christian community to shame. It is shrugged off by the churches who claim they are only obligated to give the gospel. There is an element of truth to that, however the gospel includes compassion, love for the unlovable, care for the needy, and a multitude of areas that the world cannot possibly fulfill, but it is a must for the Christian to be all inclusive. When you witness those in the church who only play service to the social order and leave God out, Jude warns that we need to pray hard about those things in order for God to allow us the wisdom to eject their type of unchristian thinking from within our believer's community.

When we allow ourselves to take the initiative to act on God's behalf we shall surely fall into true Holiness before him. That is the place where we will practice true humility as we allow others needs to take precedent over our preconceived ideas of what would make us better people. We will then acknowledge the fact that we can change no one, as only God can change people. Those people will not have the change to transformation until they are able to accept Jesus Christ as their personal saviour.

The preacher here does not denounce, rather he seeks to win, and save, the great objective of the gospel to establish it's ambassadors as men called to be reconciled to a living God of love.

Matthew 5: 17b; I am not come to destroy, but to fulfill.

Jude simply says, do not be taken off guard by what is happening; be realistic, these things have happened before. When Christians face opposition it is an indication of the reality of the issues between Christ and his enemies. People themselves often fail in appropriating God's mercy, and receive his meaningful blessings. Christian controversy can be creative, but Jude admonishes us to build on our faith by praying. A strong faith alone can make the infection of heresy sterile. Continue building your life on a Holy Faith, a faith set aside from all else. Build on the foundation that has been laid, Jesus Christ. The uninformed mind is usually captured by dangerous propaganda. Uncommitted emotions are easily swayed, and the will becomes enslaved to false Masters.

Pray in the Holy Spirit; meaning be aware that you are indwelt with the Spirit as we ask in Christ's name. The Holy Spirit alone can teach persons how to pray and what to pray. Somewhere a theologian named Calvin states that the Spirit arouses men to pray. The Holy Spirit is the inward teacher of the Christian who helps us to discern deep things of God, and the Spirit leads us into all truth, and brings us into a proper dependence upon God. Keep yourselves in the love of God, looking for the mercy of our Lord Jesus Christ unto eternal life.

What a challenge we face in this statement to keep ourselves in the love of God. This involves laborious activity. No room here for those who wish to play games with religion. There is claimed here a consciousness of love that will never let us go. To believe in it is to defeat the elements that oppose our Christian walk. It requires effort if God's love and power are to be effective in us. Jude affirms that we are to continue to look for the mercy of Jesus our Lord and saviour. The Christ that gives to us a crowning glory. Be humble, be expectant, be confident and of some having compassion, making a difference. Be compassionate to the poor in spirit, the victim of lies and heresies.

V 23; And others save with fear, pulling them out of the fire; hating even the garment spotted by flesh.

Convince some of their worldly wretchedness; snatch some from the fiery pits of hell. But in all things have mercy with fear, and love the person, while hating the manner of person they have become. Love the sinner - Hate the sin. The Christian is his brother's keeper. He is identified with all his brothers and sisters in sin, and salvation. Believers, are duty bound to bring the gospel to unbelievers in such a way that it becomes a real way for each one who takes time to hear. Even though we need to be cognizant of our own salvation there arises the need to groom our lives to lift others to God's platform of life everlasting. For their sake, we too must consecrate ourselves, as did our Lord. We are not to be saved to glory in our religion; we are saved to serve.

1 Corinthians 9: 20 - 22; *And unto the Jews I became as a Jew, that I might gain the Jews, to them that are under the law, as under the law, that I might gain them that are under the law; 21To them that are without law, as without law, [being not without law to God, but under the law to Christ,] that I might gain them that are without law. 22To the weak became I as weak, that I might gain the weak: I am made all things to all men, that I might by all means save some.*

This verse capsules the need we have to serve God to a greater degree. It leaves us without excuse for reluctant witness. The final word on the deviant, is not condemnation; But Redemption,- through a convincing argument, identifying mercy vigorous encounter, strong exposure of error to the clear penetration of light, and truth, about the one and only true God, and his Son Jesus Christ our Lord and saviour.

Know ye not that they which run a race run all, but one receives the prize? So run that ye may obtain.

The last word in this letter to praise God. The need for Jesus, the only one who can present you faultless before God. the only one who is able to keep you from falling, is the wise god who has in the first instant given you a new life with strength to carry on the fight. He challenges each of us to be competent in our following by taking serious our responsibilities to further the Gospel of the son of the living god.

Without his saving blood; all our hoping, working, praying, is in vain.

Psalm 127: 1; *Except the Lord build the house, they labour in vain that build it; except the Lord keep the city, the watchman wakes but in vain*

* * * * *

Favour With God

—◁∅∅∅▷—

And in the sixth month the angel Gabriel was sent from God unto a city of Galilee, named Nazareth, to a virgin espoused to a man whose name was Joseph, of the house of David; and the virgin's name was Mary. And the Angel came unto her, and said, Hail, thou that art highly favoured, the Lord is with thee: blessed art thou among women. Luke 1: 26-28.

The Christian life is a complicated life, and does not wreak of the simplicity that some preachers and evangelists would lead you to believe. The Christian story is far less than simple. The Christian walk is a walk of complexities, and it will take you through crisis, frustration, sorrow, gladness and joy. The Christian life requires thoughtfulness, and much patience as we consider God in his fullness. To be Christian one must embrace a magnetism, and be constantly drawn as a follower to implement those actions, which please God.

Luke 1: 30, reads, And the angel said unto her, Fear not, Mary: for thou hast found favour with God.

To raise the ire of the armchair theologian, let me point out that Mary is not and was never intended by God to be, selected over and above us. She was simply the person selected to fulfill God's purpose in a special way within a particular time frame; similar to those God chooses today to further his will through the gospel or good news of his son and his mission. At the same time, or a few months previous, he had also selected Elizabeth to mother John the Baptist. It is without error that we see Elizabeth had also found favour with God. We read later in the new testament of John himself finding favour with God; yet in humility he conceded that the one who comes after him, meaning Christ, he was not worthy to unlatch his shoe laces. The fact remains that two women are brought to our attention having found favour with God. It appears we are drawn to these stories that we may see the completeness of Christ entering into the human realm.

The world would lead you to believe, that favour with God leads to a life of ease and prosperity, and much pleasure. Oftentimes we find the Christian community living out this myth, and failing miserably to come to grips with the reality of serving Christ in a Christless society. More than likely you will see God's blessings, and favour come through desperately difficult times. God's favour will come at a time the unbelieving worlds advice to you is to leave the church because of the insensitivity of Jobs friends found there. When you are challenged for your witness, you must, as Jacob as he wrestled with the angel, cling for a blessing, and you will find favour with God.

People accept God's favour in the disappointments found on the road to success, where they find elements that direct them to summon a lost courage that allows them to endure, and when they reach their pinnacle, will wonder how they ever accomplished so much. Thus it may be attributed to the favour of God rather than the direction in our walk.

In saying that, I do believe that the Christian can be oppressed by Satan but never possessed for Satan cannot dwell in the same temple as the Holy Spirit. It is then we may find the favour of God as we are delivered from that oppression. We can be emotionally fractured, and spiritually bruised, but submitting to the Holy Spirit, who dwells within us we can be healed from broken dreams as we find favour with God.

The world in consternation seeks a solution other than God. There is the ever present idea of comfort and ease that will be the ultimate in peace. But God's favour quite often brings us to the place of challenge that may come in a crisis situation. One that the world cannot handle, and most Christians may believe that God would not allow. However, we must realize that crisis does not come from Satan, but from God, as he continues to mould us to what he would have us be. When our faith is put to a real test we recognize the favour of God. We must be careful not to label the happenings in our life as spiritual experiences, because we generate a transformation in Christ, and not an experience.

Transformation in our lives can be summed up in verses found after the visitation of the Angel to Mary First the question, what manner of salutation, or of what spirit is this?

Secondly the question, of how, in verification of the action; Thirdly, the identification of the giver, God of the impossible; and the final act for transformation, complete submission to the living God. When we are careful to recognize God where he is at, dealing with us at our level, we will not need to reach some unreachable height nor level of achievement, he will transform our lives into living lights with his word. Sometimes we are blinded by our new consciousness of God. If you have ever been put upon by a camera bug that likes to catch you by surprise and snaps your picture with a flashbulb, you will have experienced a momentary blindness. So it is when God comes into our lives to use us in his work, we may suffer from his light with a momentary blindness, then we see clearly our surroundings, that will include the image of God with the task he has laid before us. Challenged by this new light a desire fills us to walk His way, and we may very well ask, how; and Christ reminds us that He is the way, the truth and the life, and that no one comes to the father but by Him. Let us share in the beauty of the Angels' answer in Luke 1: 35; *the Holy Ghost shall come upon thee, and the power of the Highest shall overshadow thee: therefore also that holy thing which shall be born of thee shall be called the Son of God.*

The voice of God speaks to our inability to achieve His goals on our own. Mary of herself was unable to perform that which God required of her. Her human frailty and lack of understanding of that which God would accomplish is very clear that she could not produce the requirement of God. But the Angel speaks to her ineptness and gives assurance, and brings peace to the soul, by that unmerited action we call grace.

The Holy Spirit shall come upon thee; here speaking to Mary of the way conception would be acquired. Mary here, given heavenly helpful information. She could not conjure up in her mind some methodology of how she would make this come to pass. There was no emotional problem here, she had not received instruction from some committee. She was having a conversation with a heavenly body, as God had planned. The Angel delivered the message, and Mary submitted her body to the Holy Spirit, because God required her to do so, and she conceived and bore the Son of God. One thing we can count on is that, nothing is impossible with God. That is a conviction that we must be ever conscious of, and allow it to remain real in the Christian life. The crowning factor here is obedience, Mary obeyed God. She did not waver with the thought of the consequence of being a downtrodden outcast of society; she simply obeyed the God of life. So we, even in crisis with rejection of man looming before us, need to humble ourselves in any event, and continue in obedience through Jesus Christ our Lord, carefully putting our lives into the hands of God.

Oh the need for the followers of Christ to respond as Mary responded in her final words to the messenger from God; 'be it unto me according to thy word'. With this statement the contemporary life of many Christians flash before us as they can only wrongly respond saying, 'we have acted according to our word, and God you had best fit into that slot.

There is an apathy to God's word that leads to a non hearing of the messenger of God. We generate a blatant disregard for Christian leaders, teachers, preachers, and evangelists. The bible tells us in 2 Timothy 4: 3, *For the time will come when they will not endure sound doctrine; but after their own lusts shall they heap to themselves teachers, having itching ears.*

The assurance of God's truth does not lie in analysis, nor speculation. The indwelling of the Holy Spirit directs in depth, and the soul knows God has called us to a new commitment. It is about knowing that God is still in control, and his laid out plan of salvation works through his son Jesus Christ. This is the door to knowledge and truth to discover the word of life, and in it find fulfillment. God's grace leads us out of a world of lies, that we might learn to speak the truth.

Christ came in love, with peace, bearing gifts. His gifts, love salvation, eternal life, and a heavenly home. Yet the world rejects these gifts and align themselves with to perpetrate lies around the birth of Christ. The sad commentary is, the contemporary Christian adds to and encourages those same lies.

So we celebrate God giving his son to give us salvation. We celebrate coming to Jesus Christ knowing whatever trespass we have committed is forgiven. Whatever has transpired in our lives, God has found favour with us. Whatever the crisis may have been, whatever tribulations, we still hear the words of God's messenger saying, God has found favour in us.

Our commitment to God is in fact to witness for him. We are to take the message of truth to the unbelieving world. That truth, Christ came to seek and to save that which is lost. The truth, *that God so loved the world, that he gave his only begotten son, that whosoever believeth in him should not perish, but have everlasting life. For God sent not his son into the world to condemn the world; but that the world through him might be saved.* John 3: 16-17.

My challenge then to you, pick up the word of God, the bible, and read; but in so doing you must tell others about Jesus Christ. That is your duty, your concern, your witness, your challenge, to present Christ to others; regardless of the consequences, or bruises, or rejection of so called friends, it is imperative that you name the name of Jesus Christ and bring his good news to others.

* * * * *

God's Morality

And that ye study to be quiet, to do your own business, and to work with your own hands, as we commanded you; That you may walk honestly to them that are without, and that you may have lack of nothing. 1 Thessalonians 4: 11-12.

There are times when we get so busy at twisting events to suit ourselves in the correcting of other's affairs that we forget the whole purpose of God calling us into eternal life with him. He calls us primarily to get our own house in order. Leave behind lies, and deceit of imagery for the success of the world in order to profess Christ before an unbelieving world. Pay more attention to our own affairs instead of meddling in the affairs of others. We cannot change any person, only God changes people. We are in God's service simply to lift others up in encouragement with the gospel. We must leave behind our "fix it" attitude to give to others a substance by which they can build their own lives upon. We must make the honest attempt to help people adjust to the transformation that takes place when they put their trust in the saviour Jesus Christ.

In many cases of worship in today's contemporary Christian community there is so much noise presented as a theatrical performance and displacement of God. Implemented in service a counterfeit methodology in the worship time, that one cannot concentrate deep enough to touch the hem of the garment with a quiet mind. Therefore searchers simply walk away without reaching that peace that is needed. They lose the ability in that theatrical nonsense to become more familiar with the life in Christ for which they search, and would desire to live. Quietness can embellish extreme patience which a Christian needs. To exercise the quietness that is talked about in God's word is lost in the adaptation to the worlds needs. The Christian in seeking out God's direction must be endowed with serious reflection on the quietness of God. Worship services with the so-called worship team appear to believe that the more noise they can make the greater impact they will make. Let me assure you , that concept is contrary to what god requires. Who has heard God roll of drums when he sets the sun, or sound a trumpet when the moon rises eloquently across the blue waters. God, in his Majesty, created the quietness for his most interesting innovations into the lives of his creation. Even the animals of the wild run in fear when noise is about them. How much less does man require a boisterous entourage for worship. In these verses, Paul states precisely what he means by walking so as to please God. how ye ought to walk and to please God, so ye would abound more and more. Herein is a definite link of morality to the Christian walk in faith. The truth of Christ in the Christian life and behaviour must go hand in hand because of that which we read in verse three, *For this is the will of God, even your sanctification, that you should abstain from fornication.*

The terminology of sanctification simply means, to be set aside for Holiness, to make free from sin, to make productive spiritual blessing. Paul is warning the Thessalonians they cannot be spiritual, and at the same time be sexually promiscuous. He reminds them their new faith embraces chastity in the unmarried, and absolute faithfulness in a monolithic relationship of marriage. This presented something of a new lifestyle to them, so was in the real sense a revolutionary teaching. For the religion from which they had turned kept at its centre, phallic rites. They worshipped the Phallus. This was a practice to pay homage to the reproductive organs of man. It was a symbol of generative power. This led to Polygamy being the rule rather than the exception. Concubines were widely accepted as a worthy part of life and was treated as honourable before God. Never had it been considered as an act of shame, rather it was given to pride as it was part and parcel to the temple worship program. However Christ's intervention in lives demanded consecration and Holiness. Paul as a servant of Jesus Christ shows in his letter an absolute with no compromise. His demands are backed with three reminders.

1. Their call to Holiness that entails a clean cut with immorality.
2. Impurity is a grave sin, and the judgment of God is upon it.
3. That no man go beyond and defraud his brother in any matter. because the Lord is the avenger of all such,

Impurity is, in the final analysis, a despising of God. Clearly here is established a relationship between religious truth, and personal conduct. The age old adage could be aptly quoted here, action speaks louder than words. It would appear that our contemporary society suffers from some of the same godlessness experienced by the Thessalonians. Some difficulty exists in defining the difference between that which is good and that which is evil. Little attention is paid to the right or wrong of many given situations. There is a tendency to sin, easily to live in terms of our lower stages. We can do no wrong. Look around, the world is in utter chaos because there is no recognition of Christ's standards. Finally when we suffer some set back, we wonder,

How does God know?

We further attempt to erode our guilt by hiding within some terminology such as neurosis, or psychosis, an action of the subconscious, frustrations at the complexity of life. Know this, which before God these hiding places of shattered excuse shall vanish and will not cover us from His judgment. It is then you shall be reminded of your rejection of the blood of His son Jesus Christ. Despite all our callousness and evasiveness, our guilt will not disappear. Continually, it breaks through our well built wall of stubbornness, and rises up before us in all it's ugliness bringing with it all its fearful consequences. Guilt is the one emotion that exposes and condemns our contemporary generations, as it did Judah.

For God hath not called us unto uncleanness, but unto Holiness. To direct those around about us to be family oriented, and to work for the pleasure of God, and not for the pleasures of sin, is our commission. The unbelieving world is obsessed with sensual advertising and display of sexual desire in an attempt to exploit mankind, driving them to seek a peace where they will find only turmoil and emptiness. Others employ the sensuality of always living on a high, or on top of the mountain; while in fact the reality of life survives in the valley for there are none that live on mountain peaks. Settlements of communities are found in the valley.

That is where Christ walks with those who will accept him as personal saviour to turn around and follow him. Yet so many choose to worship the non lasting entity of a high of sensation rather than the ever present God of transformation who gives an everlasting settled heart of peace. It was in the homes of the first Christian disciples where congregations where formed, and Christians were organized. To them the home became the social unit upon which the church builds. It is the only enduring and healthy foundation on which any country's stability can be built. History proves that when the family unit breaks down, so then does the structure of the nation.

What can the church do, and further what must each Christian contribute to save the moral destruction of our people?

What can we do to save the family home unit?

How can we help our Nation to survive the moral holocaust?

[a] We must be consistent in emphasizing God's expectations according to His word, the bible. We must be relentless about the fact that God has called us unto Holiness. We must indeed show that God is consistent in His judgment on an immoral lifestyle. We must continue to put forth the message that God is a God of love, and live it out to others. To refuse to do so is in fact a denial of the very existence of a living God.

[b] We must teach the necessity of the way through Jesus Christ, who claimed to be the Son of God and said ' I am the way, the truth, and the life, and no man comes unto the Father except by me'. We must be ever ready to teach Christ, as the forerunner in our communities as well as our personal lives.

[c] With Christ as our central focus we must encourage all to establish the family as the root of our society as God has originally planned.

[d] We must encourage members of the church to spend more family quality time and cease fragmenting the fellowship into other factions. The church must come to grips with the break-up of the family unit. When we arrive to worship we are quickly dispersed into men's groups, women's groups, youth groups, as low as the

nursery groups. We have become an organisation that is bent on separation rather than obligating ourselves to build together for the strength in worship to a Holy God.

The Church is not without guilt for its contribution to the breakdown of family worship, and family togetherness. We chomp at the bit to follow the unbelieving world's example rather than to allow God's type of family building to happen within our church. We must encourage our member's back to the family altar in the home, and to refill the family pew in the church as we together worship our God. Herein is an element many modern day churches close their ears, and eyes to, in their obvious greed to perform in a theatrical manner hoping to impress attendance. We read, that you study to be quiet, and to do your own business, and to work with your own hands, as we commanded you.

[a] Be still and know that I am God; Quietness is a requirement of God. We see many churches so busy making noise for man God gets left out in the cold. We are not called to shout and holler in the worship place, nor to make great guttural sounds that are unacceptable to hearers. Here the writer points out that we are to study to be quiet.

[b] Also we are admonished to attend to our own affairs. In other words, mind your own business, make yourself sufficient in the community where you exist.

[c] Work with your hands; not flailing at the air like unto some shadow boxer, but to do work with them, not reaching up to God; but reaching out to your community to help build and preserve the family unit. Work with your hands to destroy the immorality of polluted Godless minds. Build with your hands the Christ founded attachment to life. A life that brings a solid structure of the family unit that will worship together. Pursue ordinary vocations with a quiet mind.

* * * * *

Go   d

But they have not all obeyed the gospel. For Isaiah saith, Lord who hath believed our report? So then faith cometh by hearing, and hearing by the word of God. But I say, Have they not heard? Yes verily, their sound went into all the earth, and their words unto the ends of the world. Romans 10: 16-18.

In years gone by we could proudly expound on the Christianity of our blessed Country, but in this day of technology with Governments who treat God as some abstract entity we can only submit that the tragedy of heedlessness has never been played out more poignantly than any time in history. They have not heeded the gospel of Jesus Christ for they have adopted the deafness of the unbeliever. We have witnessed those of an public demeanour have blatantly ignored the proclamation of God's message. Even in the small segments of scattered Christian Communities we find unnumbered people grow up with only a nodding acquaintance with the Jesus of the Christian faith. They often adopt the lingo of religious orientation learning a essential survival vocabulary, but misunderstand its essential affirmations. In accepting the outward form they refuse the truth which allows the transformation to take place within their own lives. Perhaps the trouble lies with the believer who refuses to be insistent in their convictions. We need to take the position of grasping more firmly the truth of our own convictions, and disallowing others to take it away from us through our negligence. Let us continue to be persistent in presenting a work with a message that awakens faith.

Sorrow of the soul, brings us to recognize the abstention of attention to the word of God. The world again on the brink of war having forged ahead with man's plans without taking heed to the disasters which will follow.

We busy ourselves with a counterfeit attempt to satisfy the plight of our Nations in the free world, but turn a deaf ear to the word of God that has reached to the ends of the earth. Paul, here quotes Isaiah when he says they have not obeyed the gospel. It appears that the world has not learned the elements that really bring disaster to the world is not wars, but deliberate disobedience to the word that God has sent forth to the people who refuse to acknowledge the realism of it. When we astutely observe that which is happening around us today one can truly identify to the same dilemma that the believers faced in Isaiah's and again in Paul's time.

As the elements of our day move with a tendency to de-christianise our society, our thought must turn to the fact of survival of the freedom to worship the Lord Jesus Christ in our Nation. At present we find a vague tolerance of the message we preach, but little in depth soul searching as to the value of the message. All must share in the blame for this intolerance to the Christian message because the similar semblance of misunderstanding is evident in many congregations of the modern day churches The nominal Christian lacks interest in the application of the word that they have heard. Most church attendees learned the colloquial version of spiritual dialogue, and rarely become knowledgeable of that personal touch with the saviour. Therefore their knowledge of Christian faith stays at a very low level. Their peripheral knowledge allows them a part in the community, but not enough to please the living God. The proclamation of Christ is declared by preaching that which differentiates itself from lecture or teaching of morals, or intellectual artistic presentation. Preaching is generally set apart by the stimulating application of the need for Jesus Christ in ones life. There needs to be the reminding influence of preaching that consistently sets Christ foremost in the minds of the hearers.

A man and woman where sitting at a sidewalk cafe, they observed the crumbs upon the ground as three small birds feasted there. Soon they were joined by a big bird, and soon another large bird joined them; seeing this the lady decided to use her crackers to toss more crumbs to the birds. It was not long until there appeared another two large birds then again four more large birds. Seeing the build up of birds she decided rather than continue to give the crumbs, she would purchase a loaf of bread, which she did.

How many birds do you think came?

Not one. We are eating the crumbs.

There is a hunger for the word of God. Statistics show that most of us choose to ignore the word of God on a daily basis. This wilful starvation simply feeds this hidden hunger which has already resulted in a kind of barren bankrupt existence for many today. We have become a people who are selfish, materialistic, and hard of hearing. The bible ought to change our thinking, our behaviour.

Evangelism needs to recapture the priorities of the gospel to put forth the word to the luke warm soul, and remind them there is a need to catch fire for the spreading of the gospel of Jesus Christ. Let us set out in boldness to deliver the message in the splendour to which it was intended. We must refuse to be passive with God's word, but be ever ready to speak out for the redemption of the lost soul.

Even in the 'Great Commission' of Matthew 28: 19 - 20; *Go ye therefore, and teach all nations, baptizing them in the name of the Father, and of the Son, and of the Holy Ghost: Teaching them to observe all things whatsoever I have commanded you: and, lo, I am with you always, even unto the end of the world. Amen*

Words from the very lips of Christ is a recurrent theme in his teaching as he integrated the world to a greater gift of life everlasting. Never before in history have we seen a more complete integration of the races of the world as we observe today. Yet there is a failure to attach it to what Christ had already put forth to in fact reach the whole world with his word. The alternative rears its ugly head in terrorism now visible as it puts upon us the indelible imprint of Christ or chaos.

We see a principle that the church is to teach the nations. Not the Nation teaching the church. Paul's warning is specific in Colossians 2: 8; *Beware lest any man spoil you through philosophy and vain deceit, after the tradition of men, after the rudiments of the world, and not after Christ.* With God, with Jesus, there is only one condition, to believe and accept that which they offer to their creation. This is an open attack on heretical teaching introduced under the banner of philosophy which lacks the substance of truth. Paul here elevates the mind to the pre-eminence of Christ to a complete world showing Christ's peacemaking power through the cross. It is now our duty to make this same statement alive within our local churches to be absorbed by every believer. There is not a movement here to criticize but simply to persuade non-believers of the truth which is put forth by the living God by his son Jesus the Christ. In order to do that there must be found a mutuality by which we may identify the truth of God. This is the high plain of wisdom born of love whereby the Christian is able to present the truth while not having to suffer from its defenders. At the same time being aware that the world will attempt to derail a belief in a living God, or as Paul says, spoil you. It must be noted that one can only get through to the unbeliever with a direct attitude of Christian love. We must consider building a bridge to their thoughts of coherent thinking, and making contact with them trust that God will build a path between us and their thinking to move into a clear focus of the truth of Christian thinking. Paul was not hostile to all philosophy. He had just concluded a noble statement of the centrality of Christ in the universe.

2 Timothy 2: 15; *Study to show thyself approved unto God, a workman that needeth not to be ashamed, rightly dividing the word of truth.*

Literally the Greek says, Cutting it straight. Again, Paul here is concerned about the sincerity with the approval of God, rather than the approval of man. We are not to treat God's word in a casual manner with an air of neglect, nor are we to taint the word of God shamefully by ignoring it's challenges. Study to give diligence, handle the word with authority, and not changing it to a suitable ear factor, but as it is written and prayfully considered. We are to be careful to handle the word of truth rightly.

Matthew 25: 13; *Watch ye therefore, for ye know neither the day nor the hour wherein the son of man cometh.*

Two hundred years ago Alexander Fraser Tyler, wrote, A democracy cannot exist as a permanent form of government. It can only exist until the voters discover that they can vote for themselves a larger share of from the public treasury. From that moment on the majority always vote for the candidates promising the most benefits from the public treasury, with the result that democracy always collapses over loose fiscal policy, always followed by a dictatorship. The average age of the world's greatest civilizations has been over two hundred years. These nations have progressed through this sequence, from bondage, to spiritual faith, from spiritual faith, to great courage, from courage, to liberty; from liberty, to abundance, from abundance, to selfishness; from selfishness, to complacency; from complacency, to apathy; from apathy, to dependence. From dependency, back to bondage,

God requires of us that we carry the message of the cross, Eternal life, Salvation through Christ, and His return for the saints. God requires us to tell others of the truth of Christ, and of the only unpardonable sin; that being the sin of unbelief. We are to warn the unbeliever of the burning fires of hell that await them if they will not accept Jesus Christ as their saviour.

The word of God, the bible, says in Romans 12: 2; *And be not conformed to this world: But be ye transformed by the renewing of your mind, that you might prove what is good, and acceptable, and perfect, will of God.*

One of the persistent threats of a dedicated life is the absorption of the blanket of our environment which engulfs us into a tangled web. Everyone around us sets out to organize their own lifestyle presupposing that they do not have to acknowledge God. Also they may determine to educate you in that same venue. The world does not wish to conform to that which we know to be created by God. The word conform to the unbelieving community simply implies a gradual process by which our alertness to evil is disarmed. Society, as it organizes itself apart from God, sets out to build the frail standards to abide by. We as believers some times think we have the right to like or dislike or act indifferent to that group. However when we truly absorb what God is saying we will see that we must even reflect more strongly that which God has asked us to do. There is no greater insult to God than for his followers to become complacent or tolerant about a Godless community. Intellectual, or social atmospheres simply do not comply with that which Christian communities are given instruction to project which is the complete ongoing truth of a holy and living God. Is it any wonder that secularism appears to have eaten away the graven imprint of grace.

Matt: 24:35; *Heaven and earth shall pass away, but my word shall not pass away.*

Straight and to the point are these words of Jesus. Man has, since they were spoken, attempted to dismantle them in every sense of the believer's faith. There has been the attempt to cast water of doubt that they were really meant to be said. But know this, that which God wanted recorded is there for all to see plainly. These words do not carry some mystical philosophy, but are a simple statement of truth which Christ illuminated by his response simply by being where he was at the time.

John 1: 1 - 3; *In the beginning was the Word, and the Word was with God, and the Word was God. The same was in the beginning with God. All things were made by him; and without him was not any thing made that was made.*

Here is a lesson in how to present Jesus Christ: To do that successfully, two things are required, [a] A big enough conception of him in our own minds. [b] A medium through which we can state that conception so that it comes home to those around us. Christ gives a mighty gospel; Christ is the express image of God's person. Himself divine, the very thought, and mind, and word of God, to us become alive. Christ, the mighty conqueror of sin, and death, and hell. By himself, meeting the full shock of their power, and trampling them beneath his feet. But, often in these latter days the gospel is whittled down into a tame affair with little thrill in it. The cutting edge has been blunted. That gracious New Testament figure, 'Christ' is belittled into a gracious soul who generously spent himself for others. It is a mighty gospel that Christ brings to us ample to cover every possible call upon it. Yet something more is needed, if Christ is to succeed. There is only one authentic gospel delivered to the world, eternal, unchangeable. If the gospel is to come home to folk with power they must hear it. Each in their own native language.

The church is slow to move, and heavy footed, and is apt to lag a half a generation behind times. Not so, with our Christ and his message to the soul. When this gospel took shape there was a habit of thought in the air in John 1: 1-3; it is now the easiest conception of Christ to follow. We stand, and share that Jesus of Nazareth does stand in the centre of human history that he has brought God, and man into a new relationship that he is of personal concern to every one of us, and to this hour he enshrines a truth that cannot be stated otherwise the Word of God that dwells with us is the foundation of our witness. One error I personally observe in most translations, other than the King James, is that the impact of scripture is lost because of a lack of understanding about legal structure. Most modern day translators do not, or have not comprehended the legal form impact, "the jot" nor "tittle," or perhaps as we would understand it as dotting the I's and crossing the T's; and in many places in translation have for some unknown reason changed the 'shall' to 'will', which in fact changes the intent of the rule set down.

Our law is based on God's law, and the word 'shall' indicates an absolute. It must be carried out. The word, will, in contemporary Federal, Provincial and Municipal law suggests a maybe, or a way out. The formulae is Shall = Absolute; Will = Maybe.

Matt 5: 18; For verily I say unto you, Till heaven and earth pass, one jot or one tittle shall in no wise pass from the law, till all be fulfilled.

Scriptures that ought to be a part and parcel of our vocabulary:

Food For the Soul;

Psalm 119: 11, 18, *thine word have I hid in my heart, that I might not sin against thee. Open thou mine eyes, that I might behold wondrous things out of thy law.*

Colossians 3: 16; *Let the Word of Christ dwell in you richly in all wisdom; teaching and admonishing one another in psalms and hymns and spiritual songs, singing with grace in your hearts to the Lord.*

Jeremiah 15: 16; *thy words were found and I did eat them; and thy word was unto me a joy and rejoicing of mine heart: for I am called by thy name O Lord God of hosts.*

1 Peter 2: 2; *As new born babes, desire the sincere milk of the word, that ye may grow thereby;*

Light; Proverbs 6: 23; *For the commandment is a lamp; and the law is light; and reproofs of instruction are the way of life.*

Influence: Hebrews 4: 12; *For the word of God is quick, and powerful, and sharper than any two-edged sword, piercing even to the dividing asunder the soul and the spirit, and the joints and marrow, and is a discerner of the thoughts and intents of the heart.*

Special: Matthew 7: 21; *Not everyone that saith unto me, Lord, Lord, shall enter into the Kingdom of heaven; but he that doeth the will of my Father which. is in heaven.*

Favour: John 14: 23; *Jesus answered and said unto him, if a man love me, he will keep my words: and my Father will love him, and we will come unto him, and make our abode with him.*

Are we still eating the crumbs when we could have the whole loaf?

* * * * *

He Is Risen

—⟨⟨⟨⟩⟩⟩—

And the Angel answered and said unto the woman, Fear not you: For I know that you seek Jesus, which was crucified. He is not here: for He is risen, Come; see the place where the Lord lay. And go quickly, and tell his disciples that he is risen from the dead; and behold he goeth before you into Galilee; there shall you see him: lo, I have told you. Matthew 28: 5-7.

The angel of the resurrection was an messenger of power. In this appearance the surrounding elements were beset by an earthquake with which the stone was rolled away. Upon that great rock that at one time covered the entrance of the tomb, sat the angel with a message of purity to shed a new light upon the whole world. He announced that magnificent message which delivered much freedom to the forgiven sinner, the Christ that was sought has risen.

This is the fact that sustains the Christian church throughout the years. The sign of our faith is not the crucifix; But an empty cross; not an hourglass of the aging hands of time; But an Angel at the door of the empty tomb. Let us consider anew the basis of our hope in eternal life. The life is in us, mixed with our nature

The reason men go on hoping despite every calamity, is they cannot help it. We are so born. We clear away the rubble of an earthquake with hope of a lesser disaster. A wrecked vehicle, a crashed plane, hope of life. A child may ask, What is beyond the sunset?

That is the final question for we cannot escape the surmise that there is another world 'round about our world. without that hope in us, the Resurrection hope would find no dwelling place in us. Even as the light has no use to those without eyes. It is worthwhile for this generation to remember it is almost an orphaned generation regarding the Hope of immortality.

We have been so busy with our hands, and eyes, that the things of the Spirit have grown dim. To past ages, the conviction of the next world has been stronger than the conviction of this world; But even with us, our over emphasis on the measure of sense, takes on a much different venue than that of serving a Holy God. The eternal hope remains under the stimulation of God, but Christ brought the light of life, and immortality through the gospel. Jesus not only traced the true nature of His nature, but also broke the bonds that hold men from it.

How can sinful man aspire to the presence of God?

He cannot! At least not on his own power. Man cannot forgive sins he hates. For sin is against God. Man cannot cancel the dark past, for only God can rule time. Jesus revealed God. God, in Christ, was wrestling with our sin upon the cross, and proving His power over it by the resurrection of Christ from the dead. Thus Christ, the real beckoning of our hope, through His presence Christ gave us entry to eternal life, because God raised Him from the dead. Jesus gives, new power, new insight, new love. Christ will change you.

"Why ?

He Is Risen, and we have that assurance through his sacrifice upon the cross.

Why is it that the human race has feared the sight of the dead?

The dead are dead, so they cannot hurt us, or can they?

Easter should inspire a certain kind of fear. We live in an enclosed valley called earth.

Easter takes us to the vast heights to show us a greater world than we have ever dared to dream. We are under a new responsibility. Our mortal days are no five year plan. Our Valley is now an eternal world. Christ, being alive breaks our fetters of judgment. His forgiveness now spoken on earth. Now God's own assurance, he is risen, death now wears a changed face.

1Corinthians 15: 20; *but now is Christ risen from the dead, and become the firstfruits of them that slept*

[1] As a result of that there arose humanities greatest institution,

the Church militant, and triumphant. That church was born the other side of an empty tomb. The one incontestable result of the life, death, and resurrection of Jesus Christ is the emergence of the Christian church. After that the message, and the ministry of the church, was Jesus and the resurrection. Something wonderful happened on that first Easter which lifted the gates of Empires off their hinges and turned the stream of civilization into new channels.

Something happened which gave a new date to time and a new dimension to the human soul. Something happened which has kept the church alive in the world as one of the greatest powers for good for almost two thousand years. As a result, the Christ believing Christian is freed from cynicism, and defeat, and their lives have become a sacred trust, and a magnificent adventure on the highway of eternal life. If Christ be not risen from the dead, then nothing matters, and the connotations of our larger life become worthless abstractions. It then is, as the Apostle Paul points out, *If in this life only we have hope of Christ, we are of all men most miserable.*

Easter means, God's evaluation of life. As a result death is defeated. The head that once was crowned with thorns is now crowned with glory. Our Christian faith is a resurrection faith. Our Lord is a living Lord, who faced sin, and death, and laid these grim spectres low. A resurrection faith by its very nature is unconquerable. The arms which where outstretched upon the cross, are uplifted to embrace those who dare to accept Jesus as their Saviour, the Son of God. He Is Risen. Easter is many things, it is a sleeping sentinel to awake to find no corpse, only the empty tomb. It is Mary Magdalene, standing bewildered, with her arms full of spices with no body to prepare. It is a young man in white speaking the greatest words of hope, that have ever been spoken, He is risen. It is the burning conversation during an afternoon walk on the road to Emmaus. It is a prayer meeting in the upper room suddenly interrupted by the entrance of the Saviour. John 20: 26; Then came Jesus and stood in their midst It is a day vibrant with faith worship, and with song around the world

Blessed be the God, and Father of our Lord Jesus Christ, which according to His abundant mercy has begotten us again unto a lively hope by the resurrection of Jesus Christ from the dead, to an inheritance incorruptible, and undefiled, and that fadeth not away, reserved in heaven for you.

All this then begs the question; Are you alive, and living for Jesus Christ your Lord and Saviour?

Or are you among the walking dead, those who disregard the resurrection of Him who conquered death that you might obtain eternal life, and that your sins are forgiven.

Make haste, for the time is at hand when we look to His return.

Are you ready??

He is not here, He is Risen, Come see the place where He lay Go tell everyone in your community.

Pray: O God our Father, Creator of the universe and giver of all good things: we thank thee for our home on earth and for the joy of living. We praise thee for thy love in Jesus Christ, who came to set things right, who died rejected on the cross, and who rose triumphant from the dead. Because He lives, we live to praise thee, Father, Son, and Holy Spirit, Our God forever.

Amen.

* * * * *

Unto You A Saviour

===⟨⟩⟨⟩⟨⟩===

And lo, the angel of the Lord came upon them, and the glory of the Lord shone round about them; and they were sore afraid. And the angel said unto them, Fear not: for, behold, I bring you good tidings of great joy, which shall be to all people. For unto you is born this day in the city of David a saviour, which is Christ the Lord Luke 2: 9-11.

Fulfillment of a lifetime of hope, was upon these people who long expected God to send them the cherished Messiah. Little did they know the avenue which God had so wisely chosen.

John 15: 22; If I had not come and spoken unto them, they had not had sin: but now they have no cloak for their sin.

We have learned that God throws out man's plan, tyranny, personal gain, material wealth, and selfishness. Man we find is prone to doubt, fails to follow convictions, man must learn to face the facts, that he needs a personal relationship with Christ. As we again come to this Christmas day, and throughout the festive season, the world appears to be celebrating a new birth. Joy bells ringing, love to one another being expressed, in word as well as in gift giving.

Kindness walks abroad like a white winged Angel. Today we see all that the Christian civilization could be if we were only willing to perpetrate our noblest moods and moments.

What is behind all this strange and mystic excitement?

What is behind this unusual forbearance, kindness, and helpfulness, what mighty force?

The answer, very simple, the event at Bethlehem.

Luke 2: 11; *For unto you is born this day in the city of David a Saviour, which is Christ the Lord.*

The chasm between heaven and earth had been spanned, The gulf between God and man had been bridged. Eternal silence had been broken, and God gave to the world a unique disclosure of himself, Christ was born. That explains it all. And haunting, hurting, humanity refuses the covering blood of the Christ of peace, and forgiveness. There is apparent continuous search that eludes the world today. With all the expenditures, with all the dazzling lights of the season; they fall into the elusive emptiness that a lonely Christless world offers.

Why?

Because they have not heard the message, "Unto You A Saviour."

They stampede away from the eternal gift, given by a living God. Our finest music, is but an echo to the angelic chorus. Our Christian kindness, is but a reflection of the eternal love of God, found in the gift of a Saviour. Let us then use our imagination, and think of the world without Christmas day Suppose Christ had not come.

1. The world of art would be sorely depleted. We would never had laid eyes upon Raphael's Madonna and child, nor Hoffman's, Child In the Temple, neither Holman Hunt's, Light of the World, nor would we have Da Vinci's, Last Supper, nor Munkacsy's Christ before Pilate, and we would lack Ruben's, Descent From the Cross. Let the critics tear from the walls every work of art that has been inspired, directly, or indirectly, by the Christian faith, and a price-less worth would be gone forever.

What of our Music if Christ had not come?

It is not easy to decide what music has done for our burdened world. It has lifted many burdened hearts from depression of the soul which brings to us many sordid things, It has comforted much wounded heart, and it has calmed many a stormy life.

It has been said that music is the language of Heaven. If Christ had not come, we would not have, Handle's Messiah, or Gonad's, Redemption, Gaul's, Holy City, Stainer's, St Paul. There would be no Christian Hymnology to give us the peace of heart as we sing praise to Christ and his Father. Lost would be familiar meaningful words as found in hymns like, 'The Old Rugged Cross', Rock Of Ages, Abide with me, Lead Kindly Light, How Great Thou art, Amazing Grace, Safe In The Arms of Jesus, What A Friend We Have In Jesus, and many, many more of your favourites would not exist to be sung. If some Evil genius could silence Christian influenced music; we would find ourselves living in a depleted world. The same applies to our literature, Tennyson, Charles Dickens Bunyan, even a different Shakespeare.

If we threw out of our Libraries what Bethlehem and Calvary have put into them, would they not be terribly depleted?

Augustine's confession, Dante's vision, Dwight L Moody's writings, Pilgrims Progress, along with the explosion of thousands of contemporary Christian writers

Others i.e Hawthorne, McDonald, Robert Browning, Pascal's thoughts, Kipling, Emerson, Scott, McCauley, and on, and on. Not to mentioned the non Christian authors who were indeed influenced by God's infinite plan from the manger. At least two-thirds of our Libraries would disappear

In what kind of literary world would we be living, If Christ had not come?

What would be the probable condition of the world?

Almost certain that slavery would still be with us. Slavery was not destroyed by Education, but by Love to our fellowman through Christ. But Alas! Today we live in a world that has witnessed a Revival of unbelief. Many have broken with the Christ faith and have repudiated the eternal truth of Christ-mass

Many people are not comfortable with the Christ message. They hang on to what they term as Humanism. Even that is a product of religion. You cannot praise the fruits, and despise the roots, which were established by the birth at Bethlehem, and perfectly completed at Calvary. Today we see womanhood in a different light. Now protected and honoured, no doorways closed, not harnessed to an Ox.

The birth of Christ, placed a new and imperishable dignity on motherhood. The word was made flesh and dwelt among us. Life, has had God enter it, dwelt in it died in it. Let us not allow the world to destroy it. So Christ entering our humanity judges, and condemns everything that hurts it. Redemption given by Christ delivers us from the down side of the world. It is not simply there by chance, certainly not implanted by some counterfeit happiness, definitely not a product of luck, these are not a product of some blind evolutionary product, or process, but it traces back to Christ,

Son of God, Saviour, Christ, Lord. Oh! How different it would be if Christ had not come to our world.

Have you allowed Christ come into your life?

Although we need to comply to experience in our Christ witness, and we have the need to experience of being born again. We need to affirm, that it is not an experience, it is a transformation.

Is He your Saviour?

Have you made him Christ of your heart?

Do you allow him to be the Lord of your life?

Is God on your Christmas list?

Unto you a Saviour! Exercise of love, to God, to Christ to Fellowman. If we say we have no sin, we deceive ourselves, and the truth is not in us. God's grace allows us to forget the past, when we yield the past to God's redeeming love, reaching forth unto things that is before. Reaching is an action word, it means to extend yourself beyond the range of comfort or ease. We must reach into the future, beyond our comfort range, so that we will grow and develop beyond our present capacities.

Pressing as Paul reached forward, he had a goal or a target. His energy was directed - challenged, and disciplined. He pressed toward the mark of the high calling of God in Jesus Christ. It is easy to get sidetracked, and lose sight of the goal, and forget the target.

Still looking for that Messiah. But Jesus has come. For Unto you is born this day in the city of David, a Saviour which is Jesus Christ the Lord.

We are in need of more shepherds today. Those who can go even now unto the hurting haunting society that needs more than ever to see Jesus in their heart. May we reach out and tell them the good news of a Loving God who gave himself to a selfish and unbelieving world that some might be saved from eternal damnation that was brought upon man by man. Let us go even now with the message, and bring our joy of the Lord to a dying world of unbelief. Let us also take this day to renew our own vows to continue to serve this wonderful forgiving God who loves us as we are, not for what we could be.

* * * * *

A Cause For Joy
[In The Service Of Our God]

———∞∞∞———

If any man lack wisdom, let him ask of God, that giveth to all men liberally, and upbraideth not; and it shall be given him. But let him ask in faith, nothing wavering. For he that wavereth is like a wave of the sea driven with the wind and tossed. For let not that man think that he shall receive anything of the Lord. James 1: 5-7.

When we see that which comes against the moral fibres of living a godly life we need to practice the discretion to warn others that this good opportunity passes, and it may not come around again.

The Bible gives us the texts whereby we find special rights to stand alone through certain great qualities.

What shall we do, we who have glimpsed the hidden battlement of eternity?

Life is a mystery, because it scales the unbalanced with it's laws, and interesting equations. It endows an appearance to submit itself to a rigid framework within which we live and move. That framework is like unto a wheel spinning on it's axis with no tangible track to lay hold of. The past is always returning, yet we are forbidden the fullness of knowledge. Eternity is in our hearts, but generates a homesickness. We have a brief understanding which ought to produce action on our part to satisfy the very brief present that we experience

Take therefore, what happiness you can, food, drink, labour, and rest, for these are truly God's gift to each person. Forget the haunting sense of the eternal, and seize the day at hand. Paul also had eternity in the heart with equal sense of mystery which trails around us, but he had a persuasion of the meaning of life. Jesus Christ had revealed the eternal, and Paul knew the qualities which belong to lives that have eternity in their hearts.

In the conventional sense of securing a secular position for the very first time with in our growth period, there is an absolute tendency to learn the task for which we were hired. Somehow we adopt the sensitivity of perfect production even when it takes us a while to reach that part of our position. The rules set out by the company, for which we work so diligently, never take on the element of bothersome. Instead we find a willingness to learn all the rules, and the right, and wrong way to function within the new found vocation. Once we learn the rules and follow the direction it leads us to we have the tendency to rally to the position in order to be the very best employee that the company has. That is a good thing. We build a positive atmosphere to allow the future work places to receive a credible resume from the firm when we wish to excel in further work experiences. For the most part we stay excited with our jobs as we learn to execute them in a proper way.

If you then be risen with Christ, seek those things which are above that fit into the timeless edict of whatsoever be true. We live in an world of disciplined order, but have been given by a living God an appointed place in it.

As a born again believer in our saviour Jesus Christ, we often expect the world to roll over at our presence, and when it doesn't happen we hide in the fog of realism. God didn't promise us an easy way as he pointed out that faith without works is dead. So Christians must cease, and desist from believing that the world owes you something because you are a Christian. It simply doesn't work that way. You are chosen to take a special role in God's plan even though the appeal often images that what we can do is not ample enough. However when we decide that God is in charge of our lives we shall see an unbelievable effect of the messenger. Life, without acknowledging Christ, only leads to dead end roads. The answer is found in our obedience to God by our submission to his will.

When a person serves people as a servant of God, there ought to be a depth of obligation that includes a quality of empathy, and care not otherwise found in man's service to man. For we find in the secular world that personal service or favour is predicated upon mutual good pleasure. In other words, many have the colloquial concept, you scratch my back and I'll scratch yours, in other words I will do you a favour, if you will do a favour for me. Nevertheless the thrust of the servant of God should more appropriately realise that being those who claim Christ as their saviour, must be benevolent, seeking the good for others, even if they prove to be unresponsive, or resentful towards us. God emphasizes that we need to love our enemies, and do good, and lend yourself to the task, hoping for nothing again. Your reward shall be great, and ye shall be the children of the highest: for he is kind unto the unthankful and to the evil. Be ye therefore merciful, as your Father is also merciful. Luke 6:35-36.

James, a servant of God was under obligation to measure his conversation very carefully, being careful to speak only the truth, even though the hearer might find it unpleasant to the ears. For as he taught God's word he knew that there were those who would seek their own benefits from this new gospel of Jesus Christ, the Messiah who had indeed come and returned to sit on the right hand of His Father. He remembered the prophet Isaiah was able to endure much criticism for the way he preached and wrote of his God from the people he knew he could save.

When a person attaches themselves to the church, for whatever reason, they should be ready with the same measure of application to serving God as they would aspire to the success of the position being filled in the secular job. At the same time realizing this is a spiritual situation that requires commitment to the nth degree. It becomes more personal with a special outreach to the downtrodden, especially to the unbeliever. There needs to be in your life an acquisition of caring that far outreaches any performance given by a secular world. Too often we allow a complacency to set in with a couldn't care less attitude because we take ownership to a self righteous attitude that does not belong in Christian servanthood. A person who portrays themselves as greater than others is not likely to encourage unbelievers to the service of the living God. It is what is perceived by the unbelieving world as a "holier than thou," attitude. Know this, God is not pleased with servants of that calibre. A true servant of God will humble themselves to the plateau that allows them to encourage sinners to come to the feast table that is enjoyed by those already in Christ. That cannot be an invitation of condemnation. It must be a gentle invitation where the unbeliever will begin to feel the touch of Christ through the love they find in you. It is because men that recognized they were indeed God's servants, and because they knew, where they were at, with God, it was impossible to discourage them. Missionaries have often found suspicion, instead of a cordial welcome, amongst those whom they have wished to help. Without the love of God in their hearts, and without belief that their prime obligation was to their Lord Jesus Christ, they would hardly persist in their service. Jesus reformed, or made over the thought of service, from something that was embraced as perhaps menial, to that which became the heart of his life style, and his plan to further the gospel.

Too often we take the word service, and reduce it to, 'that right of mine', to receive from the community level in the Super Market, or at the hairdresser, or the service station, or from other persons that give to me convenience for what I desire to have. A high conception of service can only be maintained when it is rooted in God. His Son Jesus Christ, as our Lord and Saviour, is the secret to happiness. Yet the ideal of happiness, which many cherish, may look to a state of ease.

James, has a different ideal of happiness, because he holds a different theory of the meaning and purpose of life. The purpose of life cannot be obtained by luxurious comfort; But only in the achievement of a Christ like character. Therefore - the Christian can count it sheer joy, when he or she meets with various trials and tribulations. When crisis is met with courage, it produces steadfastness of character. Christians are not distinguished by their immunity from trials, which are common to the secular unbelieving world; but in the way they accept and absorb the handling of those difficulties with patience and understanding, by the transposing of adversity, into a spiritual victory.

James 1:4; *But let patience have her perfect work, that ye may be perfect and entire, wanting nothing.*

Here, that which is set apart from the material universe, becomes the goal that does not allow us to settle for less. With our Christ likeness, we shall not settle for a complacent self righteousness, derived from false satisfaction, that somehow builds a hope that we have already arrived at Holiness.

To remind God as the man in Mark 10:20; Master, *'all these have I observed from my youth'*. is simply not enough. The perfection, to which we are called, is not the negative absence of transgression, but the positive presence of inclusive love.

James 1:5-8; *if any of you lack wisdom, let him ask of God, that giveth to all men liberally, and upbraideth not; and it shall be given him. But let him ask in faith, nothing wavering. For he that wavereth is like a wave of the sea driven with the wind and tossed. For let not that man think he shall receive any thing of the Lord. A double minded man is unstable in all his ways.*

The word here tells of God who does not upbraid his creation and does not wish that those who believe in his son as saviour have the right to do that which he abhors. To upbraid is to chastise, scold for some wrongdoing, offence, or error, to take to task . Synonym, reproach. As we witness the ongoing temperament of church gatherings and listen to the leaders in those growing numbers, all we hear is the continuity of upbraiding those who fail to live up to their standards called constitution. They need to be in fear of the living God whom they claim to serve while they preach against his word.

Prayer is the recourse of those who desire wisdom.

Why is prayer necessary for gaining this wisdom?

Because, in the Christian understanding, prayer involves confession of moral insufficiency, and inadequacy, and aspiration, towards the perfection of God.

James 1:12 *Blessed is the man that endureth temptation: For when he is tried, he shall receive the crown of life, which the Lord has promised to them that love him.*

For the whole person to embrace the element of enjoyment it leads ultimately to the serving a living God with all which he has already given to us. Man cannot altar anything in God's world of eternal government, because the settings have been put into place to keep man humble. Not only are those things put in place by God, but all things recurrent, for God seeks that which is pursued. The betterment of our community comes to mind when we attach ourselves to an action that will produce righteousness.

Goodness for the sake of furthering the gospel of Jesus Christ, brings the ultimate

reward, the crown of life. We will not receive the reward just because we have been good, rather it will be because of the consistency in humbleness that amplifies salvation for the lost, and rest for the weary, with a place of peace in finality for the seeker in the presence of God. The Christian life must always be one of extreme moral endeavour. Faith in God does not exempt any one believer from struggle. It simply enables one to endure unto victory.

Wisdom is the substance of our pattern to adjustment, nevertheless we must wrestle with the entanglements that come into our lives. We need to adopt positive thinking while producing that which is good for the whole community.

James 1:13; *let no man say when he is tempted, I am tempted of God: for God cannot be tempted with evil, neither tempteth he any man*:

Who is to blame?

From Adam to Eve, to contemporary man, the alibi for succumbing to temptation is invariably, 'It wasn't my fault'.

If God made me this way, why should I be held responsible for acting according to my nature?

In today's social structure we are taught to adopt the ideology that someone else is to blame for my bad behaviour. My moral decadence must be plied to the feet of those who trained me, for I am not to take the blame for my derelict attitude. Besides all that these moral attributes deny me my freedom of choice. And if I take it upon myself to live a better more loving life style, how then will I revoke all my responsibilities. James here is uttering a warning to his fellow Christians. That warning is against using worn out old excuses for wicked conduct, that God has never accepted, and will not now accept. In other words, don't blame God for your inability to grasp the truth. Furthermore do not blame the nature that he has given you for the sin that you may commit.

In becoming a Christian, does one have less of life or more?

It is all too common an impression; that we must lose more than we can gain. These verses in James suggest that obedience to the word of God, is truly the only path to freedom.

James 1:26-27; *If any man among you seem to be religious, and bridleth not his tongue, but deceiveth his own heart, this man's religion is vain. Pure religion and undefiled before God and the Father is this, To visit the fatherless in their affliction, and to keep himself unspotted from the world.*

Scripture is very clear, showing us that ritualistic action in no way brings you closer to God, because following God is based solely upon a simple and sincere devotion based upon our comprehensive understanding of the needs of our surrounding communities. That need being the salvation of lost souls which does not materialize from preconceived ideas of how to reach up to God. It is to accept his free gift of grace that entails the total forgiveness of sin, because God has already reached down to man through his son Jesus Christ.

Jesus in directing man's relationship, is based upon a simple and sincere devotion to a living, loving, God. How else could I impress upon you the sincerity of God's requirements, than to close with this verse from Micah 6: 8; *He hath showed thee, O man, what is good; and what does the Lord require of thee, But to do justly, and to love mercy, and to walk humbly with thy God.*

* * * * *

Children of Light

———⟐⟐⟐———

For ye were sometimes darkness, but now are ye light in the Lord: walk as children of the light: [For the fruit of the spirit is in all goodness and righteousness and truth;] Proving what is acceptable unto the Lord. And have no fellowship with the unfruitful works of darkness, but rather reprove them. Ephesians 5:8-11.

This section of scripture is probably one of the most fractured and fragmented scriptures of the day. Preachers, and interpreters alike seem to live on the impassionate delight of destroying the actual otherwise meaningful word from God. If you take into the darkness a book of matches, and strike the head of one of those sulphur beaded cardboard matches upon the friction band there will appear a light that drives away the darkness. If you know Jesus as your saviour, and you without fear, strike his infallible word on the roughness of darkness of the world, it will produce a light more brilliant than sulphur flame. In other words you must be an active believer without fear or favour with God's manual before you, his word.

Ephesians 4: ends in an appropriative manner as we read verse 32; *Be ye kind one to another, tender hearted, forgiving one another, even as God for Christ's sake has forgiven you.*

The last clause here has become the point of departure for a wider thought, that is that God here becomes the model for us to imitate. The ASV translates the first verse of chapter 5, to read, 'Therefore are imitators of God, as beloved children.

Imitating God can be applied to our following of Jesus as the ethical example and applying to our lifestyle.

What Would Jesus do?

This may be a very good direction of thought to take when seeking to continue in that which you know that God has set before you.

Imitation is a legitimate, and powerful motive in human behaviour. Children imitate parents, or someone whom they are impressed with, such as their favourite TV character, or there neighbour, or teacher. Leaders of our nations are often successful because they imitate some impressive leader in history. To imitate God is a good practice. Let this mind be in you.

Eph 5:2; *Walk in love.*

Here is another endearing phrase that could be taken as walking in the imitation of Christ. No one can follow Christ's example except they who by faith have found Christ by agreeing to accept his plan of salvation verified by his death on the cross. One then acknowledges this Christ as Mediator, and Redeemer, by the regeneration of their soul. Also acknowledging His saving Grace is armed with power to set them forth on a newness in their journey through life after His example. The author points out a very definite danger in the early Christian church. Christian love is not a product of ethical self culture, but a response to an act of God, Christ loved us and gave Himself up for us.

A wrong impression of Christian freedom gives rise to revolt against strict moral demands of religion. This has been a frequently practiced fact of past history in which we need to be cognizant that it only takes away what God has tried to present to us for the following of a better and more tolerant lifestyle.

In the ancient world it took common form in spirituality which thought matters pertaining to the body as indifferent. Hence laxness in sexual morality could be condoned as bodily indulgence which need not touch the spiritual attainments.

This can indicate how dangerous the word Spirit, and Spiritual, is if loosely employed.

The contrast between Spirit, and body, when the former is ranked higher than the latter is derivative of Greek philosophy, and not of the thought world of the Bible. The Bible knows nothing of the Spiritual religion in the Greek sense. That is why the body realism of the bible is so often shocking to us. The bible does not accept the worship of beauty, or of truth, or of goodness, for a substitute for a worship of a personal living God of righteousness and Holiness. No one in the Bible is excused from the humbling appearance before God as a sinner. There is no evasion of moral matters.

Eph 5:6; *Let no man deceive you with vain words: for because of these things cometh the wrath of God upon the children of disobedience.*

The wrath of God is not a very popular theme in modern preaching. The New Testament is often interpreted as picturing a kind of new God, who can be controlled with the God of the Old Testament. By abolishing the wrath of God, one robs God of His righteousness. The writers of the New Testament never dreamed of repudiating the Old Testament. The new in the New Testament is simply God's sacrificial Love as revealed on the cross. We would do well whenever we speak of God's love to always prefix the adjective 'Holy' "Holy Love."

Forgiveness before God is so costly precisely because it dare not be immoral. We are simply sinners saved by Grace suggesting that we remove ourselves as far from sin as possible. Wrong has not been turned into right because of God's forgiveness. Nor have God's standards of righteousness been lowered to the level where divine wrath no longer applies.

Forgiveness is the gift across the chasm of violated Holiness. Repentance on man's side makes the giving of the gift of salvation possible. But where there is no repentance, the wrath of God comes upon the disobedient.

Eph 5:8-14; *.For ye were sometimes darkness, but now are ye light in the Lord: Walk as children of light: [For the fruit of the spirit is in all goodness and righteousness and truth;] Proving that which is acceptable unto the Lord. And have no fellowship with the unfruitful works of darkness, but rather reprove them. For it is a shame even to speak of those things done of them in secret. But all things that are reproved are made manifest by the light: for whatsoever doth make manifest is light. Wherefore he saith awake thou that sleepest, and arise from the dead, and Christ shall give thee light.*

Here the contrast between paganism and Christianity; the important verb in this passage is "walk" Another contrast is found in the second chapter of Ephesians;

Eph 2:12-14; *That at that time ye where without Christ, being aliens from the commonwealth of Israel, and strangers from the covenant of promise, having no hope, and without God in the world: But now in Christ Jesus ye who sometimes were far off are made nigh by the blood of Christ. For He is our peace, who hath made both one, and hath broken down the middle wall of partition between us.*

In the former passage from chapter 5, we see the contrast between the past and present conditions was stated in terms of relationship to God, and to the community of God's people; here it is stated in terms of character and social influence.

You were in darkness. Darkness was not merely their environment, they themselves shared the nature of the Evil world, which surrounded them. Conversely; You are the Light. Not merely enlightened, but partaking of that nature of light which now surrounds them. And so giving light to others.

Matthew 5:14-16; *Ye are the light of the world. A city set upon a hill cannot be hid. Neither do men light a candle, and put it under a bushel, but on a candlestick; and it giveth light to all that are in the house. Let your light so shine before men, that they may see your good works, and glorify your Father which is in heaven.*

These are the words of our Lord Jesus.

Philippians 2:15; *That ye may be blameless and harmless, the sons of God, without rebuke, in the midst of a crooked and perverse nation, among whom ye shine as lights of the world;*

Live as befits your nature, let your light shine. The writer is insisting on the moral significance of light as opposed to false mystic interpretation.

Why?

Eph 5:10; *Proving what is acceptable unto the Lord.*

No observer of human life can fail to note how desperate, for most men, and women, is the fear of exposure. We wear masks to hide our real selves. For the Saint it may be the mask of humility. The criminal fears betrayal. The adulterer fears retaliation of jealousy

The sense of shame is of great importance to man, and that

creates self delusion in the hearts of men. The Christian is a person who has exposed themselves to the light.

John 3:20-21; we read the words of Jesus, *For every one that doeth evil hateth the light, neither cometh to the light, lest his deeds be reproved. But he that doeth truth cometh to the light, that his deeds may be made manifest, that they are wrought of God.*

Judgment is the very thing Christians have learned to accept as the gateway into a new life with Christ.

Repentance can be joyous acceptance of the searching light of God's Holiness. The Grace given to Christians can bring with it a shaking off of burdens. Christians walking in the light can taste the glorious liberty of the Children of God.

Romans 8:21; *Because the creature itself also shall be delivered from the bondage of corruption into the glorious liberty of the children of God.*

A forgiven sinful past is in the hands of God, and need not be paraded before men.

Christians who wish to indulge in the unseemly autobiography might well heed the message in verse 12 of Ephesians 5:12, *For it is a shame even to speak of those things which are done of them in secret. But all things that are reproved are made manifest by light.*

By that instruction by that reminder in God's word we then set out to be witnesses as shining as lights in the world.

. For whosoever doth make manifest is light, and accordingly it becomes those who are the children of light, who are light in the Lord, to discover to others light which is diffused by the Holiness of your lives, and by your exemplary walk in their lives

* * * * *

Living For Christ

Whereas you know not what should be on the morrow. For what is your life? it is even as a vapour, that appeareth for a little time, and then vanisheth away. For that you ought to say, if the Lord will, we shall live, and do this, or that. But now you rejoice in your boastings: all such rejoicing is evil. Therefore to him that knoweth to do good and doeth it not, to him it is sin. James 4:14-17.

I have fellowshipped with those who were perfectly whole in the morning, and discovered in the latter part of the day their bodies had been deteriated, and invalidated by damaging action from stroke. I have prayed, and fellowshipped with persons who in the next few hours were killed on the highway through no fault of their own. Each time has reminded me of this leading scripture in the book of James. Life is but a wisp of smoke, or steam, a vapour, they were here this fraction of time, and gone in the next instance.

When we are young we have the idea that we shall live forever, but God warns us that there is a cautionary method which he has chosen for us to be aware of, "If the Lord will."

Pitting life on earth against the eternity offered by God, we see that our time is short even if we are blessed to live out our allocation of such, four score and ten years. As society becomes more concerned about death control as well as birth control, it is now not unusual to see many living to eighty and ninety years of age. Although we see many living a longer span today, there is no less of uncertainty to the span in which God allocated to us. Nevertheless we are constantly reminded of how little control we have over those short years allocated to us. As a matter of fact we are told that after three score years and ten [70] years, we are living on borrowed time.

As God challenges us to live it as Holy there are three specific areas to consider.

First, Christ's reminder, Luke 12:19b take thine ease, eat, drink, and be merry. But God said unto him, Thou fool, this night, thy soul shall be required of thee:

God, and man's life is linked to the eternal, and is required to act in respect of that with the summation of, so be it thy will Lord.

The secret of man's being is, not only to live, but to have something to live for. without a stable conception of the object of life, man would not consent to go on living, and would rather destroy himself than go on living even though he had bread in abundance. Someday people will learn that material things do not bring happiness, and are little use in making men and women creative or powerful. Then the scientists of the world will turn their laboratories over to the study of God, and prayer, and spiritual forces.

James 4:17; *Therefore to him that knoweth to do good, and doeth it not, to him it is sin.*

Luke puts it another way; Luke 12: 47; *And that servant, which knew his Lord's will, and prepared not himself, neither did according to his will, shall be beaten with many stripes.*

In other words, if you know how to serve God through his Son Jesus, and you fail to do so, your punishment will be greater than those who did not know. When one becomes a Christian, one voluntarily takes upon themselves, responsibilities, and obligations, which ordinary people do not acknowledge. The unbeliever recognizes responsibility within the circle of certain limited relationships, but what lies beyond that circle, is of little or no concern to them.

No one can be forced to become a believer in the Son of God. The duties of the followers of Christ can only be assumed willingly. No one need to be in the dark as to what is involved. Christ does not want a surging crowd of blind followers; for his accusation of that day was to those who where blind leaders of the blind. Blind to responsibilities to a living God that had sent message upon message that his Son was coming; but when he arrived they refused to see him. When you make that, free will choice, of adherence to Christ, you cannot refuse to carry out that obligation of that relationship without sinning against God, and our Lord Jesus Christ.

Often the Christian vocation is equated with respectability. However the Christ like life is what Jesus asserted it to be in his challenge to his disciples. Then it is a different matter, for the conditions of discipleship which were laid down are not easy.

Matt: 16:24; *Then Jesus said unto his disciples, If any man will come after me, let him deny himself, and take up his cross, and follow me*;

Many contemporary believers refuse to live under the shadow of the cross. They are brazen enough to remove it from the church, or set it aside to allow the theatrics of the unbelieving public to replace that which God requires.

To refer to only one of the conditions, "to take up his cross" is precisely to assume responsibility towards God, and man, which unbelievers do not acknowledge.

Jesus did not have to leave Nazareth and go to Jerusalem in order to gain respectability. No one can be required by law, to go the second mile. No one can be forced to accept responsibility beyond the family or Nation.

But anyone who follows Christ, cannot close their ears to the call recorded in the gospel according to Mark 16:15; *Go ye into all the world and preach the gospel to every creature.*

The missionary obligation upon the church as a whole cannot be refused by the individual believer and follower of Christ, without perpetrating a disloyalty to our Lord and saviour. It is a sin. Perhaps the reason for irresponsibility on the part of many church members, lies in the failure to make plain in many instances, the seriousness of the obligations which are involved in the membership of the body of Christ. I speak in general terms.

There needs to be an adopted caring that automatically reveals submission in obedience to the will of God. What is that will? It is complete and comprehensive as written in His word, the Bible.

Isaiah cries -

Isaiah 52: 7; *How beautiful upon the mountains are the feet of him that bringeth good tidings, that publisheth peace; that bringeth good tidings of good, that publisheth salvation; that saith unto Zion, Thy God reigneth!*

Jesus gives his blessings to the peace makers:

2 Cor 5:18; *And all things are of God, who has reconciled us unto himself by Jesus Christ, and has given to us the ministry of reconciliation;*

The ministry of reconciliation, can the churches ministry be made more plain.

Let me introduce three Chinese characters similarly translated "peace" were no one seeks to dominate another. Peace obtained when homes are unmolested and tranquil. Peace obtained when all have sufficient to eat. Righteousness implies right relationships between human beings.

If the farmer gave no more thought or time, or effort, to secure his harvest, than many members of the church of Christ give to the establishing a Christ like community; would he ever reap the harvest?

Let us make peace in our territory that God has given to us.

James 4: 8; *Draw nigh unto God, and he will draw nigh unto you. Cleanse your hands, ye sinners; and purify your hearts, ye double minded.*

Here appears the seeming paradox stated by James, but a closer examination of what he portrays here indicates the call of God to repent of those wayward things we were doing to keep us out of spiritual circles with only an odd bump against the peripheral rim of the spiritual. And here God says, wash your hands to leave behind that corruption you are involved in, hate, lust, decaying morals, and filthiness of the mind. Purify your hearts you double minded people that try to portray your imagery of God by being simply an attendee of spiritual functions without giving yourself fully to the service of Jesus Christ while knowing him as the son of the living God.

In the gospel the final word is not condemnation; But an appeal for change of mind and heart. No matter how defiant and rebellious a person has been. If you will turn to God, if you will submit yourself to the Lord of life, he will welcome you, and you shall be lifted up. When the cheap joys of self indulgence, turn into the sadness of disgust.

When laughter turns into tears; as those things you falsely prize, turn into ashes, only then will you be able to draw near to God

James 1:5; *If any of you lack wisdom, let him ask of God, that giveth to all men liberally, and upbraideth not; and it shall be given him.* For thou hast made us for thyself and our hearts can never find repose until they rest in thee.

James 4:14; *Whereas ye know not what shall be on the morrow. For what is your life? It is even a vapour, that appeareth for a little time, and then vanisheth away.*

Here God and man's life linked to the eternal. There is the seen and the unseen, there is the temporary, there is the Eternal. For the great illusion of human history has been precisely this, the belief that man can be satisfied with bread. He can be bought with it, subordinated by it, and corrupted by it, But he eats thereof and fails to be satisfied. If he were the beast of the field, he might be; but he is man, made in the image of God.

Not to be satisfied with substance; but by every word that proceeds out of the mouth of God. Alienated from the world.

James 4:4 *Ye adulterers and adulteresses, know ye not that friendship of the world is enmity with God? Whosoever therefore will be a friend of the world is the enemy of God.*

If your only wish is that others should take off and leave you alone, you are defying God. I n Christ's way there is a joy unspeakable untainted by the dregs of dissipation.

How about you today?

Are you still setting God aside, and being a friend with the world?

Only what's done for Christ will last. Let him pilot you through the storm.

* * * * *

Mutual Responsibility
For Building

Wherefore, holy brethren, partakers of the heavenly calling, consider the Apostle and High Priest of our profession, Christ Jesus: Heb 3:1

H ere the writer reminds us of our relationship to God. We are considered by Him to be Holy, literally meaning, set apart unto God in an exclusive servanthood with others who have been called to consider God in every facet of their lives. There is no intent here to consider what you may become, rather it determines God's favour to us as He separates us unto His own endearment as we are. As we abide in His Holiness we will be transformed by the blood of Christ because of that forgiveness of sin God bestows upon us. Through that embracement of His creation we are expected to minister to the needs of all. We are given the desire to encourage believers while we minister to the unbeliever. There is no authority given to any of us to shut anyone out of the circle of believers. God has not given the authority to question with, should we, or shouldn't we, for He is not willing that any should perish, and has called you to give His word to those who are outside the fold.

For every house is builded by some man; but he that built all things is God. Heb 3:4.

Here is a confirmation that God has built life for each of us. He is a builder who desires those that are called by Him to build not only houses, but communities, believers, attitudes, and a great edifice of obedience to Him.

For we are made partakers of Christ, if we hold the beginning of our confidence steadfast unto the end. Hebrews 3:14.

A firm reminder here that *God would like us to finish the race* that He invited us to start hoping that we would run, and to build to the end. Perseverance is a magnificent strength with which to serve our Holy God. When we are idealistic enough to restore the faith of persons to the point that they too shall persevere with us all shall be winners. When we enjoy our nourishment from God we can go a long distance without the desire to go back or quit the thing we set out to do.

These are days of pressure, and tension, and everyone feels it in some way. Marriages are broken, and taking on a sinful concept, homes are divided, friendships are severed, and everywhere there is hurting lonely people. Many Christians are finding it hard to act like Christians because they do not have joy, peace, or satisfaction. The problem is they have not grown strong enough in faith to experience full surrender of their life to Christ.

Condensed in this first verse of Hebrews chapter three, is a reminder to people of who they are, and who Christ is in contrast. We find here that we are privileged as, Holy brethren. Holy, literally translated means "set apart unto God," and that being done in the very exclusive sense. The writer here is not referring to human perfection, only that we who believe in Christ as our saviour being the Son of God enters us into a whole perspective with God to be set apart for the purpose of serving him.

A people set apart for God is a part of the biblical emphasis on the priesthood of all believers. This doctrine is not so much a right as it is a placement in God's plan to measure unto each of us a certain responsibility to help carry out spreading the word throughout the world. It is not enough to set apart a gathering of symbolized persons for the service of God, to call them priests. All God's people are consecrated, and whatever their vocation, their service ought to be directed to him, and he says we are of his priesthood.

Hebrews 3:1; —- *partakers in a heavenly calling* —- . Herein is deemed to be a call to us from God himself.

We find a central emphasis here that is often neglected in teaching, and receiving of instruction. New Testament teaching is quite clear that the Christian life does not rest merely upon some human decision.

We read in John 15:16 *You have not chosen me, but I have chosen you, and ordained you, that you should go and bring forth fruit, and that your fruit should remain: and whatsoever you should ask of the Father in my name, he may give it you.*

Here we see that nothing we have from this transition of spirit is of our own making. He emphatically implies that it is because he chose us, What a truly unmerited mercy this is. Although we may have decided to follow we need to know that he chose each one of us on his merit. Thereby we understand when God claims us by his grace.

The RSV says, "that your fruit may abide." The NIV says, "fruit that will last."

It is an absolute that the Christian' s faith rests in God. Each Christian must understand that their responsibility is personal. The invitation from God is directed to them. God himself is calling them to a life which has been redeemed by the blood of the Lamb, God's only Son, Jesus Christ.

An aggressive Christian faith can rest on no other argument than the foundation laid by our Lord and Saviour, Jesus Christ at Calvary where he shed his blood for your sin and mine. To be an Apostle, one who is sent; not a mere envoy, but an Ambassador, authorized to speak in the name of one who sent him. Christ who is superior to Angels was not ashamed to call us brethren. The word "consider" used in Hebrews 3: v 1 literally means, to look at carefully, or regard attentively; examine.

Theoretically it may suggest that you fix your mind upon Jesus, hold him in your mind, and let him live in your thoughts. However I believe if you are to thoroughly examine Christ you will find the solution to many of your wayward questions, and you will begin to absorb the quality that God has prepared for you. It is simply that you adopt this quality, and begin the application to your own lifestyle. Living the Christ way, will make others see you in a changed light. Every step you take to absorb your portion of quality life will allow you to settle the question of right or wrong in the sanctioning of any action that may deter you from being a visible living of a Christian testimony.

Again, hear Christ, Mark 14:36b; *Father, take away this cup from me: nevertheless not what I will, but what thou wilt.*

John 4:34; *My meat is to do the will of him who sent me, and to finish his work.*

Moses was faithful in all his house Hebrews 3:2; possibly identifies the family tree. The head of the house gathered his family, and in no uncertain terms made God known to them. There are some who would bend this portion in suggesting there somehow is a reference to God's house encompassing all creation. Nevertheless I believe the strong emphasis on being Godly, meant being a close family that knew they would be worshipping together at the Altar of a living God. We of the body of Christ who claim to be born again believers need to identify with the gathering family concept.

Hebrews 3: 4; states, *For every house is builded by some man; but he that built all things is God.*

Here we find the element that Christ attempted to portray. That is to say each action we take becomes a process of building. If we perform a task that negates God's word, then we build with faulty material, and our building will crumble, but when we move with the knowledge of Christ in a positive action, we build with an indestructible product. Nothing can stand against it.

Moses was that kind of faithful servant. As he approached God knowing that his people rebelled, he sought only redemption for them, and God entrusted the Ten Commandments to him. Descending the Mountain where he had come to grips with meeting the awesome living God, he confronted the sin filled people below and directed them to follow the commandments of his God. He did so without an apologetic preliminary. He simply told of the consequences for rejecting this loving God, and the people submitted, as they believed the servant.

Christ was faithful to the mission for which he was sent to accomplish. He cared for God's house, the church, for as they believed on him they were Baptized, and added unto the church daily. Christ was faithful in attendance of the Temple where he could read, and minister the written word. Through this we are admonished to obey the gospel beginning at the house of God.

1 Peter 4:17; *for the time is come that judgment must begin at the house of God: and if it first begin at us, and what shall the end be of them that obey not the gospel of God*

1 Timothy 3:15; *But if I tarry long, that thou mayest know how thou oughtest to behave thyself in the house of God, which is the church of the living God, the pillar and the ground of truth.*

Some may take liberties with a statement such as this to break it down to segregate functional action from others, however it is my firm belief that Christ points out the necessity of building the truth of God as written in the scriptures, and not some wayward mindless interpretation. It states here that the truth must be adhered to in order to make a strong and lasting building. We are his house in the organized church that presents the gospel of Jesus Christ, and his salvation through the shed blood of Calvary's cross. We represent the home where God delights to dwell. The active practicing born again believer in the house of God will be the cohesion of joyous family fellowship. Each servant of God shall work to insure the safety of the light of Christ, and feed the soul with spiritual food, with the ultimate in Christlike love for one another.

When the unbelieving world observes our actions one toward another they shall see Christ in us. They shall identify our intimate relationship to God because of our high regard for the essential action of caring for others to a greater degree than ourselves. That is the source of our strength and our peace of heart. We are God's house if we hold fast; Hebrews 3:6; reads as follows; *But Christ as a son over his own house; whose house are we, if we hold fast the confidence and rejoicing of the hope firm unto the end.*

We live with a faith that never needs to look back if we hold fast in confidence. A firm belief in ones own ability to build for God a lasting house. An absolute assurance that we are forgiven through the blood of Christ. A trusting relationship as a servant of the living God because he sent his only son to redeem us from our sin and trespasses. With firm belief, trust, and reliance, we can build God's house with our profession of Christ before many, even as the apostles presented him so can we. We must find within a new boldness for the furtherance of God's plan to redeem all mankind, as well as a renewed boldness in our approach to God himself. It is to have and exercise a confidence that is forthright, without bluster and without apology. There is a constant reminder in the Christian circles that pride goeth before a fall. This is a truth in that of itself constitutes a false Godless pride.

Nevertheless there is the paradox here that pride is one of the essential ingredients of success of our testimony of God and his righteousness. If then we have confidence in our servanthood of God, pride becomes essential to our success of a worthy life. For without pride, and confidence, we cease to be stable persons. If a person puts their confidence in unworthy actions, and clandestine affairs, you will turn out to be that kind of a person.

Although we are warned as to the wrongful placement of pride, it is one of God's greatest gifts to his followers. The New Testament never belittles pride. Never in God's word do we find that the backward shall inherit the earth, nor shall the slovenly enter the straight and narrow. In fact the best of God's servants take pride that they are the followers of a living God, and are proud to be redeemed by his Son Jesus Christ.

The pride exercised by followers, and believers, in our Saviour, generates a greater capacity for loyalty, and devotion, to the gospel. One thing we ought to be aware of is, that all the highly valued spiritual gifts carry with them an edge to spiritual danger. We must be wise in our use of each gift that has been bestowed upon us by our God. Yet we must realize that pride of self is the basic sin of man. This is why you will find the instruction in 1 Corinthians 1: 31; that if we glory at all we are to glory in the Lord. Most of the chapter deals with our giving over to the Lord all things accomplished. Simply put, take pride in God's work, and in God who allowed us to be a part of that which he would further for eternal life of those who would accept and believe. Our confidence and our pride is to be in our hope. When we adhere to placing our hope in Jesus, we shall be on a steady course. For only then our hope in God triumphs over sin and death. By our consistent hope in Jesus Christ, we shall build the house of God by the profession of our faith in his Son and the redemptive work on the cross of Calvary. We need to consider Jesus. Heb 3:1. *Take care, lest there should be in any one of you an evil, unbelieving heart, in falling away from the living God.* Heb

3:12-13, *Encourage one another day after day, lest any one of you be hardened by the deceitfulness of sin. Let us fear, lest while a promise remains entering His rest, any one of you should seem to come short of it.* Heb 4:1, *Let us, be diligent to enter that rest.* Heb 4:11, *By faith and obedience.*

In v14, we are admonished to hold our confidence in Christ toward God eluding of course to holding fast to the end. A strong commitment in our walk with Christ to the perseverance of that which drew us to him in the first place. A strong devotion will not hold unless you build it to depend upon the living God to make it so.

Building to accommodate God is not necessarily entertaining the thought of some edifice being erected to his memory. I believe that this scripture more likely refers to the gathering around us of those that will hold to the sending out of God's word to the unbeliever. With that we build a strong bond with other believer. Only in that way can we sustain our belief in the living God and make his gift of Jesus available to every wayward soul.

* * * * *

He Is Going Before You

———— ✽ ————

And when they looked, and saw that the stone was rolled away: for it was very great. And entering into the sepulchre, they saw a young man sitting on the right side, clothed in a long white garment; and they were affrighted. And he saith unto them, Be not affrighted: ye seek Jesus of Nazareth, which was crucified: he is risen; he is not here: behold the place where they laid him. Mark 16: 4-6

These women had purchased spices for the body of Jesus because they had watched as he was laid in the tomb. When the sun had risen they ventured to the tomb in all likelihood to prepare the body to lay away after death which was the custom. As they walked toward the place where the tomb was at they recalled together about the huge stone that covered the entrance, thus the question amongst them was , "Who shall roll away the stone, for it was one of unusual size and weight. It was a natural conversation as they wondered from whence they would get help in order to administer the spices to the body of Christ. they were quite aware of their own physical weakness, and it was an exceedingly great stone. Common sense alerted them that by themselves it was an impossible task for them to remove the stone.

Imagine the surprise on their faces when they looked up and saw that the stone was rolled away from the entrance, but when they entered the tomb something was terribly amiss, there was no body. Instead there was a youthful looking figure sitting atop of the stone, garbed in white apparel. to say the least they were somewhat amazed. until the heavenly figure addressed them saying, "*Be not amazed, you seek Jesus the Nazarene, who hath been crucified, he is not here, for he has risen as he promised he would."*

How often we make the trek to the empty tomb of life seeking some retribution to compensate for all the difficult times that have come our way, but indeed it is empty. For as the women came to prepare with the right spices, they came with heavy hearts in that Jesus had been taken from their lives. We too, come with the wrong hearts, and Jesus is not there behind any mountainous stone, for he has risen. When our hearts seek solace we need to go to God in the name of Jesus to have him restock our strength and righteousness with a deeper understanding of the task fulfillment.

The heavenly voice continued to give them the direction they needed to find the risen saviour. We are often given the voice of direction, but we seldom follow the instructions, and we fall into the trap that draws us away from God's whispers, into the wrongful direction of Satan.

After Peter's denial with Christ's look of forgiveness, this guardian of the entrance of the tomb knew about Peter for he directs the ladies to go and tell the other disciples and Peter. An example here of the great love that Christ brought to God's creation for when Peter shed his penitent tears, all heaven was made aware of his forgiveness. The Angel continues with his message about Christ, *"He goes before you into Galilee, there you shall see him as he promised you."*

If one could only grasp this fact in every phase of their living, "He is going before you," it may deliver us from deep concern that need not materialize as he protects us in the way when we follow.. Instead we too often find ourselves in fear and trembling not realizing the realism of the situation that has been set into our lives by God's sanction.

The stone having been rolled back was not the supreme attraction, rather only an indication that drew attention to the real event itself. For it is my contention that the stone was rolled away after the fact of the resurrection itself. It needed not to be rolled away for Christ to make his way out of the tomb, for he had left the tomb before the gate was left open. Therefore the stone was rolled away to bring the attention of the living into the reality that Christ was who he said he was, the son of the living God, and his purpose in being here was to lay down his life in propitiation for our sin.

Matthew gives a different account of the event when he says there was a great earthquake, and an Angel appeared as lightening, and his raiment was as white as snow, and the keepers that were set by Pilate to watch the tomb did quake, and become as dead men when the stone was rolled back.

Whatever the account given, one fact remained in tact, Jesus Christ had risen from the dead. He emerged from all material bondage, and bandages. He had passed into new life while at the same time passing eternal life on to the believers. Here Jesus conquered death, and the grave in the same instance as he tried earlier to explain to his disciples what he was about to do, and they didn't understand his sayings, but now those very talks became absolutely real to his followers. They saw the miracle take form in that which they found difficult to perceive in their walk with Jesus. Here we are given a glimpse of the meaning to be born again. First we do not understand this Jesus, but when we believe on him, and walk with him we shall see the transformation of new life in our walk. This is a central fact of Christianity throughout the ages, in our believing in him there must be a visible transformation in our lives. It is not something that we configure, it is what the acceptance of Christ as saviour will bring to our life. Only the ignorant deny the resurrection of Jesus Christ. The conclusive fact is that God's word has remained viable throughout the ensuing century of the actual event. People who accept Christ as their saviour today are still experiencing the transformation from the old life to the new life given because of Christ's action over two thousand years ago.

Everything for which Christ stood came alive unto God in his resurrection, and that old worldly sinful way lies dead in the tomb. In his resurrection he taught us the glory of holiness as he claimed the power to heal the broken heart, and forgive the sins of mankind. The sacrifice of Jesus is today the symbol to men everywhere that God had put forth in a visible way the mystery of the atoning work for the redemption of sin for his created being. Jesus taught the beauty of sacrifice, and even the world had to look at him to either accept him or reject him. To those who accept him he gives them eternal life with his Father in heaven. To those who reject him , they receive eternal life in a lake of fire and brimstone in eternal damnation.

We come to that which makes the senses supreme, the resurrection gave a whole new interpretation to life, and eternity. Before the cross people always wandered in the desert of time having difficulty finding God seeking his forgiveness while never assured that he had heard. Now Jesus gives new life with the assurance that he lets God hear the cry of the sinner as he gives the assurance of eternal life in heaven with him. Now they gained intellectual wisdom that failed to deny the son of God his place in their lives.

Are you standing at the empty tomb still seeking Jesus? He has gone on before you, follow him to that meeting place where he will give you place at the Father's throne. Do not waste time seeking other ways for Christ was emphatic when he stated, "I am the way, the truth, and the life, no man cometh unto the Father except by me." Accept him today for he awaits you to say, "I come."

* * * * *

Power For Living

——《❦》——

And the Angel answered and said unto the women, Fear you not: for I know that you seek Jesus who was crucified. He is not here: he is risen, as he said. Come, see the place where the Lord Matthew 28:5-6

Power is one of the chief cornerstones upon which civilization rests. As a man has discovered new sources of power, civilization has reached new proportions.

Earlier cultures were simple, and uncomplicated, and human muscle was the only source of power. Man learned to utilize the Mule, Horse, or Oxen. New horizons were opened to civilizations. The invention of the wheel, lever, steam engine, diesel engine, internal combustion, electricity, nuclear energy, computers, robots, etc.

Our source of spiritual power is extremely important. We need power for spiritual vitality to be the kind of men and women God wants us to be, to face life courageously, to meet its challenges, to make the most of our opportunities, to live the Christian life in all it's purity and holiness. These things are possible only as we use the power our God has made available to us.

It takes power to face the problems, and burdens which life confronts us with to endure disappointments, pain, or unpleasant circumstance. Power for living is indispensable. Most of us are aware of our own personal inadequacy to cope with life's most difficult crisis. We need help, God's help. It is possible for the Christian to live to the glory of God, to enjoy, peace, satisfaction, fruitfulness, as well as victory over sin, victory over temptation through the divine energy, through the divine commitment, to Jesus Christ. The resurrection is unfailing evidence that Christ is adequate power to equip the Christian to deal with their life in any phase.

Chapter 27, and 28, of Matthew are of two opposites of despair and joy. In 27, we find our Christ falsely accused, convicted, mocked, and rejected by believers, and put to death. Here a scene that had robbed men of hope. Chapter 28: Christ's resurrection, the very foundation of Christianity, their Joy restored; we read in v 2; *And, behold there was a great earthquake: for the angel of the Lord descended from Heaven, and came and rolled back the stone from the door, and sat upon it.*

The same supernatural power that raised Christ, rolled away the stone, is available to roll away the stones before us as we serve him.

Some stones hinder the church, multitudes who have not heard, Communism, [neo -socialism], Social Injustice, Economic rivalry, Materialism, Apostate religion. Other stones stand in our way, fear of unemployment, poor health, difficult personality trait, habits that destroy our witness, enemies within the fellowship, as well as those who will rise up against the believer in the salvation message of Jesus Christ, the son of a living God.

The resurrection itself is not described in scripture, only that it positively took place. It probably took place in the early hours of Sunday morning, the first day of the week. The stone was not rolled away for Jesus to get out, but for his followers to see in. The very word resurrection means, 'standing up again'. Resurrection is the uniting of spirit and body. Jesus had promised that his body would rise. If it had not risen it would determine that Jesus was an impostor as well as a failure.

The angel's words, 'He is risen!' Has been called the greatest watershed in history. The greatest sacrificial gift in history. Even under Paul's ministry people had the same criticism as does the world today; however, we find the rebuttal to this criticism written in 1 Corinthians 15:12-18. Probably capsuled in v v 16-17, as it reads, *For if the dead rise not, then is Christ not raised, and if Christ be not raised, your faith is vain; ye are yet in your sins.*

Unbelief is the single greatest barrier between people and blessings.

Why then are there so many Christians that never grow in their spiritual life?

Because they do not feed on the word; 1: Peter 2:2; *As new born babes, desire the sincere milk of the word, that ye may grow thereby.*

Why do they lack wisdom?

Because they do not ask for it. James 1:5; *If any of you lack wisdom, let him ask of God, that giveth to all men liberally, and upbraideth not; and it shall be given him.*

Why do they not become soul winners?

Because they are really not following Christ. Mark 1:17; *And Jesus said unto them, Come ye after me, and I will make ye to become fishers of men.*

Then there are those who have never had a life changing experience with the Lord Jesus Christ. There has been no transformation: Romans 12:2; *And be not conformed to this world: but be ye transformed by the renewing of your mind, that ye may prove what is that good, and acceptable, and perfect will of God.*

Many accept the reality of religion. They also accept the reality and facts about the gospel. Well that is nice, but so does the devil. James 2:19;*Thou believest that there is one God; thou doest well: the devils also believe, and tremble.*

Before a person can receive God's power they must receive Christ as saviour.

John 1: 12; *But as many as received him, to them gave he power to become the sons of God, even to them that believe on his name.*

You must be vitally related to God through a commitment to Jesus Christ. Professing Christians, backslidden, taken away by worldly love, by visions of grandeur in accumulating material goods, by influence of friends who convey the lack of importance of worship. Others who are truly Christian, weak in the faith, somehow cannot find the strength to claim his power; Remember the Holy Spirit makes intercession for us.

Romans 8:26-27; *Likewise the spirit also helpeth our infirmities: for we know not what we should pray for as we ought: but the spirit itself maketh intercession for us with groanings which cannot be uttered. And he that searcheth the heart knoweth the mind of the spirit, because he maketh intercession for the saints according to the will of God.*

Claiming God's mighty power and knowing it's reality is not a matter of emotions or feelings, it is a matter of setting ones mind on God. Having a God consciousness. Giving him first place in your life; depending explicitly on him, and the Holy Spirits power. This must be a personal decision. People who live in the power of the resurrection, set up by God, through the shed blood of his Son Jesus Christ for the element of the forgiveness of your sin, by submission to an almighty and living God, should be, Mature, seasoned servants of their Lord. No Christian needs to live in defeat or discouragement! Each should be victoriously confident in the day of testing. I came, said Jesus, that my people might have life, and might have it abundantly. John 10:10.

* * * * *

Pride And Lowliness

—<del>⟨⟩⟨⟩⟨⟩</del>—

Be merciful unto me, O God: for man would swallow me up; he fighting daily oppresses me. Mine enemies would daily swallow me up: for they be many that fight against me, O thou most high. What time I am afraid, I will trust in thee. In God I will praise his word, in God I have put my trust; I will not fear what flesh can do unto me. Psalm 56:1-4.

It appears somewhat evident here that the Psalmist was a vibrant testimony to his living God, and his worship of him. Non believers were persecuting him for his stand, but he was not deterred, rather it made him to write about it and defy those who would challenge him in his belief. Also this person recognizes his inadequacies and throws his entire dependency upon the supremacy of God with a knowledge that he will be delivered from his tormentors. Unbelievers, and those who practice religion in a self satisfying role were in fact exercising deliberate excrtion to destroy this believer in an unresting pursuit. Nevertheless, he had not relinquished the truth that he nourished with his soul. He saw his frailty as he searched for the mercy of God.

Attacked by the enemy, he reached down to scrape the walls of his heart to rally the courage to stand firm in the hollow of God's hand. How often we need to shed the fear of the overcoming world to lay our head into the breast of a loving God. We need to be lifted up to march forward to the victory over that which drags us into the moralistic mire. When other believers doubt our role with God, and choose to condemn rather than to reach out a helping hand to lift up a soul. It is time to say with the Psalmist, I put my trust in thee without fear.

Only then we can realize our true discipleship to God through the Lord Jesus Christ, son and saviour. Discipleship, and Evangelism, go hand in hand. We need discipling, in order to venture into the evangelism for the whole world. We have secularism that is recognized as life without God. The secular sees no need for God in their lifestyle. They without a doubt are the enemy of the faith of the Christian. We have Relativism whereby we do our own thing, but in that the truth does not exist, and it becomes an enemy of the Faith. We have Pluralism that of which we include all social structure within, where diversity exists, however this is far from being the friend of the Faith while we co-exist with those that think different and live different than me. There was an intent to intimidate this believer who gives himself into God's hand for protection, so we here are confronted with the need to disarm intimidation.

Working as a labourer in an insulation factory, I was introduced as a preacher to a fellow who had come to visit someone in the factory just as our shift was changing. His response to me was to say the least, extra negative. He refused to shake hands with me, and proceeded to tell me that we of the Christ regime acting as essential clergymen were all phoney.

I said, "Okay, I accept that." To which he began to carry on informing me why he believed that. I stopped cold in my tracks, and glared at him straight in the eye and asked a key question,

" Why should I listen to you?" I have accepted the fact that you believe all preachers are phoney?

"But," he stammered, " I wanted to let you know why."

I again responded to his ignorance as I said, "I'm not interested in your story, so shut up and quit bothering me."

With that I headed off to the showers which were about a quarter of a block away from where we had been standing. As I strode along the way, here beside me was this fellow doing his best with short quick steps trying to keep up to me and trying to get my attention in order that I would lend an ear to his story. Finally he begged forgiveness of his rude approach and blistering condemnation statement, and begged me to stop and talk with him. So I did, come to a halt to let him stride along side of me. The conversation now went like this.

He said, "I want my children to have a choice when they grow up, that is why I don't take them to church now."

I said. 'You are a liar, and con artist."

He asked, 'Why do you say that?"

I replied, "If you truthfully wanted a choice for your kids, you would have them in Sunday school and church now. Only then when they were older would they truly have a choice. Now I have no more time to listen to your tripe."

He began to plead all the more for me to listen to his tale. I consistently refused. He finally broke down, and began to weep while he pleaded with me to hear his story. Only then was I able to give him in no uncertain terms the whole story of God's message of salvation, and tell him about the shed blood of Christ while other workers stood around, and watched, and listened. I have never seen that man again. Approximately six months later I was in Toronto Ontario when I received a phone call from one of the young men that had introduced me to this fellow. I was surprised at the call coming to me at that time for I would be back in Edmonton within the month, and the fellow could have conferred with me about whatever it was he needed. I apprised him of that fact, but on the line he said, no, no, you don't understand, I wanted to tell you that after the way you handled the fellow I introduced you to, I have accepted Christ as my saviour. Then he went on to inform me about all his sinful habits, drugs, alcohol, shoplifting, lying, cheating, stealing; and he had confessed his sin and set out to make restitution to all the businesses that he had stolen from. He also informed me that the fellow that he had introduced me to was the number one gangster in whom he had encountered through his own sinful actions, and the man he introduced me to had been this young fellows hero. The idea of him introducing this person to me who was high within the gangster element was to have me stumped about my Christian life, and his intent was to glory in the fact that his hero would be the victor as he put me down in front of a crowd. However, he had not counted on God being my keeper, to fill my mouth with the words to handle such an evil man. When this young fellow observed me as I verbally cut his hero to ribbons with the word of God, he lost all respect for his hero, and went home to attend church with his wife who had asked him to go with her earlier, but he had refused. Now he literally humbled himself, and consented to attend the church with her. The hand of God was indeed in all the action, for as he sat under the sound of the gospel that day he came under conviction of the Holy Spirit, and gave his heart to the Lord, and is now an active servant for the Lord.

He had invited his gangster friend to try and intimidate me into losing a battle for Christ. And God had planted in my heart the need to disarm intimidation. God's people are becoming introverted. Remaining silent, instead of open, and verbal. Christians allow the surrounding culture to impose upon them silence.

I would ask, how do you expect to give account to God for failing to witness to the unsaved for him?

God says in his word, open your mouth and it shall be filled. We must not comply with the up and coming younger generations who try to emulate a philosophy of the failed church. Jesus Christ cannot fail. We who are believers in Him shall not fail when we are about God's business. There must be Discipling, to Produce Distinctiveness. It is increasingly difficult to find the difference between the unbelieving world and those who claim to be living for Christ.

We must wrestle biblically; what does modern Holiness look like?

What are the consequences of conversion?

If we do not have a distinctiveness, we must address the problem of excessive sameness.

What does transformation in Christ produce?

Without distinctiveness, faith will be eroded, we must Disciple to create Global Christians. Our modern world is a globalized society, but we must be cognizant of the fact that God's world is our world. God is not provincial nor is God in any sense of the word Parochial, truly God is multi-national. We live under a man's created image of a small God. You are an ambassador for Christ. You are not to fear the world. The Psalmist puts it well in Psalm 56:3; *What time I am afraid, I will trust in thee.*

Here is a sure way to conquer fear. Faith in the true sense is alive, and well, to the tragic problem of evil. Faith sees all the ugly disturbing facts of life, but it also sees the saving purpose of God, and his Grace through his Son and our Saviour, Jesus Christ. Faith knows that in his cross and resurrection, God broke the power of Evil, and that his purpose for the world cannot fail. Instead of being fearful of the future, let us go forth, putting our trust in him who holds the future. We look wistfully down the dim curtained corridors of the future, and we ask,

What does it hold for us?

Is it bright with the sunshine of hope?

Is it dark with vague and ugly fears?

Show me! we cry; But, God is too merciful to grant us that request. He simply asks that we go forth to meet the shadowy future, not with fear, but with trust! The very uncertainty's of life, should remind us of our helplessness, and keep us reverently humble and prayerful.

They should compel us to live the simple life of trust; which after all is only a venture on the promises of God the Father, as revealed in our Lord Jesus Christ.

* * * * *

Right Ambition

——◦◦◦——

That I may know him, and the power of his resurrection, and the
fellowship of his sufferings, being made conformable into his death;
If by any means I might attain unto the resurrection of the dead.
Philippians 4:10-11.

Each of us at some point are caught up in the ambition spectrum.

Ambition, as defined by Webster, means going around collecting votes; 1. Strong desire to succeed or to achieve something as
fame, power, or wealth; 2 the thing so desired.

Ambitious Synonym - implies a striving for advancement, and
is used with both favourable and unfavourable connotation.
Aspiring, suggests striving to reach some lofty end regarded as
somewhat beyond ones normal expectations.

Enterprising, implies an energetic readiness to take risks, or
undertake new projects in order to succeed. Emulous, suggests
ambition characterized by competitive desire to equal or surpass
another.

An ambitious person stole my car when I was visiting my father
at Callander Ontario, and we found it where the thief had ran out of
gas at Sudbury, Ontario. I had it towed into a gas station where I
met a young man about eleven years of age, jumping to the pumps.
It seemed quite normal for me to inquire as to what he was going to
be when he grew up, but just then another car drove in, the driver
stepped out from behind the wheel, the young man stared at him,
and at the same time answered my question by saying, "Ain't none
of us goin' to be anythin' if'n that jerk don't put out his cigarette."

You see he had ambition to live.

Many of you recognize that question.

"What do you want to be when you grow up?"

[Some still ask me that] Let me point out, that while goals, and ambitions, may not be wrong, they may certainly prove to be inadequate It is not wrong to have goals, and ambition that drive us; Jesus was very clear about Talents. The New Testament speaks about Godly ambition; but we need to realize that ambition can be misplaced, and misdirected.

From Philippians 3, I want to spend some time on Godly Ambition. We desire to serve God with mixed motives, and our ambition can be misplaced. Within all of us, and certainly within myself, there is a desire and need for recognition, a need for affirmation, and indeed a search for a measure of security in the things we do. That is basically is the introduction of this chapter. Paul is speaking about Holy Ambition. He goes on in some length to describe the changes in his life since he has found Christ, as opposed to how he thought in the past. In essence he states, I have goals and values totally different from what I used to have.

The major message he leaves here is that we need to fully lean on Christ, and trust him implicitly, by faith, not by our own great actions [works]. We are justified by the finished work of Christ on the cross. Compare; Galatians 2:16, *Knowing that a man is not justified by works of the law, but by faith of Jesus Christ, even we have believed in Jesus Christ, that we might be justified by the faith of Christ, and not by works of the law: for by the works of the law shall no man be justified.* and Romans 1:16, *For I am not ashamed of the gospel of Christ: for it is the power of God unto salvation to everyone that believeth; to the Jew first and also to the Greek.*

Knowing that major truth then I must deal with a man looking back on his life, [Paul] and saying, the ambitions that used to drive me are inadequate, and I have discovered better ambitions.

Whatever else Paul may be saying here, he most certainly points out that he puts no confidence in the flesh. He does say, I could put confidence in the flesh, you should see my credentials. Just take a look at what I had, I made sure that I stayed a Jew, not only that I belong to the strictest sect; I was sold out to God. I know the Torah from cover to cover. In doctrine, and effort I was faultless.

Paul, before becoming a follower of Christ, had that now cherished Christian trait, that arrogant sense that God must be really pleased with me, but he persecuted the church. He did point out an important factor as he says, but whatever was my profit, I consider loss for Christ's sake; that I might be found in him. I am concentrating on the new sense of ambition.

We know that Paul was dramatically met on the Damascus road when God challenged him as to his actions. Paul made the complete turn around at the cost of his vision.

I have come to realize, that in our so-called western world, the great tension for our Christianity, is not that we travel the Damascus road, but that we too are willing to allow our vision to be taken away before we see the real picture of absolute commitment to our living God through his son Jesus Christ to spend eternity in heaven. At sometime along our road of tribulation we must be born again out of a selfish womb we must be born again into eternal life to embrace the new life given to us through Christ. Only then shall we gain strength in the transformation from sinner to saint.

The tension is that it never really somehow gets into our psyche. That sort of conversion demands change in the most fundamental way in which we think, in values, in goals, in ambition of our lives. We buy into the culture into which we are converted. Paul says, 'I have suffered loss of all things'. By the same token, he kept his keen mind with his sense of vision with his indispensable energy and family ties. He no longer had the status he once had in the community. He was now a poor itinerant preacher, and he now had a prison record, and was hardly likely to be selected as a candidate for a good evangelical church pulpit.

That I may know him, and the power of his resurrection, and the fellowship of his sufferings, being made conformable unto his death;

Things can happen to us socially that will radically change our way of life, as well as our ambitions. There are circumstances in life that come to us, do not think that you can map it all out, because you cannot that is why our ambition has to be right from the beginning. Death can radically change our values, and ambitions. Ill health, bankruptcy, divorce, and our world can tumble in upon us, and around us. We do not plan things that way, but circumstance can hit us in the face, and turn our ambitions one hundred and eighty degrees. How changed are my ambitions?

I want to know Christ. I want to know the power of his resurrection. I want to know the fellowship of his suffering. Not in his head, but in his heart. We can have no truck with prosperity gospel that turns us all out looking like models. The gospel must cease being demeaned as a slick presentation. It must talk of the cross; where God exercised his ambition in love.

* * * * *

Strengthen My Hands

—⁓∾⁓—

For they all made us afraid, saying, their hands shall be weakened from the work, that it be not done. Now therefore, O God, strengthen my hands. Nehemiah 6:9.

The Prophet of God had just received a nasty letter of false accusation from someone who attempted to intimidate him, and stop his work for the living God he worshiped, and served. Here was a workman worth his weight in gold because of his commitment to God. He had gone to this place by himself on horseback to look over the situation which existed because of no fault of his own, but he was determined to build the urgently needed facility for those who needed it under God. The enemy made it a point to intimidate those who would help him build for their safety as God had directed. He sought no compensation for the work directive. Nehemiah only wanted to carry out God's will for his people, but the tirade of the enemy insisted that they should bring him down. It is for that reason here we read of the receiving of a false accusation against the prophet, where he cries unto God to strengthen his hands in order that he would be able to complete the work.

Were we to find the modern churches under such wild accusations today the greater part of our congregations would become shrinking violets. There would be a rush by some committee to have this builder removed from their midst. If there was at least one person that might suggest he was being treated unfairly, the committee may concede with the amendment to simply ask him to step aside until all this was cleared up. Knowing full well that problems of the church are never cleared up. Many times the ungodly action is witnessed as false accusation linger on forever. Inevitably there may be subdued hope that it will eventually go away by itself . Hoping that the person, though falsely, accused will die a natural death before there actually needs to be an honest to goodness thrust from believers to act as Jesus would act. For often it is as he said to the woman who brought before him having sinned, neither do I condemn thee.

The prophet also was surrounded by weak kneed ninnies that wanted to cash in their chips to let the loud mouthed false accusers have their own way, but he went out to convince them that the letter had no substance, and that they must continue to finish the project because God desired it. He went on with a multitude of tribulation created by the enemy who hated him.

A man lost his car keys, he managed to start his car by 'hot wiring' the ignition; But when the wires loosened the motor stopped. He asked a bystander to sit in and step on the accelerator while he adjusted the wires, but as soon as the car started again, the man at the wheel drove off. The owner ran to the phone booth to call the police, the police asked where he was, when he stuck his head out to inquire of someone, he was hit over the head with a wrench, and they took his wallet.

Sometimes misfortunes crowd in on us so rapidly, that the result is overwhelming. It is hard to put up with obstacles that originate with ones enemies. It is even more discouraging to face opposition from those that one regards as fellow workers. Nehemiah had already felt that the effects of discouragement among the Jews, because of the rigor or hard pace of the work they were doing. Now he was called to deal with the entire selfishness that seriously undermined the wall building project. They had dropped the normal routine, i.e. employment, business, worship, to devote all their attention to the rebuilding of the wall. God's work always demands priority. Unsaved people may die before we tell them about God's grace. Doors in some parts of the world are closing to the gospel. Christ may return at any time. The Jews who were building the wall, did not carry on business as usual, during this emergency period, about two months, and we must expect that at times we will be called upon to make special sacrifices that may interfere, temporarily, with normal living. The wall builders at Jerusalem voiced a great outcry to Nehemiah. The complaint had to do with the well to-do rulers and Nobles. The haves of every generation face the temptation to further improve themselves at the expense of the have nots.

Chapter 5: 3; tells us, the people of Israel suffered a serious shortage of food. They mortgaged everything they had to buy corn for nourishment. The poorer Jews had been forced to sell their children into bondage to their wealthy fellow Jews. No wonder they cried out against their creditors who, contrary to God's law, had taken over their real estate, and now were exacting slave labour from their sons and daughters. Opposition and ridicule from outside can hinder the work of a group of God's people, but faithlessness, on the part of the groups own members, does even greater harm.

Men and women, who profess to be God's people, have greater responsibilities, than those who make no such a profession. Since the oppressors in this case were prominent Jews in the city, Nobles, and Rulers, a less principled man than Nehemiah might have chosen to look the other way. Some people accept corruption as inevitable among those who are in position to get away with it. One who fears the Lord, however, is not afraid to administer justice, and let the chips fall where they may. A less courageous leader might have hesitated in putting his subordinates in an embarrassing position for fear of losing their support. One who fears the Lord however is not afraid to administer justice and let the chips fall where they may. The people where over taxed; His conduct had been beyond reproach. He did not blame past rulers, whether Senators, or Premiers, or Prime Ministers. Nehemiah gave up his perks.

And I sent messengers unto them, saying, I am doing here a great work, so that I cannot come down: why should the work cease, whilst I leave it, and come down to you? Yet they sent unto me four times after this sort; and I answered them after the same manner. Nehemiah 6;3-4.

Treachery raised it's ugly head as the wall was being completed the war of mockery was being waged against it, only to become in today's terminology, a war of nerves. Sanballot invited Nehemiah to a meeting to be held about 20 miles from Jerusalem on the plain of Ono. Nehemiah however saw through these plans and immediately said, "Oh, No!

What good would come of such a meeting?

What was there to discuss?

He was not about to compromise with his enemies, and he did not expect that they would make concessions either. A conference meeting at this point was a waste of time, and he had no time to waste foolishly. His job was to complete the wall, not to work outside the camp. People who realize that they are doing a great work for God, do not, as a rule, tolerate, unnecessary interruptions.

Nehemiah Chapter 6: 5 - 9; Slander, after failure to lure Nehemiah out, the enemies tried another ruse, they sent a servant to him with an open letter, *Wherein was written, It is reported among the heathen, and Gasmu saith it, That thou and the Jews think to rebel: for which cause thou buildest the wall, that thou mayest be their King, according to these words. And thou hast also appointed prophets to preach of thee at Jerusalem, saying, There is a King in Judah: and now shall it be reported to the King according to these words. Come now therefore let us take counsel together.*

This of course was sheer fabrication. Careless, and unprincipled reporters, may use the phrase, 'it is reported' to cover up their lack of research or the fact that they have concocted the story. But it doesn't make the story true. Sanballat knew the malicious rumour would spread rapidly. This was an absolute, and deliberate attempt to undermine the integrity of a great man of God which surfaced because of jealousy in the ranks. He was one who accomplished what he had set out to do, and the enemy went to great lengths to tear him down by undermine his intent, or as the game players of the mind would put it, we shall destroy his self esteem

Jealousy often allows people to build lies, against successful people

Some people say, gossip is like mud, if we try to wipe it off immediately, it will only smear, therefore we should allow it to dry. Others say it is like an infection, and unless we deal with it immediately it will spread.

Nehemiah made a simple, and prompt denial of the allegation, but here he let the matter rest. Neither the threat of armed attack nor the smear campaign put Nehemiah so strongly on the defensive that he was detoured from putting first things first.

His fear of God kept him from fear of those who plotted against him, but Nehemiah did not pray, Lord defend my reputation, he pointed out all the things that he had already accomplished, then told God of his expectations; then he put it into action, and built the needed wall.

We are responsible for our own actions. God requires we take the risk. After we have done what is reasonable, and proper, we can leave to the Lord, the baseless slander, of our enemies. Nehemiah's prayer was on a more positive note. O God, he says, strengthen my hands. When people retreat from life however, they become useless in the Lord's service. The antidote for such fear is, the Fear of God. Fear of displeasing Him by abandoning a task he has assigned. When we followers of Christ fear God the way we should, we are then able to conquer other fears. Allow me to share with you a true story.

A German Battalion marched in the below zero temperatures of winter succeeding to arrive at the outskirts of Moscow. They had little food left from the long march, and very little ammunition. Some of the soldiers wounded, and frost bitten, and many overcome with flagging morale. They awaited their Captains orders to march in to capture the city for which they had painfully marched so long. They where resigned to defeat, and capture, ready to suffer the final outcome. But the decision to die in the attempt was up to their leader. The Captain realizing that they had so little ammunition ordered his troops to begin the long and painful trek to, return to their camp, only to find out later that Moscow had been evacuated, and they had only to march in and take possession of the city. Had he been without fear of his enemy, he would have captured Moscow.

How do I know that story; because I have a friend who became a born again Christian who was a part of that Battalion.

We so much fear today. Violence, perceived, or otherwise, makes many people fear. Some are afraid to leave their homes by night. Fears of personal safety. Fear of Nuclear war, economic disaster, loss of employment, Fear of family problems. We live, I believe, in one of the most frightened generation since Christ's time. The antidote to fear, is the same today as it was in Nehemiah's time. Have faith in God, as Nehemiah feared God more than he feared that which may happen to him as he trusted the outcome into God's hands.

Fear of God was more to him than some theological term, it was a way of life.

Such fear of God as Nehemiah had is not terror, it is, reverential trust, in God, and a reluctance to displease Him. Solomon puts it best in Proverbs 9: 10; The fear of God is the beginning of wisdom. Only a person who fears God is able to live with the values of eternity in view and with an awareness of the great truth that 'the things which are seen are temporal, Paul, who also feared God, wrote; 'we are more than conquerors through Him that loved us. Romans 8:37.

* * * * *

On The Road To Emmaus
[The Basic Truth]

———⟨•/•/•⟩———

And they talked together of all those things which had happened. And it came to pass, that, while they communed together and reasoned, Jesus himself drew near, and went with them. Luke 24: 14-15.

A natural event was taking place after the extraordinary loss of leadership had transpired in the minds of the believers. They gathered together to console one another as they talked about the current events of the day. The top story, was the crucifixion of an innocent man over thieves, and murderers. A man whom they knew to be the Messiah sent to them by the living God whom they had trusted over the years, however it appeared to them that their Father in heaven had called the Master home, and there was to be a meeting to decide where to go from here. As they talked, the unrecognizable Christ joined in their walk, and encouraged them in the word.

Many of the modern day worshipers are unable to identify with this kind of uplifting to those who are down. We allow the disappointed people to wallow in self pity with no thought of encouragement in the word.

The foolishness of man's law. 1 John 2:22; Who is a liar but he that denieth that Jesus is the Christ?

Stop Checks perpetrated by man's law, make a claim that it will keep drunk drivers off the road. The truth of the check is that it was implemented in order to give police a socialist arm to stop and check all people at any time. The backroom decision had nothing to do with alcohol consumed by the general public. Then we must ask the question; has it worked?

The answer, 'absolutely not.

Hear some sporadic statistics; Over Christmas of '81 there were 31000 cars stopped, averaging three persons per car. That is a total of 93000 people affected by this lie promoted by the powers that be. Impaired out of that mass there were 45 persons. This leaves 92,955 unduly harassed by our police state, who claim this is a good law. The word 'abuse' quickly comes to mind as this law causes emotional damage, psychological damage, and mental damage. The point, they would have you believe it is right, for they have been educated by authority to embrace lies, and to further impose those lies upon the general public. In 2002 the percentages of people charged remained almost the same but the percentage of people unnecessarily harassed increased because of a perpetrated lie that the law structure wishes to keep alive. The sad truth is, that they couldn't care less about the drinking driver as long as they don't have to tell the truth of why this law is in existence at all. It is simply because the stunted imagination of the law makers believe it is a method of control over all people. As long as they promote the lie that they are trying to protect you, there is no outcry and the innocent people suffer the humilities, and fear of reprisal from a new order of the Roman Empire who continue to slay the innocent as a measure of controlling people.

The educational system has taken away the right of the Christian with more lies of socialism; saying that religion has no place in the class room, when in fact it was due to the Christian philosophy that schools were finally established with good moral base that included the preservation of the Christian teaching. As they take away the Christians rights, they impose the religion of an unbelieving world upon us in the form of Santa Clause, Easter Bunny, witches, and goblins; the religion of humanism, or as they have titled it 'The New Age'.

On the TV program W5, they gave a story of a fourteen year old girl, who in tears, sobbed out the story of babies taken from incubators and the incubators being stolen. Her tears swayed the Nation to go to war, only to find that it was a terrible hoax, it was all a lie.

We must then ask the question; What of the Holocaust? Is it

also a terrible political hoax? So needful for the politicians to keep this story alive as true, that they have made laws to punish those who speak against this obvious political hoax.

Lies, lies, lies, the world continues to deal in lies. Although we should not be surprised at this; because the bible tells us that Satan is the Father of lies, and the unbelieving secular world have nothing else to draw from. The world's blindness perpetrates the thought, it's okay.

Let us interject Jesus into the tradition of these hypocritical traditions of men. Their tradition of perpetual deceit shall crumble. God sent His only Son with this message; "I am the way, the truth, and the life." God deserves nothing but the best. He is the King, and worship means serving Him. Surely there has never been a life that seems to be more lonely, and alien, than the life of Jesus Christ. He came with a heavenly language, yet moved upon the common street, with the poor, and downcast, and hungry. Yet whose life is it that is alien, and lonely in a world of God.

Is it His or ours?

Whose customs are strange?

We shall never find ourselves at home until we learn from Christ, of His Holiness, of that which He left behind for our salvation, and of the pain, and suffering, that He took upon Himself for those that had no hope.

Luke, Chapter 24, tells about two people talking, as they walked, about Jesus. It was apparently the third day after the crucifixion. As they were walking along the highway talking about the events that had taken place, also lamenting about their dashed hopes of deliverance by this great leader. They had counted on Jesus that they had come to place much confidence in. Obviously their hopes had been dashed as they mourned the loss of their Christ. They were indeed believers in crisis. They had not found any solutions at Calvary. Not many of us appear to feel fully content with what our lives got out of that transaction at Golgotha. The average result runs every where from restlessness to downright discouragement, but to those who have seen nothing is often because their vital energies are spent in some other direction. Many are unable to comprehend what Jesus did for living, by dying. If a loving, living God, had not imposed his love upon us in such a generous portion, and offered up His only Son Jesus Christ as a sacrifice on the cross at Calvary, social ethics would not matter that much. The right, and wrong, of anything would be redundant. Without the sacrifice of the cross, which Christianity is, right does not and cannot exist. We can never look forward until we recognize the keeping of our focus toward the cross. Man's best has fallen short. Our God is too great for our small hearts. So God sent Jesus to be the bridge of man, to God the Father. Accepting Christ into ones life there will be found new desires. You will discover love, and care that you never dreamed existed. There will awake within you a new zeal with a magnetic need to share and care for others.

Luke 24: 21; *But we trusted that it had been he which should have redeemed Israel*:

The two walkers, perhaps friends of Jesus, saw that the cross had spelled failure. They had not yet pieced together the whole story. Even now as Jesus walked with them they failed to recognize him. As they related the event to him because they thought he was a stranger to the country; Jesus challenged them. Luke 24: 25; *O fools, and slow of heart to believe all that the prophets have spoken:*

How often we listen, but fail to hear what is spoken of the word to us. When scripture delivers a scathing rebuke to us, we would rather denigrate the deliverer of the message than to accept God's direction; But we as these two friends, out walking, we lower the substance of the message to our lack of understanding. We too become slow of heart to believe. Christ continues in verse twenty-six with His challenge, whoever said that the going is not rough?

Is it not right that Christ should have suffered these things to enter into His glory? Here he was trying to make them come to grips with the fact that Christ had laid down His life because there was no other way for God to channel to us the forgiveness of sin. Because there is something absurd about the world that could never understand Christianity. The unbelieving secular world is like unto the sick who take medicine to make the illness disappear forever, in hopes that it will never return. A man's heart must be in tune with Christ, the Son of God who became man to bear our sins on the cross at Calvary.

Listen, hear the whisper of a stricken God, still stumbling towards the cross, not to lose, but to win an important victory over death and the grave, to conquer sin. He never asserts himself, nor crowds anything upon anyone. When Adam fell, he could have cancelled Adam. When Abraham lied, when Jacob stole, when David committed adultery; God could have eliminated them out of his precious plan of outreach to his creation, but he didn't. He continued in their lives until they repented to become great, and honourable men of God. He allowed himself to be a prisoner innocently accused, and came himself to the sacrifice at the cross of Calvary. He said, I will not make you listen, I shall not use my power, but shall put my life in the hands of your power. I shall stand in front of all your little Pilates, as helpless as can be, as poor, and friendless, and we shall see that God takes no shortcuts. He [Jesus] appeared to be going further in verse twenty-eight, because there were other lonely despairing folks that would desire comforting from the same initial events that were being discussed here. The Basic Truth is only a Christ centred life will allow you to go forward.

Are you living the world's lie; or are you serving Christ?

You cannot have it both ways. Jesus must be Lord of your life, saviour from your sin, Christ of your heart.

How many have you invited to worship with you that they too might come to know Jesus as their Lord and Saviour?

Are you seen as a Christ like person, or only as a church attendee?

Again, the Basic Truth is that we need to be seen as workers for a living God to the point that others will be touched as they witness the evidence of the work of the Holy Spirit in us.

* * * * *

The Grace Givers

—◦◦◦—

Be kindly affectionate one to another with brotherly love; in honour preferring one another; Not slothful in business; fervent in spirit; serving the Lord; Rejoicing in hope; patient in tribulation; continuing instant in prayer; Distributing to the necessity of the saints; given to hospitality. Bless them which persecute you: bless, and curse not. Romans 12: 10-14.

The book of Romans is a writing to be revered by the Christian Community as a document that gives us instructions on how to live with ourselves, and others. In these writings the Apostle Paul challenges each follower of Christ in the way that a person ought to live. Also he challenges each believer on how we ought to treat our neighbour, the person beside us. The challenge of these writings of Paul, is to love the unlovely. The people that our secular society would cast out because of the poor image, or lack of a success story, good enough to fit in with the elite. We need to love others in a very special way. We need to love them as Christ loved us. He was willing to die for us.

Are you willing to die for someone you know, today?

How do we do a thing like that, love as though we would give ourselves for someone?

Instead of referring to ourselves as Christian, we need to think of ourselves as grace givers.

You see Christ saved us by his grace. For it is by the grace of God you have been saved. It is by that very same grace that we need to learn to reach out and touch others. Forgiveness locked silently within our hearts. No big scene of showmanship surrounding us.

Just a simple touch of love to those that the world has cast aside, and the Christian has built up a tolerance for. We need to make an attempt to reach out and touch someone for our Lord. The fact is, I often find that the unbeliever has become more tolerance motivated than the confessing believer. What a catastrophic witness for our Christian community. We need to see the renewing of our minds to a true God consciousness to become a generation of grace givers. I see two major hindrances to being a grace giver; 1. We attempt to control others.

2. We make a comparison of others to ourselves. To those we think we would like to or should associate ourselves with, then we too reject the lost soul.

Attempting to control others that may act according to my assessment, will lead to rigid, and legalistic living under man's law. There is no justice under man's law, neither is there any mercy, love, or concern, or caring, and totally without empathy. That type of thinking is not what Christ intended for man. Christ commanded us to love one another with love that expects absolutely nothing in return, charity.

The comparison game leads into some real negative alleys. You may consider somebody better than yourself, and that is envy, and envy is an empty emotion that only damages those who exercise it.

Secondly, we in comparing become judgmental of actions of friends that others keep. We dislike places they frequent, or the type of clothes they wear to special events.

Judging others leads to a third position, and that is a position of prejudice. It is easy to shy away from a culture that you do not understand, sometimes we justify our prejudices with the erroneous statement that God has not yet opened the door for us to understand those people, I say, woe there, look at the words of Jesus, *"Behold I stand at the door and knock, if any man hear my voice, and open the door, I will come in and sup with him, and he with me. Rev 3: 20.*

Oh dear! He went away because he didn't look like the kind of person I wanted in my home. And besides that, I didn't know God wanted me to open the door. After all you are God, and you could have opened the door.

No! No! a thousand times no! God does not work that way.

Time and again throughout the scriptures you will find that God requires you to act on your own steam. When we envy, or are judgmental, or practice prejudice against any one person or sect, whether in church as believers, or in the world as unbelievers. It will ultimately nullify God's grace. I shall attempt to leave with you some guidelines on being a grace giver.

1. Accept others: It is my firm belief that every person you meet is put in front of you for a purpose that God wants you to fulfill. If you name the name of Christ, and claim to be a follower of that Christ, as a servant to him, then remember the person in front of you is there for a reason in which God expects you to act. You are needed by heaven to speak for the king.

What greater task could you be called to?

Do not mutter and stumble about thinking you do not have the authority, God in saving you, gave you the authority to speak his gospel to every creature. You do not need to look for some gift, God has already chosen you to serve the moment you said yes to Jesus, make no mistake about that.

You may say, well preacher I'm waiting for God's leading. Listen my friend, he has already led you to the cross, he has led you to the plan of salvation, he led you to his son's shed blood, he has led you to the grave, he has led you to the resurrection.

What exactly do you mean when you say you are waiting for God's leading?

Listen, he is so far ahead of you now you best get a jump start, and get on with his plan to have the gospel preached to all nations.

What are you really waiting for?

Another star in the East. Well, my brother, sister, it isn't going to happen. God wants you to get the job done with the tools he has already delivered to you, and he wants it done now. Open that door with your action while he is still knocking.

There are those who talk about leading in their Christian life as though Christ, and God, are sitting in heaven having a conversation about will we, or won't we allow such, and such a thing to happen for so, and so. Let me assure you my friends that God's plan is already in motion, and he is beckoning you to come aboard under your own steam. I for one thank him that he is not waiting for some

Christian group to make up their minds as to will they or wont they. God's plan is in motion, and it is time for the church to catch up to God. The way they can do that is by teaching their people to be grace givers. To those in need of your grace from God, pass it on in compassion for the entire community.

In my compassion to help others, I sometimes find myself getting left behind, or so I think. There is a measure of truth in that, but I believe that oftentimes God expects of us that we need to take that risk.

Three of my favourite men in the bible are, Shadrach, Meshach, and Abendago. They took the risk with their lives as they informed the king of their stand. I believe I can hear them saying these words, *If it be so, our God whom we serve is able to deliver us from the burning fiery furnace, and he will deliver us out of your hand, o king. But if not, be it known unto thee, o king, that we will not serve thy Gods nor worship the golden image which thou hast set up.* Daniel3: 17-18.

Allow God to assume the direction as the action goes on. we must never assume a position that we are not qualified for. According to the scriptures, the only position that we are not allowed to fill is the position of judge.

There are six reasons why we are not qualified to judge other people.

1. We do not know all the facts.
2. We are unable to read the motives.
3. It is impossible to be totally objective.
4. We lack the big picture.
5. We have blind spots.
6. We are imperfect ourselves.

We need in all these things to be wise, and above all to be sensitive making ourselves qualified to be grace givers.

What is grace?

This question in and of itself promotes a sermon.

Acts 15:11, *But that we believe that through the grace of our Lord Jesus Christ we shall be saved, even as they.*

Romans 4: 4, *now to him that worketh is the reward not reckoned of grace, but of debt.*

Favour or kindness shown without regard to worth or merit of the one who receives it. Mercy is a separate action from God's grace, love, compassion, and patience as a source of help, and deliverance from distress. Although the grace of God is free, it must not be taken for granted for grace is only enjoyed from within the covenant. Grace is the measure of God's holy love. We often relegate love to an unreal world of false emotion. It has been said that love is blind, but I believe when exercised in the purest form it can be claimed to be the only element that truly opens ones eyes of the heart with absolute and proper vision to see all correctly.

To love with a Christlike zeal can only be supported in the context of the spirit, and only then man's spirit catches fire in being touched by God's spirit. It is God's holy spirit that inspires, and sustains our zeal.

Proverbs 20: 27, says, *The Spirit of man is the candle of the Lord.* Verse 12, of Romans chapter 12 tells us that *we must be continuing in instant prayer.* [a] We are to rejoice in hope.(b) We are to be patient in tribulation . (c) We are to be constant in prayer.

Life is not merely a matter of right response, it also requires appropriate expression.

We need to develop a new vocabulary. The world does not understand our language. It is up to us to teach the unbelieving world the language of God by being grace givers.

1st Peter 1: 3b, tells us that, we must be thrust into a lively hope by the resurrection of Jesus Christ from the dead.

We see here, God himself quickens our spiritual apathy. We may at times mount up with wings as eagles, other times we must be content to run, and not be weary, even to walk and not to faint. Is 40: 31.

Faith is not a guarantee that we shall be delivered from misfortune, it's only a guarantee of eternal life for those who follow Christ in obedience. Those who will not accept the rigorous demands in following Christ, need not begin.

Matt 10: 37-39, *He that loveth father or mother more than me is not worthy of me, he that loveth son or daughter more than me, is not worthy of me: and he that taketh not his cross and followeth not after me, is not worthy of me. He that findeth his life shall lose it, and he that loveth his life for my sake shall find it.*

We ought to give others honour rather than to take it away from them. When Roman soldiers set upon a foreign soil to conquer, it is said that they burned their ships to remove any thought of retreat, or any attitude of defeat. We in our daily Christian walk must set the same course. No attitude of defeat. Always claim the victory. Live for Christ without looking for an escape route.

Simply, it is called commitment. Know the culture of the people round about you. God put them beside you that you would give of his grace to them. Never fear, you cannot run out of grace. The fact is, the more you exercise it, the larger it will appear, and the faster it will spread, and God's people will rejoice in it.

I received a call bringing my attention to a lady named, Tammy Baker. I turned on my TV to listen with interest the way she handled the questions put to her. One of her comments was this, Years ago they threw the Christians to the lions, today they just throw them to the press." She then went on defending many situations that had been thrust upon her. Whether you liked her or didn't like her, is not the question. It is the fact that she gave God the credit, even for her crisis.

Where do you stand today?

Can you praise God for where you are at?.

You do not need an in depth theological background to be a saver of souls. You do not need to understand all of the social ills of society in order to be sensitive to needy, hurting people. God forbid that you would accept that psychology has the answer. That is an ungodly, man made philosophy, and the bible warns against following man's philosophy. Remember people need encouragement. You can help lift them up to God with positive words of love. Be concerned, do not be nosy. Do not be simply a builder of knowledge even though we know that knowledge is good, but even more is needed so be an ambassador of Jesus Christ.

Generate a real and lasting love for the person on a one to one basis. Do not expect them to love you back. Many of them will, just remember it was Christ who gave his life, and the world has not yet learned to love him back. You are not of this world therefore do not attempt to hurt God's work over pettiness. You are called to be a builder, not to tear down existing structure, for if something needs to be removed for you to surge ahead, God will remove it in his own time. Finally, focus your heart, and soul, with a generous portion of love for God, and his creation who wait for you to give them grace as Christ has given it to you.

* * * * *

The Lord Has Need Of It

Jesus saith unto them, Go your way into the village over against you: and as soon as ye be entered into it, ye shall find a colt tied, whereon never a man sat; loose him, and bring him. And if any man say unto you, Why do ye this? say ye that the Lord has need of him; and straightway he will send him hither. Mark 11: 2-3.

Although I am not an artist, I would have you bear with me while I draw you a picture of the Cross. There hang the blessings upon a nail, Christ Jesus, but being short of stature, we cannot reach them; the Spirit of God takes them down, and hands them to us, one by one, and thus they become totally ours. In Spirit let us walk lovingly toward Him, and tremble at the thought of grieving Him.

The owner of the colt allowed the claim. Either he was acquainted with Jesus and his disciples or there was something about the request that carried persuasive power.

If the teacher, prophet, of Galilee, here for the only time in Mark called Lord, had need of the colt, he would acknowledge the priority.

This surely ought to be our response to God's need of anything we have. There are so many powers, and capacities, and aptitudes, as well as possessions of which it can be said; "The Lord has need of it." There are skills that can be put to use for the Kingdom, personalities, that can be put to use as the instrument of His truth, feet, that can go on His errands, hands, that can lift the burdens. If this man in Jerusalem, who owned the colt, had treated the disciples who came for it as we often treat God's calls for help, the conversation might have been,

What are you doing with my colt?

The same response; The Lord has need of it!

What do I care, I need it myself, get away, and leave me alone.

There may even be a rougher language. We may never put our polite refusals of God's demands in such blunt terms, we may even be careful to be 'politically correct'; but there is no doubt about the refusal.

God needs our time! Sorry, but my time is limited; besides, it is my time, and I shall do as I please with it.

God needs our strength! Sorry, I cannot take on a single thing more; I am almost exhausted as it is.

God needs our minds! Sorry, But I have all that I can possibly give my attention to - and more. I have troubles enough of my own to think about.

What kind of priority does God get with us?

And many spread their garments in the way: and others cut down branches off the trees, and strewed them in the way. Mark 11: 8.

An impressive picture of putting self aside caused by great enthusiasm. There was no debate about it. No cautious trial balance to see whether or not there was a risk to the clothes was really called for. No wondering at a show of respect at a cheaper price that might be enough. These people were lifted on a tide of hope, and joy, and love.

Spontaneous enthusiasm is like a flood tide, life has nothing to match it for exhilaration, and zest. The life that never forgets itself in a great lift of devotion is poor.

Such spontaneous enthusiasm is indispensable to the work of Christianity in the world, and in ones own community. Many spread their garments on the road.

Do we ever spread anything costly before Him?

Like perhaps a maximum offering of mind, heart, skill, without any bookkeeping wisdom to determine the minimum would be enough. Jesus had often been greeted with a question mark beside Him, we read in Mark 6:2b from whence has this man these things? And what wisdom is this which is given unto Him that even such mighty works are wrought by his hands?

John the Baptist did it to him as well when he considered the question in Matthew 11:3; And he said unto him, Art thou he that should come, or do we look for another?

And again Pilate in John 18:37; Pilate therefore said unto him, Art thou a King then?

The world has had it's millions of question marks about Jesus, is he really the way?

This journey with Jesus cannot be made by thought alone, but there must be action. When we follow him, we do the things He says, like, love your enemy, go without scrip or purse, Go into the highways and byways and compel them to come in, or take no thought of tomorrow. Do we freely allow ourselves to bless them that curse you and revile you and despitefully use you and say all manner of evil against you for my sake.

Mark 11: 11; *and Jesus entered into Jerusalem and into the Temple: and when he had looked round about upon all things, and now the eventide was come, He went out unto Bethany with the twelve.*

The picture here well relates to our community.

How much in our hometown could we show our Lord Jesus Christ?

Could we show him the old schoolhouse where prayer has been established in spite of the regulations set by some ungodly body of unbelievers?

Maybe we could take Him to the courthouse where the law is upheld to God's Glory. Perhaps we could show Him the social service office that helps those who are troubled by giving them the message of the Son of God. Better yet, we could just take Him to the community centre where many good people gather to help their neighbours. Surely, such loving hearts would hold up the message of the shed blood of our Lord Jesus Christ for Him to see while He visited with us.

Where would you take him?

What would you be excited about showing Him in your community?

In this verse we find a transition, From entry into the city, to rest in Bethany. In, and out, because there where only sacrilegious acts to see. Nothing in respect to the Son of God; nor his generous gift of Salvation. Would you be embarrassed to show Him around our environment of a Christless community, which has a total lack of God consciousness.

An unforgettable picture here. Christ going about the community looking at everything that took his eye, and awesome disclosure as he witnessed the abuse of the Temple. Not a business place, not an entertainment place, but a house of prayer, in distortion.

A place of worship, not meeting God's needs, but only the assemblance of secular mind, and He went out and rested, because the Lord had need of it.

Where do you stand today?

Are you holding back that which God has need of?

Are you giving him your all?.

Your strength, your mind, your priority, your worship, because the Lord has need of it.

The Lord has need of your faith in the shed blood of His Son on the cross of Calvary. God has need of your faith in His forgiveness of your sin by the sacrifice paid on Calvary's hill. The Lord is in need of your belief in the resurrection from the grave, and the ascension of Christ to seal for us life eternal. The Lord has need of a faith that knows Jesus sits on the right hand of the Father interceding on our behalf. With faith I can do all things; without faith I shall never have the inclination nor the power to do anything in the service of God. Little faith will go to heaven, but it then must hide itself in a small compartment, and it frequently loses all but its goals. Little faith says, "It is a rough road, set in sharp thorns, and full of dangers, I am afraid to go."

Great faith says, remember the promise; thy shoes shall be irons, and brass, as thy days, so shall thy strength be" so boldly we can venture into the unknown call of his master.

Little Faith stands pondering, should I, or shouldn't I, and becomes despondent in the floods of the world's cares and woe. Great faith sings; "When thou passeth through the waters, I shall be with thee: and through the rivers I shall not overflow thee.

Are you looking for success as a servant of God, with joy free from gloom. Then have great faith in God. If you love darkness and wish to play in the Little faith league by looking only for that comfort zone, then your life will be full of misery. So I challenge you, put to work the greatest gift of God, "Your Great Faith" by proclaiming to others the message that Jesus Saves. Because the Lord has need of it.

* * * * *

The Wonder Of
The Christian Family

—≈⟨०/०/०⟩≈—

*For thus saith the Lord God; behold, I, even I, will both search my
sheep, and seek them out. As a shepherd seeketh out his flock in the
day that he is among his sheep that are scattered; so will I seek out
my sheep, and will deliver them out of all places where they have
been scattered in the cloudy and dark day.* Ezekiel 34: 11-12.

The wonder of the Christian family. Caring, sharing, rejoicing,
even so I worry about the prodigals older brother, and I want
to touch on the meanings of some of this so called Christian Spirit,
and renewal.

There is little doubt that we need a rediscovery of the
indwelling of the Holy Spirit in our churches or we are bound for
entrapment of a cult perversion of the teaching that is now often
portrayed under the guise of charismatic. Nothing is real, and lasting except it be touched by the Spirit. We find ourselves involved in
the church game of, moralistic uptightness. In our fallen nature, we
need the cross, and the transaction of Jesus. The A.A. programme
has a mystical attraction similar to what the church used to be.
Everyone attends because there is a need, and they have that need.

We need a new movement within the church to portray the
worlds need for a risen saviour. When our language, and our life, is
able to project Christ to the Nation, they will see their need, and the
churches would be overflowing. I am afraid that we have become so
disoriented as to the word of God that we have forgotten about the
world, and turned our focus inward to self, buried in ways, and

means, rather than a genuine outreach for the salvation of lost souls.

Luke, and Johns emphasis, as Paul, speaks out is the one that makes it clear that the Spirit gives the commission of Mission. At the birth of Christ, Mary was told that she would bear the seed of God. How? The power of God will come upon you, she was told by the Angel.

As Christ was Baptized in the river of Jordan, the Spirit descended like a Dove.

Luke 4: 16; Jesus went into the synagogue as was his custom. The Spirit of the Lord is upon me. Isa: 56, Because he anointed me to preach the gospel. I am going to send you what my father promised Luke 24: 49. No evidence of them asking or seeking the Holy Spirit. Acts talks of the spirit the community of believers. Acts 1:4; there was absolutely nothing they could do to make the event occur. A survey taken, shows that percentage of bartenders voting, is higher than the percentage of pastors who vote.

Waiting, and urgency, about the Christian life. First there needs to be an incredible sense of Community, one senses over, and over, in the book of Acts. However we need to realize, we do not achieve the Unity; we do not wire it together. We enter into union when we accept Christ as our saviour. That is a given. It is the Spirit that creates [gives] that unity of me, and Christ to God. It is not the brilliance of some Pastor, not the power of Deacons, not the power of some man made structure, not the power of our church: It is a given at our acceptance of Jesus Christ who then allows us to enter with our full measure of salvation whereby we will know him and be transformed into the family of God.

Our churches are either closed or open. The fire, and flame, of openness draws people in. The young have a problem when we draw the line of demarcation. The most common metaphor Paul used for the church is, body. We, with our belief, measure with a common denominator, something we received by grace, and not by works.

Church is organic living tower of God's light, not an institution with a set of rules, to be changed at the whim of those who cannot conform to God's criteria as laid down in his word. We tend always to struggle with the term of spiritual superiority. We are members of one another. There are people who come to church Sunday after Sunday who are cold, frozen, and dead, and all around the people have no idea the battles they are fighting. Every member has its own function. All are not one ear, nor one eye, as Paul so aptly points out. Yet we have the tendency to try to redo each other, and rearrange each other. The tongue does the damage to the soul. Many churches today wouldn't know what to do with a red hot genuine convert. It relates somewhat to putting a live chick under a dead hen. We cannot say to any part of the body, we do not need you. One damaged little finger, and the whole body hurts. I smashed my little finger while working in a sawmill, believe me the whole body suffers from the damage. If you where to lose your big toe you would fall flat on your face when trying to navigate without help or warning. Every part of our body is essential to the perfect function given us.

The same applies to the fellowship of the church body. Each person has been placed by God to function with the whole body that there may be a visible co-ordinated action for Christ. Each soul plays a valuable part in the administering of the word.

Secondly the Holy Spirit gives us the power for witness. That power was made available by God because the total community was of one mind. They had waited some ten days whilst they sorted out their dirty linen, and confessed their sins unto God. Witness is not divorced from congregational life. The church must begin to train people to witness.

How long is it since you have told someone about the change that Christ has made in your life?

Perhaps you fail to speak because you know that others cannot see that change because of your lifestyle. On the other hand your lifestyle may have changed, but you are attached to the same worldly language you are used to.

You may ask, 'To whom can I witness?' Why not start with the meter reader, the garbage man, your insurance agent, the mechanic who works on your car, Avon lady, grocery clerk, cashier, bagger. When they ask you if that will be all, say no, I want you to accept my Jesus as your saviour too. Or more closely related talk to your fishing buddy, or your golf partner. Take someone bowling with you, and witness even by the good attitude with which you lose, on, and on, the list goes, for there are many around you who have not yet received Christ as saviour. Even greater, you will find those who where once committed, but for some reason have fallen away, and you may be the very one that God has put in place to give them an invitation to come and worship with you.

After parking my car I walked a block past a row of houses to a church that I was Pastoring, in London Ontario, and every Sunday there sat a man on the veranda of one of those houses, rocking to and fro in his old wicker rocking chair, and I would greet him with a cheery good morning each Sunday, Finally one morning I stopped to talk with him, and ask him to come to church with me. He jumped out of his chair so fast that it startled me. He pulled on his beautiful beige cardigan, limped to the steps, and said, 'you bet' I've been rocking on this veranda for forty years watching people come, and go in this church, and you are the first one who has invited me to come.

What a shame to the Christian body when we walk by those who may come, and we fail to ask them to join us. What a blemish on the church of Christ. The lesson here is that we need to learn to share our saviour with the unsaved as well as the saved.

After the stoning of Stephen, they went abroad preaching the gospel everywhere.

Phillip preached to the Samaritans, and he preached to an individual Eunuch. We must, by the Holy Spirit cross over culture. Witness to the drug addict, users, pushers, pimps, and prostitutes, boozers, as well as friends at a simple coffee party

The third element that the Holy Spirit leads us, is to worship. Remember the Holy Spirit in no way acts to displace Christ. We find a number of organizations that hold the Holy Spirit in greater esteem than that of Christ, and his work. God, is a God of order; and the order is as such, God the Father, Christ the Son, and last is the Holy Spirit the comforter, and edifier, of Christ. Always in the same order; Father, Son, and Holy Spirit.

Area number four in which we are directed by the Holy Spirit allows us to build our own open agenda to lead other lost souls to Christ while heeding the call from God the Father.

Peter and John going into the temple, confronted by a beggar, they gave him the testimony about Jesus Christ the Son of God. Then the trouble started.

What is your vision?

You might well ask, How do I achieve a vision?

See the many unsaved souls around about you. See the one unsaved soul you need to give testimony to. Think on that unsaved person you need to make a phone call to.

Ephesians 5: 18; *And be not drunk with wine, wherein is excess; but be filled with the Spirit;*

This is our mandate; the question is not, how much of the spirit do we have a hold of?

The question is, How much of us does the spirit have a hold of?

Strange that drunkenness, and being filled with the spirit are mentioned in the same verse. When someone gets drunk it effects the whole body. The body will wobble, it reflects a slowness of action as well as the mind, the speech often slurs, and all in all, the drunken body produces the ultimate in inability to function in the so called normal way.

What happens when we are Spirit filled?

Well it also effects the whole body. It most certainly will effect the speech, for there will come words of praise, love, and comfort to others. It will effect the eyes, for you will see others in a different light. Your brain will be effected because it will change your thinking to concern rather than prejudice; it may even effect the way you present that body to others in cleanliness, and dress. Most certainly it will effect your attitude. For your outlook upon a tragic world will be changed. The Holy Spirit within you will show you that it is impossible for you to change the whole world, but that you may contribute to the saving of lost souls simply by telling your story how Jesus changed your life, to someone who has not yet made that step.

Did you know that you are filled with the Spirit when you accept Christ as your saviour?

It is not some kind of bonus to be added at a later date if your works prove satisfactory. The spirit is given as part of the package with God's grace to begin your transformation.

Ephesians 4: 30; *And grieve not the Holy Spirit of God, whereby ye are sealed until the day of redemption.*

Herein lies a warning, not to insult God by the rejection of his leading, and do not put Christ down by leaving him out of your conversation that is to be Godly.

A great Christian theologian, F.B. Meyer, had a dream that Christ came and wanted the keys to his life and as he gave them to him he saw the nail prints in his hand. Christ asked, him, are these all the keys? and he said yes, all except one little one to a small room. Christ gave back his keys, and said, If I cannot have all your keys, I do not want any of them.

Meyer said he woke up with hot tears running down his cheeks. I knew what it was, there was a pastor down the street having greater services than me, and I was jealous of him. I got on my knees, and ask the Lord to forgive me, and I gave him my last key.

Each of us needs to give that last key over to the Lord. We need the spirit of forgiveness in our own lives before our life can effect others. Follow that open agenda that allows others a first spot in your life; because you refuse to take any action that would grieve the spirit.

Do not promote spiritual leprosy in the church. Lot's wife looked back and suffered the consequences of it. Let us not look back on the life we used to live: But look forward to a new life filled with the power of the Holy Spirit and the love of God that enables us to care for the lost and dying of a sin filled world. Go today, and give the message of salvation to some lost soul. You will not have to seek them out. God will place them before you.

Grieve not the Holy Spirit by suggesting that the timing is not right, for we find the bible says, behold, now is the accepted time; behold, now is the day of salvation. 2 Corinthians 6: 2b.

* * * * *

To Be Involved

―⟨o/o⟩―

I beseech thee, O Lord God of heaven, the great and terrible God, that keepeth covenant and mercy for them that love him and observe his commandments; Let thine ear now be attentive, and thine eyes open, that thou mayest hear the prayer of thy servant, which I pray before thee now, day and night, for the children of Israel thy servants, and confess the sins of the children of Israel, which have sinned against thee: Both I and my Father's house have sinned. Now these are thy servants, and thy people whom thou hast redeemed by thy great power, and thy strong hand Nehemiah. 1: 5-6, 10,

A leader seeing the despair of the people felt the need to approach the living God in fervent meaningful prayer from the depths of his soul. While talking to God about the situation, this man was not afraid to bring to the attention of his God that these were indeed his people that he had delivered out of Egypt, but now there was another real need for God to rescue Nehemiah from those who would destroy the work that he had set out to do for God's people.

Before I was saved, I was walking along a city street of Sarnia Ontario when I discovered a man, and a women, who where shouting at the top of their lungs at each other. It appeared to be a most ludicrous argument, and it was apparent to me that both had been drinking heavily. Of a sudden, the man began to thump the women with his fists. I, youthful, and valiant, came to the rescue, and became involved, attempting to subdue the man to stop his attack upon this frail little woman, but much to my surprise, she began to curse and swear, and to beat on me for touching her husband. It was a no win situation, and it was a long time before I ever got involved in taking sides in a street fight whether it was man to man or women to man or whatever.

It is usually from human perspective that we within ourselves decide that it is none of our business, and we fail to get involved. We adopt the tendency to look the other way when we encounter someone in trouble, or find a situation that needs to be corrected. Victims have suffered at the hands of others while people deliberately refused to help, lest they themselves become the victims. I know because I became that kind of a person after my experience, but since then I allowed Christ to take charge of my life, and he shows me that I must continue to take the risk to deliver persons from a sinful nature to salvation of their soul.

It is not so much that they lack empathy for the one in need, as it is a self pity section of life that says, poor me, might have to take on some consequences.

Thank God we can look to history and find great men who have felt otherwise. People like Menno Simons, John Wesley, John Knox, David Livingston, Martin Luther, along with many unsung heroes of Christianity, that busied themselves years hence in church planting from East to West, while spreading the gospel before the erection of any wooden or stone frame. They made it a normal function to have the Altar in the home, and there to worship God as family. After which neighbours came together to fellowship, and worship in log houses under sod roofs. Imagery was not a factor, only worship was essential.

These people got involved without concern or fret of what people would think. In the building of communities in those days it was an accepted event knowing that others would react in a very positive sense. They, as Nehemiah, simply went out and put into action a clear vision received from God. Not some apparition appearing, nor some vague man made fortune telling prophet, but the simple knowledge that they where in fact servants of a living God, who had sacrificed his son for their redemption. They received the word, and acted upon it, by being immediately involved in their community. Aware of dormant communities, they made them come alive with the work of Christ. When there was resistance they did something about it. They became victors over difficult, and adverse situations.

Nehemiah was a man such as this. He eventually appointed as Governor by the King because of his boldness to approach the situation at hand. The bible tells us that he was a cupbearer for the King. This was a position of some prestige. Probably parallel to a diplomat who could apply the Ambassador technique in today's standard. One who was a good public relations expert who was able to set the agenda for festivities of the King and the protocol for those who would be invited to the Royal festivities of the day. The cupbearer was to serve the wine to special guests, and taste it to make sure it was properly fermented as not to offend special guests of the King. Nehemiah was compassionate, and supporter of his fellow believers, and looked to God for guidance as well as for his provisions.

In chapter one, Nehemiah has upon his heart a direction from God with concern for the destroyed walls of Jerusalem, or which he goes to God in prayer. In this prayer he reminds God who is before him in prayer, and of a promise made by God to his people whom had been scattered. In a very real sense he tells God what an important position he was leaving to be a builder of Jerusalem's walls. He understood the culture of the day. For a city without walls was a none entity in the eyes of the political arena. We find in verse three, he had inquired about the people, when he was informed about the burned gates and the destruction of the walls from those that gave him the information that he sought, he was overcome with grief of the disaster.

Verse four tells us that he sat down and wept, and mourned for several days, and fasted, and prayed to God in heaven. I grieve that the heart of today's Christian does not grieve so in depth about the evils that take place around us in today's society. If we would be so committed to Christ that we would be thrice accountable to weep over the disaster, fast, and pray, to the living God through His Son Jesus Christ, tell him that we are about to act in a way he expects us to. To build for the Kingdom of God by showing compassion for the souls of men that we may love them into the heavens above.

In verse seven, we find this great man of God, first confessing his sin before God after he had wept over the crisis. Nehemiah cared about the suffering of God's people and he was not afraid to show it. Too often the Christian is so caught up in the, 'what will people think' syndrome, that they are unable to allow the emotional side to show. When we are unable to give emotional expression because of evil action of an unbelieving world, we lose the capacity to feel sorrow for sin. Evangelical Christians commitment to servitude of today is a far cry from the empathy for God practiced by men like Nehemiah.

Salvationists have become the remnant from the church of today, scattered to, and fro, not knowing what stand they should take, and not caring too much about the individual as long as their program is in place. However it is essential that they find strength to give testimony to a dying world. That testimony being of the change Jesus Christ can make in ones life with the gospel message of eternal life. We must be careful not to be caught up in the world's skepticism that embraces the ungodly secularism, and woeful materialism.

Nehemiah 2: 12; shows us how with a few trusted souls the work plan began to take shape. It was not broadcast abroad; but the action was taken, the important first step had been made. After prayer. and due consideration of the need for the project to begin, Nehemiah, in verse 18, of chapter two, shared his clear direction from God with the fellowship of brethren, and their families, requesting aid from them for this mega construction to take place. God's man had followed the order without chaos, putting into place God's plan. He grieved, he fasted, he prayed. In praying we must needs to plead the word of God, and cling to his promises. If we are devoted to the pursuit of saving of souls for Christ we shall follow Nehemiah's Godly plan. When you have received Jesus Christ as your personal Saviour and committed your life into his care, do not wait to be asked, take the initiative even as Nehemiah did. There are many of God's servants out there who will help you to build under the most difficult circumstances. If someone refuses to help you walk for God, leave them behind and seek another who is more committed to God's eternal structure. The only caution I must give is, be careful not to get wrapped up in your personal likes and dislikes, remember you are in God's Work, and you may not like what **or** where he directs you but when you accept the assignment, you will be blessed.

We live in an age of scanning, so let us quickly scan the beginning of Nehemiah's task:

Chapter 1: vs. 1-4, Here we see the interest taken in the people of his life, and as he finds out the facts are overwhelmed by concern for the situation. 5-11 Immediately prayer is involved, requesting God's intervention, forgiveness of sin, removing doubt as to direction, knowing his position in life, willingness to abandon all, for God's people.

Chapter 2:1-4; Heaviness of heart in great thought perception of the King as they shared. Thoughts made known. 5-8: Encouragement from unexpected source, support of a friend. 9-12: Implementation of action First and foremost, interested in God's people, and their needs, then a genuine interest in the salvation of the soul, by delivering the gospel message of the need to be born again, to the unbeliever, that they too might have access to eternal life through Jesus Christ. We being the redeemed of Christ by the shed blood, must adorn the responsibility to carry the good news of eternal life to those who have not yet heard and understood. To carry to those that have heard the message of another chance to accept our Jesus as the Son of the living God. It is our imperative duty to warn them of the awesome fires of hell, that await those who reject him, and refuse an ear to hear. The born again Christian must learn to be persistent in the message, by word, deed, and lifestyle.

Nehemiah was aware that sin, not position, had to be dealt with. He maintained a strong forward movement in his Godly action to get the job done. He made no mistake about being involved. Criticism, and slander where hurled at him in defiance of his work for God, but he did not falter. Instead he found a way to handle each and every situation that confronted him. Least of all he refused to allow others to take the blame. He shouldered the responsibility well and without complaint. He was aware of God's availability. He was not ashamed to become personally involved in God's building. A job needed to be accomplished, and he was visible in his desire to be victorious in accomplishment.

Do you really want God to use you?

Then take hold of this Nehemiah formula and put it to work in your life.

* * * * *

Vision In Action

———⟨☙⟩———

If it be so, our God whom we serve is able to deliver us from the burning fiery furnace, and he will deliver us out of thy hand, O king. But if not, be it known unto thee, O king, that we will not serve thy gods, nor worship the golden image which thou hast set up. I see four men loose, walking in the midst of the fire, and they have no hurt; and the form of the fourth is like the son of God. Daniel, 3: 17-18, 25.

Herein lies three of my favourite people. Today we know the outcome of their refusal to serve other than a living God, but they did not know until they were delivered even though they knew that God was able if it were his wish. Still they stayed tried and true to that to which they were dedicated, the living God.

Contemporary gatherings of today are often heard to flaunt the same expression of why does God allow such a thing. They are not truly interested in the deliverance that is sustained by faith in a living God. Oft-times it provokes them to anger as it did this king of yesteryear. It is of worthy notation that God even showed the unbeliever his power to answer a stalwart faith. They believed, and God honoured their firm stand before the powerhouse of the secular world.

When our faith is challenged there is no need for the argument that entails all the nit picking elements of substantiation. One simply needs to stand firm on the direction God would have you go, and he will act on your behalf, just get the thing done.

How then can we relate to this Christ, the Son of God, who gave himself for us, if not through our eyes of mission?

Your commission is mission. Whether it be your next door

neighbour, town or country, home or abroad.

Vision in action; Psalm 42: 2; My soul thirsteth for God, for the living God: When shall I come and appear before God?

This verse is one of those verses, which justify the highest degree of action. Perhaps there is no passage that is more searching, more telling, more touching, or more expressive, than the solemn, and exalted sentiment which is spoken in this text. My soul thirsteth for God.

When shall I come to appear before God?

This verse then is justification, rationale, and motivation, of the action of the Christian. God's word, the bible, our foundation, a directive to go tell the good news. There is no book that expresses that deep inner serious fact of my being, of my soul, of myself. It is the fact that lives, when the world's facts are dying. The Bible, the fact that insists on asserting itself, when the noise of the world is still. The Bible, the fact that does not care about daylight only, but comes up in the dark. The Bible, the fact that whispers low, when I am in a crowd, but speaks loud in the darkest night. The Bible, with asserted facts that cannot be contradicted. There is nothing that can speak that fact of facts, that thirst, that longing, that desolation, that desire, that hope, that activity. There is nothing like the bible that does that. The very word the bible says, determines, and insists, upon the truth, the soul is thirsty for God.

The action of attraction to natural beauty exists only a short distance where one can be deep into the foothills to enjoy the beauty of the Alberta in the breathtaking drive through the Canadian Rockies, with their majestic snow covered peaks. In that journey one enjoys the glimmering Emerald lakes and torrid rivers flowing in their might, dashing over rocks into a misty waterfall, as they are joined by rushing gentle waters of the creeks. We can appreciate the soaring flight of the ever present hawk, or the dominance of the occasional eagle, to establish his territory. Locally we appreciate the attractiveness of the swan, the robin, the blue jay, a bob-o-link, ever present the red winged black bird.

We appreciate the stagger of the new born fawn, in it's attempt to be swift upon it's weak new limbs, we are even caught up in tenderness of the new born calf, or colt.

Nature is beauty you say; and you are right, as you gaze upon it you are stimulated, delighted, consoled, but you are not satisfied.

Again there is an activity of commercial instinct that will stimulate, delight, attract, and intoxicate us, with dazzling lights, and great merchandising advertisements. Places such as the largest shopping centre in all the world, the West Edmonton Mall, for which I possess the unheralded privilege of setting the idea into motion, with all it's glitter and glamour. Even the lesser Malls in cities across our rich land, resort to brilliant methods to attract the crowds. Winter games, summer games, hockey, and baseball, stimulate with a supposed magic in being there. Many will spend their last dollar to gain access to any or all of these magnificent commercial actions. Yet there remains one thing that they will not, nor cannot do, that is to satisfy, embracing all that they offer to the yielding public, they cannot satisfy.

Then we find there to be the pure intellect action, falling back upon the cells of the brain, traversing the corridor of thought. Falling into that labyrinth of instinct or association, or accumulative learning. There is that in the mere exercise of intellect which is intoxicating, and consoling, if not challenging. Yet there is one thing about intellect that is perfectly appalling, and that, of course, is the fact it does not satisfy.

There is yet another area of action embraced by society as a whole, and that is the region, of action of affection

In the world of affections that we become wrapped up in, the branch of contrast prevails. We are moved at the sight of a starving child. We might even sponsor one. We have affection for those who suffer loss of material through storms or earthquake. Or we may just feel affection for that cute kid, when in essence, they are real brats. Affection can stimulate, console, delight, and even lead to delirium, but it does not satisfy.

My bothers, and sisters in the Lord, we are not born for a moment, but for infinite moments. Not for the struggle of time, but for that great platform, and career of eternity.

So it is we must act as Shadrach, Meshach, Abednego, who refused to absent themselves from attending the mission that God set forth. Daniel 3: 25; —- Lo, I see four men loose, walking in the midst of the fire, and they have no hurt;

It was not until there had been a commitment made that the fourth figure was available.

There is a spiritual truth here, we say, show me what I shall win, and then I shall risk it!

But there is no answer until we have decided to do it God's way. The Angel of the Lord stands beside us, to strengthen, and comfort. It is the unseen power that upsets the plans of despots.

So it is with that power we take up the Mission of telling others about the Christ of the gospel, about the God who so loved the world that he gave his only begotten son.

Vision in Action, let us have the deep roots in God's word, faith believing in the love of Jesus Christ, when he says, come unto me all ye that labour and are heavy laden, and I will give you rest.

Deep roots stop erosion.

Some years ago, CBC, had a tidbit of news about an elderly lady who lived on an island on which was built a lighthouse that had been established there for many years on the East coast of Canada. She tried in vain to get the attention of government officials to note the erosion of the soil that would eventually destroy the lighthouse if nothing were done to stop this erosion. Well, as government officials usually do, they formed a committee of environmentalists, and erosion experts, to determine what might be done, and as per usual after spending much time, and too much tax payers money, they arrived at a negative conclusion, and sat like unto braying donkeys, determined to hold more bureaucratic meetings to consider this problem. In the meantime, this frail seventy seven year old lady, wishing to simply stop the erosion, began working on the soil, and planted seed that would manufacture deep grabbing roots. She said as the roots took effect upon the soil that it would stop the erosion.

That is Vision in action.

There is an erosion of the fundamental gospel. Your Mission needs to be the reworking of the soil. Plant the seed of deep-rooted strength, and nurture the growth of the new believer. Manufacture that deep grabbing root of salvation. Make that ultimate commitment that holds the risk. Say with the Psalmist, my soul is thirsty for God.

Trust Christ. Trust God's Grace! Remember, the value of the gift is determined by the giver.

Salvation, a gift beyond price. God's gift. No self merit in God's word.

* * * * *

What Think Ye Of Christ

—⟨⟨⟨⟩⟩⟩—

In the beginning was the word, and the word was with God, and the word was God. The same was in the beginning with God. All things were made by him; and without him was not anything made that was made. In him was life; and the life was the light of men. John 1: 1-4.

Where I to ask you what you think of your Senator, MP, or your MLA, or your Mayor; and where I bold enough to ask what you thought of our Premier, or Prime Minister, in the U.S.A. it would be the Senate or State Rep, you would tell me freely of your support, or your criticism, of any one of these people. You have made up your minds about each one of them.

Christ hung the truth upon everything; a fox, a sower, a bird, have you made up your mind about Christ?

Was he really the Son of God?

Was he really the great God man?

Did he leave heaven to come to the world for a purpose?

Was it really to seek, and to save?

What do you think of him as a teacher?

He spake, as never a man spake. He makes the sparrow to preach to us.

What do you think of him as a physician?

No man has the reputation for curing as Christ did. Nothing to him was incurable.

What think ye of Christ as comforter?

Mary, and Martha, called him for Lazarus. He calmed widows and children. He raised others from the dead. If you want to find out something about someone, you go to people who know the person.

Let us go to those who knew Christ. Enemies, the Pharisees, their hue and cry was, this man receives sinners. He saved others, but himself he cannot save. Caiphas screams, he claimed to be the Son of God. Then Pilate declares in the courts, I find in him no fault at all. Pilate's wife attempts to interfere with the courts decision by telling her husband the forthright truth, have thou nothing to do with this just man. A repenting, and broken Judas recanted his thirty Shekels of silver testimony as he says, I have betrayed innocent blood. One can almost hear the money falling heavily upon the table as he returns it to the elders trying to disrobe of the guilt that was now encompassing him in a shroud.

The thief on the cross attempted to warn the nay sayers, this man has done nothing amiss. The Centurion who was guilty of abuse by ordering the nails driven, made Christ carry his own cross, saw his own base of inhumanity cried in recognition, truly this man is the Son of God. The Demons who are unable to stand in the presence of the son of the living God began to cry, Jesus, thou son of the most high, you have come before your time, what would you have to do with us, for they knew his presence meant their destruction.

But let us go to his friends, John the Baptist introducing him as the one to take his place says, Behold the Lamb of God which takes away the sin of the world. Then there was Thomas the doubter who was asked to put his fingers into the nail prints of the hand of the saviour, and simply responded with the statement of belief, my Lord, and my God. He who at one point had set out to persecute this Christ, now an apostle, Paul, who was given by inspiration of the Holy Spirit, to pen chapter upon chapter leaving with those of us who would accept Christ, and become followers in our day. John; who was exiled to the Isle of Patmos because of his extreme loyalty to the Lord Jesus Christ. Matthew; who was willing to jeopardize his high calling as a tax collector, to serve his heavenly King.

Peter; he who denied knowing Christ, it is said that he asked to be crucified upside down because of his unworthiness to be given anything of credit that may even make him somehow equal to his Lord after his own repentance. But there is still another witness.

Some think that the God of the old testament, is the Christ of the New Testament, but when Jesus came up out of the Jordan river while being baptized by John, there came a voice from heaven, God the Father spoke his testimony to Christ, this is my beloved Son in whom I am well pleased. Again, that same God upon the mount of transfiguration, he cried again, this is my beloved Son, hear Him. And that voice is echoing still, hear Him, hear Him!

These first four verses in the gospel according to John are especially important for what they teach about the nature of Christ. We discover, the Word, [Jesus Christ] was with God the Father in the beginning. The preposition here indicates a one on one, face to face communication. The word was God, yet the word was also distinct from the Father.

The picture here, God the Father, and God the Son, two distinct persons.

John calls Jesus, the Word. The Greek for word is Logos. There was in that time a Doctrine of Logos.

Peer into the dark past as far as you may, you will never come upon God alone. Always from beginningless beginning, there has been God, and always there has been another with Him, who is to God, what man's word and thought are to man.

The Greek word Logos, means reason, or mind, or expression, Jesus is God's expression to us. God's full revelation of Himself to us.

Life, and light, are two key words in John's gospel. They encompass for us reason, memory, conscience, and a hunger for God.

As the light penetrates the darkness, so the light, or revelation of God in Christ, penetrates human ignorance, and sinfulness. These are gifts to us from Logos - Christ, breaking through to us into a deeper love for our fellowman, yet lifts us higher in that we are drawn unto God the Father through Christ. Darkness has not been eliminated nor vanquished, nor done away with. He who is light is always groping, feeling for an opening into the mind and soul, seeking to fill our lives with the glory of God. Christ as light has made great gaps in that darkness. God's word has encountered resistance from the world. There are those who preferred darkness to light, falsehood to truth, their own will, as opposed to the will of

God. The rejection of God's will is described in three stages in John 1. The darkness did not comprehend it. The world did not know Him. His own did not receive Him.

Comprehend is a translation of a word that means, grasp. The picture presented here, is not a student wrestling with a problem, and failing to grasp it, but an enemy bent on destruction of the truth, and unable to accomplish it. Know simply means, recognize. Despite His miracles and teachings, the world did not perceive who Jesus was, nor would it acknowledge His claims.

Is the step that is most serious. For centuries God had been preparing His people to receive His supreme revelation through worship at the Tabernacle, and the Temple, the precepts of the law, Prophets teaching. But when the living word finally came, at the appointed time and place, his own people did not receive him. Those who rejected Christ were not Pagan, nor Agnostic, nor Atheistic, they were Jews, who prided themselves in knowing, and keeping the law of the Living God. They missed God's revelation, because they did not want to receive it. Understanding God's message results from us knowing Christ as a guest is welcomed into a home, so Christ is welcomed into the heart and life of the believer. By so doing we become the children of God, and partakers of a divine nature. Christ reached out to the ordinary. When it happens, it is natural for us to want to tell others.

But why would these men have none of Christ?

It is very likely that they instituted the same reason then as keep many people of today from dealing with him now. It is because Divine originality confused them. They had been expecting something quite different. To them Christ did not look the part, and did not fit what they perceived to be a part of God's promises.

Again to the Mount of transfiguration, hear him for this is God's cry!

Will you hear him today?

What think ye of Christ?

What says Christ to you?

Come unto me all ye that labour and are heavy laden and I will give you rest. Take up your cross and follow me. My yoke is easy, my burden is light. It is appointed unto man once to die - after this the judgment. All have sinned and come short of the glory of God. I am the way the truth and the life. No man cometh unto the father but by me.

* * * * *

Son Of God

—⫷⦿⫸—

He said, I am the voice of one crying in the wilderness, make straight the way of the Lord, as says the prophet Esaias And they which were sent were of the Pharisees. And they asked him, why baptizest thou then, if thou be not that Christ, nor Elias, neither that prophet? John answered them, saying, I baptize with water; but there standeth one among you, whom ye know not; He it is, who coming after me is preferred before me, whose shoe-latchet I am not worthy to unloose. John 1: 23-27.

It was quite evident that John knew his calling as his worth was acknowledged by the work he performed. At the same time he was able to grasp the element that literally changed his strategic ministry. He knew he had been chosen to introduce the master without resentment or pride standing in his way. Christ had been revealed to him, and he understood his changing mission in the presence of Christ therefore without fear or favour steps aside, and introduces the person for whom he had been called to set the stage.

What it is Christ calls us to do?

Once we have been visited by the Holy Spirit, and I mean simply by us believing in Jesus Christ, and having the Holy Spirit dwelling within us by our acceptance of Jesus Christ as our saviour, our duty, our business, to witness, and our actual commitment to God to witness. I would like to talk about commitment today rather than witness, yet in my mind it is difficult to separate the two, but there are multitudes because Jesus taught, lived and died who have shaken off unworthiness, and you know that my hue and cry here is that there are so many Christian organizations that put the onus upon the person even after they are saved, that they are to stay unworthy, that they ought to be down, and keep that ever present negative to keep feeling bad about their own existence, when in fact Jesus Christ said, I have paid for your sin I have made you worthy. If God is not worthy, then you are not worthy. When God makes you worthy, that means He has sent his son Jesus to die on the cross to lift you up to make you worthy because he has now forgiven you for your trespasses, and sin, against him. It is not anything that you by yourself can do. You cannot reach out to God and prove something of your lifestyle that allows you access to heaven. God has already reached down to man, and proven to man that he has been lifted up and made worthy through the blood of Christ.

There are multitudes, because Jesus taught, and lived, and died, have shaken off unworthiness that used to beset them, and have risen above what had become an inherent part of their personality.

There is a peace of conscience that they did not know before coming to Calvary. They are better, and cleaner, and stronger, because Christ has taken away that which had soiled, and shamed them.

All this at a tremendous price to Christ that we cannot begin to reckon up, but the thought of which moves us to the very soul. He loved me, and gave himself for me.

I believe that we need to come to a more in depth grip upon this very fact of the gospel

But, Alas! There are those times when we are too casual, ours is a great salvation. We have a tendency to state, oh well, everything will turn out okay. God's in control. If my friend wants to live that way I will let him /her because I want to keep them as a friend, and would not upset them. What you are really saying is that you want them to spend eternity in a burning fiery Hell. We have become too casual about this Salvation that is so great, verses 29-34: there is a threefold declaration, v29 A. The sin bearing Lamb of God, Jesus Christ who took upon himself our sin so we would be free from sin, we do not have to confess anything to man, but that we had to confess before God, we were sinners, and now, as we accept Jesus Christ we are sinners saved by Grace. v33.b. The one who is to Baptize with the spirit the moment I believe. Not hours, days, weeks or months later, but when we accept the freely given salvation that Christ put his whole being on the line for, we then are given the indwelling of the holy spirit.

I want to be very clear on this, you may be in a community whereby you hear of the baptizing of the Spirit, which is in the absolute sense is false cult oriented, because the Spirit does not baptize, Jesus always baptizes. The bible says, here is the one who is to baptize with the spirit. Jesus is always in control. There is no such thing as a second blessing. When you start talking about second blessings then you insult God because God says, if you worship me, and serve Jesus as my son, and saviour, I will open up the windows of heaven, and pour out thousands of blessings upon you. Let us be careful not to insult God. Do not be sidetracked by some misunderstood theological indifference. We cannot say to others that we are undivided if they do not adhere to God's way of Salvation. We are divided if you do not believe if Jesus Christ is the Son of God. We are divided if you do not believe that the scriptures are the inspired word of God. We are divided if you begin to worship the Virgin Mary instead of Jesus Christ. We are divided when you say I cannot have communion with you, and you are not allowed to have communion with me. We are divided.

Why?

Because God has already set the plan in place. When you come to grips with Jesus Christ, and throw yourself at his feet at the foot of the cross, and say Jesus take me I am yours. I have left aside all that man can offer. Accept me Christ, and clean me that the old may die here at the cross, and that I may rise a new person to serve you. Then we are not divided. Son of God, And I saw and bare record that this is the Son of God We are the body of Christ, his feet that must run for Him, his hands that must carry for Him, his body through which His will gets done.

If Christ is all that we say He is, we cannot keep it to ourselves.

If you really love Christ, how can you keep it to your self?

We must share him with others. When we begin to share him with others they will begin to look at our lives and ask, how are you committed to this Jesus Christ?

You say oh well I go to church every Sunday, and I listen to the preacher, and even sometimes I disagree with him to help you out.

But God doesn't talk about that does he?

Then you must say I am kind of religious, I sing the hymns, sometimes I even read the scriptures, and sometimes I teach, and sometimes I listen to the Sunday school teacher, and sometimes I never disagree with the preacher.

They say yes but how do you really relate to this Christ that you impress others, and how many people since you have known Jesus Christ have you led to the Lord?

How many people have come to you to say, I know that you serve a Lord that I don't understand. How many people have come to you because of your life style, because of your commitment, and said to you, well now you have something that I don't have. And I would like that something. How often are you are able to take them down the line and lead them to everlasting life in Jesus Christ. Because they are lost in sin, and you can show them how Jesus Christ paid the price, and you can lead them out of that sin, and bring them into worship because God said remember the assembling of yourselves together. I know there are many who try to relate to you by suggesting that they can be just as good a Christian at home as they can by attending the church. That is a lot of hogwash. Because if a person believes in God, and that person believes in Jesus Christ as saviour, what is the first thing that happened, they are saved, and added unto the church daily.

What was the church then?

It was not simply were two or three were gathered together. It consisted of many thousands of bodies worshipping the living God. Muslims, Islamic Siekes, or other cults. If you look at these cults that do not worship Christ as Saviour, and any one who does not worship Him, as saviour is a false cult. As far as we are concerned they are not Christian in any sense of the word. Christianity is a way of life, life eternal. But when you observe these cults as to how they get down to the committed life to worship the false God whom they serve, then I wonder where the Christian is coming from. The Muslim, kneels upon the floor on his hands, and knees with his head bowed down as he works his way to the altar of sacrifice to make himself worthy. The Jew, whose fist hammer beats upon the stone wall, and wails to a God that does not hear him.

How much more does the Christian need to get excited, and commit their lives to a Christ who makes them worthy?

If lost people can be so committed to ungodly acts why can the Christian not see the need to be deeply committed to a Christ who delivers, that others may see Him in us and our lives. Commitment to the Glory of God the Father, is not to be content with ones own Salvation, while others around you are perishing in the storm, But you are to take your life in hand, and spend it relentlessly in an eager effort to bring others along with you, home, to God.

Not home to a Baptist Church, not home to a preacher, that you may like or dislike, look beyond the human element. See God almighty in love, with His creation, as he has created mankind in his own image, and if God would create us in his own image, that means I am worthy to witness.

Did you know there are people out there in your community that are waiting for you to speak up about your Jesus, your Christ?

Those same people will respect you for your values of Christianity. Some congregations take on the image of religious clubs, run for the benefits of its members, not to win the world for Christ. Religions, not a few, are a mere spiritually self centred gathering of those with no interest in reaching out to the lost, which spiritual or not shall receive the wage of selfishness.

I know a pastor who always berates his people because he himself has a spirit of condemnation whereby he is literally unable to implement the love of God toward others.

The most effective portion of the church, is the Christ - like home

v37- two disciples followed Jesus.

v40-41- Andrew spoke to his brother. Here we find an immediate commitment to soul winning. Andrew has no prominence in the gospels; but when we do glimpse him, he is always doing the same thing, bringing others to Christ. Simple folk with no particular gift of their own can do wonderful things for Christ.

Luke 2:15; the Shepherds made a commitment to go to Bethlehem

Luke 2: 18; and all those who heard wondered at these things which were told by the shepherds.

We need more shepherds today!

You need to be an Andrew - bringing others to Christ. Make your commitment today

* * * * *

The Four Soils

—⌘—

For this peoplès heart is waxed gross, and their ears dull of hearing, and their eyes have closed; lest at any time they should see with their eyes, and hear with their ears, and should understand with their heart, and should be converted, and I should heal them. But blessed are your eyes, for they see: and your ears, for they hear. Matthew 13: 15-16.

Challenged by the immediate followers whom we know as Christ's disciples, Jesus sets out his apparent reason for speaking to unbelievers in the method he chose called parables. Many of our contemporary age seekers have become followers of the church, or religious organization to which they belong, rather than to be followers of Christ. There is today an apparent need to get back to the basics of speaking Gods word in the methodology that can be understood by those who refuse, to this point in their lives, to disbelieve the message of growth in salvation given by Christ.

To anyone who fancies that he can reduce the reality of God's world to a neat formula, or who fondly thinks that he can dispose of all the hopes, faiths, and devotions of the race with a few "hard facts" we might say, *"Thou hast nothing to draw with, and the well is deep."* John 4: 11a.

The seed was a good seed, and the sower was a faithful man, but the soil determined the success, or failure, of the seed.

The soil, not the sower, is closely described. The teller of the good news was not the main concern. The parable here portrays the congregation. We find that there are four main groups that arise from the assembly of believers. Some are dull, indifferent, and calloused towards the word of God, and they have only attended for appearance sake to their fellowman. The soil in their lives can be likened to a pathway through a field. Everything goes over it; weddings, trade, pleasures, shortcuts, and children in play. The path is trodden down with our own desires. Seed cannot penetrate the hard surface. This path can only dissipate by the cultivator of some tragic experience that takes hold upon our life. Our own loss, or the loss someone close, is that which can break through this stubborn soil.

We are shown another group, and they are those who are shallow in nature. They are good soil, but lack depth. As a rule those people will have a real sentimental fervour, and will act with instant response. The grain springs up, but soon sags under the heat.

How can shallow people ever become sound, or profound ?

I believe the answer can be found in Matthew 27: 36; when Jesus had been taken to the cross, it says, And sitting down they watched Him there. Only at the cross, the long patient suffering of God can give them depth. We must get back to where we can stop at the cross, and watch again Jesus.

Christ in his emphatic love moves on to point out a third group who live a divided life. I believe farmers would call it unprepared soil. A soil full of rocks, and roots. They have potential gifts, they have potential zeal, but they crave the world, and will not surrender it. Sin, mixed with consecration and worldliness, will stifle the true life until cleansed by some tragedy.

Fortunately for us there is recognized in Christ's story, the fourth type of soil which proves to be very interesting. Some seed falls on ground that is clear and good.

It multiplies, thirty fold, and sixty fold, hundred fold. This is the meat of the whole parable that we who know Gods word must readily share it with others. John 13: 23, gives the package information of this total formulae. But he that received seed into the good ground is he that heareth the word, and understandeth it; which also beareth fruit, and bringeth forth, some a hundred-fold, some sixty, and some thirty.

There is a tendency to get caught up in the world of the Academic soil which tends to fragment the things of God. In afterthought, this is perhaps the thistle that chokes it out of society leaving a definitive void. therefore it behooves us to make certain that our ears are open to truly hear what the scriptures have to say to us as we set out to put that dent in the social order of the day.

Hebrews 6: 10; For God is not unrighteous to forget your work, and labour of love, which you have shown toward His name, in that you have ministered to the Saints, and do minister.

The gospel appears to be a very small seed falling upon an alien world as we might consider the question as to what chance does it have ?

In shallowness, in worldliness, and cruel "ism's" that rise up as cactus in the desert. But, take heart, it has a secret life that cannot fail, and will not fail. The sower must sow, even knowing that some seed will fall on stones, and roots. The soil still determines the success of the seed.

Jesus gave the message of Matthew 13: 9, urgent meaning, Who hath ears to hear, let him hear.

We must now mark a lesser heeded plea about the responsibility of hearing.

Oftentimes we like to blame the Prophet, because he does not speak a better truth, and what we hear goes in one ear and out the other. Our claim, we don't like the style, we don't like the delivery, we don't like the stance, or the nervous twitch. We cannot believe that God would speak through a person we do not approve of, either logistically, nor Profile wise, and such a short resume.

Do we really want God to speak at all ?

That is the real question. Strength is a responsibility, Romans 15: 1; We then that are strong ought to bear the infirmities of the weak, and not to please ourselves. Money is a responsibility. 1 John 3: 17; But whoso has this world's good, and seeth his brother have need, and shutteth up his bowels of compassion from him, how dwelleth the love o God in him.

However we do not believe what we hear in the message, a challenge of responsibility. Rather we choose not to hear anything with a directive that may take us out of the shell we have learned to live within. The hearer has the power to thwart the gospel, or to bring it to fulfillment.

The secret of the Kingdom lies in Matthew 13:12; For whosoever hath, to him shall be given, and he shall have more abundance But whosoever hath not, from him shall be taken away even that he hath.

The old saying here rings true, the rich get richer, and the poor get poorer; in money, in knowledge, in talents, in the saving knowledge of our Lord Jesus Christ. What a joy to know the secret of Christ is like a seed. There is a multiplied joy of harvest to each of us. Not only to the Apostles, but to you and me as believers who have accepted the salvation prepared by God through his son Jesus..

Matthew 13: 11, —-But it is given unto you to know the mysteries of the kingdom of Heaven, —- .

To all seeking souls, it is given, and especially to you who believe and are committed to follow the Saviour, and to teach, and preach His gospel.

John 15: 11; These things have I spoken unto you, that my joy might remain in you, and that your joy might be full.

Sin is still sin, Hell still exists, it is still appointed unto man once to die, and after this the judgment, eternal life still exists, Heaven still is a reality. Death and life are one, as the river and the Sea are one.

Will the voice of God be sweet to your ears as he says?

Well done thou good and faithful servant.

Or will it be as vinegar?

Depart from me ye worker's of iniquity'.

Some men continue seeking after gifts, but are unable to recognize, and use the gifts that God has already given, the gift of Salvation, the gift of love, of hearing, of telling others of the miraculous Christ. Your commission, is related to my commission, to tell others.

We read in Luke 8: 22-25. This story of stilling the Tempest. As people grow older they must depend more and more upon the Lord Jesus for victory over the "storms" of life. i.e Poverty, handicaps, poor health, bereavement; separation from loved ones, and the indifference and neglect of others. We must never be obsessed with Satan's error, but struggling against emotional problems that overwhelm people such as, bitterness, fear, uncertainty, regret, and guilt. We must instead experience the freedom of Jesus. When we consider Physical healing as found in Luke 8: 41-48, We must remember that such healing is always within God's power, but it may or may not be His divine will for the individual. It is always Gods will however, that a believer lives above their ailments to know real joy of their relationship to their Lord, in spite of weaknesses, sickness, handicaps, failure of vision, failure of hearing, or other disabilities that many older adults endure.

Even when they deny it, older Christians sometime fear death, or at least dying. If the Lord tarries we shall all walk the Valley of the Shadow, but believers can look forward to the Lord's company. Psalm 23: 4. With the assurance that the Valley leads to that beautiful place that Jesus has gone to prepare a place for His people.

What kind of a soil are you?

Hardened beside the road, trampled, devoured by the weeds of life, fruitless showing no production. Or are you simply shallow, on that rocky soil, grew for a short time and withered from the heat of tribulation and indifference of the day. Perhaps you would be identified as the soil who was distracted by the enticing presentation of the contemporary look at the thistle, and was choked out of existence as you struggled to survive amongst the thorns. Little growth, no fruit desperate to survive your own way. Or can you readily identify with the receptive soil as one who heard with open ears to grow in the word, and produce a quality fruit that can withstand the ultimate scrutiny of inspection by your living God. The seed depends upon the quality of the soil in order to produce a hundred fold, or sixty, or thirty as Christ himself suggests. We are not to work to perfection, rather we are to hear the word and continue to plant it as the seed understanding the preperation of the field could be of the utmost importance to the success of the seed.

What does the size of the crop depend upon?

On the quality of the soil. "He who hath ears to hear let him hear" Jesus, Lord of Lords, deliverer of Salvation, giver of grace. Tell others this great news. Do not wait for a leading.

* * * * *

Pathways

by J. A. [Jim] Watson

I walk down the narrow pathway of life
Impenetrable jungle to my left
Enemy in the dark, to my right
In solitude my soul bereft

As God comes to take away the night.

Tall Cedars, grown a thousand years and more
Though picturesque against yon sky
They are rotten to the core
Man does not understand, asks the question why?

As Paul upon Damascus blinded by the light

The wagging tongue, blocks the open trail,
Knowledge here but dung
As savers of environment wail
By their own desires for living are hung

To find that others are more correct in flight

So be careful of the pathway you take
If you find it narrow with love
Instead of employing ideas that are fake
Stay true to our living God above

For HE has created all things for man's right

* * * * *.

God's All Things

And we know that all things work together for good to them that love God, to them who are called according to his purpose. Romans 8: 28.

One day a man took his little boy atop of a high hill. He pointed in every direction; North, East, South, West, "My boy," said he, "God's love is as big as all that."

"Yes Dad," said the little boy, "and we are right in the middle of it."

Much of the trouble in the world today, stems from the fact that men believe in a small God, and a big humanity. Man tries to take God's place with humanism by serving the false god of academics rather than the inspirational spirit of the living God. With all man's technological society of progress, and inventions there lies an impending thought of doom, and that is, that he is outgrowing a living God of creation. Man is being glorified, and God is being pushed into the background, but my friends have no fear, God will not be left out.

He will make himself known and felt. He is still the great sovereign God. He made all things, and they are his.

Personally, I have stood upon one ten thousand foot peak of the majestic Canadian Rocky Mountains, high, and overshadowing the torrent streams, and gaping valleys below. The world appeared to stretch for miles upon miles, without interruption or direction, and one absorbs the greatness of God in a setting such as that. Knowing that God created beauty with such magnificence, one feels quite small, and highly inadequate in the presence of His Majesty. I realized amidst this awesome beauty that I was unable to bring into view the magnificent prairie, nor was I able to view from where I stood, the absolute beauty of the valleys below. Yet I was engulfed by the absorbing beauty of the sea of mountain peaks that had been created by our majestic living God. Amidst all the beauty before me I could in my minds eye include all of his creation. The ever reaching and powerful seas, the emerald of the inland lakes, the high soaring birds, and the swiftness of the animals, in the forests beneath this plateau. A never ending desert of amazing creation flooded my soul when all I could visualize was a very small segment of what God had created to supply the needs for his very own creation.

The Psalmist felt that way, for he says in his writing of Psalm 8: 3- 4, When I consider thy heavens, the work of thy fingers, the moon and the stars, which thou hast ordained; what is man, that thou art mindful of him? And the son of man, that thou visiteth him.

The subject, God's All Things'

I am referring four scriptures in the bible where we will find these words used. These four scriptures in capsule form cover everything from creation, to final victory in our Christ.

1. *All things were made by him; and without him was not any thing made that was made.* John 1: 3.

Man can do some wonderful things, build canoes, to cabin cruisers, gigantic steamers to roam the seas, trains to spread across continents, jet planes, rocket ships, highways, bridges, Moon landings. All types of communication devices, telephone, radio, TV, CB'S, Fax machines, and now a sea of a multitude of computers. Yes man builds many wonderful things, but he builds from already created materials. Not so with God, He spoke, and there was light, and land was, and rivers formed, and seas took shape, and mountains thrust into existence. He spoke, and the sun and moon, and stars glittered, and the world filled with light, he moved his hand, and animals, and birds of the air, and fish of every shape, and size filled the lakes, and seas. He spoke, and created man, and breathed into him the breath of life, and he stood in God's own image.

Modern day technology with which man continues to build unbelievably marvelous. things to benefit humanity, and we know that which they allow us to see is twenty years behind that which is on the drawing board. Yet in all of those things, man still constructs everything from existing materials. Whereas, God simply spoke it into existence.

Therefore if any man be in Christ, he is a new creature: old things are passed away; behold all things are become new. And all things are of God, who hath reconciled us unto himself by Jesus Christ, and hath given to us the ministry of reconciliation; 2 Corinthians 5:17-18.

As each person finds their new life in Christ, they soon recognize the fact that God does not treat the disease of sin, rather he treats the patient. The believer who finds Christ and applying to their own walk will discover a new loyalty, to walk in new places, to follow new paths. In all of this each person will discover a new love for their fellowman under the light of the gospel. One who takes upon themselves the servanthood of Christ will look at the church in an absolutely new light that beams to them a whole different meaning as to what the church is. They will command a new longing to serve the living God while pleasing their saviour Jesus Christ.

Here we see man has a new life to which Jesus provokes us. The old things referred to possibly were dealing with the self centeredness of the individual. For when we see things in a different light, or from a different slant, we get a whole new picture, and all seems different. So as we leave the self centred attitude to enter the Christ centred outlook things do change for the better in our lives. Jesus does not treat the disease of sin, he treats the patient. Man has a new loyalty allows him he walks into new places, and follows new paths. Man has a new love, he sees his fellowman in a new light. Church takes on a new meaning. Man has a new longing, he longs to serve Christ, and in his newness, thoughts and action dovetail to God's perfection to please him. The person will no longer be ashamed to talk of Christ.

3. And he that searches the heart knoweth what is the mind of the Spirit, because he makes intercession for the saints according to the will of God.

And we know that all things work together for good, to them that love God, to them who are called according to his purpose. Romans 8: 28.

This is one of the most blessed promises of the bible, but men do not believe it. They cannot understand why troubles come. But they need to look up into the light out of their darkness, and say, I know not why this came. But I know it will work out for my good because I love and serve a living God..

The text does not say to all people, nor does it infer that evil is good. However, God co-operates in all things for good with those who love him. That leads to the discovery that even the sufferings of the present times, become a source of blessings. The promise is to the believer, no one else. The text says, all things, not just some things.

We see the good things working together for us but let me assure you, the bad things, the crisis things, the unlovely things, work around us for good too.

A diamond rock fresh from the mines must be cut to bring out its true beauty. Gold must be refined under a major portion of heat, to bring out it's purity. The vine must be pruned to bear fruit; the clay must be moulded to make a fit vessel. So must the child of God be, cut, refined, pruned, and moulded.

Let us not be in despair over the condition of the world. Let us simply remember that all things work together to the good, to them that love God and are called according to his purpose..

4. And he is before all things, and by him all things consist. And he is the head of the body, the church: who is the beginning, the firstborn from the dead; that in all things he might have pre-eminence. Colossians 1:17-18.

There have been some great men in the world, they came, they saw, they conquered; but there has never been anyone like Jesus. He walked among men to conquer death, and the grave, and Arose again. He is pre-eminent in history. He lets the world go so far before he stretches forth his hand, and sets things right. He is pr-eminent in nature. The heavens declare the glory of God. He is the creator, and sustainer. He is pre-eminent in prophecy. The greatest actor in the final drama will be Jesus. He will come from heaven with a shout, and he will gather all his loved ones and take them home to glory with him. He is the centre of all that is going to happen.

Are you among that number that knows the Lord Jesus as

your personal saviour who has shed his blood for the remission of your sin?

There is going to be a day of happening when Jesus returns for his own.

Are you at the centre of that great love?

Can you say, because of all things in your life, 'I am included in God's all things?

You can be! Today is the day of salvation. Now is the time. Accept him into your life today. Know a personal relationship with Jesus. Those of you who have professed Jesus as saviour; renew your commitment to him right now where you are at.

* * * * *

God's Guarantees

The eyes of your understanding being enlightened; that ye may know what is the hope of his calling, and what the riches of the glory of his inheritance in the saints Ephesians 2: 18

Greetings in the name of Jesus Christ our Lord. We celebrate the gospel, to share that gospel of God's undying love with relevance to empower us with the sense of God's guarantees. Those guarantees are not left to our own devices, and not dependent upon our own ideas.

When you make a purchase from the store of any product, you get a guarantee.

If this product proves to be defective you may return it. Now one thing is sure it is not worth the paper it is written on. In the final small print it reads the company is not liable for any loss damage or failure due to fact they're not covered by the warranty.

I wish to share briefly with you a sense God's guarantees clear, and unequivocal, and without fine print.

God does not guarantee us position to inflate our ego as tremendous word of reassurance to the weak, faltering, inadequate, Christian, who knows that if left to himself will never make it to God's satisfaction.

According as he hath chosen us in him before the foundation of the world, that we should be Holy, and without blame before him in love. Having predestinated us unto the adoption of children by Jesus Christ to himself, according to the good pleasure of his will, To the praise of the glory of his grace, wherein he hath made us accepted in the beloved. In whom we have redemption through his

425

blood, the forgiveness of sins, according to the riches of his grace; Ephesians 1:4-7.

We must never forget that God chose us in love, with all our disqualifications, all our irregularities, all our deficiencies, all our moral weaknesses, and all our downright sinfulness, he adopted us to be his children. He chose us in Christ to be his son's, and daughters. God adopted us to be his children. Nothing to qualify, nothing to commend, nothing that was attractive. We neither deserve, nor could achieve by ourselves. It was an action that was wholly, and only God's initiated plan to include us into his total family.

But as many as received him, to them gave he power to become the sons of God, even to them that believe on his name: John 1: 12.

Mystery of the Gospel

Ephesians 3: 6; That the gentiles should be fellowheirs, and of the same body, and partakers of his promise in Christ by the gospel:

Gentiles heirs together with Israel position of heir. Here is a family picture a relational picture, he has chosen, he adopted, he gave the right to sonship. He made us heirs, and initiated the adoption into the Christian family. This is the security of the Christian, as long as God is God, my position is secure.

Not by the strength of my hold on him, but by the strength of his hold on me. Heirs of God, joint heirs with Christ Jesus. A peculiar people, God chosen along with his son Jesus who also chose the most unlikely people to join in the walk with him.

We have a tendency to glamorize the disciples. Yet when you look at them, they were rough, they were very unpromising, they were very untalented, aggressive, unpredictable, and two of them were always in trouble because of their pride, and grasping for power. Then there was Peter who almost invariably did the wrong thing before he did the right thing. The marvelous news is Jesus didn't give up on them. In love he chose you, in love that he made you his own, in love he called you to a responsive faith. If you feel disheartened, know that God has no intention of giving up on you.

2. Guaranteed Power, the concept of power keeps reappearing. We must never underestimate the power of God's word. [a] there is the power of word, it is alive and active it can be dynamic.

When the Holy Spirit is at work in the witness of the church;

and through the direction of the church. Power is assured, by the same token it is by the word that we deny the power.

A great many of us deprive ourselves of the dynamism that is available to us of our Christian transformation because we will not rest on the direction and the power of his word, as God speaks to us through it.

We have become so sophisticated, intellectualized, critical, that instead of listening for the word of God, we are consistently trying to analyze it. If you did that with your breakfast cereal you would never eat it. Stop doing it with the word of God.

The Christian needs to discover the enormous release of power for living, through His word. The inner witness of the Holy Spirit of God, takes the word of God, and empowers us for his work, and for his service.

I am not ashamed of the gospel of Christ: for it is the power of God unto salvation to everyone that believeth; to the Jew first, and also to the Greek. Romans 1: 16;

The gospel is good news and carries a rich and enlightening message to the soul. It is Power. The good news is God can do something with sinful broken lives. He can remake them [b] Power of the risen Christ is the power of the gospel, not just the power of ideas, but the power of Jesus Christ alive, and active in our lives. The power of the risen Christ is the guarantee that God gives us is this. If we bear our witness by our lives, and by our words, to Jesus Christ in dependence upon the Holy Spirit, he will give us power to become the sons of God. Now that does not mean we will all become fast talkers, it does not mean that we will all become articulate because we know that some of the most effective witnesses for Jesus Christ are those who have greatest difficulty with words while some of the poorest witnesses are those who can speak endlessly never knowing when to quit, and are without sensitivity. [c] Power of His Spirit. Christian witness is a mandate laid upon believers. We are not all gifted to be evangelists, but we all are challenged to be witnesses. Not by my vocabulary, but my dependence upon the Holy Spirit, a source of power, and although I am inarticulate, and bumbling, the Holy Spirit takes over in spite of my inability to execute a form of verbal gymnastics.

3. Presence, he guarantees, Lo I am with you always. As you go make disciples hear his commission put discipling at the top of the list. Christ's commission to us is to Baptize, not to make Baptists, with a confession of faith to, I am with you all the way. Baptism shows our total dependence in commitment on God.

Do you believe that ?

Does your life give evidence to that ?

Many live the opposite to that in which they pay lip service to. If God has said something to you do not keep it to yourself, share it with someone.

Therefore, my beloved brethren, be ye steadfast, unmovable, always abounding in the work of the Lord, forasmuch as ye know that your labour is not in vain in the Lord. 1 Corinthians 15: 58;

Speed the cross through all nations and you will spread the victory across the nation

Rest on God's guarantees, God is with us. It is not God's way to desert what he has once undertaken. How fortunate we are that we have a power that draws all men. We are fortunate that we do not have to advertise as the world advertises. Come to our church, home of nine percent tithe, eight out of ten Commandments, take your choice, softer pews, and shorter sermon, new revision of do's and don'ts, only the finest comfortable word here, visit our sanctuary of weekly theatrical performances.

Be thankful that as men desire change, we serve a living God who does not change, he is the same yesterday, today and forever. All the same rules are in place without compromise. Thou shalt not, is a very real direction for the believer.

For God so loved the world he gave his only begotten son that whosoever believeth in him shall have everlasting life. For God sent not his son into the world to condemn the world; but that the world through him might be saved. John 3:16-17.

The man who discovered his life surrounded by God's love, and transformed by God's grace, is not content to regard this as an accidental benefit on which he has happened to stumble. It is the manifestation, within the limits of his life of a purpose, which lies behind all things, and is older than creation itself. The heart of Paul's faith so far as foreknowledge can express it, is the conviction that our salvation springs from an unceasing activity of God. Here let me assure you, this does not give the individual right to denial of that individual responsibility.

Those who desire to truly live to please God need to put the spirit of condemnation behind them, and go forward with absolute commitment to telling of the Jesus gift of salvation. Give to those round about you a chance to live this new way of life put into place by God himself. Set your sites on destroying the disillusion of de-christianizing our nation. Remember with each step you take, only what is done for Christ will last.

* * * * *

Remember The Assembling Of Yourselves

And let us consider one another to provoke unto love and to good works: Not forsaking the assembling of ourselves together, as the manner of some is; but exhorting one another: and so the much more as you see the day approaching. For if we sin willfully after that we have received the knowledge of truth, there remaineth no more sacrifice for sins. Hebrews 10: 24-26.

When one person confronts another whether with good will or in conflict, there is a provoking that takes place. While employed as a clerk in one of our mega-supermarkets, we were told to address each customer with, good morning, or good afternoon, or good evening, the idea was that if several employees spoke to the person, that customer would be provoked into shopping again in our establishment, because they were recognized by that store. In fact as the customer was greeted we were to provoke them to feel as though they had become a part of our organization. Today it is simply recognized as, Customer Relations. In more professional circles it is often referred to as, Public Relations, and we are often provoked into liking or disliking places, and people by the very philosophy of relationship communications. Indeed it is more simply put here in Hebrews 10: 24; we are told to provoke unto love, and good works. What a marvelous provocation. It is an area that we can and will benefit from when put into practice. When I meet you and sincerely greet you, I need your positive response; because when we are cordial to one another, we lift each other up in the name of Christ.

If a godless organization is able to exercise such awareness of strangers that come to buy their wares, how much more sensitive ought the confessing Christian be to those who have come to share with them in worship. After all, their God, and their saviour is whom we worship also. We need to provoke one another unto love and good works. Take special care to greet those that have a habit of slip ping out quickly after the service. They probably need to be noticed and to be greeted joyfully, with a positive, and meaningful tone in your voice. You will find it to be overwhelmingly rewarding. As we enter the sanctuary fully in the attitude of worshipping our living God through his son Jesus Christ, so afterward, we ought to be as intent on greeting others with love in our hearts. Do not hang back to see how many are greeted by others, but measure your attitude of heart to see how many more you are able to greet this week than what you where able to accomplish last week or last service time. It is a good habit to get into. Do not approach another person as though they need you, rather approach them as though you need them. Marvelous things begin to happen for you when that approach is taken. When one responds to another you will find that an uplifting occurs. I like to deem it as the gravitation of the soul.

There are those who may render a fearful atmosphere, and will instill that fear to others, as they attempt to isolate themselves from those that would love them without question. We must then over-come our fear to distil the other fear of being involved, or being too close to someone, and so on. There are also those who will attempt to avoid God's love with deceit, or selfishness, or they may see it as a weakness. Whatever the reason or the perceived action of others we who love God must not allow any of those human elements of fear to deter us from reaching out a generous hand of hospitality. Greeting to others ought to come natural to the Christian. For Paul says 'I can do all things through Christ who strengthens me'. We need to be able to say hello, glad to see you, I love you, I needed that you be here, I needed that you talk to me. Once you build that solid relationship with other believers, you can be filled with confidence simply by their smile. And as you look at the person, in that built up relationship, you cannot help but to be lifted up yourself.

Those who live by the rule of doing it their way or doing your own thing, will not please God, and shall not experience the peace of God from the depth of the soul. The very essence of God's word from Genesis to Revelation, is to put others first, to love them, cherish them, nurture them, disciple and train them as servants to a living God, because of Christ's sacrifice upon the cross of Calvary. The whole perspective of being Christian is to subordinate one's self. Not to dwell on our needs or wants or that which we may gain for ourselves, but to have primary concern for what God has already done for us through Jesus Christ, his only son.

In the parable of the rich young ruler as Christ witnessed to him. He recognized Christ for who he was. He ran to him. He did not hang in with the crowd and say oh well, maybe I'll get to him. No, he ran to him, acknowledged him, knelt down before him, and asked,

What must I do to inherit eternal life?

Jesus demanded that he let go of all his material possessions, only then could he follow him. The young man refused, and walked away. Jesus sorrowed in his heart for the young man, but could do nothing else to persuade him to follow, because the young man was not willing to commit only to Christ. In essence, Jesus here lost his man. He turned him away. With all our accomplishments, all our achievements, all our worldly possessions, we cannot come to Christ as though it is another accomplishment added to our lives. We must be willing to leave 'all' behind, and recognize that when we accept Christ as our saviour, and follow him, that, is His accomplishment. Many young Christians fail, because they believe they can save the whole world, instead of accepting that God has already done that, but each person must accept on an individual basis the shed blood of Calvary, then go, and tell others that they too may accept this Christ and receive forgiveness of sins, and receive eternal life.

Only love can awaken love; 'Let us provoke one another to love' the bible says. Too often this message is bypassed by the Christian community. We must remember, a bitter word stirs up bitterness in others. An honest word produces or provokes compliments, a kind word provokes kindness. The hard unloving word provokes anything but virtue. Only patience with surrounding humanity can stir up good works.

We see, in verse twenty-five of Hebrews, in the King James version, the word 'exhorting', rather than the word 'encouraging', as some newer translations use. Exhorting is the proper translation, and exceeds the action of encouraging. For it is taking the infant in arms, to hold them and caress them to the point they feel safe and secure from all the uncomfortable things that enter their lives. Here there is no intent to have you take everyone into your arms, I only use this illustration to point out the security one must receive when being exhorted in the love of Christ. Every believer must go beyond the encouragement point to reach out to others, and expect nothing in return. This verse is a direct transition to a direct warning found in the following verses, v26, For if we sin willfully after that we have received the knowledge of truth, there remaineth no more sacrifice for sins.v31, It is a fearful thing to fall into the hands of the living God. Here indicating, of course, the truth of Jesus Christ. Again here is the exclusive claim of the gospel that refutes salvation by works. The work has already been accomplished we need only to follow, and in that following fellowship together with one another, and in that fellowship we must only exercise the ultimate love of God. For there is nothing else we are able to do to maintain our salvation. You may burn all other altars, you may do away with the many false cults, you may disparage any other religion, but God shall not honour those things. Why? Because there is no more sacrifice for sin other than what God has allowed his only son to put in place at Calvary. He paid the price.

Many believers continue their life treating God as though he where out there somewhere in space. They want him to be at a distance, so as not to become to involved with the requirements on which God persists. We have become a society of believers wishing to keep God at a distance. Sometimes we fall into that mode after our initial 'first love'. Instead of allowing God the foremost front of our lives, we allow other things to take his place. After all the 'church' takes first place, or the pastor's great personality or work ethic, captures our attention, and our own demands give him first place. (a good pastor will attempt to steer you away from this pitfall). We pay tribute to the song, and well we ought to, perhaps we simply like the singing ,and the praise, and that which we deem to be worship. I must admit, the church would not be much without all of these contributory divine factions. However we must never lose sight of the fact of the non chaotic order of our Father in heaven, who sent Jesus Christ, who in turn sent the Holy Spirit, and commands us to fellowship together, and to provoke one another unto love and good works together. Many have left the church assemblies, and failed to be adhesive within the congregation. There appears to be a new turn back to the church in these last days, not having found any other worldly store that offers such a peace, as does our living God. We can still hold our faith and preserve our loyalties. Those who have left draw unto themselves strange rules; they do not know why they left the church in the first place. They do not wish to talk about it. They allow, we need the church in our community. We need the proverbial 'good preacher', and of course we must have a good entertaining music programme, but you see all this is O.K., as long as I am allowed to work amongst the world's labour force, and I can visit with my neighbour, no matter how ungodly they may be, as long as I do not have to speak to them about the gospel of my saviour, as long as I do not have to talk about God. Let a person break fellowship with their church, and that person is on their way to denying Christ. For it is my belief that there is not a more effective denial of Christ than that of cutting one's self from the fellowship of other believers in the church assembly. That is the real tragedy of disunity in the Church. Remember if your unity with God is in the proper vertical position, you will not harm the church by refusing to fellowship, and worship with other believers of Christ. When someone misses a Sunday worship service occasionally without a legitimate reason such as travel, or being hospitalized, you can rest assured, there is sin in their life. They borrow a feeling of condemnation, forgetting they are redeemed and forgiven already. Sometimes you will find those that refuse to fellowship, blame the church for their non attendance. The reason they blame the church for everything is because they are unable to take the blame for their own inadequacies. If they would place the blame where it belongs, 'upon themselves' they would then come to grips with making things right with God, and knowing his forgiveness, would be back in the congregation to fellowship with the believers of the gospel of Jesus Christ.

Many Christians plead that their voice will make no difference. That is a devil's lie. Dwight L. Moody one of God's greatest of the twentieth century of Chicago Illinois where he established the Moody Bible Institute, was the only person that was led to the Lord by a certain mild mannered Christian. Feast your spiritual eyes upon the results. Millions have been reached through the Moody Institute. You possess that seemly mysterious power to lead some soul to Christ. One of my favourite stories of the great evangelist Moody is where he had called on one of Chicago's leading citizens to persuade him to accept Christ. As the story goes, they were seated in the parlour of the man's home, it was wintertime, the coals were heaped in the fireplace, and they both sat enjoying that setting. Moody apparently gave him the message of Christ, and invited him to be a Christian. The man's response was objectionable, claiming he could be just as good a Christian outside the church as he could within the church. Moody made no reply, he simply stepped over to the fireplace, picked up the tongs, he reached in pulled out a live flaming coal, set it aside in the hearth; the two men sat and watched the flame go out. The coal turned black. 'I see" said the man ' I see."

Exhorting, encouraging one another; how desperately we all need that. For if we sin willfully after that we have received the truth there remaineth no more sacrifice for sin. That is the encouragement of a friend who does not hesitate to point out our flaws in our Christian faith and conduct. The finest encouragement is only possible with friends who can challenge us, because we trust them in their walk.

Do you have that trust in the Christian community with your neighbour, to the point where you can share with them to know all you share will not become gossip?

Are you able to challenge them on their Christian witness to the point where they will stand stronger because of your challenge?

Do you know your neighbour well enough to laugh together at each other's expense?

The creation of this type of fellowship is surely the most urgent need of our churches today.

As you look to the last portion in v25 it says, 'as you see the day approaching'.

What day?

Christ had come and been seen and was gone. It talks of the day of judgment when Christ shall return for his own, all believers. We lack a sense of the speed in which that day is approaching. We may be in the last times now as we witness one prophecy heaped upon another being fulfilled. That sense of urgency must become real within our service to God through Jesus Christ. Instead of saying 'Christ is coming' it may be more appropriate to say, 'He is on his way'. Christ began preaching in Mark1:15; The time is fulfilled, and the Kingdom of God is at hand: repent ye, and believe the gospel.

The grace of God may now enter the human heart; the urgency is real. Again we read in Isaiah 59:1; Behold, the Lord's hand is not shortened, that it cannot save; neither his ear heavy, that he cannot hear:

When we begin to recognize this way to encourage, the urgency of it will make itself quite clear. The love of Christ within us will allow each of us to reach out and touch someone with the word. We are assured of this as we hear Christ's own word. They who confess me before men so will I confess them before my Father which is in heaven.

Have you confessed Christ before men?

The following of Christ demands it. The scripture explains it, and God rewards for it. There is no way around it. We need to tell others outside our circle, about our Christ who changes people's lives. The Christian life is a work of love, whereby we reach out to encourage and uplift one another. As we prepare ourselves to witness we help those around us to be witnesses also. Be assured of this one thing, God has trusted you with His gospel, and he has directed you to tell others. God in His magnificent power works through the common person, the poor, the needy, the new believer; He trusts you to deliver His work of the cross to a dying world that some might be saved. What then have you done for God? Allow me to leave you with this great poem that has meant much to many throughout their lives and has a special spot in my heart as well, it simply called,

The Touch Of The Master's Hand
Myra Brooks Welch

'Twas battered and scarred, and the Auctioneer thought it scarcely worth his while to waste much time with the old violin, but held it up with a smile, 'What am I bidden good folks,' he cried, 'Who'll start the bidding for me'? 'A dollar, a dollar', then, 'Two! Only two? Two dollars, and who'll make it three?'

Three dollars once; three dollars twice; going for three - ', but no, from the room, far back, a gray haired man came forward and picked up the bow; then wiping the dust from the old violin, and tightening the loose strings, he played a melody, as pure and sweet as the Angels sings.

The music ceased, and the auctioneer, with a voice that was quiet and low, said, 'What am I bid for the old violin', and he held it up with the bow, 'A thousand dollars, and who'll make it two? Two thousand! and who'll make it three? Three thousand, once; three thousand, twice; and going, and gone,' said he. The people cheered, but some of them cried, 'We do not quite understand what changed its worth' Swift came the reply: 'The touch of a Master's hand.'

And many a man with his life out of tune, and battered and scarred with sin, is auctioned cheap to a thoughtless crowd, Much like the old violin, a 'Mess of pottage', a glass of wine; a game - and he travels on. He is 'going' once; and 'going' twice, he's 'going' and almost 'gone'. But the Master comes, and the foolish crowd never can quite understand the worth of a soul and the change that's wrought by the touch of the Master's hand.

* * * * *

When The Angels Have Gone Away

—◦◦◦—

And she brought forth her first born son, and wrapped him in swaddling clothes, and laid him in the manger; because there was no room for them in the Inn. and there were in the same country shepherds abiding in the field, keeping watch over their flock by night. And, lo, the angel of the Lord came upon them, and the glory of the Lord shone around about them: and they were sore afraid. And it came to pass that as the Angels were gone away from them into heaven, the shepherds said to one another, Let us go now even unto Bethlehem, and see these things which is come to pass, which the Lord has made known unto us. Luke 2: 8-9, 15

I would that you where able to grasp even a mite of this happening. The night had settled, shepherds were seated on the cold damp ground in the black of night, perhaps sitting around a not so romantic open bonfire. They were not being entertained by singing of choruses, nor the strumming of guitars. At best they may have been in deep conversation about the crisis times they were forced to live in. They may very well have been sharing about their God, and wondering when he would fulfill His promise to them to send the messiah.

These men were not dressed in suits and ties; nor were they ready for a celebration or feast. No, they were unbathed smelly shepherds who spent most of their time away from the city dwellers; alone, in the fields with sheep of their masters. This was a period of crisis; when the Angels flooded the fields with their radiance, in the land, surrounding Bethlehem. It was not difficult to believe in the reality of God, and the truth of religion. Faith seemed easy because it was expected of each family to seek the will of God, and almost spontaneous, amid such conditions. The shepherds had no problem believing that the old testament prophecy was being fulfilled, and that now that infinite love was upon the earth. It was not difficult for them to accept that the resources of the spiritual world, had come forward, to meet the needs of humanity.

In that hour of tremendous visitation from the living God, all skepticisms, and prejudices, concerning spiritual reality, vanished from the souls of these men. Belief, devotion, worship, service. All these things that entered into the soul of religion, were not difficult, in the presence of the Angels. I am glad that the story did not close with verse fourteen because the sight of the Angels was spectacular to say the least. But think what happened when the Angels had gone away.

That was the hour of reaction, and possible relapse in the aftermath

of this heavenly event. How strangely silent the fields of Bethlehem were, after the Angels had gone away. The closest you could possibly come to relating to the likeness of the aftermath is if you have ever been blinded by the bright lights of an oncoming car when the driver flicks his bright lights up just when meeting him. Perhaps you have been shopping in a huge grocery store when the power outage hits, and it is silent and black until your eyes adjust to the dullness of candle light. Perhaps the blinding instant flash of a camera's bulb, that gives you momentary blindness. This was a period of test, with a crisis in inky black emptiness.

Angels who appear on Gods behalf apparently are never given a great length of time to meander amongst earthly bodies so consequently never stay for lengthy time. Periods of heavenly visitations throughout scriptures, prove that the visits where always brief.

This is why we need worship as perhaps the world never needed it before.

We have plenty of ideas, but they are accompanied with a famine of deep assurance. We may even have great ambition upon which we ride, as children ride horses upon a merry-go-round, or as they ready their imaginations with their space orientation that engulfs man in dreams.

We like the motion and thrill to the music, but when we climb down from the ride we discover that we have gone through many resolutions, only to arrive nowhere. We like to hear people talk, providing they will give us a series of new impressions, so rapid that we do not have to concentrate on any one. What we must learn, is to be quiet before the voices, which speak to us of the unseen reality of life. Those forms may come to us in forms no more impressive than the shepherds, but they come

Someone has given us the incentive to believe that there is more to life than it's everyday appearance.

Before such wonders, as that of messenger Angels, or some real direction from God, there can at least be wonder; and it is wonder that opens the mind and heart to truth.

The spell, of some searching, special sermon, or some spiritual leadership, Followed by reaction. Oh! But, the bleakness of the night. After the Angels had gone away. It begs the question,

What would we have done, had we been in the place of the shepherds?

Well! For sure, we would have initiated a group discussion. We might have said, let us be careful, we must not do anything rash. After all we had better analyze this, and rehash it all from the beginning. Then again we may question the happening,

Is it all real?

Where those really Angels?

Real beings?

Shepherds with names like Jacob, Samuel, Zechariah, their conversation could have sounded like this;

Did you see that Jake?

What exactly did you see Sam?

Did it appear that way to you Zach?

Do you think it was an optical illusion?

Is it likely that a divine Saviour come and be born in such an unlikely place as Bethlehem?'

Even so would God really send a heavenly envoy to us lowly shepherds?'

We may have been careful to caution ourselves, and each other, to be careful before committing ourselves to such a strange announcement. We again may have cherished suspicions concerning the whole underlying principle of the angelic song. We may have said, this involves the principle of Divine Incarnation, and then discussed it at some length.

How can eternal enter into time?

How can divine enter into the limitations of human?

How can we commit ourselves to an Evangel, which philosophy has not been endorsed, and to which it will never be approved?

We might have suggested that we return to our normal life, get on the best we can with this phenomena, and say nothing of this whole affair. After all we could make ourselves look pretty foolish, and we don't want to be laughed at the rest of our days. Let's play it safe. And so would have dishonoured the greatest event in human history.

How often good people follow the prompting of their fears, rather than the summons of their faith?

When the Angels had gone away; when the period of emotion had passed - then what?

Luke 2: 15b tells us, Let us go now even unto Bethlehem, and see this thing which is come to pass, which the Lord has made known unto us. Intellectual and moral honesty compels us to face some very unfriendly facts, in the life of this age. We are face to face, not only with a good deal of mistrust of religion; but there is much hostility towards it.

Many now assert their doubt about the reality of God, or the Devine authority of Jesus, and the idea of a personal immortality of man. They look upon these things as a projection of man's hopes and wishes into the infinite. Their unbelief is caused by those who have never taken upon themselves the attitude of the shepherds. They have never said we will go and see. The shepherds tried it out, and that is all Christianity asks, 'A fair trial'

After a bridge is built in any Municipalty, there is required a test to know its strength.

Would it not be wise to apply a reasonable test to the unbeliever to see the strength of the gospel of Jesus Christ?

We need the Attitude of the shepherd, to treat God with all reverence, and treat man as his child.

Verse 16; the shepherds made a discovery; they came with haste, and found Mary and Joseph, and the babe lying in a manger. There the spiritual certainty of Christians. One does not need to enter the monastery, or a convent, or a retreat, nor does one need to join some pilgrimage to the ends of the earth. The mother can find it in the nursery, the farmer can find it in the field, the nurse can find it in a hospital, the pilot can find it in the wild blue yonder, the builder can find it in construction. In common walks of life, we can verify the teachings of our Saviour, Christ, Lord.

Follow the highest light; be true to the deepest convictions, and you shall ultimately come to that Bethlehem where God is revealed in Christ. The shepherds made a proclamation; Verse 17; and when they had seen it, they made it known abroad the saying which was told them concerning the child.

They risked contradiction, mockery, ridicule, and even hostility. Think on the vast truths unused Think on the vast convictions, never uttered. Think on converting and transforming truths which are never voiced. We have taken refuge in the horrible heresy, that the priest at the altar, the preacher in the pulpit, the evangelist in the forum, can convert the world, and solve the problem to which the whole church of God is committed, but it was the Shepherds, it was the layman, today, as in those days, it will take more than the songs of the Angels, we must have the testimony of the Shepherds.

* * * * *

One Thing Christ Could Not Do

——⊙⁄⊙⁄⊙——

He saved others, himself he cannot save. Matthew 27: 42.

The human element of Christ could have given thought to the challenge of giving up the sacrifice as he suffered upon that cruel cross of Calvary. However he had come for a purpose, and that purpose was to lay down his life as a supreme sacrifice for those whom his father had created. His determination to carry through the portion that was so difficult, gave to us eternal life, that we might spend eternity in heaven with our living God.

Even though the crowd before him jeered, and taunted, about his position of saviour, he stayed the course, and shed his blood for the remission of sin. May God continue to forgive each one for their doubting, and for their slowness to comprehend the vital act that took place at Calvary that awesome day.

I can think of no picture of injustice that compares with that which was thrust upon the son of god that day at Calvary.

Christ, the blameless one, having done nothing but good to build each persons character to the fullest, bringing them to the most wholesome practice in life building. Yet in all that we find him dying on the cross between two thieves, with a jeering, gloating, bloodthirsty crowd, not understanding who he was and why he chose to finish his work there.

At the height of their slander and abuse, voices rose above the noise giving this challenge, "he cannot save himself." the claim was, if he would come down from the cross this instant, they would believe in his kingship, but Christ knew of their false accusations which kept their lies alive.

History has recorded no greater poignancy of injustice, yet for the sinner who is in need of deliverance, as for followers of the living God there is no more wonderful news than this. For here at the cross my life begins anew. I was dead in trespasses and sin until I learned of this sacrifice that he had made for me at Calvary. Here in that frightful day the world found the superlative of mercy. It was here that the blood of bullock, and the goat, carried no more meaning, for the blood of Christ, God's perfect sacrifice paid in full the eternal debt of the trespasser's sin.

Yes, Christ could have come down from that cross, even as a king would step down from a throne, but he chose to die for you. Christ knew the human heart, and had he chosen to step down, the crowd would only have marveled at the strength of the man tearing himself from the cross, but they still would have failed to accept his deity. Their unbelief in this man as the son of God would not have been brought to a more convincing climax about the why of his being there. So, Christ, uttered a prayer for the frenzied crowd before him as he clenched the gruesome spikes with his hands, and remained on the cross.

His reason for remaining on the cross was more than just provide an escape for the sinful person. For over thirty years Christ lived a life conducive to winning the world, and to convince people that he was the son of God, the prophesied redeemer, the Messiah whom they had been looking for over the centuries. He attempted to live his life to extend the confirmation being given to the Jews, as well as his disciples, that the Angel of the Lord spoke the truth when he said to Joseph, "Fear not to take unto thee Mary thy wife - - - and she shall bring forth a son and thou shalt call his name Jesus; for he shall save his people from their sin."

Through parables, and miracles, Jesus traveled all over the country establishing the reason for coming , and telling of the ultimate sacrifice that must be administered for salvation, but few understood. The only way to initiate a cleansing of the soul was to perform the greatest miracle of all, that was for him to die, and be raised up from the dead in order to be declared to be the son of God with power, according to the spirit of holiness, by the resurrection from the dead. Romans 1: 4.

Here the resurrection gives every believer boldness and assurance that all was accomplished that Christ set out to accomplish as in agreement with God, his father. The resurrected Christ meant redemption, complete and proof positive. The words spit out at the cross, was to challenge Jesus to act contrary to his father's will, were uttered in sarcasm, and ridicule, without realizing that they spoke a basic truth. Saving others he had to refuse to save himself from the particular situation, in which he placed himself for mankind. If Christ had saved himself, it would have been impossible to save others, because his redemptive errand would have remained incomplete. The fact that he came to save others is paramount in that his life and death were dedicated to this purpose. He not only claimed to be saviour, and redeemer, he verified his claim with the act upon the cross.

There was an instant where Christ healed a man who had palsy, and the Pharisees who witnessed this were highly incensed when they heard Jesus say to the man, "Thy sins be forgiven thee." They were astonished at this action and immediately brought on their criticism by asking, "Who can forgive sins except God?" Christ reading their thoughts asked, "Why reason you this thing in your heart - - -, but that you may know that the son of man has the power on earth to forgive sins - - -, I say unto thee arise, go take up thy bed , and go into thine house."

Not only could he say to blind Bartimaeus, "Thy faith hath made thee whole," but he could follow it up with, "receive thy sight."

Yes he saved others, and he saved them from their lifestyle as they were. The thief, for instance, surely unfit for heaven by any of the contemporary modern day standards, but Christ saved him. The thief, was by his own testimony, deserving of the fate in which he was found in. Even so, he was able to witness to his fellow gangster on the other cross. "Dost thou not fear God, seeing that thou art in the same condemnation, and we justly? For we receive the due reward of our deeds, but this man has done nothing amiss. The thief, at his best, was miserable and undone. Clearly, he had no merit of his own, Christ, looked upon this man and saved him.

My friend, God does not wish you to waste time by cleaning up to the best of your ability, he wants to make the change in your life, and says for you to come, as you are, and he will do the clean up.

Again Christ says, "They that be whole need not a physician, but they that are sick. I am come not to call righteous, but sinners to repentance."

One of the most demanding lies that keep us from surrendering to Christ is the common excuse that I must conquer all my bad habits to reform my daily living before giving myself to Christ.

Supposing I am in the field preparing it for the seeding in order that I could produce a harvest, and I was diagnosed as having been stricken by appendicitis. Someone tells me that they would drive me to the hospital where an operation would save me, however if I refused I would die. Refusing to follow the direction I had been given, would be looked upon as sheer stupidity, because I would suffer, and die, right there in my field.

Statistics show that today there are millions who are following the wrong course , while the Holy Spirit pleads with them to let Christ do his perfect work in their lives. I plead with you to let Christ do his perfect work of grace in your life as he readies you to reach the unsaved around you. He wants you to be a witness for which he died and rose again. He wants you to yield to him just as you are now. For you see my friends, Jesus, is in the saving business, the cross, and the empty tomb, bear witness to that fact.

He is the receiver of destructive souls, he is the transformer of God's creation. His specialty is saving the moral, and the immoral, the decent and the indecent, the clean and the unclean. He can do far more for you in a minute than you will accomplish for a lifetime. Everything worthwhile demands sacrifice. Strike a match, it burns. Light a candle, and it melts away. Turn on your houselights, and somewhere generators grind away and wires hum in order for you to see. Everything you have or own has been sacrificed for. If you made no sacrifice to obtain that which you enjoy in life, someone else did. Nothing worthwhile can be obtained without sacrifice.

Eternal life with the living God for the believer, came only after that unwarranted sacrifice of his son Jesus Christ as he shed his blood upon the cross at Calvary for your sins, and mine. Only

Christ could measure up to the value given by God to make that sacrifice. Without spot or blemish. he was the lamb of God, slain from the foundation of the world.

He made the sacrifice, the job is done. If we believe in the redemptive work on Calvary, God will welcome us with open arms when we meet him in his heavenly home as we enter eternity. There is only one way to make reservations in heaven, that is to accept Christ as saviour now.

Just as Christ could not come down from the cross if we were to be saved, so we, cannot be saved except we go by the way of the redemptive plan that was successfully put into place on that cross. People must believe in Jesus Christ's redemption plan today, even in this world filled with falsehood. Christ's words stand in the never changing drawing board of God, as they stand true in the demanding swirl of time in today's whirlwind of lies. You cannot lean to your own evaluation for the scripture bluntly reminds us of the way, *"Trust in the Lord with all thine heart; Lean not unto thine own understanding. In all thy ways acknowledge him, and he shall direct thy paths."* Proverbs 3:5-6.

Take the promise of God and believe in his work repenting of all your sin and unbelief. His resurrection becomes our hope of a glorious future with a sweet reunion of our loved ones who also believed in him.

Truly he saved others, but saying he cannot save himself is to lose the whole concept of the sinless Christ who did not require saving because of his guiltless nature, and sinless life. Instead he paid an awesome high price for you to have eternal life.

Will you allow him into your life that he might save you today?

* * * * *

New Creature For New Life

—◦/◦/◦—

Jesus said unto him, I am the way, the truth, and the life: no man cometh unto the Father but by me. John 14: 6.

In the bushland wilderness of Northern Ontario there existed many eerie lays of swampland within the parameters of the tall tamarack timber stands. In the changing temperatures of the season they would be blanketed with thick fog, primarily in the forenoon, and as the warmth of the day rose, the fog would be vanquished. Such was the case on our farm as we looked out across the fields the fog blocked our view. In its own spectacle of beauty, the warmth caused it to rise toward the noon hour to uncover a certain wilderness beauty all its own making clear the road we needed to follow. In the wintertime we logged the timber from the bush by building a winding trail through the swamp to haul logs to the mill to be cut into lumber. It worked well over frozen tundra. In the summer time we were still able to travel through the swamp on the well padded, but twisting trail that had been built for travel in the winter months. If there were morning fog, one could not find the curves so we were not allowed to travel until the fog cleared from the warmth of the day, for if one were to run off the road into the bog you would be a goner. All residents of the area were quite aware of the danger of traveling the swamp in the fog, and avoided travel when it was evident that it was unsafe to do so .

I believe, the unbelieving world lives with that kind of fog towards the message of salvation before their eyes. If they would seek, and watch for Christ, the fog would lift from the warmness of their heart, and the road for them to travel would be clearly visible to see the way, which is Christ.

The whole of Christ's existence summed up in this one statement, here is life in all it's complexities simplified in the acceptance of Christ, here and in the hereafter. The gateway to eternity stands before us in the body of Christ. He is the straight way, the way of truth that goes on forever. He is the format by which the way, and the truth lead to the life that goes on forever.

Jesus said, Except a man be born again he cannot see the kingdom of God. Which prompted the question from Nicodemus, How can a man be born when he is old? can he enter the second time into his mother's womb, and be born. *Jesus answered, Verily, verily, I say unto thee, except a man be born of water and of spirit he cannot enter into the kingdom of God. That which is born of flesh is flesh; that which is born of spirit is spirit.* John 3: 3-6.

Jesus faced a seeker who happened to be a ruler of the Jews, he was interested in answers from Jesus because he was concerned about eternal life thinking perhaps this new teacher could deliver some consolation to his soul.

Life in the flesh begins with birth, so Jesus points out to the ruler that life in the spirit begins with birth in the spirit. A precisely logical answer to the seeker. It is not a phenomena of scholarship, nor some scientific discovery, it is a simple fact of having life in the spiritual world through Christ's formula of being born again. You may not fully understand the reason of the blowing winds, but only an idiot would adamantly deny that they do blow.

It was an honest question of a sincere seeker, and Jesus took time to explain to Nicodemus in his answer. Jesus pointed to the fact that he had brought new life down from heaven with him. He explains further that he is that life announcing the initial step of entrance into the new birth. Jesus makes it clear that to enter heaven to be with the Father you must enter through him for he is the way, or the door through which one must pass. He points out again, that he has come that we might have life.

The sinner finds the way by faith, the truth by faith, and now when he receives Christ by faith he will receive life. for Christ, and Christ alone, can impart everlasting spiritual life. The Jesus way of life will be important to you if you wish to be born again.

The tragedy of our churches of this contemporary age, is that there are multitudes on the membership rolls that have never been born again.

They may be altogether loyal to the church, and they may be without question meticulously law abiding citizens highly respected on the social ladder of success. They may give generously to their church to the point the organization is dependant upon their support. They may even attend services consistently giving that extra push for special services that are needed for church growth. They may even worship as people have always worshipped traditionally. they may even take a stand on the side of righteousness as they make the show of opposing every evil that seeks to undermine the moral fibre of the nation. They may even have kept the whole law as perfectly as people claim to keep the law of God. But if Christ meant what he said to Nicodemus, they are undone sinners, without hope, in time or eternity if they are not born again.

Except a man be born again he cannot see the kingdom of God, are the words of Jesus Christ the son of the living God. This is the process by which people will be brought unto God, there is no other way. Christ proclaimed it, God has sanctioned it, believers must preach it. For this is the only way of eternal life that will allow you to win the race and receive the reward.

People have come to rely on the fact that they belong to a church organization. They encase themselves into false respectability of academic prowess. They rely heavily on good works with righteous attitude. A drunkard or a beggar with little in their lives may be easier to convince of their need than people bathed in religiosity or self appointed righteousness. If you are only committed to the church attendance scene because of the social impact that gives you an appearance of respectability, you need to examine these words, You must be born again.

A secular statement exists saying that the so-called Christian is one who puts on the cloak of religion to produce an image that is acceptable to society.

Some people get involved in one of the more acceptable humanism channels. That is to be involved in all sorts of youth activities, because along with our cloak of religion it portrays a more perfect image of a person in the community. However as people involve themselves in the community of youth today, we fail them as a coach to life. People are not honest with the young people whom they attempt to influence in some direction. People lack honesty in telling the youth how to play the game of all games, the game of life. For here is where their goal is to reach eternity with it's rich rewards from a committed life of obedience for our living God.

In many churches the social hour of mixed entertainment draws a bigger crowd than a prayer meeting. The table games become more important than to attend a bible study. People do not give the youth the truth, because they do not want to hear the truth themselves, therefore they teach others that they do not have to accept the truth of God, and here the church has failed miserably.

This does not mean that the church does not have the way to life, as given by God, it only means that they have found a convenient way to amalgamate the world with the church. It has not worked in the past, and it will never work to the advantage of Christ, but when you compromise God's word for an unbelieving world, it will destroy the church, and take away it's life.

Churches need to implement a concern that the up and coming youth, learn that Christ, and the life the world lives, are two absolutely different ways of living. One way leads to destruction, the other way leads to eternal life in heaven. Christ, and life, are inseparable, and the recipe cannot handle any added ingredients.

When you allow Christ into your life he will motivate you, choose winning paths for you, he will give you purpose for your life, he will direct you to valuable acts to favour your walk. We are the only vehicle through which Christ ultimately delivers his message to the unsaved. Let him take control of your life today.

One of the difficulties we face, is that we undertake to live a life that we do not have. We attempt to do our own thinking, we believe we choose our own paths, and map our own courses. Even though we exercise the ability to achieve we muddy up the process by our rejection of Christ as saviour of our life.

Christ says, God has given us eternal life. Nation, upon Nation, and tribe upon tribe discovered by the Christian workers found that each in their peculiar way, believed in eternal life. God gave us life at creation, and Jesus brought new life for the eternal.

God did not leave this mighty truism to College, Universities, libraries, medical laboratories. He did not even leave it to some inspired book. He purposed in his creation to give an absolute certainty that all created in his likeness would have the knowledge that life is eternal.

For God so loved - - - that whosoever believeth in him, should have everlasting life .

Why don't you sit down and accept that eternal life now?

* * * * *

The Homeless Saviour

—◦◦◦—

And it came to pass, that, as they went on the way, a certain man said unto him, Lord, I will follow thee withersoever thou goest. And Jesus said unto him, Foxes have holes, and birds of the air have nests; but the son of man has nought where to lay his head. Luke 9: 57-58.

The beginning of another century has brought into focus the growing numbers of homeless people who are in all probability that way because of their own wrong choices that are in conflict with a social order that would feed and house them. But they continually refuse to accept the generosity of the do-gooders of our society. Nevertheless, as they attempt to portray the fact that they believe that society has rejected them, they lose sight of the fact that they are the ones who have also practiced the emotional rejection of those who would fulfill their needs without question. They refuse to believe enough to accept the goods and services offered to them on a platter as they continue their rejection.

In these scripture we see that Christ knew where this type of people were headed. He points out that his own experiences included the lack of insight of his necessity to be there as he too experienced being without.

The sin of rejection of Christ as personal saviour, is the sin that is condemning the world. People refuse to entertain Jesus in their homes, or in their lives they seek comradeship elsewhere as they slam the door in the face of Christ.

From the manger to the cross, from the cross to an empty tomb, Jesus has experienced aloneness. He walked alone on the road to Emmaus. He walked alone from the garden to his cell. He stood alone in the courts that applied the false accusations of the religious order. He stood alone as the ruler from the Roman Empire found him not guilty, but still sentenced him to death. Ascending into heaven alone, he promised to send someone to comfort those few who lost his personal companionship for a short time.

Luke says a certain man offered to follow Christ, but he was given a thought provoking response to the offer. In the truest sense it made him to search himself to see if he was truly willing to follow, or if he was only struck in the heart sorrow by the rejection by some to such a fine person as Jesus proved to be. Jesus perceived that this fellow was not ready with self denying devotion to take up the cross to ingratiate himself to the kingdom of God. Although this man appeared to be filled with a new enthusiasm as he stepped out from the crowd to at least appear make the effort to become a follower. I suppose we should give him merit because of a one time action to submit to following.

But herein lies the fault of those who fall away to stay with the sin of the world. He thought it to costly to continue, to find himself without home or family by committing himself ultimately to the furtherance of the gospel to lift up the son of God. He would not be able to appear as a successful religious person at Christ's expense, so he fell away. The once in a lifetime right move or correctness, does not give you salvation. There needs to be an unquestionable commitment without seeking gain for self position. Feeling sorry for those who have had a bad deal in religious circles does not constitute salvation. Only at the acceptance of Christ will salvation be applied to your life.

Perhaps this man was satisfied with the answer that Jesus gave when he showed no sign of retaliation to punish his enemies. At least it seems reasonable to assume this man was moved emotionally as he made ready to become a disciple of Christ.

The in depth love of Christ for the sinner shows forth here when he made no bones about telling the man exactly how it was, if he was sincere in following in his decision. Jesus pointed out to this certain man, that if he was serious he must consider he was joining a homeless man, and the trip was to be tough to start with nothing, and carry on.

View well, the modern church of our day. See all the activities that have absolutely nothing to do with Christ, and his salvation of the soul. They have invited the ways of the world into the sanctuary and moved the cross out. They insult God to his face, but to their own death, and they drink damnation to their own souls. Who shall deliver them out of Christless rituals of adolescent mockery by ritualistic pantomimes in the place of holiness. Only Jesus Christ who measures unto each the grace of God in their hour of belief in the only son of God.

The modern believer lacks in absolute willingness to give of themselves to God. Again add their distasteful attitude of self satisfaction while they fail to deny self, and give absolute devotion to a living God. With worship in the sanctuary people today deny their absolute priority to God. They seek and do not find because they are lost in the ignorance of that which is required of God. When they finally come to grips with the fact that God requires exclusive attention, because he has given his only begotten son on the cross of Calvary to shed his blood for their sins. They wallow in the joys of ritual, and do not heed the exclusiveness of God, never realizing the road has no pillows or rest stops. Only a rocky trail where we need to be willing to undergo all the trials that come our way, and still pay to God our tribute of worship for rendering unto us eternal life.

What keeps people doing those things that separate them from God?

It is because they cannot lose concern for themselves, because they are overly concerned for their own comfort. Another road to a Christless eternity is working with closed groups. They not only shut out other would be workers, but they shut God out of their circle, because God's own son implores each one to preach the gospel to the world, not to a select group where your loyalty has the infection of narrowness. Human nature ply's us around with the thought of protecting one another from a nothingness position which shuts out the kingdom of God. So we allow Jesus to travel his course without us for it has proven too costly.

With all our indifferences, we need to ask ourselves, are we fit for the kingdom of God?

What would be Christ's response when we offer to follow with a shallow base of trial and error. I believe that he would also discourage us as he points out the cost of in depth integrity it takes to be remotely Christ like.

Jesus, who left his throne with his power, and presence in the creation of the world, attended his advent in human form, as a child, loved and cuddled by a carpenter with his young wife Mary bedded down in a stable. They had been told the cost, and they accepted God's will in their lives to bring Jesus to the world that the world might be saved. Their trials started in a stable, but had to flee to a foreign land to protect this child. God sent news of the death of their enemy with a message that it would be safe for them to return. Christ's messengers were Angels from heaven sent to direct those involved in his life. God had started his plan in motion. Jesus returned to Nazareth as a young preacher knowing full well his course, and the outcome that was to be apparent to others at a later date. His sermon was not well received in his home town. They asked, is not this the carpenter's son, and is not his mother Mary?

I imagine his sermon was compelling, but they didn't like him because of the personal conviction that was brought by his message. Jesus was walking in the wilderness when he was accosted by his adversary Satan who tried to persuade him to do things his way with exotic rewards as he spent some quiet time before God the Father, and accredited him with all things that Satan attempted to claim possession of. Jesus, who took upon himself the responsibility of a ministry to evangelize the then known world. He took unto himself twelve faithful men to help with his work He touched many as they believed not only n his miracles, but in his touch as they were lifted up by his word. He rode into Jerusalem as the king surrounded by a crowd of those rejected by a selfish world, yet Christ embraced them, and cherished their presence.

Royalty was absent, wealth was absent, yet the king of kings, rode through Jerusalem amongst believers who were there to cheer him on, even though they little understood the total significance of the gathering until some time later. Later he withdraws to a place of prayer by himself, and he wept over Jerusalem's rejection. He knew that it would not compare to what he still had to face. In his prayer he asks, Father, if thou be willing let this cup pass from me. What was that cup? It was a cup that would be filled with blood, bitterness, and pain of the sin of the world to be cast upon his shoulders at the cross of Calvary. An affair with the Father where they had agreed for him to carry this load to deliver salvation to the created being that had wandered so far from God.

Today men still reject the saviour as they turn a deaf ear to the message of eternal salvation that the preacher brings. Perhaps at one time you have said the words, I believe, but you have allowed it to be a shallow echo of the past. You have refused to carry the message to others. If that is so, remember the blood of the unsaved will be upon your hands, and God will hold you responsible for their souls. There is still time for you to discontinue your neglect of the saviour Jesus Christ, and put yourself into the place where God can deliver the reward to you when you are with him in heaven.

* * * * *

Love And Fulfillment

—⟨⟨⟨⟩⟩⟩—

And he answering said, Thou shalt love the Lord thy God with all thy heart, and with all thy soul, and with all thy strength, and with all thy mind; and thy neighbour as thyself. Luke 10: 27.

Consider these facts, life is short, eternity is long, sin is black, hell is certain, and heaven can be yours if you learn to exercise forgiveness to your fellowman.

What does forgiveness mean?

According to Webster's dictionary, Forgive - 1. to give up resentment against, or desire to punish; to stop being angry with; pardon. 2. to give up all claim to punish or exact penalty for (an offence); overlook. 3. to cancel or remit (a debt).

You see, God has forgiven you. By what criteria should we allow another Christian into our lives?

Let us again take a close look at what Webster says. We read in his reference, the Synonym Absolve. which implies a setting free from responsibility or obligations from penalties for their violation: Acquit, means to release from a specific charge by a judicial system usually for lack of evidence, to exonerate from wrong doing: to pardon is to release from punishment as well as any resentment or vengeful feelings, to vindicate is to clear (a person or thing under attack) through evidence of the unfairness of the charge.

God has already forgiven. Christ said, If I make you free you shall be free indeed.

Can you produce anything positive about your brother in Christ?

If not, then it is wisdom to consider keeping your mouth shut. In conversation with a lady who believed herself to be less than what she really was, stopped to tell me how she appreciated my work for the Lord at the same time she said, "Of course you are more Christian than me," I put my hand on her shoulder, looked her straight in the eye to respond, "There is no such thing as a greater or lesser Christian. If you are a believer, you are as much a Christian as myself, or anyone else that claims the name of Christ. I may, because of my learning, possess at this time a greater knowledge of scripture than you, only because I have had the opportunity that has not availed it's self to you, but more Christian than you, absolutely not."

As a Christian you must be careful not to get caught up in your own greatness by holding up others to ridicule for lack of learning. The bible says, even those who believe on the name of Jesus shall be saved. There is a tendency to bypass the word of God when it does not comply with our own thinking. God knew this and gave us the story of the good Samaritan in Luke 10: 25-37. Let us first take a glance at those who passed by the wounded man. A man of the church came by and saw the man lying there, and instead of allowing it to cut into his time factor he crossed over to the other side of the road, deliberately ignoring the need, he left the troubled man by the wayside, for the church couldn't get involved. So the Church was not there. Then appeared the Levite, a supposed keeper of the law, or member of the board at the temple. Often, used to police communities, for people breaking the law of God. The Levite knew how God had delivered his people in a spirit of forgiveness for their sin against him. Even the knowledge of God's love did not direct him to take action to the person in desperate need. He also left the wounded by the side of the road.. Then a common traveler came by, a Samaritan. This man in the eyes of the community had little status for he was unimpressive, and certainly not of Royalty. He made no colourful showmanship, nor was religion important to him. He was an inconspicuous character that made no display of pomp, and ceremony, but he was a man who cared. He immediately recognized a problem to which he began to share the solution by his action toward the individual.

Here was someone who knew how to put himself last, and the need of others first. This type of caring has become a lost art in the modern day congregations that call themselves Christian. The Samaritan made no excuses to get away on his own business. He did not sit back to make some logical sense of why a man would lay on the side of the road. He did not reason out some logic of informing someone else to come by and pick him up. The most blessed part of this story is the fact that, he took the "now" action, and gave the remedy for the survival of the injured man who was left to die. The scripture shows he had compassion, and bound up his wounds, he lifted the man to his own beast, and took him to the Inn where he again stayed to look after him. When he left he paid the Inn keeper extra money to continue the care, promising him that if there was added expense he would cover it on his next trip.

Can you identify with the action taken here, or are you with those who pass by ignoring the need to save the soul of the individual by the wayside?

And grieve not the Holy Spirit of God, whereby ye are sealed unto the day of redemption. Let all bitterness and wrath, and anger, and clamour, and evil speaking, be put away from you with all malice; and be ye kind to one another, even as God for Christ's sake has forgiven you. Ephesians 4: 30-32. Forgiveness of those who have wronged you is very difficult. I am fully aware of this from very personal experiences in church leadership, and civic politics with community leadership. For there are and always will be those who will work towards your demise. When you are strong on producing a God oriented success with Christ in your foremost picture presentation. There will always be a group of agitators that will be ready to put you down for the things you accomplish, but you must never dwell on those things. Rather you must embrace God's way, and forgive them without any thought of getting even.

That is God's way. That is Christ's way. True forgiveness with no apologies for the practice of it. God's infinite mercy, and patience with each other, should lead us to be kind one to another, even when we see the defects.

* * * * *

Unbelief

by J. A. [Jim] Watson

I heard the fluttering of wings
I saw the pool of broken Kings
I heard the screams
Of broken dreams
And saw the souls that fell
Politicians promise in the fire of hell

Others robed in white
An awesome sight
Followers of the Son
Paraded the throne one by one
Followed by Him on a great white horse
Suffered by man , ran the course

Can those cries be subdued
By man's claim of being good
Open eyes the blind yet unable to see
Have not yet bowed Oh God to thee
And continue the pageant myth to tell
To find only they too shall end up in hell

God's measure of the human race
Unbelief, refusing to see His face
Turning away from Jesus' gift
The only way to find a lift
That takes you to heaven's pace
With salvation for the human race.

* * * * *

What Shall I Cry

—oⁿoⁿoⁿ—

And the glory of the Lord shall be revealed, and all flesh shall see it together: for the mouth of the Lord has spoken it. The voice said, Cry. And he said, What shall I cry? All flesh is grass, and all the goodliness thereof is the flower of the field. Isaiah 40:5-6.

Many years ago when sporting boats, worthy of our lakes for fishing, were made of cedar slats carefully constructed by the boat builders into a beautiful floating device that we called a prize to own. Many of them would be decked out with red paint for the top half with the bottom a shining varnish to show off the cedar craftsmanship This was years before the fibre glass, and other synthetic materials were usable.

I had moved to a city were my brother lived. The company he worked for required that he travel on the road during the week, but he always had the weekend off. In his travels he discovered a beat up old cedar boat for sale. It was such a good price he couldn't refuse it. He asked if he could store it in my back yard, of course I conceded to his request. When he delivered it into the back yard, I could see why he got it so cheap. It required a major amount of work. With so much traveling time he didn't have time to work on his boat to make it seaworthy, so I decided to surprise him and fix it up myself. I scrubbed, and I sanded, I varnished, and I shellacked, and painted, being very careful to produce a super special finish in order that my brother would have the prettiest cedar bottomed boat in the valley, and it was. Finally the day come when I applied the paint and varnish to let it dry, and if I do say so myself it looked like new. I was pleased with the outcome of all my labour. Then came the moment as I called him to come and visit. When he arrived I directed him to the now renewed finished product. Needless to say he was absolutely delighted and overwhelmed by my surprise when he saw the beauty of his newly acquired toy. He was excited, and could not wait to load it on the trailer to take it to a lake about an hour away. I followed him to the lake to witness the launching of his now exciting beautiful vessel. He backed the trailer to the edge of the lake, jumped out of the car to unwrap all the fetters that held the boat locked to the trailer. We both stood together with family and friends watching in joyful exuberance with big smiles on our faces as we watched the launch. It slid majestically from the trailer into the beautiful blue water of Clear Lake, as it should, bobbling, rocking back and forth as we moved it further into the lake away from the trailer, and lo, before our very eyes it sank directly to the bottom. You see with all my diligence to make the vessel look beautiful, I had forgotten the most important step. that was to calk all the strips before painting and it would not repel the water. In my meticulous effort I had overlooked a most important step of securing the area against seepage. I had forgotten that the sealing process needed to come before the beauty process.

What shall I cry?

Everyone broke out in laughter, and it turned out not to be serious enough to cause any damage. Although we could find the humour in this, and redid the boat before any lasting damage had been done, I often think about how the Christian life is built.

So often we attempt to build that which will produce a glossy shining shell that looks beautiful to the outside world, but when our works are put to the test, they will it sink to the bottom of the lake, and be unusable. Many lives can be destroyed by our selfish interest in how we appear to others as we allow those of our nurturing communities to fall apart from the Christian element, never to be put back together when we forget the most important factor of sealing their salvation by the regeneration of the soul. That was a discovery I shall never forget.

There is another discovery that has become real to me, and that is from the secular world. There are those who are without Christ, who love, trust, share, and care for others in a more binding, and loyal way than many who name the name of Christ while calling themselves Christian. For they have varnished themselves with a coating of looking good as they hide beneath the imaging lacquer of religious cloak to look good to their fellow man.

What then do we present to those who seek that peace that passes all understanding?

I have made another discovery, that is not all who name the name of Christ have that inner peace, and cannot experience that inner joy, while they present a good image to others, they are full of anger, and ungodliness within, and seldom tell their friends or family about the Christ who is able to save the soul with his new forgiving way that gives freely, salvation to the soul, to prepare us for our home in heaven with a living God

. What then shall I cry?

There are those who frequent the sanctuary to use it simply to seek out weaknesses of the active Christians to cry before Satan using their appetite to de-christianise the community to elevate their position or build their ego. The bible relates to them that it be better that a millstone be hung about their neck, and they be cast into the sea rather than to harm God's children.

Another discovery that I have made, is that God never promises that which he cannot deliver, and he always delivers in abundance.

Have you been too busy tearing down that which God has built, or have you been praising him as you ought?

Have you discovered the greatness of God's love?

What then should I cry? says the voice.

We must cry unto men the word of God, about the blessed eternity to which he draws us. God proclaimed the gospel to have us pass it on to others in order that they too might believe in the only begotten son of God as the way to salvation, and a new life for all mankind. A greater love hath no man, than that he lay down his life for a friend. Forgiveness such a troubled step for man. Yet if followed according to the instructions laid down in the scriptures, such a short step.

How very selfish we have become when we envy the gain of our fellowman. Somewhere along the way we chose to believe that we were God's deliberate choice as a measure above others. In the process we expect God to give us all things to add to our life. When it does not come we are resentful of the success of others while losing sight of our shortfall before God.

What shall I cry?

God wants us to rejoice over the success of others. We allow pettiness to split the body of believers. We need to cry out of despair for our own short-sightedness, and our failure to listen to God as to how it is. Christian, stop trying to please the human element, and hear God's cry to love those alongside of you. Yes, God has made you different in order to fulfill the application of furthering the gospel of Christ.

What must I cry?

Cry this, that the foot cannot clap. The hand cannot run the race. The nose cannot hear the word. And the ear cannot smell the sweet savour of his love, Know this then, that each individual item is essential to make the body completely whole. When one part of that body suffers, the whole body goes out of kilter, therefore let us be at peace with one another, to love one another, recognizing the need of each individual as needed to make the whole body operative in a functional manner that presents Christ to the unbeliever with a pure message.

You may be the eyes for seeing, or you may be the heart, unseen but a very vital portion of the body to make it function properly. Rejoice if you have been chosen to be the feet to deliver the message swiftly in the strongest fashion. Whatever part of the body you have been chosen to function as, remember that when you refuse to function in harmony you go against God's will, and the whole body becomes inefficient or crippled with limited functional ability. Hear the voice that cries, and identify your place within the body. Find out which part you are, learn of your proper function within the parameters of God's direction, and begin to reveal, disclose and uncover the thing that holds you back. Remove the obstacle in your way to serve God to the fullest. Your life will change to hear the cry of peace, and perfect love, destined for the journey onward to heaven to spend eternity with your saviour. The frailty of the human being is worthy of the watchful eye It is because we are frail we need to move as close to God as we can move. Fear of failure, although not a sin will sometimes direct us to spiritual laziness when it comes to carrying out the work that God has designated us to do.

Our youth rise up with false fears of adopting tradition refusing to follow the way that is set before them. They decide to change things without examining God's word. They turn thumbs down on what is passed on to them by their elders who have been appointed to the Holy of Holies. Few think on the invisible factor of the Christ that has gone before. Some view the tragic events of the world, and attempt to put the blame on God for it being that way. When they hear the cry they will know that man has stumbled by himself into the atrocities of life. It is only when they return to their place with God there begins to be a change with greater understanding.

Behold, the Lord god will come with strong hand, and his arm shall rule for him: behold, his reward is with him, and his work before him. He shall feed his flock like a shepherd: he shall gather the lambs with his arms, and carry them in his bosom, and shall gently lead those that are with young. Isa 40: 10-11.

A restful and full acceptance pictured here of God. He is all caring, coach and manager, and still the gentle nursemaid to each believer that is dedicated to the servanthood for Jesus. The people of God would have trouble denying his creativity if they would accept his gentle embrace. The mystery is why man continues to ignore the message of a living God who is lofty and mighty as the creator of the ends of the earth. He does not grow weary of man's alienation from him. He, all the more searches, for those who have a misunderstanding of who he is in order for us to tell them the story. Have you not known the everlasting God? Man in his inadequacies of understanding needs to reach out to allow God to embrace him into a newness of life that will allow you to know the cry that God makes to his creation. And when you hear God's voice telling you to cry, you can ask the question, And what shall I cry, and God will tell you to cry, repent, and be saved, for the kingdom of God is at hand.

* * * * *

They Went Up To Pray

—⟨⟨⟨⟩⟩⟩—

Two men went up into the temple to pray; the one was a Pharisee, and the other a publican. The Pharisee stood and prayed thus with himself, God, I thank thee, that I am not as other men are, extortioners, unjust, adulterer's, or even as this publican. I fast twice a week, I give tithes of all that I possess. And the publican standing afar off, would not lift up so much as his eyes unto heaven, but smote his breast saying, God be merciful to me a sinner. I tell you, this man went down to his house justified rather than the other: for everyone that exalteth himself shall be abased; and he that humbleth himself shall be exalted. Luke 18: 10-14.

As I sit in on gatherings of prayer, I sometimes feel as though those speaking to God are giving him their personal resume rather than petitioning him for the need of others. This particular parable was addressed to certain self satisfied souls that trusted in themselves, and hated others. When the self righteous review this scripture message it should cut them like a sword. However those who recognize their own incapability's as sinners before God, should find this as the golden key of acceptance. those that are aware of their unworthiness can know there is a way to enter into God's grace. There are three sharp contrasts in this parable, first there is a contrast between the men. Secondly there is a sharp and poignant contrast between their prayers. The most surprising contrast to most would be the tangible answer to their prayers.

We see two men of different calibre, the first one, was the habitual church goer who preformed well all the ecclesiastical mechanics of being a good member. He was for all intents and purposes a good neighbour, and a successful business man, as well as a conscientious church goer. The other fellow, was a poorly equipped labourer who knew his need of God's forgiveness. No works involved on his part. Only the knowledge that he was a sinner and needed to cry unto God for forgiveness.

The first man makes sure that everyone sees him as he sits in a conspicuous place to offer up his prayer. Somehow we resent him, but we must not conclude that there was no good in him. If he is not all good, then neither can he be all bad in spite of his glaring defects, we see in him some virtue. He is after all, a devoutly religious man, and has joined the church to give it some healthy support. so he outwardly casts his vote on the side of spiritual interpretation of living. He openly confirms his belief that man cannot live by bread alone, but by every word that proceeds out of the mouth of God. Also he is probably here proclaiming publicly his faith. With that we must realize that profession doesn't always guarantee performance. Church membership does not a sainthood make, but in acknowledging that we must be quite sure that in belonging he has carried out the disciplinary elements required of servanthood within the religious structure. In other words, he was not shy in carrying out his required duty. He again is decent and upright, and honest in business. He even dares to boast that he is not an extortioner. Another commendable virtues, that he is generous with his wealth. there is no doubt that he does not short-change the church in his giving. In so doing he walks safely within the perimeters of the church organization. He could probably teach us much about the grace of God and how it should minister to our stinginess. Because of his generosity, and his loyalty to the church, his general decency has much to say for himself.

Nevertheless the Publican's prayer was much more accepted. Let us take a look at him. The general gathering of worshippers didn't give him much credence. He wore clothing from a foreign power, and he was looked upon as a traitor to his nation as well as to God. He has allowed himself to become a pawn of the civil authority that ruled. All this he has done to satisfy his master passion of life for monetary gain. Upon the altar of greed, he has sacrificed all. Neither can he claim not to be an extortioner for in this very prayer time there were those present that he in all probability had stolen from. He was at the bottom of the social ladder, while the Pharisee was considered to be at the top.

Why then does Jesus differentiate between these two men so drastically?

Let us again consider the prayer of the Pharisee. He is a man with a good eye on himself, and a critical eye on all of his fellowman, with no eye to the Lord at all. He says he is comprehensively different, and extremely unique. After all, he has arrived at the pinnacle while his fellowman is floundering around the bottom. Nevertheless with all the superficial differences he is very much the same. He is flesh, and bone, with likes and dislikes, with victories and failures. He is to be compared with the difference between the dewdrop, and the ocean. The dewdrop is much smaller than the ocean, but they both are water.

We too are like our neighbours. we are quick to condemn for situations that we do not understand, and never take time to find out all the circumstances that surround the action that we so readily condemn. Robbie Burns said it well, If God would only gives us the gift to see ourselves as others see us. We are like the Pharisee, who believes that their way is the best, and only way. we get caught up in more than self esteem, we wallow in self love, and pretend that we are better than our neighbour ever thought of being. There are those that are racial Pharisees, while others are social Pharisees. Then there are the intellectual Pharisees who speak in contempt of the illiterate instead of helping to work out a plan to be a catalyst from their dilemma.

Planted in our contemporary day religious gatherings we quite often find the religious Pharisee who prides themselves in their own goodness with their adherence to church principles in following tradition, and producing all the good works that nations should approve of. Aside from that let us not forget about the pagan Pharisee who thanks God that while he makes no pretence at religion, he is so far ahead of those who belong to a church that there appears to be no reason why he should attend..

At any stage of the game we hate the Pharisee for his arrogant showmanship, but let me remind you of the challenge put forth by

Christ, he who is without sin, cast the first stone. It seems the greater we set ourselves up, the greater we condemn those who cannot see it our way.

Are we sure of a sense of divine presence? Are we right with God?

If your answer is yes to these questions, then why are you at the place of condemnation. For Christ points very clearly, that he has not come to condemn the world, but to seek and to save that which is lost. Are you seeking and saving the lost?

If you claim to walk as Christ walked, you had better be telling of the plan of salvation with the true forgiveness of sin.

How beautiful is the difference in the prayer of the publican. He had been driven to this place of prayer with a sense of need. He claims no superiority to his fellowman, and his only uniqueness is that his need is greater than any other. He does not look around for someone who is a greater sinner than he, nor does he flee from the words of the belligerent Pharisee. His goal was to seek God's forgiveness, not to find an element to which he could use as a hiding place He prays with his confession of being a sinner Here is a style that needs to be adopted by those who come to the altar in our modern churches. This man in prayer offers no excuse for being wrong, he just admits to God that he has indeed done wrong as he prays for forgiveness. What transpired in the lives of these two men whose prayers have just been offered up to God. For the Pharisee, absolutely nothing. It was not because God did not love him, it was because he refused to accept what God had to give him. "If any man thirst, let him come to me and I will give him to drink," said Jesus.

When a person is too full of self there is no room for Jesus. The Pharisee here goes to church, reads his bible, pays his tithes and offerings, but shuts God out by loathing his fellowship team of believers around about him. Somehow we can deliberate upon our own fellowship with others. Not how long we spend in the prayer room, or how many services we attend, and not even how many sermons we attempt to drink in, but it depends on what we do with what we have already been given. We need to take out of all our activities, a time to get to know Christ better. there is an urgent need to attempt the application of that which we have already learned about the cross of Calvary and the reason for the shed blood of Christ. Prayer can change you if you desire to tell the gospel message as God has laid it down in his word.

There is a need to make your presence to God a genuine factor of action for the saving of souls If your attitude remains on the same line as the Pharisee, you have no part in the gospel of Jesus Christ. He came, not to call the righteous, but sinners to repentance.

* * * * *

Christian Giving

—◈◈◈—

Bring ye all the tithes into the storehouse, that there may be meat in my house, and prove me now herewith, saith the Lord of hosts, if I will not open you the windows of heaven, and pour you out a blessing, that there shall not be room enough to receive it. Micah 3: 10.

The Christian is often faced with the question of how much they should give. We recognize that everything belongs to God, but how much should be given to his work?

As much as we can assume the time element, it was about four thousand years ago that Abraham gave tithes. Jacob, Abraham's grandson. made a vow one day recorded in Genesis chapter twenty-eight.

And Jacob vowed a vow, saying, If God will be with me, and will keep me in this way that I go, and will give me bread to eat, and raiment to put on, So that I come again to my father's house in peace; then shall the Lord be my God: And this stone, which I have set for a pillar, shall be God's house: and all that thou shalt give me I will surely give a tenth unto thee. Genesis 29: 20-22.

Here we see that Jacob made a vow to give a tenth to God, and we know that God held him to that promise. This presents to you that the idea of tithing was God's method as practiced but God's people many years ago with knowledge that God required them to adhere to the element of tithes and offerings, often strayed from what they had promised, and God had to bring them to task. God gave the whole law of practical living through his servant Moses. Tithing was incorporated into that law, and although this type of offering was the first there were also twelve other types of offerings. Hence the statement in Malachi that they had robbed God of both tithes, and offerings. Some displace this law by suggesting that it is old testament teaching, but you will remember also that Christ was firm in his assertion that he had not come to do away with the law, but to fulfill those laws. Therefore the new testament has truly kept them in place in order that we may know the direction that God requires us to walk. Let me include several passages of scripture that give credence to setting aside a portion for God. *Upon the first day of the week let every one of you lay by him in store as God has prospered him, that there be no gatherings when I come.* 1 Corinthians 16: 2. The scripture in Hebrews 7: 4-8 seems to be the most convincing proof that the principle of giving is carried into this dispensation in which we are now living. Now consider how great this man was, unto whom even the patriarch Abraham gave the tenth of his spoils. Hebrews 7: 4.

New Testament Christians should realize that it was God who lay down the principle for tithing. Let us consider why people should give proportionately unto the Lord. First of all, we find it to be a command, as the scripture puts forth the evidence for the need of obedience, because God can only use people who are willing to be obedient to him. We who have accepted Christ as our saviour know full well that we are not God's because of any work we produce, or still produce, we are simply his by the gift of his grace. It is a serious enough act if we would be required to face a judge for stealing from our neighbours, but think of the seriousness of robbing God. Consider tithes and offerings as our first debt to God, therefore we must render to him the firstfruits of our harvest.

A very special reason to increase our giving is not only because we love God, but consider how God loves us. Christians who fail to honour God in this way really do not love God. Yet we should be so moved by his love for us that the very gratitude of our hearts would move us to surrender tithes and offerings. God emptied heaven of it's greatest treasure for you, and me, as he gave his only begotten son to die so that we could have eternal life with our father in heaven.. Today I am on my way to heaven, I will be spared from hell.

Will you be there too?

Honour the Lord with thy substance and with the first fruits of thine increase. So shall thy barns be filled with plenty, and thy presses shall burst out with new wine. Proverbs 3: 9-10.

Some say, it takes all I have just for living, I cannot make it on my small income. The person who declares that is leaving God out of the picture altogether. You cannot leave his share until the last for he has said, you must give me the first fruits of your labour. We should be prompted to generosity, because you know in your heart if you are faithful in your giving, you cannot out give God.

Give and it shall be given unto you, good measure, pressed down, and shaken together, and running over, shall men give into your bosom, for with what measure ye mete withal it shall be measured to you again. Luke 6: 38.

There is an all encompassing message in these scriptures of giving. that is one must be honestly dedicated to the work of our living God. When we dedicate our all to Jesus Christ our saviour, we then will find it less difficult to adhere to the principle of giving in the material sense. Remember this, it is required of God whom we love, and serve to the fullest.

Are you in tune with my God?

If so your giving will not be painful, but your blessings will be a hundred fold.

* * * * *

What To Do With Another Gift

—⧽∞∞⧼—

Though I speak with the tongues of men and of angels, and have not charity, I am become as sounding brass, or a tinkling cymbal. And though I have the gift of prophecy preaching, and understand all mysteries, and all knowledge; and though I have all faith, so that I could remove mountains, and have not charity, I am nothing. 1 Corinthians 13: 1-2.

The word charity, has been transliterated by many that record the word they downgrade it to the word love, which does this portion of scripture irreparable damage. Although the original word declared a measure of love, contemporary worshipers have lost sight of the true meaning which was placed by the direction of God in these Corinthian scriptures. The reasoning behind the translation of the word to, charity, was rendered with the intent of measuring the absolute definition of love in its original context, and that meaning being the action of love to our fellowman without expecting anything in return, which is the type of love that God gave to his creation.

As a member of the body of Christ, because of our unquestionable desire to serve him in our love for others with the ever pressing message of salvation. We should desire to be a blessing to be used of God in giving the gospel to a lost world. This privilege of action is given to us when we accept Jesus Christ's gift of salvation that transforms the soul into Christ like action. It always is in the Christians best interest to act wisely in seeking the best for God. When we are born again into the family of God we do not automatically become some sort of super monster with alien abilities to perform scary tasks.

One must be sure not to abrogate the desire of God. For it is his intent to have us settle in as those who will fellowship with him. We are not to presume that he will open a Pandora's box of tricks for us to perform. First up we need to remember that we must seek wisdom in prayer. We are cautioned, they who desire wisdom let them ask, and it shall be given to them.

Every gift that is given is done so for the benefit of the whole Christian body, and is never a personal application for ones own benefit, with the exception of the gift of salvation. In the church gathering where there is fellowship of the believers there is no place for selfish fleshly display. If I am gifted to preach, I am in no way to take advantage of that gift for the soul purpose of displaying my ability. If a person is gifted to sing the beautiful hymns of the Christian community, they are not to use their voice in a manufactured theatrical sense to attract attention to their ability to do so. Neither are they to display the God given gift as a power of entertainment. The church sanctuary is not a place of entertainment, but a separate place, set aside for the worship of a holy and living God. Rather, the gift is to be used to give out a great message to move the human heart of the unbeliever to repentance, and turning their soul to Christ. If someone is gifted to teach the holy scriptures, they are not to exercise that gift to display their academic prowess to show others how great they are, but with that teaching gift, they are required to make things as plain, and as simple as possible. Remembering, those that they teach need instruction to allow them to grow in the knowledge of God. Also when the unbeliever gathers under that persons teaching they should be able to discover that Christ is the way, the truth, and the life. This criteria is the standard for using the gifts that God has been so gracious to endow you with. All gifts are to be used for the edification of others in that very special spirit of love. A love from the believer without expecting any return for the exercising of their God given love. Herein, that God has shown in giving to each of us how we ought to reach out to touch the unbelieving community around us.

The apostle points out that we should prophesy, meaning to teach religious matters, to preach by foretelling the outcome of serving Christ. We are challenged to reveal the results, according to scripture, of not serving the living God. To do this we need to read, and absorb the seventeen prophetic books of the old testament. When you complete that heavy task you will find that prophesying has very little to do with fortune telling of the future. For you will find that the prophetic books are taken up with endeavouring to bring home the truth of God to the hearts, and consciousness of the believers in God. there is in fact a difference between the prophet and the teacher. The teacher is to expound the scripture to illuminate the mind in understanding what God has to say about your total living habits. Whereas the prophet brings home the truth to the conscience that it might be exercised before God.

I may be able to take the writings of Paul to the Corinthians, through divine help, being able to expound it that hearers may thoroughly understand what that it is the spirit of God teaching. Yet their conscience may not be exercised in the least degree. In other words, their heart may not be lifted to God, even though they had been edified completely, and intellectually. However if I had the gift of prophecy I might take the same scripture, always helped by the spirit, to enable me to press home to the heart and conscience, so that those who hear will attempt to find a secret place to kneel down while they search themselves while asking God to enable them to live the truth they had been learning.

He that speaketh in an unknown tongue speaketh not unto men, but unto God: for no man understandeth him; howbeit in the spirit he speaketh mysteries. 1 Cor 14:2.

Paul, goes on to indicate that the gift of tongues causes confusion, and for all intents and purposes displays lack of intelligence. Again he says, *Wherefore tongues are for a sign, not to them that believe, but to them that believe not*: 1 Cor 14:22.

In the light of this it is a wonder that there is any approach to attempt to apply it to the believing Christian. I would much rather spend time in attempting to deliver the message of salvation for the receiving of souls for Jesus Christ, than to waste time with some element that is not applicable to the believer.

The man who is gifted by divine authority to give a message of God, is to deliver it to the people of God for edification, [i.e. moral and spiritual improvement]. The person who comes for learning should receive a word that will be good for their walk with the Lord.

The prophetic message is for exhortation, [i. e. to do what is proper or required]. Some have a tendency to wait until tomorrow to get things done. Exhortation must be a message to show the urgency of getting things done. One must impose within a message of exhortation, a need to press forward vigorously by earnestly persuading the drive of emergency of doing that which needs to be accomplished in championing the message of Jesus Christ.

The true ministry by direction of the holy spirit is to give comfort in the time of tribulation, but not allowing workers to remain in a comfort zone which emanates danger to the gospel. Also to generate encouragement when we appear to be slowing down because of lack of the vision towards the victory in Christ. Exhortation will give the substance within comforting encouragement to keep believers lifted up as they walk the walk to identify the talk.

We should only seek that spiritual gift that will make us quicker to profess Christ before men, and help us give the gospel to the saving of souls. Be careful when asking for a gift from God, for he will give you a gift that will edify the whole church, not just one individual who is only interested in acting out some self fulfilling fantasy.

* * * * *

Christ's Hometown Visit

—⟨⟩⟨⟩⟨⟩—

And he could do there no mighty work, save that he laid his hands upon a few sick folk, and he healed them. And he marveled because of their unbelief. And he went round about the village teaching. Mark 6: 5-6.

Christ's work was rejected by his neighbours and friends because they knew him as a carpenter's son. The unbelief of the community rendered him powerless. It is interesting to learn here that our belief in Jesus acts as a generator for his power. The more that believe the greater his power becomes. According to this record, this is Christ's second visit to his homeland. The first time there were a group that tried to throw him off a cliff, and he immediately departed. This second visit allows him to heal a few sick and go about the area teaching. His notoriety had grown, and been brought to the attention of the dwellers in this area., but his power was still stymied.

This was a new revelation for his disciples as they now witnessed the very thing that limited his exciting power. There is little doubt about Christ wanting his disciples to witness this account in order to strengthen them in their own ministry.

Let us compare the unbelief of the residents of Nazareth as to the unbelief that we witness today in the modern socialistic society in which we live to witness the de-christianisation of our communities.

There is testimony that they were quite familiar with Jesus, as they faced him at his homecoming. There was possibly the neighbour hood gossip of all the things that he was supposed to have done, Also they would interact with the stretched stories, as well as those things that were supposed to be. After all, wasn't this the carpenter's boy that they played with in their youth. There were the elders who would admit that they hadn't exactly followed his particular field of expertise, and had lost track of what he was actually doing. Although they had heard some strange things about him they had put it aside with no action one way or another to verify, or discard.

Now they had many bothersome questions. Like, since when does this man have these things?

Where did he get all this wisdom, and how come he is able to do these mighty things? After all they should be told for they had employed this same man as a carpenter to build, or repair their homes. They say he has unrealistic powers.

Why would he come home with so little notice?

Is he in trouble somewhere?

It was however, impossible to deny these powers for he is well known throughout the land, and there must be some truth to the stories we hear. But he looks so ordinary. There is no halo bouncing around his head. There are no supernatural flashing lights dancing in the sky. There is absolutely no outward indication that he is different now than when he lived amongst us. A little older perhaps, but to claim that much wisdom, I think we must be careful in sanctioning all his activities.

Had they believed Mary, and Joseph, when they told their story, how then could they react so negative?

Had they accepted that Jesus was in the fellowship of the living God, they would have opened his secret, but they were so busy trying to display their own knowledge, they as many today in their fact finding tours, shut God out. They were offended with him because they refused to understand the source his power. They also refused to submit to his wisdom, or to the appeal of his works, because they had it fixed in their small minds that they knew all about him, when they knew nothing of his relationship with God.

Although Jesus, may have been disappointed in their reaction he did say, *A prophet is not without honour in his own house, save in his own country, and among his own kin, and in his own house.* Mark 6: 4.

The reason for their unbelief was envy which is part, and parcel with jealousy. We understand those false emotions so well, because it's small town interaction where everyone is related to everyone else by some means. It is part and parcel of the vulgarity that persists through many centuries. It is a part of humanities contempt for itself with the inerrant ability to work by your side, and ever believe that you could amount to some stature that was recognizable by the rest of the world.

The wisdom they admitted, the power they acknowledged, but refuse to accept while they listened to the teaching. Their excuse, he is one of us.

Their criticism of Jesus was their very own condemnation as they withdrew saying this man who worked beside me cannot teach me. How unconsciously they uncovered to lay bare their own limitations. In Jerusalem they asked, Whence hath this man letters?

His appeal was to the underlying motive, and passion, with desire of the heart, however it might be, crippled, broken, or paralyzed he would deal with the person to deliver from that state. The men of Nazareth were wrong in their thinking. They were without desire, therefore their central motive in life was wrong, and they lacked the ability to discern spiritual things. Instead of wanting to do the will of God, they wanted to be involved in actions to please themselves, and were blinded by their own selfish ambitions. They belonged to the club of avid disbelief, or if I didn't think of it, it won't work, attitude.

He could do there no mighty work because God had been excluded from the central desire, and motive of life. They loved darkness rather than light, therefore they shut God out.

The final effect of their disbelief is that he left, and never again returned. The hardness of the inhabitants of the country where he once lived paralyzed his power.

Let us then turn away from this strange story of the country where Jesus lived, and relate to our modern day society of unbelief. We almost want to bypass that word modern because the word is almost passe'. The terminology we would rather implement today is "progress" As a matter of fact we pay homage to it while technology becomes our dead mechanical God.

The modern mind is trying in it's fitful anxiety to proportion and accommodate faiths declaration as well as the whole revelation of the bible. God's word, to the modern mind

What do I mean by the modern mind, and what is the modern mind?

Modern, simply means present time, and coming from that the very simple Latin word Modo, which means, just now. Let us then substitute the modern mind for the just now mind. However modern the mind may be, we need to carefully remember the continuity of some elements in men, and the human mind.

What does, the just now mind, know about Jesus?

There is first the fact of association with Jesus with persistent spiritual revolutions. Secondly, associations with Jesus through moral transitions. Finally the transition of association with Jesus through materiel benefit. We name the name of Jesus, and we think of it as a name found in the new testament, or we think of it as a name held in high reverence. Another thing that the unbelieving critics must deal with are all the facts related to Jesus.

Modern belief is seeking to reconstruct the cause of hope, of love, and understanding, but it takes Jesus Christ of the gospel and denies the implication that he brings transformation to the soul.. They want to deny the fact that because of Christ, churches were established, hospitals curing the sick, came into being under the Christian message brought by Jesus. Modern, belief is left to face the facts of Christ victorious without sufficient cause to deny his impact upon the world today. If Jesus is not the man that the gospel presents him to be, then woe unto man.

What is the effect of this modern belief?

He could do there no mighty work, no spiritual revolution, no transformation of the soul, and definitely no material betterment for our society.

The mighty works of Jesus Christ have moulded all history that men ask again, and again, Whence has this man these things?

Jesus says, "The very works that I do bear witness of me, that the Father hath sent me."

Where do you stand today?

Are you on the side of unbelief?

Do you only enjoy the practice of religion?

The time to believe is now. Jesus will not reject you because of your past error of misunderstanding, for he has already forgiven you for that, and now awaits you to come in faith believing that he is the Christ who will deliver you from eternal damnation into eternal love with his father God, in heaven.

In your belief he will perform mighty works for you by the transforming of your soul to be fit for the kingdom of heaven. Faith will allow the mighty work of our Lord Jesus Christ to begin within our own parameters. As we see the transformation of our lives take place we shall also know the consistency of the work of God who is able to deliver to them who ask and receive that which he offers.

As Jesus calls us to serve in faith, he will also give us the ministry to go and present his gospel to the unbelieving world and for the uplifting of the believers to encourage and edify.

* * * * *

How Are The Dead Raised Up

But some men will say, How are the dead raised up? and with what body do they come? 1 Cor 15:35.

The Apostle Paul here having settled the question of Christ's resurrection finds himself faced with another perplexing question, If there is going to be a resurrection of the dead in what kind of body will they rise?

With his answer comes a special divine revelation. Yet we are just as ignorant today as to what comes after death as the philosophers of five-hundred years before Christ were. Always men of high estate have been searching after that truth. Men like Plato, and Aristotle or Socrates did not solve that question for themselves nor anyone else. Had God not rendered unto us his word it would remain as mere speculation, *But God has spoken, All scripture is given by inspiration of God, and is profitable for doctrine, for reproof, for correction and for instruction in righteousness.* 2 Tim 3: 16.

In the eighth chapter of the book of Romans, Paul's comes to a close with his wonderful exposition of our three-fold salvation. Salvation from guilt and sin, salvation from the power of sin, and salvation from the presence of sin, as he looks to the time of the redemption of our bodies.

We know the soul is redeemed for those under Adam will die. But thank God, our bodies will be redeemed also, for the Lord Jesus will return to change our bodies unto righteousness to those who believe. This creates an unreal difficulty to the unbeliever's mind, but to us who are redeemed ,we know this as Christ's promise.

How can he change us?

He will change us in the twinkling of an eye, and we shall have new bodies.

Let us take a lesson from nature. Observe the ugly caterpillar as he winds himself into a cocoon and dies, and in some miraculous way he comes out a beautiful butterfly. Surely this creature was created to give us the picture of true resurrection ability of the body change. We as God's creation have become wrapped up in the ugly sin of the world seeking seclusion under the name of Jesus we will be resurrected with a beautiful new body. Jesus took upon him the sin of the world, and descended into hell to arise the third day, victorious over death. Also he passes that to us as we too shall have resurrection to be with him in heaven with new and indestructible bodies.

Paul uses the illustration of the farmer growing grain, and when it begins as a seed to break through the ground you cannot see the grain. First it is a tiny blade of green foliage as it draws food from the root it becomes a sturdy stalk with it's production increasing. then what is termed as the head of the stalk takes form, only then can you see the grain. Again another parable comes into play, what we sow we shall also reap. If we sow wheat we shall reap, wheat. If we sow barley we shall reap barley, and so on. You must indeed sow the seed of the grain you would like to yield.

Skeptical science tells the world that they change their body every three years. I am not sure of the accuracy of that, but this I do know that when the body does change, I am still the person I was before, still me. As we gain in the age factor the body takes on new lines, and the hair sometimes a new colour, and we change as we gain weight or lose it, but within that flesh you are still you and I am still me.

The scriptures under Paul's hand stresses the different kinds of flesh. here is the flesh of men that makes us comfortable here on earth, then there is the flesh of beasts although a much different structure in body they too are comfortable on the earth. Then there is another flesh of the fish of the sea, and another flesh of the fowl of the air, and he goes on to point out the celestial bodies, and terrestrial bodies of a heavenly flesh.

The risen Lord Jesus Christ took on a celestial body to ascend into heaven to be in the very presence of the living God.

When Jesus was talking with the Sadducees they presented what they thought to be a problem for him. They asked about a women who had been married seven times to seven different brothers and as each husband died before her, they wanted to know who would be her husband in heaven. Christ was quick to remind them that they knew little about heaven or they would have known that there was no such ritual to be produced in heaven for there is neither marriage no those to be given in marriage Christ said to them, "You do greatly err, not knowing the scripture."

All the change of time will come to an end and our bodies will be glorified like Jesus. In that day there may be differences in glory according to our devotedness. We all saved by the same grace, and that very same grace will allow us to be raised and changed at the coming of our Lord Jesus Christ. The rewards will likely vary because of that which we have already submitted to the Lord. Wholehearted surrender to God will bring the greatest joy, and greatest blessing that can come to anyone's life.

There is not one soul with Jesus that will be able to look back on this old earth with regret because God has washed away the whole burden of sin. It is not a question of whether or not we get to heaven, for all who are saved will be there. Only the rewards will show the difference of commitment.

I pray God your whole spirit, soul, and body be preserved and blameless unto the coming of the Lord 1 Thessalonians 5: 23.

Therefore we should be under control of the spirit instead of under control of the soul, that is moved by emotion and easily influenced. And so it is written, the first Adam was made a living soul, and the last Adam was a quickening spirit. An interesting note here, the word Adam means "red clay." As we bear the image of the earthy, so shall we in resurrection bear the image of the heavenly. We should observe the now difference, and strive to perfection of Christ.

The infinite variety of creation is marvelous, even amazing. When you know that there is so little to work with, two ears, one nose, two eyes, one mouth. Science tells us that there are two billion different specimens that they are able to account for. Yet we find only seven notes of music, that brings literally thousands of renditions that are listenable too, and a multitude that is unacceptable at any stage, all out of only seven notes.

In the resurrection body there will also be an infinite variety all in harmony one with the other, for we shall all be like him, Jesus, with incorruptible bodies, and everyone different. What a wonderful hope the scripture puts before the believers, but beware for sin can keep you out of the picture. What is sin? It is the rejection of Jesus by the rejection of those who bring his word with the message of salvation. Before you take a look at your fellowman, take a look at yourself to see how far away from Christ you have walked. Make thing right with your Lord now by correcting your relationship with your neighbour, or you will not be received into the kingdom of God. For to be in heaven with peace, love and joy, you must first generate that love on earth to be allowed into God's perfect harmony.

* * * * *

They Crucified Him

—◦◦◦—

And when they were come to the place, which is called Calvary, there they crucified him, and the malefactors, one on the right hand, and the other on the left. Luke 23: 33.

It is said that God is no respecter of persons, and it is ruled further that he is no respecter of places. There is one place, that will always remain dear to the heart of God, that being Calvary. This is the place of the skull. Here tragic lives of lawbreakers like thieves and murders along with other transgressors suffered under the penalty of the law. Many were here bludgeoned to their death. Here often was the shedding of blood and the meeting of death. Calvary, the place of the cross where innocent blood was shed for the sins of God's creation, man. I , personally have never been there as many of our traveling preachers have, along with their Christian counterparts. But oft times I imagine looking into the very compassionate eyes of Christ from that cross, and am more able to drink in the absorbing forgiveness of the wayward soul. I thank God for the gift of that hour, and that he died there for me. I do not try to understand the thoughtless unruly crowd of that day. I can however feel the milling around of their thoughtlessness, and picture in my minds eye how removed they were from the actual changing of history as God set out salvation for the world. I close my eyes as I perceive in my minds eye the three wooden crosses and in the centre the merciful Christ who suffered there to take away my sin. I feel those powerful eyes that say without words that you are wholly mine, love me as I love you, and in that show our love to my Father's creation.

Here dies the only perfect man who ever lived, with a record whiter than the driven snow. His question to his persecutioners, Which of you convicted me of sin? His lips spoke the greatest sermons ever preached, with the wisest lessons ever taught. Soldiers who took him from the garden said, never a man spake like this. And the judge said, I find no fault in him at all.

Now he is a mangled form upon the cross, bruised and battered his lips form a prayer, Father forgive them, they know not what they do. God was in Christ reconciling the world unto himself.

There is no other explanation for him who thirsted, yet quieted the troubled sea, who hungered, yet held the power to feed thousands. Only here he was being crucified by the religion of the day, believers in a holy God, but failed to recognize his son. It is a familiar picture of our modern churches of today, they fail to recognize the expertise of God.

The prophets title was not misleading when he said, his name shall be Emmanuel which means, God with us.

God in his finite form sleeping in the womb of Mary, God at the mercy of the wicked Herod, God, with blistered feet on the road to Nazareth, God, with calloused hands wielding the carpenter's tools, God, in agony at Gethsemane, God, with the bleeding back in the judgment hall, God, crushed beneath the heavy cross. He whose dying lips gasped, "It is finished." Was the incarnate God dying that men might live.

The miracles and teachings, and noble deeds of Jesus were only incidental to the main purpose of his advent here on earth, he came to die. John the Baptist knew this and introduced the statement of truth that needs to be adopted by every believer today, for he said, "He must increase and I must decrease."

When John introduced Christ, it would have been accepted if he had used the old testament terminology of the Prophet Isaiah, to say, here is the wonderful councilor. the mighty God, the everlasting father, the prince of peace, and he would not have spoken improperly. All these titles were in fact owned by the Christ to come as saviour. John knowing the situation had probably considered that phraseology, however his knowledge of Christ's presence was very intimate. His introduction had to include blood with anticipated heavy pain, because Jesus was born in the shadow of the cross. So

John's introduction was one that was very revealing, Behold the lamb of God which taketh away the sins of the world.

Jesus lived for the cross. One day staggering up to Golgotha, he felt his body pressed to the ground beneath that cross, and he knew that his supreme purpose was nearing fulfillment. It was a day of darkest gloom when the bleeding body of Jesus was lifted up to die on that cross. An elegant confirmation was made when Christ said, "For this hour I have come, to pour out my life for many,"

Those who deny the fact of sin must meet with God's irrevocable reply, "If we say we have no sin we deceive ourselves and the truth is not in us."

Let us set the stage more completely, there are two great morals that receive the spotlight in the scriptures, one is "sin," and the other is "Holiness." The word Holy, simply means separate. God can have no company with sin or the sinner. Holiness of God separates the sinner from his presence.

Behold, the Lord's hand is not shortened, that it cannot save; neither is his ear heavy, that it cannot hear: But your iniquities have separated between you and your God, and your sins have hid his face from you, that he will not hear. Is 59: 1-2.

Here is Isaiah's declaration of total separation from God, not because of God's desire but because of each persons own sin for which they refuse to seek forgiveness for. There are two direct opposites at work here, sinful man as opposed to the Holy God, and herein lies our need for atonement which is found only through Christ's sacrifice on the cross of Calvary. His death as a substitute in my place places the required demand on my life to accept him as my saviour. For God so loved even me that he allowed the sacrifice of his only son on the cross for my freedom from sin. In other words he paid the price for my trespasses.

The climaxing truth of all the scripture is that God is love, and God's hatred for sin, and ungodly acts, is only matched by his love for the sinner. He formed the infinite system of redemption, whereby those who have fallen by the wayside simply can believe that he is available through Christ, and he will reach down and touch their souls to redeem them from the depths of sin and bring them high into the heavenly places. Truly he opens the way to those who will seek him out. Some have tried to come into God's presence by other doors, but that is an impossible route and simply will not work. Salvation is in Christ, Jesus, not of ourselves. The old testament and the new testament met together at Calvary. The old testament says that it is the blood that makes atonement for the soul, and the new testament states emphatically, that without the shedding of blood there is no remission of sin.

Let God be true, and every man a liar. God has established it, the blood of his son cleanses us from all sin. Jesus prayed, Father let this cup pass from me, and in my imagination I can almost here the gentle words of God as he explains to his son that this is the only way and he asks him, "Are you ready." And Jesus in affirmation considers his plight with a vibrating summation to his father. Father I have never sinned, I have not tasted of the forbidden fruit, and I have kept my record clean and pure. I am one with eternity and thee, I stood upon the mountain top of infinity with you beside me. We looked down through the valley of space and declared let there be light. Creation is the work of my fingers, I carved out the valleys, I put the seas into place, I am holy as thou art holy, yet now I must drink this polluted cup of bitterness. Must I also take on all the sin of your creation?

And God replies softly, "Yes my son, it is the only way to give them eternal life."

Many years before this moment a prophet takes his pen in hand to write this just observation pertaining to the sacrifice of God. All we like sheep have gone astray, we have turned everyone to his own way, and the Lord has laid on him the iniquity of us all.

Beaten and bruised they make a crown for him, not of gold, but of thorns thrust into the flesh of his head. They stripped him naked and bound him to be scourged, meaning to flog severely, to punish, chastise, or afflict severe torment upon him. His last friend had fled and forsaken him.

Again the prophet Isaiah had foretold the incensed happenings of the crucifixion, as he wrote, He is despised and rejected of men; a man of sorrows, and acquainted with grief: and we hid as it were our faces from him; he was despised ,and we esteemed him not. But he was wounded for our transgressions, he was bruised for our iniquities: the chastisement of our peace was upon him; and with his stripes we are healed. All we like sheep have gone astray; we have turned every one to our own way; and the Lord has laid on him the iniquity of us all. He was oppressed, and he was afflicted, yet he opened not his mouth: he is brought as a lamb to the slaughter, and as a sheep before her Shearer's is dumb, so he opened not his mouth. Isaiah 53:3,5-7.

Human execution is not a pretty sight, and more often than should happen innocent men are obliterated from our society. But here is a man who was falsely accused by the religious order of the day to be put to death, thinking that it would be the end of the story. But praise be to God, because he had a plan in place to redeem mankind, the anti Christ element have not succeeded in obliterating his name from society, but have proven truly he is the Christ, the son of the living God who lay down his life for the redemption of God's creation.

Although the cross itself is not a thing of beauty, splintered with spikes in the hands of Jesus, and smeared with human blood the worst torment that could be imposed upon man. Yet Jesus implores us to take up our cross to follow him. A church with out the emphasis upon the cross is no church that belongs to Christ. Many churches of today tries to make the cross of a lesser necessity than what Christ intended for it to be. Your duty is to hold the cross of Christ before all generations to come. Do not fail Christ by relegating the cross into oblivion from the existence in the church where you worship,

I would make one observation of this picture at the cross where Jesus laid down his life for you. On that great day of atonement, when God's back was turned to blacken the sky, and the Messiah lifted his bleeding lacerated face to the heavens to cry out, "My God, my God, why hast thou forsaken me?" The sun beheld that sight though it was a darkened noon and the earth was drenched in the darkest of night, it was the greatest time in history for the unbelieving world.

How much he suffered, I cannot tell. But this I know, he drank the cup, and he walked the burning corridors of hell, he plucked the sting from death, and robbed the grave of victory. He led captivity captive, and climbed the stairways of the stars to mount his throne to take again his place in the eternal kingdom of God.

There behold him, the king of kings, adored of God, blessed by angels and worshipped by the saints of glory. Jesus, man's only saviour, and the keys of death and hell are in his hands. With the gift of eternal life held out to each one who would accept him as their personal saviour. Won't you accept him now.

* * * * *

The Prodigal Son

—◦∞◦—

A nd when he came to himself, he said, How many hired servants of my father's have enough bread to spare, and I perish with hunger!

Here is a confession that has torn the hearts of many throughout the centuries. The absolute terrorism cast into the household of faith when the child believes that their plight elsewhere would be far better than what they have at home. There is a nonsensical assumption that somehow the child knows best as to what will be suitable, and nothing can be further from the truth. In today's world of modernism the parent is made out to be the criminal when they disagree with the child. Yet the child's confession of sin is mechanical and lifeless. Too often they are sadly lacking in reality, and the sense of spiritual hunger has never been more evident than it is today We are confronted with it every day in the church, among the great and the small. Even the rich and the poor have been trapped by the nonsensical claim of the child who believes they know more than the parents. Everywhere there is the social thrust to solve the dilemma of the youth without, who refuses to recognize their need to make amends with those whom they have treated belligerently with an attempt to damage the soul. Refusing to ask forgiveness they quietly starve while eating the husks. consequently from major portions of the element of youth we hear this articulate dry, "I perish with hunger."

The story of the prodigal of course is only a parable told by Jesus while trying to convince people of their need to draw closer to God, but he has become the best known literary character in history, as the prodigal son. Every man in the truest sense is prodigal if he is making his way in the world, but living outside of life in the will with God. Never again from now till the end of time can the decision to follow Christ mean as much to you as it will mean right now. The urgency is evident for you to say, "I will rise and go to my Father."

How do you find the way to the Father?

Christ is the way. He says with compassion, come unto me and I shall give you rest.

Have you not wandered long enough, abdicating your responsibility to the father?

You say you are satisfied being the servant where you do not have to make any decisions, but God wants you for a child unto himself. Are you not tired of your subjection to an unbelieving world, and feeding only on the husks of life?

Then you must make that crucial decision now, and follow the saviour to assure yourself of life eternal in heaven with the living God.

* * * * *

The Eighth
Beatitude - Persecuted

Blessed are they which are persecuted for righteousness sake: for theirs is the kingdom of heaven. Blessed are ye, when men shall revile you, and persecute you, and shall say all manner of evil against you, for my sake. Rejoice and be exceeding glad: for great is your reward in heaven: for so persecuted they the prophets which were before you. Matthew 5:10-12.

In this last beatitude, Jesus speaks about the kind of reception that genuine working Christians are certain to encounter in their new lifestyle for Christ. In the practice of the previous beatitudes one would rather suspect that the meeting of the minds together would in fact be able to comprehend the style set up by Christ would be a welcome starting point for all to share. Sad to say the meeting of the Christian minds and the minds of the unbeliever will promote a gathering contrary to what it ought to be when we are following the laid down plan of Christ. However when it comes to the world accepting Christian principles it creates an immediate conflict because we live in godless world.

Christians have so dropped behind in the work of a living for God, that the world calls foul when we bring the moral issues to the forefront. They care not that the plan has substance, but if somehow they see it related to the living God it will be cast aside, and the Christian, will be berated for attempting to establish good Christian biblical principles within the structure of the unbelieving world. and we are to remember these words of Christ, blessed are ye - - -.

But, you say, the modern world is a generation of understanding. Not so when it relates to our almighty and supreme God, and conflict will be there if and when you work well for Christ. The Christian element has always produced opposition along side of persecution, and the fact that the Christian proposal provokes opposition, does not mean that this opposition is universal.

Everyone who names the name of Christ will win friends, and some of those Christians will generate loyalty and generous love of a few. Jesus was not in any way advocating that we work to be hated, nor should we generate that attitude amongst new believers. Even though the scriptures warn us to be careful when all men speak well of us, but I believe that venue was aimed at deceivers of the Christian faith who tried to put on a front to join the ranks with intent to destroy the element of Christianity that was perceived to be strong. I would suggest that we need to be concerned when all men speak evil of us.

Jesus not only spoke with these beatitudes, but he lived them to the point of perfection. He was meek, he was peaceful, he was tender of heart, and gave himself in full with the purest type of love for each individual.

While Jesus gathered unto him those who loved him deeply for his way with them, there were also present those who hated Jesus enough to seek to take his life. They manufactured derogatory names for him because of their lack of understanding of him. That inward blackness was sin that dwelt in their hearts as they continued to plot his downfall as they tagged him with demeaning names. They called him, gluttoness, and a winebibber, they claimed he was blasphemous, while they tried to make out he was of unstable mind. People still clamoured to meet this saviour, even under all the competition that set out to destroy to his goodness. They dared to suggest that he was in league with the devil. Finally they crowned him with a crown of thorns. Not for any evil he had done, but for all the good that he had bestowed even upon his enemies.

I often remark to my colleagues with the lament that the church is becoming more like the world today, but there is one redeeming factor in that thought, and that is that the world is becoming more like the church.

The Christian provokes opposition because they are different from the in believing world. The bible says, "a peculiar people." Being different arouses suspicion, as well as opposition. Society consistently seeks to rob us of our individuality, because if the individual Christian is successful the secular world cannot understand it, and furthermore abhors dealing with it.

If ye were of the world, the world would love his own; but I have chosen you out of the world, therefore the world hateth you. John 15:19.

The world promotes the slogan, "dare to be different" but when that means being someone who lives for Christ, they withdraw saying under their breath, "I didn't mean that." To de-christianise our community the world has to promote lies accompanied with the rebuke of the believing Christian. The Christian arouses opposition because when they are in tune with God, there life is a constant rebuke to the selfishness, and sin of the godless world.

Living these beatitudes in the power of Christ, you become the incarnate conscience that rebukes the sinner as they see their souls in condemnation by your pure actions.

Finally, the true Christ like person stirs opposition to the world's abstract prominence in the self righteous attitude, to everything is right, and there is no wrong. The Christian knows by their own experience that everything is wrong, and only Christ can make it right with our confession of sin. We are redeemed, and the world still struggles in hate, and disbelief.

The world said about Jesus, he meddles in our affairs, he rebukes our prejudices, he reminds us that God is our father, and accepts men of all races, colour, and creed, to live under the acceptance of our saviour Jesus Christ.

The genuine Christian interferes with some of our pleasures, and sometimes interferes in our business practices. Now the nature of interference, and opposition is somewhat different today from what it was in the days of Jesus, Persecution then had the stimulation of physical violence. Christians were thrown into prison, burned at the stake, and fed to the wild beasts, as well as being sent to their death by being hung upon crosses. Although the law disallows such inhumane treatment today, the world puts the Christian in the corner with their psychological wickedness, still trying to prove that serving Christ is an unacceptable practice.

Many Christians face persecution today. To examine that truth ask anyone who works in the social services of the country. They are not allowed to use their testimony of Christ to point the way of life. If they do they would face dismissal as unfit for that type of employment. Ask the Christian police officer, and when he is out of earshot of his superiors he will tell you that he is not allowed to tell his prisoners about the Christ he serves. Christians appearing in courts are frowned upon for wearing a cross, as a lapel pin, or carrying any artifacts that may depict their Christian stand in the courtroom. Yes Christianity is still under attack even in the countries we like to think of as democratic. Christians do not have the democratic right to pray in our schoolrooms. We have lost the right to teach our children as we wish to have them taught.

Who are these people protecting?

The liars, the godless, the apostles of debt, the money mongers. Yet, those who are elected stand to tell the world that they are doing the best they can, when in fact they will not make a move to give the Christian the right to have our children pray.

When they are confronted they try to avoid dealing with the issue head on by making excuses that they have been saddled with so many other things that they have no time for that. Nevertheless they have time to go to war, but not time for to allow our children to pray. They have time for those who practice the lust of the flesh, whom we know as homosexual. Same sex marriage is definitely not right in the eyes of God, yet our leaders have a tendency to promote it. And again, they stop our children from praying in public schools which is paid for by our taxes. Rise up my Christian friends, and let them hear loud and clear our protest as they attempt time and again to de-christianize our country by throwing out all the elements that we have worked so hard to put in place.

There are at least two modes of persecution from yesteryears that are still with us today, blessed are you when men shall persecute you and revile you. Secondly we can still revile, and reproach, and we can still be narrow and fanatical. We can still shrug our shoulders, and laugh at them as cranks, and there is still the weapon of slander that is initiated by even the modern churches of today.

When you are having that initial time of persecution, God will not feel sorry for you, nor will he take pity on you, rather he will extend his hand, and say let me congratulate you. Rejoice, says God, for they so persecuted the prophets before you.

The challenge then is to be so noticeably Christian, that it embarrasses the non Christian. For if they can only dish out persecution, rejoice, for God loved you while you where yet in sin, and he suffered making the supreme sacrifice, his only son, Jesus, on the cross for you.

Enter thou into the joy of the Lord.

* * * * *

Diversion From Christianity

And I will appoint over them four kinds, saith the Lord: the sword to slay, and the dogs to tear, and the fouls of the heavens, and the beasts of the earth, to devour and destroy. And I will cause them to be removed into all kingdoms of the earth, because of Manasseh the son of Hezekiah king of Judah, for that which he did in Jerusalem.
Jeremiah 15:3-4.

Here God's word fixes responsibility for damage inflicted by Manasseh who rejected God in early life, but came to serve at a late time after afflicting a nation with his atrocious besiege upon followers of the living God. This indeed is a startling verdict for Manasseh in his later years was a good man who finally served God. Nevertheless the full influence of his life was not a blessing, but a curse.

I believe that the total of our world of Christian youth communities should become totally aware of the particular outcome administered by God. It holds up in boldness the need to come to God through Jesus Christ, early in our life by putting away false conceptions of sin. This particular event should press home the urgency of the truth of the need of salvation.

There also is revealed here the danger of disaster when allowing a novice to lead others who are already committed to the kingdom. Service to his Lord was short lived and seldom practiced as he began to wallow in every imaginable type of contribution to sin. He readily entertained with generous hospitality, every false belief that was practiced within his boundaries. It is recorded that there was very few ungodly practices that he was not guilty of participating in.

Manasseh was raised by a generous God fearing father. He was without excuse for the irresponsible actions of his lifestyle. He turned his back on God, but God desired his return to his service, thus never gave up on him. Actually God sent him messenger after messenger with the attempt to make his guilt vivid and realistic to his thinking. God tried to invite him back to pardon and peace of his father's presence. However the more he was directed away from such a wayward life, the deeper he plunged into sin. In his youthful years he had turned a deaf ear to the way of the living God, but God persevered to deliver him back to the right track.

You who have wandered away from God to fall back into sin probably are as guilty as Manasseh as God attempts to call you back to the fold only to be treated as though you are deaf to the warnings and the rebuke. He has called you through your conscience, and through your wretchedness. He has spoken to your heart through your restlessness, and your hunger of loneliness for companionship that would be uplifting. He has called you through sorrow and pain as you long to find the success of usefulness. His call to your soul lingers in the shadow of your rejection of all that is good, and you refuse to turn around to accept the mercies of the living God. Your need is not for more light, but for a stronger courage to enable you to live up to the light which you already possess.

Your life may not carry the influence as many leading personalities of the day, but however obscure your life may be know this to be an absolute truth, that whatever influence you may initiate from your Godless stance that it will set in motion actions that will literally outlast the world. You may have control over your own actions before it is visible, but once you put it into motion there is no way that you will be able to control it. Suffering because of our sin does not always come immediately, but it will come as did for the king many years after he had returned to God.

There are those who believe that because they have not been punished immediately, God has put it on the back burner and forgotten about it, nevertheless there will be ramifications return from your misleading deeds of sin. The sooner one realizes that by confessing those trespasses to God the easier the road will be in your lifestyle. God is faithful and just to forgive us for all our sins.

Jesus paid the price.

When we permit one travesty after another we begin to harden our hearts, and too often we end up blaming God for where we are at. It is only when our thinking sends us to a private spot in seclusion of sincere prayer that we are able to reconcile with God.

Then we can face the real issue of repentance which will restore our salvation. There is however one thing that repentance cannot do, and that is to save us from the consequences of that which we have sown. You can go into the field of life and grow tares if you dare, even then God will forgive you. Nevertheless, there is one thing that God will not do, and that is to change the tares that you have sown. That which you have sown will remain until harvest time when the tares shall be burned.

How about your influence, is it good, or is it bad? Or is it Christ like?

Only you can answer that now, but someday you will have to account for the tares you have sown, not to man, but to god. However if you wish to have a favourable hearing for your influence from hereon in, God is willing, and just to forgive you for your wandering. He pleads with you to come back to him now. Make your stand to be a good influence for the living God through your saviour Jesus Christ.

* * * * *

Areas Of Consideration

—⦿—

For when you were servants of sin, you were free from righteous-
ness. What fruit had you then in those things of which you are now
ashamed? for the end of those things is death. But now being made
free from sin, and become servants of God, you have your fruit unto
holiness, and the end everlasting life. For the wages of sin is death;
but the gift of God is eternal life through Jesus Christ our Lord.
Romans 6:20-23.

Here we find that change of position of service brings a greater change of satisfaction into our walk with Christ. The time is now for that decision to take up your position in the path that follows the evangelism of the son of God. In grasping the element of the now time to follow, we must apply to our sensitivity of the shortness of time that ensues our privilege to serve. The scriptures are very definite in this area as God points out in his word that you cannot know what will take place tomorrow. The question is asked, What is your life? It is even as a vapour, that appeareth for a little time, and then vanisheth away. To him that knoweth to do good, and doeth it not, to him it is sin. James 4:14, 17.

We must therefore make haste to transfer our allegiance from the ruthless unbelieving world, to the living God, in order to bring the secular world to the saving knowledge through the gospel of Jesus Christ. Some of us are busy at making plans for our own space in life, but God has said, Thou fool, tonight thy soul shall be required of thee. So we must indeed consider the shortness of life, and putting God first we may accomplish a great deal, but he only requires our honest acceptance of his word through his son. In our short life span we need to pay absolute attention to the direction that we have chosen. If we have made the right choice we will spend eternity with the living God, and know that eternity is long.

The bible tells us that the span of life is three score and ten years long, which, in man terms, is seventy years after which, we are told, is borrowed time. When a person is fifty years old they have lived over half their lifespan in half a century. With salvation which assures us of eternal life we can look at fifty years and be assured that we have another fifty to go. After that a hundred we look at another hundred to go, then two hundred another two, and so on, and so on. Life never ending.

The bible tells us about the heavenly place for the believer, and it also informs us about hell with all it's eternal torment for the unbeliever. Those who have rejected God's plan of salvation by turning their backs on his only son, Jesus Christ. Eternity there will be the same length of time, and there is no escape. The people who live for Christ will find perfect peace where there is no more heartache, or tears, no pain nor sorrow. It all seems to good to be true, but God has promised us to spend eternity with him to enjoy all the amenities that he has planned for us never to fade away.

For the believer it is difficult to imagine those people who have heard the word being unable to dedicate themselves to such a worthy expectation in eternity. Although we are told that Satan is the father of lies and he blinds man's eyes to the truth. They in their unbelief would rather have darkness than light for their deeds are evil. The bible also tells us that we are born in sin and conceived in iniquity. Ps 51:5. For all have sinned and fallen short of the glory of God. Romans 3:23. All we like sheep have gone astray, and we have each turned to our own way. Isaiah 53:6.

Sin is the transgression of the law. God's law. It is rebellion against the living god. Damning sin that sends us to the lake of fire and brimstone is the sin of unbelief. The soul that sinneth shall surely die, and this is the second death that sends us into a Christless eternity of eternal torment.

If you were riding a galloping horse across the field and realized that you were heading to a precipice that would take your life you would take extreme measures to guide the beast away to safety for both of you. If you saw a friend heading down a road with the bridge out you would take time to flag them down to warn them of the danger. So it is that the believing Christian must warn others of the disaster that awaits them if they refuse to stop and accept Jesus as their saviour. The true preacher of the gospel will not lose the word of hell out of their vocabulary as they sound out the warning.

Then shall he say also to them on the left hand, depart from me , ye cursed into everlasting fire, prepared for the devil and his angels: Matthew 26:41.

Here we see that hell is a place of separation where the fire is not quenched, and the suffering never ends. Also read the story of the rich man and Lazarus as the rich man cries out, "I am tortured in this flame." But, you say, this is only figurative language and cannot be taken literally. Let me assure you that the real thing is always worse than the picture.

I once took pictures of a devastating fire as a sawmill burned to the ground. It was literally burned to the ground before my eyes to the point that every inch of it had to be reconstructed. I could not capture the real devastation in the pictures I snapped on film, nor could I capture the pain of the men who where burned in that fire. that did not make the scene less devastating or less costly to the owner who had to replace the total building and machinery. Nevertheless it was quite a real happening.

With the picture that Christ painted with his words gives such a vivid portrait in a literal sense to show the unbelievers how real it will be when we arrive at an eternal destination without Christ. No picture that Christ drew here can bring us to the reality of the torment will be as we suffer the separation from the living God. Think about this, if Christ can give us this picture that depicts such a vivid portrait that attempts to make us see what it would be like from his word, then just try to imagine what the real thing would be. Truly a place to be avoided at all costs.

But the fearful and the unbelieving, and the abominable, and murderers, and whoremongers, [lesbians & homosexuals] and sorcerers, and idolaters, and all liars, shall have their part in the lake that burneth with fire and brimstone, which is the second death. Revelation 21:8.

Would you like to spend an eternity with any one of these types of people? Then why are you doing it with your short life here on earth?

You have unlimited access to heaven's gate to be at peace in eternity with your saviour Jesus Christ. So why would you stay the course on the road to hell rather than accept Jesus and be redeemed. Jesus said, "I am the way, the truth, and the life, no man cometh unto the father except by me. John 14:6.

God rises above the judgment of men. He will elevate you while others will be ready to suppress you. Look at God through the eyes of Christ, not the eyes of man. Here are five simple truths that can make a difference in your life.

1. Life is short.
2. Eternity is long.
3. Sin is black.
4. Hell is certain.
5. Heaven can be yours.

Abide by them, believe in them, and they will keep you in the safety of the arms of Jesus, and the ever growing grace of the living God that is not willing that any should perish, but that all should have eternal life.

* * * * *

In The Beginning - the Gospel

The beginning of the gospel of Jesus Christ, the son of God; As it is written to the prophets, Behold I send my messenger before thy face, which shall prepare thy way for thee. The voice of one crying in the wilderness, Prepare ye the way of the Lord, make his paths straight. Mark 1:1-3.

The book of Mark, in all likelihood was written the earliest of any of the recorded gospels, and gives only the brief accounts of that which transpired during this period. The difference between Mark and Matthew is primarily the brief way in which the writer depicts the circumstances. The writer here starts with a peculiar statement, because the known Christian community accepts the fact that the gospel begins with God's creation recorded in Genesis. therefore we need to assume that the writer simply dramatizes the fact of John the Baptist's presentation when he directed his followers to Jesus as one who came after him whom he was not worthy to unlace his shoes. Neither does the writer here refer to simply a book of the gospel, but indeed refers to the thrust of the prolific Christian proclamation of the salvation of Jesus Christ as the son of God.

The word gospel simply implies to evangelize which is derived from a Greek word that first meant a reward given to the bearer of good news, until finally it was used of the good news in and of itself. When we think of it today it is primarily used in the New Testament sense. The gospel in itself is a message of salvation, a message of comfort, hope, joy, that should always thrill to the depths of the innermost soul. It is a message that has nothing to do with condemnation and when accepted the message itself will denounce sin.

The gospel is good news to sinning people for it is the way to be delivered from a weight burdened life of darkness into a free eternal light of forgiveness. Thus generating in each person a new beginning as they accept the transformation of the new life. In that we are at once caught up in the central gospel of Jesus Christ himself. The charm of the gospel is that we will be following Jesus, We will in the very real sense, walk with him, watching every gesture as we capture the method to relate to our fellowman. Christ administers the salvation proclamation as God the father witnesses with him to verify his claim to be the son, the Messiah sent by the living God.

The beginning of the gospel statement becomes redundant until a person accepts Christ the son of the living God as their saviour believing that through him they have eternal life because of the forgiveness of their sin by that same Christ. Only then can there be a beginning of the gospel as each begins to proclaim it and personally identify with the new transformation that takes place in their lives. In your personal beginning of the gospel you will adopt in a very real sense the need to prepare the for Christ in the lives of those who surround you. I like to think of it as paving the way for others. When I was involved in Municipal politics there was a protocol to follow in order to have streets paved or to contribute to the building of highways across the country. Always there needed to be a set of guidelines set down to properly build that street or highway in that the conveyance of vehicles would be a transition to easier traffic flow to handle a greater number of vehicles in the areas considered in the project. So it is when Christ is the beginning of your new life. You need to follow the instructions as laid down in God's word, the bible, to make sure that the way you construct with your life will allow others to follow you while making a smooth transition into the life of Christ. One must take added care to read the blueprints correctly. Too often we find fragmented lives because they choose to fragment the scripture rather than to follow the blueprint to the letter.

When municipalities build roads they do not attempt to put a lesser quantity of material into the laid down plan for the mixture. They not only follow the plan to the exact formulae, but they also seek ways to add to the strength of the project to enhance the products they use for building. If the believer would adopt that simple criteria there would be evidence of the winning of souls that would be unprecedented, and the gap in the message would stop those who would purposely de-christianize our society.

We find in the book of Mark, Jesus, the servant of God creating the gospel, the good news of salvation. He came with a soul full of perfect love, holding the most sacred virtues, inspired by his father God, to build a future for people here on the earth to prepare for eternity with him in heaven. Jesus bent over the corpse of a dead world to whisper a word of hope, and faith. He breathed into that dead corpse of the world, new life. The dead arose as the world again began to hear the words of their living God to rise up as a Christian community with a new beginning of a true presentation which must be applied first to self that others may live. The soul of that new beginning must become saturated in the image of God to spread the good news of a saviour who came with a plan of redemption for all mankind.

The voice of one crying in the wilderness, prepare ye the way of the Lord, make his paths straight. Mark 1: 3.

There is in our modern day a wilderness of unbelief along with those who claim godliness without living up to it. Here we see how important it is that we follow the implied structural formulae of Christ to make sure that we present to that wilderness a straight path of righteousness with interwoven purity which will pave a solid road to a living God. First we need to have a receptive mind to prepare a positive asphalt in building the way. We find in Isaiah and Malachi how god deals with those that fall away. However we have the new ingredient to improve the road in which we lay before the fallen and unbelievers. That ingredient is the salvation that Christ has paid for upon the cross of Calvary. This love of God is the indispensable ingredient that assures that our, building of the way, project will not crumble into useless brokenness.

Truly, the beginning of the gospel to any community begins with you playing an active part. Those around you are seeking, and they look to you for the correct answer in following a living God. There is a real spiritual hunger, and God has called you to fill the need of seekers. Use your manual for life, the bible, and you will be able to lead them into eternity with Christ.

Accept it, follow it, apply it to your personal life that others might see Christ in you. While observing the righteousness within your life they too might pursue the kingdom of God. You have a great responsibility to those around you to know this Jesus so well that they will accept him because of your life.

* * * * *

That I May Know Him

Yea doubtless I count all things but loss for the excellency of knowledge of Christ Jesus my Lord: For whom I have suffered the loss of all things, and do count them but dung, that I may win Christ, and be found in him, not having mine own righteousness, which is of the law, but that which is through the faith of Christ, the righteousness which is of God by faith: That I may know him, and the power of his resurrection, and the fellowship of his sufferings, being made conformable unto death; Philippians 3:8-10

Here is Paul's testimony with an attempt to relate his special closeness while expounding the gospel of his saviour. In doing so he immediately cultivates fertile ground for each believer to find room to stand with him because of happenings of unforeseen events in ones life that lie beyond the suffering, and tragedy of human existence. One cannot have these events fully revealed, except in those that truly suffered the loss of all things. We envy those who attain a comfortable life in this world, but we keep our final admiration for those suffering, and contemporary morally crucified lives. For therein lies a manifestation of the stalwart soul who finds the ability to withstand all that has found its way into their lives, and they have been able to more deeply relate to the God of all things to portray a stand, that living for Jesus, is allowing your life to become invincible which is unable to transcend the element of understanding in an easy life.

The realm of experience is hardly glimpsed by the contemporary conventional Christians, who live in the tame areas of respectability. We need to care, we need to have pity for lost souls, we need to have empathy for saved souls, to the point that we realize the, loving, forgiving, saving, came from God, through Jesus Christ, who came down from heaven for the redemption of the lost soul by generating the plan of salvation for the lost through others who already believe. When you claim that stand for Christ with the thought put to action where any factor that could dismay you will not disturb your stand for Christ. No matter what comes against you or interferes in your lifestyle, you will only find it right and proper to continue with your firm stand for Christ as directed by Gods word through the scriptures.

Philippians 3: Paul's assertion is made to emphasize a contrast. Firstly, it is my belief that one must get a firm grip on the nature of Paul's stand that we only obtain righteousness by trying. Again we must acknowledge there is a righteousness we catch through contact of life, with life, as the grace of God is mediated. Often from the outside these two look exactly alike, but their motivations are utterly different, and the truth about life always raises the ire of those who do not wish to hear the truth, and they are many.

The self-made righteousness is produced by adding one virtue to another, and by restraining selfishness, lust, moral decay, and other vices. We might even list the virtues we seek to attain, and the evils we seek to avoid. The righteousness that is caught, or given, comes from seeing the best foot put forward within the close community within your walk with the Lord.

The revelation of God in Christ, was first of all an action. Only words could describe the action, but they could not convey its power. We do not own it, but it blesses us while leaving our wills free. Although Christ made the statement that if he makes us free we shall be free indeed, this does not by any figment of the imagination, allow us to do our own will, for Christ emphasizes only that we are free from sin.

Good things do happen to good people, however we must simply adhere to the knowledge that, what is God given, cannot lead to self-glorification. In ^pointing that out I would caution you that this is not a reason to put yourself down, but on the other hand you must make what you have been given, to be a very satisfying positive element for your lifestyle. Christ was not a defeatist. I know this because in his word he teaches about being uplifted, and about how we need to uplift one another. You cannot be uplifting to someone when you are down on yourself

We often forget one root cause of our contrasting estimates of human nature is the unevenness of human experience. Sometimes children are very, very, good, and sometimes they are terrible rascals, and switch between the angelic, to the devilish, is all in a day's work. Some days we are easy to live with, and again we will crucify the thing we love. We go to bed like a Lamb we wake up like a lion. We like to think of our own person as when we are on our best behaviour, but we are still our own self when we are on our worst behaviour. Our self-loving ego seems to invent it's owned standard of goodness, by which we condemn all others to inferiority.

There is a free enterprise kind of righteousness that denounces the Christian planning as a tyranny against all non Christians, yet does not acknowledge the tyranny of their own social planning by holding governments up as the culprit; thus we find ourselves regimented by a totalitarian police state kind of righteousness, that would dominate the world in the place of God;

And in between is the do nothing kind of righteousness, of ordinary citizens who see what is wrong with all parties, and just look out for number one.

What is good about acquired righteousness?

1. It can stand guard against easy Salvation
2. No neat line drawn
3. We realize the limits of trying our own way.

Christ's revelation remains the final correction of all human efforts because it constantly reminds us that men knowing to do right, do that which is wrong, and man's ability to save himself soon turns into evil, which brings human life to the brink of destruction.

I have heard it repeated at times the most common source of wrong thinking is self defence while according to the courts guilt or innocence is not a relevant factor, because it is only which lawyer presents the best argument.

We try to justify a partial view as though it was God's full view, and close our eyes to new truth that might disturb us. The chief source of evil stems from the Father of lies, Satan, with his attempt to make some relative opinion, or interest, an absolute, putting it in first place, as he attempts to have the thinker put God into the last place instead of where he belongs out front in first place in any part of our lives.

When anything human is exalted to divine level, it becomes a devilish source of confusion, and terror. The one hope of source in the Christian belief, is the continuous fearlessness of the believer to present it in every possible manner given to them, in the continuous building, and creation of a lifestyle that is fit for the servanthood to Jesus Christ.

Once we realize that we cannot make anything human as absolutely right, we are in a position to see that our creator is forever ready to take us as we are, and provided that we are willing to do some new thing with our life, he will accept us, and embrace us, and direct us, into the life that we need to live to worship a living God.

Philippians 3:10; That I may know him, and the power of His resurrection, and the fellowship of his suffering, being made conformable unto his death;

Sharing a love even unto death is a special way Paul shows it as a lifetime decision. A scientific specialist may know about chemistry, businessman knows about the marketing and sales production, but what they both know about their family, and friends, equals two kinds of knowledge.

Resurrection is just a continuation of all that mystery that runs through life.

We are always aware of self, which has no power to transform itself into what God designed it to be. God's transforming power by our simple belief in Christ, as Saviour, makes it well with my soul. Open my eyes that I may see the simplicity of the righteousness of the living God who will make me to walk in a special positive way that I may with my life direct others to him.

* * * * *

Church Will Fail When Humans Run it Their Way

—=/o/o/o=—

Filled with pompous ceremonies, affected by the Architect's dictatorial imposition of an ominous sprawling edifice without a steeple. A church without a steeple is like a train without a caboose. It simply depicts the changing times. The temple is a lost artifact to the contemporary Christian community.

The "Church" by definition is the Bride of Christ further defined as the Body of Christ of which Christ is the head. Colossians 1;18, it is a people gathered together to worship the living God, with Christ being the head.

Throughout the transcending years people have dissimilated the worship, the music, the Godliness, to the point that some believe that it is just another functional social order.

Pastors are no longer leaders in their communities, and followers are no longer attempt to be a lasting influence upon the world with the revelation of the gospel as presented by our saviour Jesus Christ. Instead they get caught up with the inward possessive political structure to maintain a public image of what a great church they are, that they became when they built when they built this new edifice of worship.

I wonder what happened to the newness of the life that Christ gave to them? Where did the church leave behind the love of Christ to such an extent that Governments had to form the social services to care for those the church rejected.

In Ephesians 5:27, we read, That he might present it to himself a glorious church, not having spot, or wrinkle, or any such thing:

but that it should be holy and without blemish.

We find that this part of God's word is being ignored as the contemporary Temple becomes a place of entertainment rather than a place of worship that allows us to give God the full credit of the created creature. Songs are sung in repetition without ever mentioning the name of Christ let alone the acknowledging God as almighty. Again we find in God's word, the bible,

2 Timothy 2:19a, And let everyone that nameth the name of Christ depart from iniquity .

Nevertheless the churches of the day seem to embrace that which God abhors as OK, rather than to depart from that which they know to be sin in God's eyes.

Churches embracing the new world's "Look at me" social structure while they shut out those whom God commanded us to seek out and to hold up above that which we are in order to save the wayward soul. Is it any wonder that they fail to produce a loving community to reach out and touch the lost souls around them. The things which they do not like they call worldly and that which they embrace they call Christian, and their actions toward others outside their organization become anything but Christian. They carry on a counterfeit Christianity as they trample their wounded to death.

One becomes a member of the invisible church when he, or she, accepts Christ into their lives as their personal Saviour.

The visible church consists of those who attend and subordinates themselves to the ritualistic membership of those who builded the frightening edifice built for worship. Some are believers, and some are not.

Here Christ's parable of the Wheat and the Tares becomes abundantly clear to the follower as God addresses it in Hebrews 10:25, telling us to not forsake the assembling of ourselves together; but exhorting one another [lift each other up by positive means] We must put on the brakes when we are considering those whom we assume we must excommunicate from our fellowship - those who are not like us, and those who do not fit our political protocol of organization, or spiritual correctness. Christ was absolute in his distinctness of repetition of offering himself to all who came to him. Can we then as an organization clearly become a functional

Church while we afford to select whom we would associate with.? I think not. After all God created even me.

True, the bible warns against allowing novices in taking office, but we with our extreme academic know how, are ready to sidestep God, and readily allow that as long as they promise to fit into our organization along with our perception of what a church should grow to be. We also allow the consistent fragmentation of the scriptures to build a counterfeit message and call it truth. After all, we must follow a more "modern day" approach for the attendee of this day of me now generation. [whatever image that may conjure up.] We pay little attention to a haunting, hurting society that surrounds us which God has allowed to cross our path, as long as our organization functions well.

Yes! The church has failed, and will continue to fail as long as the human element insists on doing it all their own way.

There is an urgent need for believers to take eyes off themselves to follow Christ's bidding to seek and save that which is lost. I asked many believers to repeat the scripture of John 3:17, you would be surprised at how very few even attempt to do that, and the many who just don't know. God's word says, " For God sent not His son to condemn the world: but that the world through him might be saved."

I hear preachers asking, "What can I do with my congregation?" I never ask that I simply ask God for strength to walk the walk He has given me, and teach me to improve myself in His word and allow me to apply that to my relationship with others in whatever state that God sends them to me. We can only reach out to touch other and lift them up to a better life by directing them with the already established manual that God has laid down, to a better life in Christ and admonish them to realize that Jesus never fails.

Why are so many leaving that to which they have been called?

There may be many excuses, but only one true reason. They have stopped adhering to God by refusing to serve as he so willed, in submission, in prayer, in putting others first, by intending to build their dream instead of building God's community.

Even God knew when it was time to rest. Genesis 2:2-3. He did not waste time attempting to fulfill all the desires of a Nation He gave the responsibilities to others. Genesis 1:28. He simply laid out the formulae. He was not attempting overshadow His creation. He simply attempted to build a continuing relationship of love with that which he had created for himself.

* * * * *

Character Of The Saints

━━⟡⟡⟡━━

Character Crisis of the Christian believer hovers in the shadows of the damned. Our goal is not to start well, But to finish well.

Read your bible- sin, greed, envy, lust, pleasure seeking, the evil one, Satan -the Father of lies. He lied to Eve in the garden of Eden - David blinding his eyes with lust after another man's wife - Demus - Born in sin - Self destructive pattern

RELATIONAL

Held accountable! We ARE each other's keeper.
Now we have received the Spirit which is of God; that we might know the things that are freely given to us of God." 1 Corinthians 2:12. Hebrews 10: 25 Eph 3: 12-14

The fellowship of the Saints

v 20; of Hebrews 10, says a new and living way
There is the thrill of rightful novelty in this verse. These words came to us long ago; yet for each believer the way is as new and fresh as it was for the writer of Hebrews.

Gone are the old despairs:

- the old burdens of dishonesty
- the old dreariness of self
- the old guilty fears
- the old defeats

It is literally a New World that the believer enters. New, because it is the world of God. It is a living way, because it is through Him that says "I am the way" John 14:6

Through Him who always makes intercession for us 7:25;

The way is never impersonal. We do not travel alone, it is in His GRACE that we walk, and with his very life flowing through our members; and it is to Him that we strive.

V 21, Hebrews 10: "A high priest over the house of God brings before us again the imagery of the family.

V 22, Hebrews 10 "Let us draw near with a true heart" with genuiness, let us mean what we say.

- We depend upon the mercy of God
- Let our reliance be complete
- Let there be no un-surrendered areas where self becomes prominent
- Let there be no part of self that stands aside to admire what the rest of self is doing
- Let not self be divided, but made one, in love, and trust.

It is never easy to be completely honest. Men sometimes use the words "absolute honesty" when the most we can do is to cry out with the psalmist, "Create in me a clean heart, Oh God. [Ps 51:10]

A child in danger literally will throw themselves into the arms of their mother; for there they have the full assurance of faith.

Only when faith is assured is the heart kept true

V 22; Hebrews 10: With our hearts sprinkled clean from an evil conscience.

or guilty conscience

We are to draw near to God as men who have been - and are - and remain - forgiven, with the dread of guilt no longer holding us back.

Our bodies washed with pure water in Baptism

Baptism is an outward washing to signify an inward cleansing of the heart.

Let us then hold fast to the profession of faith.

Ephesians 3: 12; In whom we have boldness and access with confidence by the faith of Him.

Do we stand in the need of the gift of boldness as we approach God?

Any man, who takes the presence of God lightly, may not be dealing with the right God.

Only through the reconciling blood of Christ can man come boldly to the throne of Grace of God's deity.

The more seriously we deal with the God of the bible, the more we shall appreciate the MARVEL of Christ's work in giving us confidence as we come into judgement.

"It is a fearful thing to fall into the hands of a living God" Heb 10: 31.

1 John 4: 17; that we may have boldness in the day of judgement

We all shrink from seeing ourselves as we really are. We are frightened of coming into judgement. We need courage and assurance - that the one who sees us as we really are - with all our inner lusts, and envying, and pride, will be able to endure the sight.

When God looked for Adam and Eve in Genesis 8: 8; in the cool of the day they hid themselves from him

The good news of the gospel of Christ is that God's love is equal to the sight of man's sin.

HE - God, will look and judge; But will not turn his face away. HE forgives ALL that repent, and repentance may mean precisely, courage to the face of God.

God in Christ is the great deliverer, the great physician, who can do what no medical expert can do -

He can give repentance, and forgiveness - only in Christ can a sinner receive the gift of courage - to come first to himself, then to the Father.

For in Christ we have boldness, and confidence, by the faith of him. Eph 3:12.

Christian courtesy can differ in kind from the politeness of the world. It is the fruit of the true Christian love; In 1 Corinthians 13 we read . . . which does not behave itself unseemly - seeketh not her own - is not easily provoked - thinketh no evil

Acts 4:12; there is none other name under heaven given among men whereby we must be saved

To present Christianity a one world religion would be to betray the gospel of Christ

Romans 2:15; All people have the divine law written in their hearts.

Eph 3:14;For this cause I bow my knees unto the Father of or Lord Jesus Christ

A M E N

CPSIA information can be obtained at www.ICGtesting.com
Printed in the USA
LVOW082109281011

252570LV00003B/28/A